A Supernatural Life

4720-SEGG

A Supernatural Life

Anne Seggerman

Library of Congress Number: 00-191497
ISBN #:   Hardcover   0-7388-2850-5
               Softcover   0-7388-2851-3

To order additional copies of this book, contact:
Xlibris Corporation
1-888-7-XLIBRIS
www.Xlibris.com
Orders@Xlibris.com

Contents

PART VI 449

To all the orthomolecular and complementary physicians, some of whom went to jail due to the Big Brother of the greedy and ignorant orthodox medical, psychiatric and drug establishment, finally beginning to give way to common sense.

What great suffering could have been avoided by paying heed to their discoveries in their own time?

ACKNOWLEDGMENTS

W riting this book has been an on-going project unfolding over a number of years, during which time I have been supported, encouraged and nurtured by many people.

First of all I must start with my family. Loving thanks to my husband Harry for quietly supporting me throughout. I also want to thank my children for being so patient with me all these years. Patricia, Henry, Marianne, Yvonne, Suzanne and John, their spouses Vera and Norm and their children Alexander, Irene, Harrison and Michael—may there be more!

I would like to express my thanks in the words of the famous Dr. Krebs: "To all the Patricia's and Michael's of this world," the handicapped, the "have nots," the abused, the forgotten, the disenfranchised, especially many thanks to our Patricia.

My warm thanks also go out to the many "good" doctors in my life, who without knowing it, inspired me to forge ahead with this book. Although they are listed in the bibliography, I must specifically mention Dr. Mike Lesser, former president of the California Orthomolecular Society, who acknowledged me in his book, and Richard Brodie, who hung in all these years as the president of the Huxley Institute in Connecticut.

My gratitude also goes out to the marvelous priests and religious who amongst other things, supported my prayer conferences (now that's a long list). Some of them were victims of communism: the late Cardinal Kung and Joseph Terelya, gratefully alive, and

Father Houle, a prison mate of Cardinal Kung, who married my nephew Patrick to the good Ruth; and to our dear friend Father Val McInnes, thanks for your friendship and scholarly advice. I would also like to gratefully acknowledge Louise Webb for her thoughtful attention and invaluable contributions to the reviewing of the manuscript; my very good friend Laurey, who, despite her present state of health also willingly agreed to share her literary skills; Will Brownell, who was my muse—somehow or other that is always good enough—but I miss him still.

I cannot thank enough my wonderful staff—what living treasures in our midst—who supported my work in so many diverse ways. They are: Agnes Rethy, an athlete, gardener extraordinaire; wonderful Stephanie who worked with me for seven years until she bore her first child; Cathy my winter helper as well as my wonderful and dependable student helpers Tanya, Katie, Melissa. Finally, David, who is truly a kindred spirit, pianist, composer and computer expert. I could write a book about him; instead he made writing this book possible in every way.

And there are the helpers over the years my loyal Peruvians, Soledad and Segundo Blas, without whom I could not have done anything, let alone write a book. Good Martha, who has given me a deeper appreciation of the Torah because she simply lives it, and her son Clinton who might become one of the greatest orthopedic surgeons of all time. Emelia, who always cheered all of us up and her valiant daughter Antoinette.

How can I possibly thank every special person that has made this book possible? To those whom I have not mentioned, my dear friends, my heartfelt thanks to you all.

Anne Seggerman
Fairfield, Connecticut
April, 2000

PART I

Czar Alexander II and Abraham Lincoln

I always wanted to be a spy. My great-great grandfather was the general in command of all the armies in Russia under the reign of his first cousin, Czar Alexander II, who freed the serfs and was assassinated by a nihilist, a proto-Bolshevik. Around the same time, Abraham Lincoln was likewise freeing the slaves, by means of a war, half a world away, and he too met the same fate as the Czar, my distant cousin. And who knows but perhaps Lincoln's assassin was a prototype for another kind of more contemporary evil.

Over the years, through events fully described in this narrative, what has transpired is that I have become a spy after all, prying into the motives and uncovering the plans of the forces of evil as some recompense for the deeds of those whose heroic actions cried out to set it straight.

I've looked back on my genealogy and early life and said to myself, "Oh! That's kind of an amazing life; I wonder why." Presently, due to my investigations into coincidences and other metaphysical questions, I feel that our genetic backgrounds are more important than we give them credit for. But for a long time I never paid much attention to them. In fact, I never paid very much attention to any of the extraordinary things that happened in my life; I took them all for granted. Some of my experiences have been unique and I'm convinced there's a reason for it, spy or no spy.

CHAPTER ONE

MY GENEALOGY AND EARLY LIFE

As it turns out, it's doubtful whether the Crellins of Pasadena really were my blood relations, the details of which will unfold later, but here are the details as I grew up knowing them. My paternal grandfather, Edward Crellin, by all accounts, was a kindly man; tall, slender, with very deep-set eyes, very gentle and gracious. My maternal grandmother, who raised me, always liked him and said he was a nice man and since she usually possessed a very good understanding of people, I generally accepted her judgments. Old Mr. Crellin was an industrialist, an inventor, and a man with a curious and inquiring mind who, according to family legend, had made some contact with many scientists and inventors, including Luther Burbank. He had some interest in Burbank's development of the nectarine, which is not a cross between a peach and a plum as commonly thought, but a distinct fruit, like the peach and plum, improved from an inferior state to its present quality through selected cross-breeding. Aside from his interest in these scientific experiments, I don't know exactly what old Mr. Crellin invented because he died when I was quite small, but he is supposed to have invented machines for the steel industry early on in his life. He amassed quite a fortune from these inventions.

The name Crellin originates from the Isle of Man but Grandfather Crellin was originally from Pittsburgh, traveled through Des Moines, Iowa, and eventually settled with his family in Pasadena, California.

On May 16, 1938, Edward Crellin was present at the dedication of the laboratory named for him, The Crellin Laboratory at Cal Tech. Dr. Linus Pauling, my grandfather's protégé, was awarded his first Nobel Prize in Chemistry in 1954 for his research into the nature of the chemical bond and its application to the elucidation of the structure of complex substances, and did his pioneering work at the Crellin Laboratory. Dr. Pauling named his youngest son, Crellin, after my grandfather.

After having been professor of genetics at Redlands University, Crellin moved to the family home in Portola Valley when his mother, Ava, died, and there he continued his work on a fascinating thesis, "The Discontinuousness of the Genetic Code."

We met for the first and only time when he came to dinner at the home of my sister-in-law, in Studio City, California where we all had a riproarious time. I shall always remember him fondly and regret that he died before I had the opportunity to further discuss his aforementioned study with him.

Later in my life—in the 70's and 80's when I became involved with my daughter's illness, Dr. Pauling, Senior, became one of my primary mentors.

During his lifetime my grandfather, Edward Crellin, generously supported Cal Tech and the Methodist Church, and in fact, on his passing these two institutions were the beneficiaries of most of his fortune.

Of my paternal grandmother, Mrs. Crellin, I don't remember very much. I think she took a back seat to her illustrious husband. My maternal grandmother didn't like her as much as she did Mr. Crellin, but that might have been a totally subjective judgment on her part. Mrs. Crellin doted on my putative father whose full name was Curtis Vergil Crellin. He was adopted by the Crellins and was their only child. Some people thought my grandmother, Mrs. Crellin, might have been related to him in some way since she was so fond of him; the truth was, my grandmother couldn't have any children of her own.

I remember the few times I went to visit old Mr. Crellin were always formal occasions. Sometimes I was scared because I was just a little child and they forced me to eat things I didn't like, such as grated carrots and raisins, phah!, and to sit up straight in my chair. I had to be on my very best behavior and it was a little awe-inspiring to be in his presence in this very strict household. I remember feeling overpowered by these very remote and unknowable adults. Obviously my mother felt the same way about them which is why she ran away to Paris for three months after my brother and I were born. Since there wasn't any commercial air travel in those days, we went by way of the Panama Canal and we supposedly got very sick, but she just had to get away.

Since Curtis was adopted by the Crellins while they had either lived in or passed through Des Moines, I conducted a nebulous search since the hall which contained the original adoption records burned down after he was adopted. But from further inquiries it appears that there's an American Indian strain involved. If I had to guess this to save my life, I'd say it's entirely possible that a cousin of old Mr. Crellin had a child by an American Indian of the Oglala Sioux Tribe from the Rosebud Reservation which is immediately adjacent to Marshalltown, Iowa, where records show the adoptee was born. The real story was kept very hush-hush.

Adoptions in those days were done under a great deal of secrecy. According to the people I spoke with in Des Moines, there was a tremendous amount of secrecy concerning this particular adoption. At that time, Des Moines was the adoption capital of the United States, which meant that Des Moines was, in that felicitous pre-abortion epoch, a place where women came to have their out of wedlock babies, probably, I suppose, because it was near the geographic center of the United States. Curtis Crellin did bear a striking resemblance to the famous holy man of the Sioux, Black Elk, as he is pictured on the cover of the book, *Black Elk Speaks* by John Neihardt. But I don't really know how much credence to give to this, that he might have been part American Indian. But I do remember that as I was growing up, my maternal grandmother made a point of giving me books about the American Indians and taught me to form a strong appreciation for them and a deep respect for their culture.

Curtis Crellin had some character defects, which may be traceable from nurture or nature. He was too spoiled, had everything his own way, and probably it was genetic too; somebody in his background had character defects, some of which I think must be genetically transmitted, but he did have a lot of natural gifts and was actually a very talented man. He was a concert pianist, the official translator for the Olympics in Germany in 1936, he spoke several languages and so he was quite intellectually gifted, although one could have also called him a bona fide dilettante.

Later on he was banished from the United States, after leaving my mother and two small children, me included.

My Grandmother

My mother's mother, was Anne Magher Lagrave, after whom I was named. She was half English, half Irish with a little Dutch thrown in for good measure. Thank goodness for her good, hearty middle class stock, and for her solid background, because she was a remarkable woman with a lot of common sense and she seems to have provided a very good grounding for me.

The French government gave her the medal of the Legion of Honor right after World War I because she conducted herself valiantly and meritoriously, taking care of many doughboys (as the American soldiers were called in World War I) in her apartment in Paris, as well as some French soldiers. Just before the shelling of Paris, she gathered her family and together they walked out of the city to their country home in Vezeney some 30 miles away—the occupying forces having commandeered all available means of transport for their own use. She went through tremendous hardships in her life and got through them amazingly well.

My grandmother had lost her mother when she was born and was raised by her father who doted on her and whom she also loved very much. When my grandmother was in her early teens she contracted malaria and her father sent her to the Ursuline Convent in Quebec, where she had to break ice in the wash basin with an ice-pick in order to wash up in the morning (a cure for malaria?). I guess that contributed to the fortitude she displayed in her later life. Many years later, while I was attending Ethel Walker School, during an Easter vacation, my grandmother and I were fortunate to be able to visit the same convent in Quebec where she had grown up. We actually got to meet the old Ursuline nun who was her teacher, a woman in her nineties who peered out from behind the iron grille that separated the cloistered nuns from the outside world. It was an emotional visit. As my grandmother and her teacher had their reunion, tears streamed out of their eyes (mine, too!).

My Grandmother and her teacher

19

When my grandmother was eighteen, she lost her fiancé in some war or other and a few years later, she married my grandfather, Alfred Gosling Lagrave, when she was 25 and he was 40.

Grandfather Lagrave's real father was a man named Gosling, an American, an old New York family of English extraction—I guess the same family as one of the fabled 40 Thieves of Bermuda, as the leading settlers in Bermuda were then called. His mother was a Russian woman with the name of Sophie von Schmetterer, the illegitimate daughter of Prince Orlov, the general in command of all the armies in Russia and first cousin of Czar Alexander II. This Russian connection may explain in part my career as a spy!? It was common in the Russian court in those days for people to have concubines. Prince Orlov's favorite concubine, my great great-grandmother, was a German Jewish cabaret singer.

The Russian Court gave Sophie, this illegitimate offspring of the royal blood, over to an Austrian family, the von Schmetterers, by way of adoption. They raised her to be a lady, to play the piano and to sing, and to be generally very grand. Sophie's royal connections provided her with an impressive array of jewels with Persian stones which only the high born Russians would have had. In fact, I have one ring left which holds a most unusual ruby—its setting is very Asian . . . quite exotic-looking.

Sophie was a very smart and talented lady, but had a reputation for being bad-tempered and cruel, especially to my tempestuous mother. We once had a photograph of her but did not keep it in the house for long because of its bad vibes. While we were living in Beverly Hills, we banished her picture to the garage, behind an enormous avocado tree and in front of a small fig tree. That's California for you.

Sophie was first married to Mr. Gosling by whom she had two sons, Alfred and Eugene. Gosling came to a tragic end by shooting himself. Sophie then remarried. This time to a Frenchman, Lagrave, who adopted her two sons, thereby giving them his name. So my grandfather, Alfred, had the French name and lived in

Paris. Grandfather Lagrave became an architect and lived in Paris. He might have had something to do with the Eiffel Tower. I'm really not sure. I've forgotten so much because I never paid any attention to those things at the time. One usually doesn't until one gets older and starts looking back.

There wasn't too much genuine love between my maternal grandparents. My grandmother was so devoted to her father that she never completely separated from him and she may also have been afraid of men. It wasn't a love match but that was true of a lot of couples in those days—arranged marriages. When she went to visit her father for three months, my grandfather had a fling with the chambermaid and she told me that she never slept with him after that. It was a tragic affair, probably contributing to his early death of a stroke on a train after the war. He must have loved my grandmother. I don't see how anyone couldn't have loved her. She was just such an amazing person. She was very beautiful, very kind, intelligent and compassionate.

My maternal grandparents' life in Paris was affluent. They were not aristocrats but they were among the upper middle class—the bourgeoisie! They had three daughters, Suzanne (who is still alive), Yvonne (my deceased mother) and Denyse, who died tragically when she was only twelve, in the World War I influenza pandemic, which, according to a recent TV documentary, was really responsible for the end of World War I. Since so many men died from this influenza, there weren't enough men left to fight. The death of her youngest child devastated my grandmother.

As I've said, my mother's family had a very rich cultural life in Paris. In fact, my aunt, my mother's older sister, a remarkably intelligent lady with a wonderfully dynamic personality, is still living and remembers those days very well; in fact she remembers everything very well. Her name is Suzanne Louppe. She studied art history to become a curator in a museum, but she married instead and raised four children. She remained in France during World War II and got her family through this crisis, escaping the Nazi occupation of Paris, which was no mean feat. To

21

escape the Nazis, they fled to a farm in Provence owned by an English woman. There, Aunt Suzanne learned how to take care of many kinds of farm animals. She knew how to slaughter a pig and how to get all the meat out, and how to dress and cure it. She also learned much about agriculture as well including the technique of pressing the most delicious grape juice. I had some right after the war. Her husband, Robert, was gentle and sweet. He was purportedly a member of the underground. My Aunt Suzanne is strong like her mother, so despite all their difficulties she and her children were able to survive by living off the land.

Eventually the Germans came south and took everything for their own use, which didn't leave my aunt and her family enough to eat, so they had to survive on snails, chestnuts and rabbit meat until they were liberated by American soldiers.

One of them, Sergeant Tom Curtin, formerly of Richmond Hills, Long Island, New York, is now residing in North Carolina. We have kept in contact with all these years.

As if to show off their survival skills, I know that when they came to visit us after the war, the four little Louppe children took great pleasure in picking snails off the bushes along our front lawn in Beverly Hills, getting up before the crack of dawn to do so, much to my personal embarrassment since I was something of a prig.

In a way my Aunt Suzanne has had an influence on my life because I'm getting increasingly interested in survival agriculture right now, for the times which may come upon us.

Yes, my aunt is definitely a survivor. She and I have not always gotten along all these years as there were some rather severe negative financial issues in our relationship, but the fact remains that Aunt Suzanne had what it took to survive and I admire her for that. She's taught me to value survival as well. Surviving sometimes means that you're not always able to be a very good person or a very nice person in the process.

I had another aunt, my mother's younger sister, Denyse, who as I've said died of influenza at the age of twelve. My grandmother's husband died shortly after that. My grandmother was in her forties when her daughter and husband passed on. I think she was grateful that I came along to fill the gap: she really doted upon me, that's for sure. She remained a widow for the rest of her life and died at the age of 76.

My mother, Yvonne Marchais Lagrave, was born in Paris. She went to a convent school, the Dupanloup, in the upscale Sixteenth Arrondissement in Paris; apparently she was the naughtiest girl in the class and quite a cut up. Although my mother didn't have any French parents, she was the most French person I've ever met in my life. She spoke with a French accent all her life; she was a short, cute, brunette with great sex appeal. I guess this is why so many men found her attractive, including the one who became her second husband, Hal Rosson, who, having an eye for very sexy women, was previously married to Jean Harlow.

My mother had, what I like to call for lack of another phrase, "strong genes." She was headstrong, willful, absolutely charming, said "yes" to everything but went her own way. I can see that she would have been a handful. There's a physiological component—she probably had hypoglycemia or hyperactivity or something of that nature. We now have physiological words to describe similar behavior, which was probably also of a genetic origin. There was no overt pathology that I could see, but there was a lot of strong behavior, what the French might call neurasthenia. The eccentricity, wherever it comes from—whether from the Russians, the Goslings or both—doesn't appear to have come from my maternal grandmother's side, which is very solid Irish-Catholic, English pioneer stock; all the good stuff from the people who settled this country. A lot of derring-do seemed to be from my maternal grandfather's side.

When my mother met Curtis Crellin and fell in love with him, this was obviously her first love affair as she was barely into puberty. She also just wanted to get out of the house, to escape the constant arguments between my grandmother and my godfather and the emotional cruelty of her grandmother, Sophie, who would constantly pick on her. Curtis was thirty. She was sixteen. I have pictures of the wedding: they had the whole treatment—the twelve bridesmaids, the flowers, the church.

Then, Mr. Curtis Crellin took my mother back to Pasadena with him, leaving the warm but frenetic environment of Paris for the cold reserve of the Crellins' Pasadena, which probably came as a terrible cultural shock. They lived in a little house in Beverly Hills. Curtis wasn't working then: he never worked, never had to work so he dabbled, and he was already losing interest in my mother, wasn't paying any attention, was self-absorbed. My mother's loneliness was tremendous and out of it she made a few friends, most notably a young Belgian Jewish doctor who could speak French to her and used to prescribe Champagne for her bouts of melancholy. Now that's a great doctor! She would sometimes go with this doctor to his cabin on the eastern slopes of the Sierra Nevada near Mono Lake. It was actually during one of these visits that I was conceived!

Several years ago, Curtis Crellin's widow, his second wife, informed my nephew, whom she had kept in contact with, (after all Curtis was his real grandfather), that right after my mother got back from a particular trip with the doctor, she insisted on having relations with her husband, obviously to cover up her relationship with the doctor. This was unusual since she was already finding him increasingly repugnant. The doctor turned out to be a neurologist at UCLA (University of California at Los Angeles). For most of my life, even before knowing anything about my real father, I have had an amazing predilection for Jewish doctors.

I was born when my mother was nineteen, and my brother Edward was born a year later. After we returned from that short trip to France, which took us through the Panama Canal, Curtis started fooling around and that sort of ended the marriage. One of my mother's earliest exploits during this marriage happened when she was at Good Samaritan Hospital in Los Angeles having my half-brother Edward. She had somehow heard that Dolores

Costello Barrymore was also there, on the same floor, giving birth to her son Johnny. Since Dolores was having all this fancy food and drink served to her, being a famous movie star married to the ineffable and self-destructive John Barrymore, one of the finest actors who ever lived, my mother somehow persuaded the nurses to bring her all the leftovers, including the champagne, of course. Little were we to know, although I was obviously just a newborn! that Dolores and Johnny would become our very good friends years later.

I have pictures of my father, the Belgian Jewish doctor, at my christening with his wife and another picture of him at the beach where my mother and I happened to be looking quite morose while he was smiling broadly. As my husband says, "men are such beasts." I didn't believe it was really he for the longest time I must admit. In this beach picture I appear to be the spitting image of this man, which explains a great deal, since I never looked at all like either my mother or Curtis.

When Curtis left us my mother didn't move back to France but stayed in California. She had a little house and a little money and went back and forth between France and California, taking me and my brother with her. I know that I frequently went to France when I was a kid and came to know the French steamship line very well, which I loved. Due to these regular trips to France at such a young age I was brought up as a bilingual child. In fact I spoke French before I spoke English. I remember poetry that I would illustrate and put together in books, which I wrote in two languages when I was three years old. For years, I never thought it much but later realized that was unusual.

My Crellin grandparents were not very supportive of my mother. They just did what they had to do and gave us very modest financial support. A few years ago Curtis seemed quite threatened when I started to investigate who his real parents were and I don't know why. I would guess that he wanted to bury everything in the past because he felt badly about it.

Through my studies of pathological behavior, I think that as a foundling infant, he must have spent a lot of time crying out of neglect, which is very bad for people and may turn many of them into sociopaths or whatever. I think he was neglected very early on and being an adopted child it had a very serious effect on him. This is what I surmise, based on some studies. I gather his mother wasn't all that warm and loving even though, as I said earlier, she loved him very much. The fact is that she was not at all demonstrative. Mr. & Mrs. Edward Crellin were two very uptight people who probably didn't show their affection for each other. It's very likely that their son was raised by a nurse or a governess, impeding his emotional development.

CHAPTER TWO

HAL ROSSON:
MY MOTHER'S SECOND HUSBAND

Once I had a visit from an art expert who came to repair my furniture and continue selling my paintings. I told him I had this amazing picture of Jean Harlow on a wall upstairs. He said that she was one of his favorite people and I said, "Good, let's take a look." It's quite a remarkable pointillist picture by a Scottish sculptor and tapestry maker and I said, "I have to tell you part of the amazing story about this as we walk back downstairs."

I told him that my step-father had been married to Jean Harlow before he married my mother. My mother was a dead ringer for Jean Harlow except for her dark brown hair. He said, "She was a very beautiful woman," and I said, "I know."

When my husband and I were on a business trip in Scotland, maybe in 1977, one of the directors, a purser to the Queen, a very charming man who is now a Lord, had a friend who was a sculptor, painter and tapestry maker, Gerald Laing. Knowing my interest in art, he suggested I visit one of his friend's shows which, very coincidentally, was currently in Edinburgh. I took a bus to the show and as I entered, right across the room from the entrance was a very large canvas, which left me totally dumbfounded. It was a very large rendition of Jean Harlow, my step-father's former wife.

A Friend of My Mother's

The director—now Sir Charles—, my husband, the painter, and I had dinner that evening. I told him I really wanted that picture and told them about my family background. He said, "You must have that picture." The title of the picture is, "A Friend of My Mother's." What a coincidence! The thing is so big that I had to hang it in the back hallway of the house where we now live, and when you drive in at night, the first thing you'd see was Jean Harlow looking out at you from the second window. I have always wondered whether it has good or bad vibrations or spirits. I still don't know.

Anyway, my step-father, Hal Rosson, was the third of a family of six siblings, all of whom emigrated from England and were involved in the motion picture business in California. They were a talented and enterprising bunch coming from a working-class background. Hal was a cinematographer of renown who photographed *The Wizard of Oz*, got an Academy Award for *The Garden Of Allah* and an Academy Award nomination for Marilyn Monroe's first film *The As-*

phalt Jungle. He was Clark Gable's "personal" cinematographer and shot many of his films at MGM in its heyday of the 30's and 40's.

Hal Rosson was also well known as the man who could make aging movie stars look young on the screen by the use of special filters. It was this same prowess that landed him the job as FDR's personal photographer for his fourth term, to disguise the extent of his feebleness. If the American people knew how sick FDR really looked, and was, perhaps they would not have elected him, and Eastern Europe would not have been sold out to the Soviets. For much of his presidency the American people didn't know he had been wheel chair bound after a bout of polio. There is a famous picture of FDR in his ubiquitous wheelchair, Winston Churchill, Stalin and Alger Hiss, FDR's adviser and a Soviet spy, implicated by Whittaker Chambers in his riveting book, *Witness*, which has since been corroborated by newly opened KGB files. This book, which I read while expecting our second child, Henry, had a profound impact on my life by putting me squarely into the world of strategic politics (a spy!) ever since.

Mr. Rosson was very fond of his siblings, especially his sister, Gladys. He was actually an extraordinary man—so talented.

After Jean Harlow died of uremia in 1937, he met my mother, who was so Parisian! He was very much taken with my mother, as were most men who met her, and so he married her in 1938. We had already moved into his house in Brentwood, California, a part of West Los Angeles, before they were married. Let's just say she was ahead of her time. I remember my mother coming into my bedroom and saying, "Darling, we just got married." I was about seven years old and was rather confused. I also remember being shaken out of that same bed in that same house by the great earthquake of 1938. Because she was married to this famous cinematographer and was a very beautiful, vivacious, interesting and charming woman, my mother was constantly featured in the local Los Angeles newspapers and later after we had moved, in the Beverly Hills newspapers. Mr. Rosson and my mother were so busy socially that they did not have too much time for me or my brother, Edward.

During those lonely years, I went to the Town & Country School in Brentwood, which seems to have been run for the movie industry's children. That school was certainly instrumental in developing me artistically or as I found out much later, my right brain activities. We were educated along the Montessori system so there was music, art and drama in the curriculum. One teacher even read the entire *Hobbit*, by Tolkein. I also remember playing with Spencer Tracy's children, Selznick's daughter, and going to Shirley Temple's birthday party.

We lived right next door to Henry Fonda and I remember Franny, the daughter from his marriage with Franny Brokaw, whom I am sorry to say, committed suicide. I remember little baby Jane, who was just a toddler then, seemingly displaying her individuality by not wearing any bathing suits, jumping into the pool. I suppose that by the age of three she may have introduced skinny-dipping to Los Angeles—she was also ahead of her time.

Right across the street from them was a very stable Irish Catholic family, the McCaughey's. I felt different with them, a settled feeling I had when I went to the first school of my choice, the Roman Catholic college, Albertus Magnus. That was like going home for me. I had that same kind of stabilizing and comforting experience when I was with those two McCaughey girls and their brother as we picked boysenberries in their front yard.

Charles Bennett was one of my mother's many gentleman friends and a very debonair British man about town who helped develop the script for the film, *Lost Horizon*, taken from the book of the same name by James Hilton. It became one of my very favorite films because of its Utopian theme. My mother humored me by arranging for me to "interview" Charles Bennett when I was nine. This did not take place at MGM, my usual haunt, but at Paramount, where Mr. Bennett hung out. Therefore it was a new experience for me and I was pretty scared, being only nine. But I bravely climbed those stairs to his second story office. If you have been to the studios as they existed in the 30's and 40's, picture those wooden buildings, which probably were in existence since the beginning of the movie industry. There was an outdoor staircase, with rows of small windows as well as tiled roofs. Their small rooms housed some of the most brilliant Hollywood minds; these were their aeries.

I was ushered from the waiting room into the inner sanctum of Mr. Charles Bennett. I don't remember clearly but I think my mother sat in the waiting room to make sure everything went O.K. I could only remember a conversation, which went something like this (since I suppose my mother must have told him to humor me). "Well, young lady, what can I do for you today?" I said, "Mr. Bennett, I would like to become a writer. Could you tell me what I have to do to become a writer?" He replied, "First of all, you must have something to write about." Since I was only nine years old, there was not much for me to write about yet! I was somewhat dismayed, and he said, "Don't worry, little lady, just be patient and persistent and *start writing*, and some day you will be a writer just like me."

Those were also the days when Mr. Rosson was filming *The Wizard of Oz*. I remember going on the set and being scared out of my wits by the rubber trees—the ones that threw apples at Ray Bolger, the scarecrow—worried that a tree would throw its apples at me.

For reasons that still remain a mystery to me, we left the Brentwood house in 1940, and moved to Beverly Hills. I have a feeling that some negative things happened in the relationship between my mother and Mr. Rosson during the last years that they were in Brentwood. In fact, I am certain of it. One reason I feel so sure is that when we moved to the house in Beverly Hills they had separate bedrooms. But Mr. Rosson was really very fond of my brother and me; he wanted to adopt us but my grandmother wouldn't let him. She did not like any of the men in my mother's life and who could blame her since my mother had so many men in her life. My grandmother was always a good Irish Catholic lady who wanted a more stable life for me.

It was in 1939 when war once again loomed over Europe that

my grandmother whisked my brother and me out of Europe on the Queen Mary. I remember that two days after we sailed from Southampton, Winston Churchill on September 3, 1939, declared war on Germany! Our ship was blacked out because of the German submarines. Our official M.C. on board was the young Bob Hope and I remember my brother and I sitting at his feet as we listened to his brave and funny jokes.

Here I have to ruminate on the coincidence of this amazing experience, of my brother and me being whisked out of Europe just in the nick of time. It is so similar to a generation earlier when my grandmother did the same for her own children, by walking out of Paris to avoid German shelling. I wonder if I will be doing the same for my children. Such a scenario might be more than remotely possible as I will explain later.

Hal Rosson with Greta Garbo
during the filming of *Camille*

CHAPTER THREE

THE 911'S IN MY LIFE

There were three 911's in my life. One is the emergency telephone number, which I have had to call too many times over the years, and the other two numbers are the addresses of houses in which we lived with my two stepfathers respectively. We lived with Stepfather # 1, Mr. Rosson, at 911 N. Rexford Drive, Beverly Hills, and with my second stepfather at 911 No. Beverly Drive, Beverly Hills.

It was circa 1941 when we moved from the house in Brentwood, West Los Angeles, to a rather strange U-shaped house at 911 Rexford Drive where my bedroom was at one end of the U. This was not a happy time for me or for the other family members for that matter. As I mentioned earlier, when we moved to Rexford Drive, my mother and Mr. Rosson had separate bedrooms.

The only way I could get to and from my bedroom was through my mother's room, which didn't give her the privacy she needed. I remember tiptoeing through my mother's room, usually when she was sound asleep, in order to catch the bus for school. My room was also very cold in winter because central heating in California, such as it was in those days, was gas heat, and the bedroom didn't receive the central heating of the rest of house. It did have an erratic electric heater, but Mr. Rosson, being the miser that he was, would not allow me to have any extra heat unless it was very cold. It was a lonely and miserable time for me.

Mr. Rosson, with all his famous Hollywood talent, also had his dark side. Among other things he was an alcoholic. I think it was when we were living in Rexford Drive, Beverly Hills, that he became a more severe alcoholic. In addition to the fact that he did not let me turn on the electric heater unless it was really cold, he also threw out all of my toys one Christmas, in one of his alcoholic rages. He was kind of miserly, whereas my mother was very extravagant. The mere attempt of a co-existence of these disparate souls was disastrous for all of us. Both of their dispositions actually came from a much deeper level of dysfunction. Neither of them was devoted to Jesus Christ, He who can provide one's being with homeostasis, that steady state of body, mind and spirit.

Nevertheless, when not under the influence of drink, Mr. Rosson was occasionally very nice and humored me in my adulation of some MGM male stars, namely Van Johnson and Peter Lawford. Most people under a certain age may not have heard of Van Johnson. He was a famous actor in the 40's and 50's who never went into the draft; I don't know why. But he was a hero in a good many movies made throughout the war including the extremely timely movie, *Thirty Minutes Over Tokyo*. This was a true story about a fighter pilot who was on a raid over Tokyo, commanded by James Doolittle, who said about the mission when questioned, "Too little, too late." The fighter pilot was played by Van Johnson. Mr. Rosson photographed the scene after Van Johnson loses his leg and when his wife came to see him, he was afraid to tell her of his missing leg but, of course, there was a very moving embrace. What a strange, amazing and agonizing synchronicity for the times to come later in my life!

Mr. Rosson gave me the opportunity to have Keenan and Ed Wynn and Jimmy McHugh help me celebrate my fourteenth birthday. I was beside myself as Jimmy McHugh played on the piano his composition, "On the Sunny Side of the Street," and "I Can't Give You Anything But Love, Baby," and other up-beat songs of the 40's. A truly unforgettable moment! Jimmy McHugh happened to come because he was the boyfriend of my mother's good friend, Felicia Pablos, a stunning Mexican beauty who went on to marry Cornelius Vanderbilt, Jr., and later the New York socialite, Clifford Klenk. When Felicia married Cornelius Vanderbilt Jr., my mother was her matron of honor, and when my mother married her third husband, Stanley, Cornelius and Felicia were her best man and best lady at her wedding which was held in the famous Riverside Wedding Chapel in Riverside, California, an area known for its irreligious and often famous people.

Anyway, back to my 14th birthday. In addition to Keenan and Ed Wynn and Jimmy McHugh, there was also Barry Fitzgerald's brother, Arthur, who had recently arrived from the Abbey Theatre in Dublin and he recited Irish poetry.

Once, in order to make up for his erratic behavior, Mr. Rosson asked me, in a fit of generosity, "Annabella, what would you like for your 15th birthday?" I said, without thinking twice, "Van Johnson." "Little lady, I will give you the person that you want," and was presented with a photo-op with Van Johnson on the set of the Esther Williams' movie, *Easy to Wed*, and it was touch and go whether I would faint or not. I was absolutely crazy about Van Johnson, especially in *Thirty Minutes Over Tokyo*.

Mr. Rosson had funny ways of addressing people. He called me, "Annabella," and sometimes, "Little lady," and my brother and I were the "Chicabiddies." I suppose Mr. Rosson spoke the way he did because of his English working-class background. He referred to his father as, "The Guvnor."

One night, Mr. Rosson, honoring another challenging request, took me out with Peter Lawford, who was amazingly charming to an ungainly 15-year-old going to hear her favorite Boogie Woogie musician of the time, Meade Lux Lewis, the King of Boogie Woogie, at the Biltmore Theatre in Los Angeles. I was frozen with fright at having the famous and handsome Peter Lawford at my side the whole time. All I could remember is telling Mr. Rosson, "Home, James," at which Peter Lawford laughed, and I practically fainted there, as well.

I also remember that Lou Ayres, my favorite of my mother's boyfriends, was the first Dr. Kildare, long before the television version. He was a very gentle man, a pacifist, and was always very nice to me, something I much appreciated since I didn't get much attention from Mr. Rosson or from my mother, for that matter. This was the first inkling that I preferred the gentle types, and later I liked them with fire in the belly, like "the Scarlet Pimpernel," a recurrent theme for a spy like myself.

Mr. Rosson had a maid named Stella who was also our so-called nanny. Every Thursday night she made wonderful Yorkshire pudding and floating island. She was very protective of Mr. Rosson but was a cruel boorish person to me and my brother and what's more, she was also an alcoholic. One morning in one of her alcoholic outbursts, she came at me with a bread knife. I wasn't even dressed yet—was still in my night gown—and I had to go hide behind the bushes on the front lawn—the same ones that had the snails on them, much to the delight of my aforementioned malnourished French cousins—until someone came and relieved her of the knife and put her to bed. Later, after I was married and we had moved back to California, she was somewhat more sober, drinking just beer. I hired her as our children's nanny for a while, out of financial desperation since she would work for practically nothing. It was all that I could afford, what with a handicapped child, a small budget, and my own health in an increasingly precarious state. The poor woman finally died of cancer many years later.

We first lived in that house in the 1940's while the war was on. My mother and Mr. Rosson, being the prominent Hollywood figure that he was, did a lot of entertaining. My mother entertained servicemen and did her bit for the war effort. She had a lot of Hungarian and Russian friends who were musicians, including Nina Koshetz, the famous lyric soprano who sang for the czar, and her daughter Marina, also a singer, and one of my mother's best friends. Even the famous Rachmaninoff, a friend of the Koshetz's, came over to play on our wonderful Knabe piano which we still have after 50 years, and a few transcontinental moves. They also had Mexican friends, one of whom was Mrs. Puig who lived next to the Blessed Sacrament Church and the Hollywood Athletic Club. She made very good bunuelos and my grandmother and I would go over to sample them, which was not very good for our figures, of course.

Once my step-father took me to the Athletic Club to learn to swim. The barbaric custom of those days was to throw the kid in the pool and he or she would either "sink or swim." I was terrified. Because of that experience I never wanted to go back to that club again. That experience also made me afraid of water for a very long time. I am still afraid of large waves. Not only was my life at 911 Rexford Drive lonely and rather miserable, I was also lonely at school since I was very religious and was called "the brain." I didn't have many friends. My best friends were serious male students and two Jewish girls, Carol Bergerman and Jill Kraft, as well as another girl, Jennifer Young, who was British and had been sent to the US during the war to escape the blitz on London. Jennifer and I would paint pictures together in the schoolyard since we were both "artists," and were joined occasionally by fellow Californian, Laurey, who has endured tremendous suffering all her life. Laurey and I are still friends to this day, almost sixty years later.

I also remember another good friend, Millicent Siegel, while I was attending the local public school in Beverly Hills. She was a very lovely, delicate looking person, much taller than me. It was rumored that her father Benjamin was a mobster. That was quite exciting, even more exciting than having a movie star for a relative, which was pretty common in Beverly Hills. A mobster was something quite different! My mother was intrigued by him, as he no doubt intrigued a lot of women. My mother simply loved greeting the dashing Bugsy Siegel, bringing his daughter to the front door! He was a suave dresser and very dashing in a kind of weird way—Beverly Hills or maybe I should say, Las Vegas style. He wore white or tan double-breasted suits and slicked down his hair, like a prototype for *Guys and Dolls*. Millicent lived in Bel Air, and I remember her dressing room lined in powder blue velvet wallpaper, which impressed me very much, and also shocked me a little. The two of us played a lot of make-believe games, probably in an attempt to temporarily escape our relatively dysfunctional lives. Millicent must have suffered as much as I had, though I didn't know it at the time. After we graduated from grammar school, I never saw Millicent again. I always wondered what happened to her.

I spent an inordinate amount of time reading and my mother took me to the ophthalmologist to get stronger glasses. The doctor said to my mother, "If your daughter reads like this much longer, she will go blind." I did not pay any attention to him, and neither did my mother for that matter, since her eyesight was worse than mine. My mother had to be hospitalized because of a detached retina, and after the operation, Carole Lombard, Clark Gable's wife, visited her and gently told her, "It's going to be all right, baby." (I wondered once why that lovely Carole Lombard and Leslie Howard, the model for the men I really loved, had to go down in a plane crash, while serving their country?) Well, the operation did not make my mother's sight all right. It was not a success; she was partially blind for the rest of her life and had to wear dark glasses.

When I was six years old, I started piano lessons with a Miss Peery whose grandfather was a chieftain of the Cheyenne nation. She was very beautiful, tall, rather slender. At that age my legs were quite short and could not reach the pedals. Added to that, being nearsighted I could not see to read the music very well, so I had to memorize everything. Miss Peery insisted that I learn to play *Lento*, the first of the *Pierrot Pieces*, by Cyril Scott. This was certainly a difficult piece of music for a mere beginner. Nevertheless, by the age of nine, I knew it very well.

Later when I went to Paris for a year, I took master classes with the foremost Romantic Style, French interpreter of Bach, Albert Lévèque. By this time he was getting on in years and besides being a family friend, the only reason he took me on was because I played the *Lento* so well, and he imagined that I also played other pieces very well!! He could see that my interpretation was very good, but my technique was not. Good right brain, bad left brain, then as now.

I am grateful to Miss Peery because she instilled in me the idea that nobody could ever progress in anything unless one undertook tasks which were much too hard. "Shoot for the stars," she would say, "so you can play *Claire de Lune*," which I did—an easy piece. My motto still is, "Always do stuff that's much too hard; that way, you can do something—sometimes anything."

The composer of the *Lento*, Cyril Scott, was British—an eccentric who wrote a very impressionist book, *Music, Its Secret Influence Throughout The Ages*. My piano teacher, Miss Peery, was the opposite of the Swiss Bach interpreter, Edwin Fischer, who was a "cold" interpreter, warm vs. cold. Walter Giesking was a warm player who played for the Nazis in Paris. When Giesking came to New York to play at a concert the Jews picketed him. The concert-goers in France, right after the war and the horrible Nazi occupation, had no qualms about such political issues. They accepted him on the basis that he was a remarkable musician.

We moved to the other 911 address, 911 North Beverly Drive, with stepfather #2, my mother's third and last husband. I avoided him like the plague. The situation became intolerable in spite of the fact that it was a gorgeous house, really gorgeous. My mother had good taste. The very high ceilings were paneled in pickled off-gray wood and the good old Knabe was refinished to match; pickled, and my mother and stepfather were also pickled sometimes, come to think of it. They had glorious parties with all kinds of assorted guests from Hollywood and a lot of French people who might be visiting as well. This contrast of the beautiful house with the intolerable living situation created a dream and night-

39

mare quality you might see in the background of *Beauty and the Beast*, certainly in the French version that could be on the Broadway stage. Notwithstanding all the tensions of living there, that was the house in which I flipped the famous coin to go East to meet the man who would eventually become my husband.

CHAPTER FOUR

GROWING UP IN HOLLYWOOD:
1931-1949

September: This is the month of catching up; the month of our last two weeks of four in which we own a timeshare in Newport, Rhode Island. You know how it is, you want to keep that vacation feeling as long as possible. And so, on returning home, I was prone to turn on a movie if a good one came along. This time that good movie was none other than *Captain from Castile*, the movie that continued the remarkable collaboration between the magnificent director, Henry King, and the *Captain from Castile*, Tyrone Power. Tyrone and Henry were good friends and worked in a total of eleven movies together. I had not known that. Tyrone Power's wife, Annabella, was a friend of my mother's. I kept mixing her up with Lily Damita, another good friend, who was once married to Errol Flynn with whom she had a son, Shawn. While they were still married, Errol Flynn had an affair with Beverley Aadland, the original Lolita—a precursor you might say to the film version of the book of that same name by Vladimir Nabokov. They subsequently got married. We old-timers remember that Errol Flynn escapade, a harbinger of the terrible goings on of these times.

Only old timers could remember that scandal. In those days the scandals that surfaced in Hollywood were few and far between. Mostly they were kept under wraps. Now, it's a scandal a day with few if any raised eyebrows, since such conduct is simply considered normal. Tyrone Power did not have too many scandals, if any, so he could work with the great, virtuous Henry King, the same Henry King who was and remains one of the most important men in my life. When I saw *Captain from Castile* for only the second time in my life, I thought, "Oh my gosh, this is a great movie!"

Alan Mowbray, the British character actor played his usual very broad comic act, not as his usual butler, but as the swash-buckler, and I thought "Good grief, Alan Mowbray! What was he doing being a swashbuckler? He's usually the butler."

When I was growing up as a child in the Chevy Chase, Beverly Hills house, which my mother moved into after she divorced Hal Rosson, our next door neighbors were the Mowbrays. I befriended Patricia Mowbray, Alan Mowbray's daughter, who was just as ec-centric as her dad. The mom, Lorraine, however, was pretty straight—or perhaps just a little tipsy!

Our little house on Chevy Chase Drive was a darling brick house, really something out of a fairytale and probably the most modest house on the block, yet my mother did succeed in rent-ing it to various, mainly British, actors because of Mr. Rosson's British connections, I guess. These were people like Claude Raines, Patricia Morrison, who was the first star of *Kiss Me Kate*, with Alfred Drake as her co-star! Now that was a great team. Interestingly enough, Vincent Price was also a tenant, who far from being a monster, in real life was a charming gentleman and a very fine chef. He actually slept in the four-poster bed that my grandmother had given me for my fourteenth birthday. He must have slept on it diagonally, since he was so tall! My daughter, Patricia, is still using that bed. I hope that it still has Mr. Price's sweetness attached to it rather than anything of the roles he played!

Patricia Mowbray and I, with our other neighbor, Alexander King's daughter, Suzanne, who lived on the corner house of Chevy

Chase, would take turns in our weekly production of Romeo and Juliet. One of us would be Juliet on the balcony, intoning her newfound love for Romeo, and then Romeo would declaim "Call me but love and I'll be new baptized". The third person, if she were there, would be either the nurse or sometimes the friar, depending on how much time we had, and if we could find the right costumes, and depending on what mood we were in—mercurial females that we were.

My mother also owned an apartment on Wilshire Boulevard which she rented, and one of her tenants was Rita Hayworth while she was married to Dick Haymes, the singer. After my mother died, I had the extremely grievous task of putting all her effects in order and came upon, in the very top of her closet, hidden away in a corner, some love poetry that Haymes had penned for Rita. The handwriting was almost illegible, but it was really amazingly lovely. I wish I still had it.

Downstairs from my mother's apartment, for a couple of years lived our beloved friend, Dolores Costello Barrymore, who in many ways was much closer to my grandmother and me (Irish Catholics that we were) than to my mother, although they were closer in age.

Dolores was really just a good Irish-Spanish Catholic girl, who in her heyday was extraordinarily beautiful, considered the most beautiful woman in Hollywood at the time, which no doubt is why Jack Barrymore fell in love with her and took her as his third wife.

His daughter, Dede and son, Johnny, were good friends of mine, especially Dede since we went to school together and were both kind of star struck types and from showbiz families.

When Dolores left that apartment building on Wilshire Boulevard, she moved to her avocado ranch in Fallbrook, east of San Diego. After I was married, we went there to see her a few times. She eventually died of emphysema since she was a heavy smoker. I think that Gilbert Roland was at her funeral which I couldn't make because we were living in the East at the time. Not surprisingly, Gilbert played the good thief in *Our Lady of Fatima*, a Warner Brothers movie that is still being played today.

Getting back to the Mowbrays, I believe it was a certain dramatic childhood event that broke up my relationship with Patricia, alas at least temporarily. Whenever the Mowbrays went out for the evening, Patricia and I sometimes joined by her younger brother, Alan Jr., tried to be mischievous within limits. Mostly this meant trying on Alan Sr.'s very expensive British clothes—Saville Row and Burberry. These were kept in a semi-secret cedar closet on the third floor, supposedly safe from any mischievous interference.

One time though, we really got mischievous and went down to the ordinarily off-limits pool room which was 20' x 40' with a very grand pool table. The high point of the evening came when we went over to the bar that had a very mysterious and remarkable lighting from below, you know the kind they had in some art noveau movie theatres in the thirties. In the bar we found some glasses, also lit up, I think they were Lalique, and the stems were nude ladies holding up the top part. This was very shocking but rather dangerous fun. It was almost too shocking for me. Alan, Junior, used to like to keep shocking me by repeating, "I don't swear, drink or smoke," and then he would say, "Damn, I left my cigarettes in the bar." He would always get a rise out of me with that well worn refrain.

That evening they dared me to play pool with them, which I accepted for some reason, probably the devil, to take their dare . . . .a serious mistake, as it turned out. With my very first attempt to push the ball to the other end of the pool table, I was not successful in that endeavor; the ball did not get there, but what I succeeded in doing was making a huge rip in that gorgeous green felt cover, about three feet long. A worse thing could not have happened to me or my friends, to say nothing of Mr. Mowbray's beautiful pool table. Many years later my husband and I attended a party at Charles Bennett's house and so, by a mere happenstance, who was there but Alan Mowbray! He had obviously forgotten about the torn up felt pool table such a long time ago when we were neighbors on Chevy Chase Drive. He just laughed. My husband then began to tell some of his wonderful British jokes. That was one of the most delightful times we had in California.

I heard that Patricia, very eccentrically, went on to marry Douglas Dumbrille. He was one of those character actors of the thirties and forties who wore those curly mustaches. He must have been years older than she! I love thinking about them; at least they must have had some serious fun.

Solace from my lonely life was found with yet another extraordinary childhood playmate, Jorie Butler. She and I, for one enchanted summer, spent the entire time together putting on our mothers' or aunts' long dresses and sometimes their high heels, as we acted and reenacted our favorite fairytales. Sometimes we made them up as we went along. That was even better. I always thought Jorie was one of the best friends I ever had. We were really kindred spirits. Later on I found out that Jorie had become a well-known equestrienne of the Chicago suburbs. I guess she's an heiress of sorts. Her brother was the producer of *Hair*, the well known sixties musical production, which was part of the sixties revolution. I think everybody was nude or something. All they had on was long hair, which is why I didn't go and see it, of course!

I had been given the opportunity during this period in the late thirties and early forties, to take advantage of those acquaintances of my step-father and mother who were mostly celebrities and athletes. I could have taken swimming lessons with Johnny Weissmuller—the first Tarzan—for instance, but that honor fell to my brother who was built much more like an athlete than me. My brother went on to become a very fine swimmer and track star. He wanted to compete in the Olympics. Unfortunately, family troubles prevented him from doing so. Alas, my brother and I were never really close. In fact he and I were sort of raised separately.

The other night while I was still watching movies, pretending that I was still on vacation, there was a documentary on Flash Gordon and, sure enough, there was old Buster Crabbe, the father of Cynthia, one of my best friends in grammar school. I had no idea old Buster was so good looking and had such enduring popularity, and was such a good role model.

When we lived in Brentwood, before moving to Beverly Hills

in the late thirties, my best friends were the daughters of Raymond Massey, who were also creative, and we enacted some fairytales on their beautiful estate. I didn't see them very often but our relationship had a dreamlike quality that permeated much of my childhood.

CHAPTER FIVE

THE FRENCH CONNECTION

One of the main themes of the life of our family has been "The French Connection," like the title of the book by my dear friend, Robin Moore, author of so many popular books. Dear Robin, I certainly do miss him. That's another story for later.

As I mentioned earlier, my great-grandmother Sophie came to Paris in the 19th century and settled there with her family. One of her sons, Alfred Lagrave who became an architect, married my grandmother and they lived in Paris. My grandmother subsequently became the co-owner of another home, with my godfather, who was my grandfather's secretary. So my maternal family settled in Paris in this building. Quite frankly, I should have come to own an apartment or two, according to a will of my grandmother's and my mother (also co-owner), and other documents. Money has never been my strong point so I lost out on that opportunity.

My first recollection of living in Paris was at the age of four when my grandmother would open the windows of the living room since we lived on the ground floor. She would pass me over the window sill to my godfather, (the same godfather who appeared to the medium, Mrs. Myers of Vermont, as recounted in another part of this book) who would then pass me over to the school bus driver.

They sent me to school at that very young age because they didn't know what else to do with me. I was a little young for that type of learning—reading, writing and arithmetic—but I did it since I had to. I had very bad eyesight even at that tender age and had trouble seeing the blackboard unless sitting in the front row.

I made a lot of French friends in my childhood; life was so pure and uncomplicated then, before the second Great War. We used to have a lot of hide-and-seek parties. Maybe they now call that game, "Sardines?" I have kept these friends over the years, until recently. Paris was always a wonderful place to which I could escape from Southern California, from my poor mother and all of her troubles. So, when things got rough around the age of 14, I escaped back to Paris with my grandmother by way of Rhode Island, where we visited the five Healey boys, sons of the one and only Dr. Joe Healey of Pawtucket.

One of those Healey sons was that wonderful Jack who used to play, "Deep Velvet" on their tinny piano, at which I was always enthralled. Poor old dear Joe used to call my mother at 2 o'clock in the morning. She could never figure out why. Maybe that's why he called.

That was a wonderful fall which followed when I was tutored in trigonometry by a Professor de Cerf in the Mathematics Dept. of the University of Paris who lived on Ave. Mozart. He was a family friend who gave me my undying love of spatial relationships. I also attended the Opera Comique workshop and art classes at the Louvre.

It was right after the war and we did not have any central heating, but I hardly noticed that since life was rigorous. Also, I got sick with colitis, so my grandmother fed me grilled Dover sole which always occasioned a trip to Pruniers, the preeminent seafood restaurant on the Ave. Victor Hugo, not too far from us, which only recently went out of business. To this day I still love Dover sole which really kept me alive through my illness. That is a great diet if you're lucky enough to get it.

I was 15 when I met Guy le Vrier for the first time. He is a

Scarlet Pimpernel type—a person of great mystery, really out of a fairy tale. (Was it because I was so nearsighted?) Nevertheless to me he was a most dashing and romantic figure. Guy was a very eclectic person. He became the private test pilot for Jacqueline Cochran, a well-known aviatrix, and friend of Amelia Earhart and Howard Hughes. Her husband owned Republic Aviation. An accident on one of his missions left him with impaired vision, so Guy went on to become the public relations person for the Principality of Monaco. He was also a good pianist. He used to play for me "La Cathedrale Engloutie" (The Sunken Cathedral) on our poorly tuned piano. For some reason I always had to hear this piece. You know some people have to have "their" pieces played. For my mother, it was *La Mer*, and for another very good friend, *The Enigma Variations*. I do not know why we couldn't keep our piano tuned. I guess it was because of the dampness on the ground floor. But Guy le Vrier reminded me of that scene from the original French *Belle et la Bête*, (Beauty and the Beast)—with the princess waiting in the dining room with pale mauve walls and candelabra and magic hands bringing you dinner while waiting for the mysterious, handsome prince (she didn't know he was still a beast).

I think Guy was slightly in love with me and maybe was thinking of marrying me some day but he didn't have any money, so my mother didn't approve of him but we always remained good friends.

During my stay in Paris I also met and befriended students at the International School of Paris including Herb Allen, an Oxonian, who was a student of international law, and a guy named Tex who came from the same town in Texas as Van Cliburn—Tyler, Texas. (Where else?) Tex and I had a very nice platonic relationship. We didn't have that much money at the time, so, when Tex suggested that he would take me to the theater on the Champs d'Elysees to hear my hero, Yves Montand, if I would take him to the Tour d'Argent, the premiere restaurant in Paris at that time and still is, with a gorgeous view of Notre Dame, I said, "yes, of course."

49

What a great night that was! I wore this beautiful dress my mother had made for me—mauve moirée; yes, mauve moirée. Strange—no? It was rather decolleté; rather beautiful. We had seats in the front row. Yves Montand liked my dress too. He was absolutely as fascinating as anyone whose real name was Yvo Montani, but much, much better than Dean Martin or Frank Sinatra. Well, that's a toss up. I was so proud of him when he became a conservative in the later years of his life; as well as being very talented and gorgeous, Yvo also had a lot of common sense, like many Italians.

Our art classes were absolutely fascinating, and the only reason I didn't stay and become an artist was because of my poor eyesight. I couldn't see the project screen when we were learning to do lettering. I had to go to the Arts Decoratifs, Arts Deco, as it was called, not the Beaux Arts, which was too much for my small talent. Frankly speaking, one of the privileges at the Arts Deco was having Bernard Cathelin as my painting professor. He was a protégé of Maurice Brianchon of the School of Paris, who was related to my aunt's husband. He was about the nicest professor I ever had and I learned a lot from him. He went on to become an immensely popular and eminent designer of tapestries as well as paintings and prints. His most famous tapestry on a Japanese theme hangs in the foyer of the French Embassy in Tokyo—a great honor for Cathelin and also for the Japanese. Years later, our daughter Suzy and two of her friends from Kenyon College were invited by Cathelin to his beautiful apartment for an impromptu Champagne toast. He was magnificent.

Much of my time was spent on the subways and buses, but since this was Paris, that was wonderful in its way. There was not the crime as there is today, right after the war. We could go anywhere on motorcycles but sometimes we just chose to walk home. That was fun, too. Everything is fun when you are young and don't have too many problems—such as those that come later to the ones God has chosen for a lifetime of suffering like my daughter, Patricia.

Of all my classes, my favorite was the History of Art classes at the Louvre. The professors were completely chauvinistic (very pro French). We still got the good sweep of how art moved from the East to Venice by the Silk Route, to the rest of Italy and on to France and then to the North. Also we were taught how first, architecture, then sculpture, then art, then music evolved. It was the way of teaching at the Louvre—so very logical and grand. My History of Art teacher at my college, Albertus Magnus, was a nun—the wisest of all the nuns, and the most beautiful. This kind of teaching enabled me to lecture while I was a student at Albertus Magnus.

This was quite natural for me because like many people in Europe, I was raised in a family that was very art conscious. As I said earlier, my aunt studied art history but decided to make marriage and family her career.

I returned to the United States and enrolled at Ethel Walker's School in Simsbury, Connecticut, in the fall of 1947 as a senior. Despite the fact that I was abroad for one year, I was still on par with my colleagues in the US, even though I had lost a lot of English but with the help of the indomitable, brilliant and kind English teacher, Miss Waite, I was able to catch up.

CHAPTER SIX

SUMMER OF 1948

In the summer of 1948, right after graduating from Ethel Walker School, I was joined by my friend Dede (Dolores Blythe) from California. She was my friend from the Marlboro School in Los Angeles, a private girls' school. Dede was the daughter of the late John Barrymore, the well-known actor, and his third wife, Dolores Costello, who later married a gynecologist, Dr. Vruink. Dede was pretty wild and I was a good balance for her because I wasn't very wild, even though I sure appreciated wildness. I guess this has not changed too much. Some kind of alter ego syndrome, no doubt.

That summer of 1948, a very fortuitous and interesting thing happened when I met John and Mary Ellen Brosnan. Their father, John Brosnan, was a lawyer who had been editor of the *Columbia Law Review*, was on the New York Board of Regents, was the brother of Father Vincent Brosnan, head of Catholic Charities, who was to become one of the three priests who officiated at my wedding, and was one of my grandmother's cronies, what else?

John, Junior, was a real intellectual; we used to have really interesting discussions on philosophy and he also wrote me beautiful love poetry. He went on to become a lawyer like his father.

His sister, Mary Ellen, was very pious, became a nun and eventually the Head of Marymount Catholic College on the Hudson River for many years. On one side of me was that wild girl, Dede and on the other, Mary Ellen, the nun.

These two friends were at the opposite ends of the spectrum; Dede was absolutely from Hollywood, Mary Ellen was destined to become a Mother Superior. Being a right-brained and rather naïve person, I really didn't realize that Dede was fairly promiscuous for that time. Anyway, the four of us went to Paris to my grandmother's where we had a wonderful time. After that we went with my French family to my grandmother's and my aunt's summer home in Brittany.

Dede's pen pal boyfriend came up from the South of France. She didn't speak any French and this guy didn't speak any English. He subsequently left, so Dede, who had attracted all the local males, took up with Bernard, a tall, sleazy, but handsome guy. They decided to go out on a sailboat all day and when she came back she was lobster red all over with no strap lines of any kind. Furthermore she was delirious—a very bad case of sunstroke. She had a temperature of 105! So we took her to the local hospital, (the same hospital to which we took my husband-to-be, Harry two years later), from which she tried to escape out of the toilet window, ranting and raving.

My aunt was furious with me for having such a friend—she grumbled about Californians and used some not very pretty epithets. She was disgusted. She said, "Why do you Californians behave so badly?" Dede had obviously been nude with this guy in the boat and been making love, oblivious to the hot sun. I really didn't put two and two together; the whole thing sort of washed over me like a dream or nightmare! I didn't know what had been going on. I was in a state of shock. French girls did not carry on like that at all, so that put us Californians in a bad light.

Dede (Dolores) Blyth (Barrymore)
and
Mary Ellen Brosnan

CHAPTER SEVEN

ALBERTUS MAGNUS

Having graduated from Ethel Walker and after spending a summer in France, I wanted to go to a Catholic college. I had never been allowed to go to a Catholic school as a child because, being a Freemason, Mr. Rosson didn't approve of things Catholic in general and Catholic schools in particular. Nevertheless, despite this opposition, even from a very young age I was very spiritual; a very strong Catholic. I never lost my faith. Looking at my own children, I don't know what's happened to faith these days. It seems a very hard thing indeed. It was my grandmother who nurtured my Catholicism and my spirituality, not my mother. My poor mother was excommunicated. They gave her a raw deal. She wasn't really a spiritual person, but she was still very kind and warm.

In preparation for college I had to take my SAT's. That was while I was at Ethel Walker's in Simsbury, Connecticut. One holiday weekend I returned to California from boarding school and spent it at my friend Dede's. Her brother, Johnny, had gotten the chicken pox and I caught it from him, just at the time I was about to take my exams. Would you believe on that trip, at age 17, Johnny taught me the facts of life? In order to hide the pock marks and make myself presentable, I used some really globby make-up for fear that they would not let me in if they knew I had chicken pox. I thought I could relax on the SATs because I wasn't trying for Bryn Mawr. We agreed on Albertus Magnus in New Haven, Connecticut because of its proximity to Yale where the Dean of the Art Department, Dean Meeks, was a friend of the family. I thought maybe I could study art at Yale which has a very good Art Department, and Theology at Albertus Magnus which also has a very good Theology Department. Those were my two major interests.

So in the fall of 1949 I went to Albertus Magnus which was really my only choice. That was a good year, my freshman year. I remember thinking to myself when I got to Albertus Magnus, "Now I'm home because I'm with Catholic girls." It was a time of real release for me—freedom and joy. I was really very comfortable there because I had the closest thing to a complete life that I'd ever had.

At Albertus, I think the education in some respects left something to be desired. It was a little bit one-sided. We studied Thomistic philosophy and G.K. Chesterton. They left out an awful lot of non-Catholic authors, but it did give us a very good education in things Catholic.

I was able to get a kind of intellectual basis for my belief which I hadn't had before. I was fascinated with so many aspects of the education there. There was a lot of humor. We had this one great professor from Providence College, the Dominican College in Providence, Rhode Island. I passed a Religion test, which amazed me. I did very well even when compared with other girls who had had a parochial education. I guess my grandmother had given me a real good basic training in the seven deadly sins, the seven virtues and the Ten Commandments. I remember once in class the professor asked, "What's the Sixth Commandment? You, there, Crellin." I replied, "Thou shalt not commit murder," I stammered in panic. He laughed and said, "Oh, you Hollywood girls. It is, "Thou shalt not kill."

There was an exchange of views between the girl from Southern California on the one hand and the Eastern middle-class girls who had been to parochial schools. They were very pious and took their religion for granted. I didn't. To me, it was kind of an adventure, since I hadn't had the same kind of exposure to it. One thing I also remember is that the history professors spoke in such tremendous terms about the Thirteenth Century. I thought they were really hooked on the Thirteenth Century. But now, peculiarly enough, after many years of reflection, there indeed seems to be something special about that Thirteenth Century: the building of Chartres Cathedral and the resurgence of spiritual energy that hasn't been matched in human history, I don't believe, since to many Christian philosophers, and an Episcopalian priest friend of ours, Rudolf Steiner et al, there was a decline in the civilization of man when he stopped building cathedrals and started building palaces. Maybe the 21st century will be different. That's a very widespread hope in these times.

The girls at Albertus were idealistic and certainly they were far more naïve than the girls I encountered at Walker's where I felt an outsider in the sense that I couldn't go along with what I considered their un-Catholic lifestyle, at least in words. I might have been thought a fairly sophisticated young girl. After all, I had been raised in Hollywood and had traveled extensively. I had lived in Paris. But I wasn't really very sophisticated. It never took. I was always extremely naïve. In fact at Walker's I was voted the most naïve, the most conscientious and gullible girl in our graduation year book. It's only in the last ten years that I have become in any true sense of the word, 'sophisticated,' which, in my view, means possessing a left brain view of things. I've always been so extremely right-brained. I still am, but just to survive, one has also to be a left-brained person to a certain extent.

I had come to Albertus Magnus with the thought of doing the next best thing to attending Yale, an impossibility for young women at the time—which was to get a Catholic education and, hopefully, study Art with a Yale professor. As it happened, we did have a Yale professor in the Art department at Albertus. I think we had three art students. I was one of them. I'm a fair artist and probably could have made a living as a commercial artist, but my eyesight was very poor. I had an extensive background in Art history by American standards, having studied at the Louvre, but not at all extensive by French standards. Europeans have a different notion of education. At Albertus, we had this Art course, a lot of Religion and Theology. We were automatically Theology majors at Albertus. You got the whole *Summa Theologica*, which was really a very good way to study theology. There are a lot worse ways today I can tell you that! We also had something called Logic. When I told my husband that I got an A in Logic, he really guffawed. Yes, laughing, good old laughs. If a marriage lacks laughs, then good luck. We've been hanging in for 48 years, joking all the way, as you will soon see.

Anyway, I was very happy that I had gone to Albertus, but I only got on with one beautiful nun who understood me, since I was kind of different from the other girls. She was the only one who was really nice to me. A couple of them gave me kind of a hard time. I don't blame them because although I was naïve, I was also really iconoclastic going to a place like that, even though going to a Catholic school had always been one of my most heartfelt goals. I was personally very happy, but they didn't understand that. How could they? My behavior was not that of an exemplary Catholic. I used to go to wild parties, had enormous hangovers the next day and once I had to go to the Infirmary. I would make a lot of ruckus on the front steps with Yale people. I had a Yale boyfriend and we were going steady for the most part. I was really very fond of him and he of me. He was a senior and when he graduated, I was really distraught because I was kind of in love with him.

At Albertus Magnus, we learned on the first day we were there, with our eager shining faces, that the Yale campus was close by. So we checked it out immediately, even before we had unpacked.

While on shipboard returning from France I had met this Yale student named Jim, who someone called, the handsomest short man she ever met, and had struck up a budding romance.

I knew that he lived at Calhoun College so we wandered around Yale looking for it and by mistake, I found myself in the office of the *Yale Daily News*. It was a huge room with very old windows and a very high ceiling, maybe thirteen feet high. At the far end of the room with his feet on the desk was a very interesting fellow, very tall, with what I think was dark blond hair like my boyfriend, Jim. His name was William Buckley, as I found out later, and he was the editor of the Yale Daily News and had just written or was about to write, *God and Man at Yale*. I was impressed as he was very humorous and friendly. He looked me over very carefully. I was pretty good looking in those days with a nice figure. I had made sure to wear a very becoming wool dress that I had recently acquired from Bonwit Teller on that special day I went looking for Jim.

I made some good friends at Albertus, one of whom, Nancy Pettee, was the reason we moved to Connecticut instead of New Jersey when we moved back East from California, after marriage. Another was once the most senior female on Capitol Hill—former Congresswoman, Margaret Heckler. She was in my class but was a much harder worker than me. Margaret was a very good student. I was as well, but decided that after being the best student for 10 years, I was going to have fun for a year or two before buckling down again. Margaret was completely different. She was very motivated to study and went on to law school, became attorney general for her state, and then congresswoman. She was appointed Secretary for Health and Human Services and Ambassador to Ireland. She is still a genius. Now many years later, she has come back into my life, an honor and a blessing.

At Albertus I sang in the a cappella choir, played the piano and also played some tennis. I was able to do some stuff the other girls didn't do just by virtue of the fact that I had had a more eclectic education than some of them. I had a B+ average or something like that. It didn't matter then anyway because I was in love with Jim, my Yale boyfriend. But a fateful trip to France in summer, at the end of my Freshman year, soon put an end to that.

CHAPTER EIGHT

BACK TO FRANCE
FOR THE SUMMER

After my first year at Albertus, my mother and I went back to France for the summer. My mother joined me in a rather small first-class cabin on the Ile de France, the ship we often used to cross the ocean. I had met Jim, my Yale boyfriend, on the De Grasse coming back a year earlier. My mother was nursing a wounded heart since she was leaving her current boyfriend. She was between relationships at the time, so she decided to go to France to see what she could find, maybe a boyfriend or even a husband for herself. Right after our going-away party, my mother sat down on a case containing my 35, 33rpm wonderful jazz records. On top was Buddy Berrigan's, "I Can't Get Started." I heard the crunch of that record along with some of the others. After that I realized I had better stop collecting jazz records, there being no future in it, because I couldn't "get started."

I was a kind of "Barbie Doll" for my mother. She liked to dress me up in beautiful clothes, some from the couturiers like Jacques Fath, Nina Ricci and even Balmain. I'm sure you get the picture. She would do this as a kind of treat, but she always had my clothes made to order whenever possible since I was a 36, 25, 38, rather on the robust side, but a perfect size 10. I looked pretty good and she always looked great. Her clothing bill was just amazing; couturier fashions, the best clothes you could buy, etc.

My mother, as I said, was between husbands, had a lot of boyfriends, was getting over an affair. I think somebody may have just died. I wasn't on top of that situation and didn't want to be. My mother was very beautiful, very young looking; she was only nineteen years older than me. We had a very close relationship. I was very sad because I had just left this Yale boyfriend and she was sad because this guy had died. So, there we were, the two of us, in first-class on the Île de France. They knew me very well on that French liner because we traveled frequently across the Atlantic. We had had a lot of good times on those trips.

Here were two lovelorn ladies, beautifully dressed. People must have thought we were Lesbians or something because no man came up to us. We were very close and tender with each other.

The only one who came up to us was a guy who might have been bisexual, a man-about-town, very well connected, by the name of Harrison Negley. He used to date Trish Baldridge who had been social secretary to a first lady and wrote a very up-to-date etiquette book. He was a very worldly, sophisticated guy. A very gentle, cosmopolitan type from California! He liked us both and struck up a friendship with us. When we arrived in Paris he would take turns dating us. We loved that, thought it was just convenient and occasionally humorous. Sometimes he'd take us both out, but he didn't like that as much. He wanted to pay attention only to me and then to fasten his attention exclusively on my mother. Meanwhile, my grandmother presided over our apartment in Paris.

Harrison Negley was apparently having lunch in a little café off the Rue de la Madeleine where they had these little outdoor cafés which were wonderful little spots for Americans. It was 1950, a super time for people our age. He saw this very handsome young man, so he sat down and had lunch with him. That evening I had asked Harrison if he wanted to go to a Bach concert with

61

me because I was a great Bachophile; I really loved Johann Sebastian Bach's music very much. I asked Harrison to come with me, but you can imagine that someone like Harrison Negley was not too crazy about Bach. He would have much preferred Bobby Short or Bobby's mentor, Mabel Mercer, whom Harry and I actually heard at the Carlyle many years later. How great she was and how great Bobby Short still is! He was trying to get out of it or at least bring somebody along to ease the strain of the experience. He was to come and have dinner with me. My grandmother was cooking and that was always a treat because she was such a great cook. He said he'd bring along this young man who likes Bach. I remember Harrison coming along with this young man whom I didn't pay any attention to at first. The three of us had dinner and Harrison said he had a bad headache and suggested the two of us go along to the concert together.

Harry on his BSA 750

So the new friend—Harry, and I went to the Bach concert and didn't pay much attention to each other. We left the Bach concert early because it was so horrible. It was in the Maison de la Pensée Française which was the official Communist cultural house in Paris. In those days I was already beginning to become anti-Communist, so hating this concert came naturally. Harry and I both liked Bach, were both interested in culture, were both young Americans and we didn't have any dates. I was still recovering from this broken heart and Harry had an English girlfriend as well as a Spanish girlfriend. He had plans to visit them both. It was an accommodation. We'd go to concerts; we weren't too interested in each other, but we dated each other anyway. That was fine until, as was our custom during summer, my family—my grandmother and my aunt, my uncle and my French cousins—rented this same lovely house in Brittany, St. Briac it is called, not too far from Dinard. It's in the neck of the woods of Mt. St. Michel, the northern part of Brittany, not the Finisterre, but north of that. This was our third summer there.

I went to this house in Brittany and Harry went to England to pick up his BSA British motorcycle, a 750 cc which was big then, big enough even by today's standards. Many years later, after we were married, Harry got one that was a 1,000 cc. Anyway, after he picked it up and because he was your typical young college grad, he liked to freeload as much as he could because he didn't have any real income yet. He had just graduated from Princeton and hadn't gotten a job. Here was this reasonably well-off young lady whose family had very fine Spanish cooks and servants, etc. She was reasonably attractive and had similar interests, so he decided to go out of his way to see her again on the way down to St. Jean de Luz, to visit his Spanish girlfriend. He had decided to write off his British girlfriend because she yawned loudly during a concert featuring the Bach *B Minor Mass*. He was turned off by anybody who yawned that loudly and especially so as she had asked, "Oh Harry, may I have a cigarette?" right in the middle of the *Crucifixus*.

Harry came to our house for two or three days. God only knows where my mother was. My grandmother was running things but allowing me every freedom. I was completely undisciplined. My disciplinarian aunt would raise her eyebrows when I would stay out late. I always hung on to my chastity, which was a pretty good thing I thought. I had this very strong moral sense. That was that. You didn't do it, period! No ifs, ands or buts about the whole thing. They trusted me. Maybe I drank a little bit too much on occasion, but by today's standards, I was pretty self-disciplined. I studied hard, got good grades, etc.

That was self-imposed discipline because no one else did it for me. No one ever told me what to do or not to do. Harry came down on his huge motorcycle. My grandmother was scared to death when I rode on the back. She had a right to worry for I know a lot of people who were killed on motorcycles. Nobody wore helmets then, either. Harry took me up to Mt. St. Michel once on rutted roads. God only knows how I survived it! I guess it's youth or something.

How could I have been so brave? I just never thought a thing about it! I used to do risky and reckless things in those days. Conversely, now sometimes I'm scared to leave my front door. There was a gypsy camp right next to the motorcycle repair shop. My grandmother would say with great emphasis, "Don't go near the gypsy camp! The gypsies, they might kidnap you!" My aunt and uncle wanted to go with their children to visit the Chateaux de la Loire and they wanted me to go with them. But I said no; I'd stick around with this guy because I liked his motorcycle. They were pretty angry with me about it. We kind of smooched a little bit because there was nobody around, but it frankly wasn't very serious at the time.

This reasonably well-off young lady

I didn't know much about Harry then. Harry Seggerman, for that is his name, was born in New York City and his parents were typical of their culture, the upper class Four Hundred, or such. However, they had an unusual situation. His mother's father, Mr. Atha had all the money. He lived with them and sort of ruled the roost. He became senile and continued living at home until his death, which was probably rather depressing for the boys. They partially grew up in Rumson, New Jersey. Harry's mother had a stroke and died when she was only 46 years old. When Mrs. Seggerman died, the father was so upset, he moved to Tuxedo Park where he met the second Mrs. Seggerman, Betty Avery Bakewell. Harry spent his teens in Tuxedo Park but had spent his childhood in Rumson, both Social Register places. They had the old homestead, with the garden. Harry got his first taste of gardening there, didn't like it and still doesn't. He learned to hate gardening which I'm sorry about because usually he won't go out to pick anything; though on a few rare occasions he has picked some tomatoes. Harry and his younger brother, Fred, reminisced: "Do you remember the victory garden?" There was this old Russian guy who apparently planted it with nothing but potatoes and some asparagus and onions thrown in, so that he could make vodka.

So Harry grew up with a step-mother during his adolescence. He had a reasonably stable childhood—riding his bike to school every day, and racing small boats on the Navesink River. Nothing was perfect; there was a lot of drinking in the family and a certain amount of infidelity, typical stuff you see in the movies of the 30's. What really helped Harry I think was being a student at the Rumson Country Day School, where his friends and colleagues were well-balanced youngsters from very stable homes, who turned out to be equally stable adults. We went back to the Fiftieth Anniversary of the Rumson Country Day School and a nicer group of people I've never met. These people he grew up with, they seemed just wonderful; straight, cheerful, well adjusted, bright and successful—or so it seemed from that one wonderful party. It provided a very good environment with a lot of physical activity, especially sailing. He always wanted to move back there but the place had changed enormously. Most of the people at the reunion weren't living there any more. Things had changed so much. There were no longer the great mansions with all the servants, etc. Estates were broken up and filled up with split- level houses.

Harry's maternal grandfather, Mr. Atha, was the dominant one in the family. He dominated the whole milieu. He had the money. I forget how old Mr. Atha made his money. The fortune dated from the early years of this century.

Harry's father came from a very prosperous German family, the Seggermans, who were food importers and merchants. They had cornered the rice market, but twice they had lost their fortunes. They were kind of happy-go-lucky types. Harry's cousin, Bonsall, is very much like Harry's father. A more liberal outlook in many respects, both good and bad I might add. Bonsall's father was very much like Harry in some respects, more straight, more Germanic, more dogmatic, more reliable. As far as I'm concerned, those characteristics in a man would make a better contribution to a successful marriage. Yes, from what I gather, the Seggermans had awfully good times and awfully bad times when the Depression was on.

Like the Seggermans, my Russian great-grandmother Sophie, also managed to lose most of the family fortunes. She was the victim of a scam. Two con men said they owned the Baku oil fields in Russia! She thought she could not make any mistakes. This crazy Sophie, my grandmother's mother-in-law, basically squandered the proceeds of her deceased husband's estate on the oil fields, and the claims, whether valid or not, were worthless because, of course, the Bolsheviks took over Russia and as I hate to say so tritely, the rest is history. As a result most of the family money went down the pipeline.

They took off with her money. She was left with a worthless paper deed showing she owned the Baku oil fields. I actually saw some of those certificates in my grandmother's trunk in her back closet in Paris, shortly after she died in 1959.

Harry always teases me about being such an anti-Communist spy because he says I just want my oil fields back. Sophie did have royal blood, even if it was bar sinister and she thought if anybody deserved the Baku oil fields, she did.

Both my mother and Harry's father had a lot in common. When they met they really hit if off. They were just like tea and tea; so similar. Both were adventurers—happy-go-lucky, warm, fun-loving, charming, attractive, gorgeous people.

Harry went to Princeton. He had started out as a Mathematics major but when he got into the major there were five other math majors who were all geniuses. And Harry thought mathematics was so abstract, too complex, so he became an English major and he really enjoyed it. Harry was happy playing golf, and bridge, too. He liked his leisure very much; he was an easy-going person. That's how he grew up. He didn't want to work too hard. In those days at Princeton you really didn't have to. It's a lot more difficult there now.

A lot of Harry's friends got thrown out for indulging themselves too much—playing too much poker—and not paying enough attention to their studies. I remember when we went back to the Princeton reunion in the classic Princeton Reunion march his class held up the banner, "This class had a C+ average." Now Princeton is getting so elitist that you have to be tops in everything. Harry also took a course which he thought would be interesting—Chinese calligraphy. It wasn't either easy or hard, it was just fascinating. He got totally immersed in Oriental culture. He subsequently went on to become an international financier. Harry was one of the first American businessmen to have a serious interest in Japan in 1960 that subsequently led to his financial success.

Did Harry's great career all start with the calligraphy course? It might well have done so. But I think there's more to it than that. I think it has to do with his karma. More on that later.

There he was, a young, handsome Princeton graduate
in that summer in Brittany with me.

But anyway, before I knew all that, there he was, a young, handsome Princeton graduate in that summer in Brittany with me. Slowly, we kind of started to like each other. I could ride on his motorcycle, and we both liked the same kind of music. He liked foreign girls much better than Americans. I was quite French in those days. My French was just as good as my English, maybe even better. Harry was my real "Scarlet Pimpernel."

On the last day of his stay, Harry was to be on his way to his Spanish girlfriend's. I was a little sad, but we had had a marvelous going-away meal which I remember to this day. We had crayfish and hard cider. A lot of hard cider! It has a certain reputation as the poor man's champagne, but it's not. Really it's great stuff. I remember I had to go on my little bicycle down a little rocky path to get the cider. This was his last free meal until he got to the south of France so he really had to load up. Feeling no pain, off he went. The next thing I knew the telephone rang two hours later. "Madame, madame! Monsieur . . . .an accident. Il est prêsque mort. Venez vite!" (He is almost dead. Come quickly).

Harry had leaned over to see if his bag was coming loose and in doing so, with the shift of weight, the motorcycle swerved and he was thrown, helmetless, onto the road. He had a concussion, was bleeding a lot when some peasants picked him up and brought him back to their little hut. They wrapped him up. He regained consciousness. My grandmother and I rented a little Model T Ford from an ancient guy. I remember those roads. Talk about Fairfield, Connecticut roads! It took us an hour to get to the peasants' hut where we found Harry bleeding, so we had to take him to the hospital.

To flash back two years before, to that memorable summer of 1948, in this same place in Brittany where we took Dede, my then best friend, to the hospital run by nuns, there was this French doctor who was in charge and treated her when she was admitted. Now two years later I turn up with another American. He obviously remembered me, because as he looked at me he said, "Oh, no! Not you again!" I think he was what you might call sadistic because he then proceeded to take care of Harry's wounds in his own special way. Harry said it was the most painful thing that ever happened in his life. (He hasn't gone through childbirth). He was howling as they stitched him up without anesthetics. I was holding his hand and it was a pretty dramatic scene.

Of course Harry was terribly fortunate that the accident had happened fairly near our house. The funny part of it is that the day before we had this farewell meal, that very morning, we had gone to the blessing of the animals. We had gone to Mass and after the blessing of the animals, Harry decided to have his motorcycle blessed. He wasn't Catholic, but he'd go to church with me. He was Episcopalian, but liked going to church with me, in France especially. No sooner had the motorcycle been blessed, in retrospect and in view of the work we're doing now, I must say that God does work in a very mysterious fashion, there is no question about it, that the accident happened, the whole thing was very well synchronized. Harry came back to our house all bandaged up and couldn't move for three weeks. I had to serve all his meals to him in bed. Of course we got much closer. As they say, he took a turn for the nurse.

So Harry was the man who came to dinner, and my aunt insisted that I had to take care of him. When he left the second time, I really did feel very sad that he was leaving this time because by then we had become much closer. We had a theme song, "Greensleeves," which I'd play on the piano after he left. Whenever I hear that tune, as popularized by Vaughn Williams, I think of that time.

Harry went down to see his Spanish girlfriend. For some reason, he thought she was too disorganized. I guess, in contrast, he thought that since I had been such a good nurse I wasn't too disorganized.

CHAPTER NINE

COURTSHIP AND MARRIAGE:
A NEW LIFE BEGINS

I went back to Albertus Magnus for my sophomore year. I had desultory dates with a few people, but at that point I was kind of interested in what Harry was doing. Harry started work at Dominick and Dominick. He had a tiny apartment on Third Avenue in New York and was pretty lonely. I would date him infrequently. He had stayed in Europe until November 4th when he returned to the United States. At this point we were kind of serious about each other, but he had New York girlfriends and I had some other boyfriends too. There was one fellow in California in whom I was very interested and he in me. I went out to California for the Christmas holidays. I also had a boyfriend at Dartmouth who was wonderful, one of 10 children, whose German dad owned the Bismark Hotel in Chicago. I also liked my California boyfriend very much. He actually would have made a very fine husband. He was from a good family, fairly wealthy, intelligent, a nice person, etc. He wanted me to stay for New Year's Eve. In those days, if you spent New Year's Eve with somebody it was like making a commitment. Harry called me up to say I had to come back to spend New Year's Eve with him. I had a hard time deciding so I ended up tossing a coin, really! Heads, Jim from California, tails, Harry. Harry won, so I had decided to return to New York. What an experience!

When I arrived, Harry didn't meet me at the train station and he didn't even meet me at the New York Port Authority Bus Terminal. So I had to take the bus to Tuxedo Park where he met me at the bus stop. Not having Harry meet me when I first arrived in New York seemed like some sort of a comedown. I had been in a gorgeous house in California with this rich California boyfriend with his own convertible and now here I was taking a bus to meet Harry Seggerman in his father's oldish car! I think Harry's father was in the car too. His father and I got along very well because he loved ladies. He was very gracious and I was fond of the old man. We drove to the gate of Tuxedo Park and I remember saying, "Oh, is this your property, Harry?"

The Seggerman men both laughed! "Well, my house has a little gate." I guess I never realized in those days that our life would take some amazing turns. But not only was I not in a luxurious suite in Beverly Hills, I was in the locker room of the squash court in which they had put a bed and with no heat! I had a drink before we went out to a New Year's Eve party. The ice cubes were still in my drink the next morning. Fortunately, I wore a beaver coat that my grandmother gave me when I was 15, which I put over me. I had left California for this?!

The Seggerman men, from left to right, Ken, Fred, old
Mr. Seggerman their father, and Harry

I wondered whether there was to be a sumptuous New Year's Eve party crowded with glittering fascinating family and guests. Well, Harry's step-mother was there, but no, we went to some dark dingy restaurant. It was really a pretty disappointing evening, but I had made a commitment, and God has moved very mysteriously through all of these events; of this I am certain right now. But at that time, I didn't know what was really in Harry's mind. Young men at that age are often prone to let things happen to them rather than the other way around.

Yet, Harry was a mature 23-year-old in some ways; in other ways he wasn't at all. But that could have been said for both of us. As far as making a living and being responsible or serieux, as they say in French, Harry was ambitious in all that the word conveys. He earned his plane passage to Europe by selling tickets to Princetonians. He never had that much money because his family had lost a lot of it. So Harry had to make his own money. He hitched across the country four times. That's very enterprising even nowadays, when it would now be too dangerous, no doubt. He got around on his motorcycle. He always had the capacity for doing what he had to do. It's been a life-saving capacity. He's always lived by his wits. He's never shirked. In fact he once delivered a little speech about the workers, not the shirkers. He's always taken on the full load of responsibility for keeping our house together. All through our horrible times Harry has been there. He's always come through.

At a very early age, Harry assumed responsibility for himself and had to make it on his own. He was not only focused, but had the ambition to succeed. He was used to hard work. He obviously was bright enough not to have to work hard academically at Princeton, but he worked hard in other areas when he focused on something. When Harry puts his mind to something he'll do it and do it very well.

I don't remember exactly how the rest of that New Year's Eve weekend went, but I do know that it was uneventful—maybe that's good? The major participants in this romance were my grandmother and Harry's father. I remember once in a cab Harry's father said to him, "Oh, she's too good for you." Another time he said, "She's got such fat legs." I still have short legs, can't really do much about that, but I had a good figure in those days and was much thinner than I am now, naturellement!

I was back at Albertus for the spring semester to finish my sophomore year, but found the time to return to New York a few weeks later to attend Harry's brother's wedding. He was older than Harry by two years, and had a great society wedding. The family he married into was very interesting. I was very fond of my sister-in-law, Helen Louise. She was terrific.

My mother had married again, her third and last time. Everyone was in New York, but I was up in New Haven in college. I went back and forth all the time. I remember once we had a snowstorm and I didn't get back to Albertus until 2 a.m. Already my reputation at Albertus was getting slightly sullied as I was considered irresponsible. By that time, either intuitively or subconsciously, I knew I was going to get married. To be very honest, I didn't want to lose my chastity and I was worried I might, so I thought I had better get married. To that end, my grandmother told me to have this young man declare his intentions.

At that moment, my mother and her new husband were in New York at the Croydon Hotel for a few months. Everyone was always traveling between Paris and Beverly Hills. My grandmother usually stayed at the Grosvenor Hotel down on 10th Street and Fifth Avenue. She knew everybody there and they knew her. She was really an old New Yorker at heart. She had Dutch, English and Irish blood. She spoke like FDR, with the same upstate New York accent. She was an exceedingly distinguished woman for as I've said she had been given the Legion d'Honneur. Of course she had great presence. She dominated me. She had amazing friends from the lowest cab drivers to chiefs of state, a truly amazing person.

My mother was also going back to the West Coast and I wanted to be with her. I sensed the relationship that she and I should have: I wasn't happy with her life and I wanted to be with her to help her. I was always reversing roles. My mother leaned on me for everything: she was an eternal child. I was really like my grandmother's child. I didn't like my second step-father as well as Mr. Rosson. In spite of what had happened, I had a real affection for Rosson after the divorce because he was, in his way, a fine man, in spite of certain weaknesses. Of course we had troubles with him and sometimes it was pretty terrible, but by and large, there was a nobility about Rosson; he had a lot of talent, a lot of strength. I came to like Rosson better after he and my mother were divorced, merely because, they were two disparate souls, as I said earlier, that just couldn't live together harmoniously. I think it was my mother's wildness that drove him to the edge. She couldn't have been too easy to live with, with her extravagance about everything.

Of the third man, the less said the better. He was manic depressive. I suspected that if ever anybody I ever met was evil, he must have been. But knowing what I know now about mental disease, that there is an element of negative presence in madness, may temper my original impressions of him. Perhaps from his mental disease or from some more sinister source, in this guy I sensed there was a whole lot of negative presence. My mother had fallen again into a tragic situation which destroyed her in more ways than one. It was tragic and I wanted to get away from it. I really didn't want to go back.

But I was going to go back anyway, back to California, because I sensed my mother needed me. One night in the car I told Harry I was going to transfer from Albertus to Scripps Institute so I could be closer to my mother. I had also decided that at Scripps I would study with Millard Sheets, one of the great art instructors at the time. I may also have had an idea of possibly getting back together with the nice boyfriend Jim, once back in California.

75

Nevertheless, remembering that my grandmother had told me to find out what were Harry's intentions, the opportunity came when Harry and I were in the back of a cab after we looked—unsuccessfully—for a place to smooch around Grant's tomb. In those days there was no place in New York for young people to court, and my grandmother didn't like me going to men's apartments unchaperoned. I remember when I first met Harry, he called me from his hotel which happened to be in the red light district in Paris, right next to the Gare St. Lazare (the St. Lazarus train station). My mother escorted me in a cab to meet him. I was a bit embarrassed but eventually I came around to seeing that it was a good idea after all.

Anyway, back to the cab in New York. I told Harry, "My grandmother said I should ask you to declare your intentions, as I am going back to California." He said, after a pause, "Well, I guess you should marry me." Then I said, "Okay, I guess I will marry you." I thought my grandmother would be pleased and certainly my mother would be very pleased. She was always trying to marry me off to people, some of whom were rather strange.

For example, there was this boy at Yale who was an heir to a witch hazel company in Connecticut whom I met in Paris. My mother actually used witch hazel for her skin and doubtless hoped that something would come of the relationship which would also be to her advantage. I remember her pouring witch hazel over herself in the bathtub. One of her idiosyncrasies was to have me sit on a chair and keep her company while she was taking a bath. Don't ask me why! She poured the witch hazel with paeans of praise for the witch hazel heir in some kind of pseudo French. My mother was very funny.

The witch hazel heir was strange indeed. Once he took me to his room at Yale and opened his closet as some special favor. It was full of whips, chains and assorted instruments, really! It was a store of sado-masochistic equipment. I didn't have the slightest notion about those things, but after seeing that closet, needless to say, when he proposed marriage, I declined as gracefully as possible.

My mother also tried to get me linked to a Prince d'Arenberg. Really! We were at the races at Long Champs and I ran the other way.

It wasn't to be any of these, it was to be Harry and that's how it happened. Harry was on the verge of pulling out a few times. We really weren't that much in love with each other. It was almost an arranged marriage through my grandmother and his father. We were both young: we didn't have any direction; I was about to go to California, Harry was lonely; he needed somebody to look after him. Then the Korean War broke out and it looked as if Harry might be drafted. However, if he were to be married before the draft, his selective service status would change. With a kind of a hurry-up situation on our hands, we got married in two months.

As I've already said, Harry and I attended his older brother's wedding, which took place in February shortly after Harry proposed. I wore this awful looking hat that resembled a flower pot, since my mother had stopped dressing me and I had no taste in clothes. My mother was having loads of problems with her new husband and simply didn't have the time. Because of that flower-pot hat, Harry joked that maybe he shouldn't marry me. I got rid of the hat, and I told him that he had to marry me because we had made all the arrangements and it was too late not to.

I got engaged in February. When I announced my engagement and showed my ring to everybody at school, the nuns said I had better leave. I agreed and left Albertus in March, in mid-semester. Wasn't that silly? In those days my mother and grandmother really wanted me to get married and I wanted to get married, so education wasn't considered as important then to young women as now. I didn't think I would need all this education anyway. I thought I'll get married, be a mother, have a family. So, I left Albertus and it was okay. Nobody cared. What was important was that I was finally going to get married.

It was to be in New York and we did want a big wedding. Behind the scenes my mother had to dredge up some money for this wedding. Her new husband wasn't about to spring for it, although he was pretty generous. There was a lot about that situation I knew nothing about. I was very spoiled—there's no question about it—and unaware of my mother's financial situation which was not good.

I just assumed I had money. I assumed also that there would always be money the way it always had been. After I left Albertus, I came to New York and stayed with a friend of the family, Jean Helm, who had a beautiful apartment on Fifth Avenue overlooking Central Park. She was a neatnik of a very tall order and I was too messy for her so she threw me out. So I moved in with my grandmother at the Grosvenor which was fine.

We were married on April 14, 1951. We had a large wedding at St. Vincent Ferrer Church with the reception at 1A East 77th around the corner from Jean's apartment. We had Ben Cutler's orchestra. It was a very nice wedding. It was frequently hilarious because there were so many diverse elements: Harry's friends and family from New York and Rumson; some of my Irish Catholic friends from Albertus Magnus; and there were three priests to marry us—all friends of my grandmother. One was Monsignor Devlin, whom she flew in from California, and was considered the "padre of the movies." Monsignor Devlin was very famous in Hollywood. He was a superb intellectual Irishman who had a vast Mozart collection among other things and was the official technical advisor for all the Catholic movies made in Hollywood. Loretta Young used to attend Mass frequently at his church in West Hollywood, St. Victor's.

At the wedding my husband's godfather, who was a car salesman in New Jersey, an alcoholic, and other things too, I think, said to the padre, "Oh, I'm a high Episcopalian," to which the padre replied, "Well, you're high all right!" That was one of the little jokes of our wedding that we remember with a smile.

My godfather, Pascal Bonetti, gave me away. He flew over
from Paris. This very distinguished man, a marvelous person
to give somebody away at a wedding, was my real father in
many ways. He looked to be so good for the part that he
might have come from Central Casting

Grandmother also had Monsignor Brosnan who was the uncle
of the girl with whom I had gone to France. My grandmother was
absolutely, completely pro-Irish! It was unbelievable! She was only
about one quarter Irish herself, and had never even been to Ireland, for heaven's sake, but as far as she saw things, the Irish could
do no wrong. It's rubbed off on me too. I finally went to Ireland and
I must say I found the country and the people to be wonderful. The
third priest was Father Ed Gaffney, an old friend from the First World
War who'd gone to Louvain University in Belgium.

My grandmother masterminded the wedding—the church ceremony part anyway. My godfather, Pascal Bonetti, gave me away. I didn't want any of my step-fathers doing that. My godfather flew over from Paris. That was very touching, wonderful. This very distinguished man, a marvelous person to give somebody away at a wedding, was my real father in many ways. He looked to be so good for the part that he might have come from Central Casting.

It was a very happy period from the time of my engagement throughout the preparation, including picking out the bridesmaids' gowns at Henri Bendel. It was very exciting and very scary. To get married! Oh, my goodness! I remember we went to the Plaza Hotel for our wedding night and then we went to Bermuda for our honeymoon. My mother, in her zany enthusiasm, had given us a newfangled suitcase where all you did was to turn something around and it locked. Naturally the suitcase fell open right in the middle of the lobby of The Plaza. All our clothes had been tied in knots and the suitcase was full of confetti, thrown in by my step-brothers who were nevertheless nice kids and with whom I always retained friendships. Who should walk in but one of Harry's distinguished old foes! It was a ludicrous, hilarious situation. We didn't stay at any swanky inn in Bermuda, but it was lovely. We got so sunburned that we couldn't go out in the sun for a whole week. I remember the wonderful vegetables, onions and carrots, at the inn. (I am too food oriented!) I always remember what people ate. Harry's family had a house in Bermuda, but because it was rented we couldn't use it. We did use the house only once with our daughter Patricia's godfather, Graham Shanley, a very witty and engaging person—Harry's only Catholic friend. Harry's mother's ashes were buried there, and we brought her tombstone back when the house was sold.

While we were away on our honeymoon, my mother, with her flamboyant extravagance, fixed up a wonderful apartment. I must say I was very pleased with myself for getting our apartment. We were on a very low budget so I read the *Sunday New York Times* on a Saturday night, no less! and saw an ad for a third story apartment at 8 East 92nd Street. A very good address, and only $165 which was $15 more than Harry's monthly rent allowance on our budget. I remember taking a cab very early in the morning and running up the stairs and beating somebody by five minutes. I signed the lease. Our landlady, Mrs. Stanley, and her dog, Johnny, would always send us a Christmas card signed from her and Johnny. She was a very nice lady and when I got pregnant, which was immediately, she would wash my dishes if I were really under the weather. We had a very good relationship.

My mother furnished the apartment as a surprise when we came home and it was beautiful. We still have some of the furniture. It still is great. It wasn't until some years later that we were able to purchase such good things for our home. The reason I liked this place was that it had a door made from a window and we had a lovely little balcony. When we had parties we'd crush 20 people on our little balcony. When Patricia was a baby I'd take her out there in the sun. I have a lot of photographs from that time: I took vast quantities of photographs of everything. As an adoring new mother I remember taking a picture of Patricia every month for the first twelve months and putting them in her baby book.

Our life in New York at that time was really fun. We were young marrieds, had this darling apartment, lots of friends and hosted many parties. We were very socially active even though we were on a very tight budget. I remember that when I shopped at the supermarket, I was to spend $19 for food for two people for one week and if I went over my $19 budget, I was in trouble, really! If my mother or grandmother were in town they would take me out to buy extra stuff, but if they weren't around, I had to stay within the budget.

CHAPTER TEN

WE MOVE TO CALIFORNIA

Yes, our first year together in New York was fun. Patricia arrived. I had another child, Henry, right after Patricia and space in our apartment rapidly became a problem. I was pregnant with my third child almost immediately, so we thought we'd better move. Our lease was up. We looked around. We had some friends who lived in Wilton, Connecticut who worked at Dominic with Harry. I didn't know anything about the East Coast so we considered moving to Wilton because these friends were there. We looked around at various places and then there was a Revolutionary War era house that formerly had been rented to Leadbelly, the great folksinger. It was at the corner of Belden Hill and Drumhill Roads.

The real estate agent told me to write to the owner who lived in Minneapolis. I write great letters sometimes (when I'm inspired by the Holy Spirit), so I wrote to say how poor we were and that we really had to live in her house, that she could live in the little guest cottage adjoining the main house. Much to my amazement and to Harry's astonishment, she said she would live in the guest cottage and she gave us quite a good deal on the rent. We were very lucky to get it.

So, after living in New York for two-and-a-half years we moved to that old 18th century house in Wilton, Connecticut. Nevertheless, when my grandmother visited, she took one look at our back porch, with its large cockroach population, and said, "My God, this place looks like the black hole of Calcutta!" I was rather bewildered, but my husband was angry. He and my grandmother did not get along very well. Of course she doted on me, since I was her replacement daughter. My grandmother didn't like it when I took my marital vows seriously, and put my husband ahead of everybody.

But after a year and a half in Wilton, Connecticut, we decided to move West to California, to my mother's house on Chevy Chase Drive, because of the possibilities of greener fields for my husband's career. My husband was willing to take a new job in a fresh financial enterprise in Los Angeles. Another consideration was that my mother's health was not very stable, and her house in Beverly Hills was to be vacated in a couple of months.

On October 5, 1954, my mother came East to take our two babies, Henry (eighteen months old) and Marianne (four months old) and fly them West. We took the oldest, Patricia, who was two-and-a-half and very precocious, in the back seat of my stepfather's Jaguar all the way across the country. The only toy I remember giving her to keep her occupied was a doctor's kit, an ominous coincidence that will be played out for the rest of our lives.

While we drove as fast as we could, with 900 pounds of books behind us in a U-Haul trailer, Hurricane Carol was coming up the coast rapidly, and was beginning to flood New Jersey. The storm came upon us just as we had turned onto the highway that went from New Jersey, through Pennsylvania. Our route would pass through Ohio, Indiana, Illinois, Iowa, Nebraska, Colorado, Arizona and finally California, our final destination. We were literally driving through the hurricane and couldn't see where we were going because the windshield wipers simply could not keep up with the amount of water that was pouring down. As we were crawling towards an underpass, not seeing where we were going, there was a thump, thump, thump on the window. We rolled it down, letting in torrents of water and there was a policeman yelling at us. He said "Don't you twerps from California have any sense? (My stepfather's car had California plates.) That underpass now has eight feet of water in it. You would have been drowned." The rest of the trip West was interesting and safer too. We met some of Harry's college friends as we made our way across the country. We made it over Wolf Pass in the Rockies, where the aspens had turned to gold. It was breathtaking, an adventure.

On our arrival in Los Angeles, we had to move into my stepfather's home since the tenants were still in my mother's house on Chevy Chase Drive, which was behind the Beverly Hills Hotel and right down the street from the Beverly Hills Women's Club.

My stepfather, Hal Rosson, had been divorced from my mother, but was still in love with her. In his way, as I've said many times already, he was a good man. He put all five of us up in his house. Of course it had enough room, because it seems as if every house in Beverly Hills had enough room! Mr. Rosson even let my husband and me use the room which belonged to his deceased sister, Gladys, who was Cecil B. DeMille's secretary, and some say occasional mistress for 35 years. Allowing us to use her room was really an honor in view of his special relationship with Gladys. But he made one stipulation in this regard, and that was that we should keep a fresh pink rose in it every day.

This was the time, alas the only time in my life when we had a really good professional nanny who also happened to be English. She occupied the room next to ours and what I remember most clearly about her is that she gave the children much attention. She took a liking to Henry because he was such a bright little boy and was practically speaking like an adult at only one and a half. This might have been due to his own emerging brilliance and/or to that of the superior nanny. However, not to disparage a really good nanny, I can't help reflecting back on that time and wondering how much better life would have been if my real father and my mother had been around to be nurturing grandparents to my children. Unfortunately, I had to rely on paid help, the kind of help that I could afford (not much). Eventually those nannies had to help with the care of a handicapped child. Alas, over the years we have had some real doozies, an understatement, to say the least.

When Harry and I were married in New York, I did not tell

him about Mr. Rosson because I was so embarrassed to admit that my mother had had three husbands. Although my mother's last husband was present at our wedding it was my godfather, Pascal Bonetti—the male figure that really raised me, thank God—who gave me away.

My grandmother had lots of Irish cronies, one of whom was a photographer for the *New York Daily News*. He took a photograph of Harry and me leaving St. Vincent Ferrer's Church and underneath was the caption, "East mates West," a mantram for our life.

EAST MATES WEST. Mr. and Mrs. Seggerman are rightfully gay after their wedding yesterday in the Church of St. Vincent Ferrér, 66th St. and Lexington Ave. Mrs. Seggerman is the former Patricia Crellin of Los Angeles, Her bridegroom is a Princeton graduate from Tuxedo Park and New York City.

Harry and Mr. Rosson finally did meet and Harry's family and Mr. Rosson got along very well because they were all culturally and otherwise Anglo-Saxon. Harry's father and step-mother lived in Tuxedo Park as well as New York City. One weekend I remember Mr. Rosson visiting us when we went to a party at the home of George A. Baker, a well-known financier. Mr. Rosson came along for the ride and was absolutely tickled pink, since his roots were working class and he kept saying how he loved the furniture there.

There was another most interesting person, Hazzard Reeves, a wealthy eccentric, who also lived in the Park. When they were removing the bed of the river to make it into the Tuxedo Park Golf Course, Hazzard Reeves took the topsoil from the river and turned it into a huge organic garden. Further, he boasted that he had the largest ham radio in the world. He certainly had the largest aerial contraption that I had ever seen on private property.

When we moved from New York City to Wilton, Connecticut for a year and a half, Mr. Rosson came to take pictures of our two oldest children who were still toddlers. He forgot to put film in his camera, which was very disappointing but typical of absent-minded geniuses. On another occasion he volunteered to rent a projector for Patricia's eighth birthday. Her special request was *Pinocchio* (not Van Johnson!). It took him almost three hours to run the movie. The invited children were having a rambunctious time while their parents sat in their cars in front of the house, getting more and more impatient. Mr. Rosson reminded me of the old Robert Benchley movies where everything goes eccentrically wrong. By the way, I sincerely recommend Benchley's, *The Sex Life of a Newt*, if you haven't seen it. I took my husband down to Greenwich Village a few years ago to see it; it still holds up very well.

Mr. Rosson had a very good heart, but it was his drinking problem that made life with him so difficult. I remember that when my mother announced that she was divorcing him, I grabbed her with joy, and danced around with her because he was very abusive to her and in some ways to my brother, Edward and me. Nevertheless, he continued to see my mother after the divorce; the relationship improved. I know I liked him better after the divorce. I think they were still friends even after she married the man who made her very unhappy—her third and last husband—a man I liked the least of all the men I have ever met, for a good number of reasons.

Mr. Rosson moved to Malibu around 1956, after we had been in California for two years. Malibu was a very devastating experience for him. In 1960 there was the famous Malibu fire and he barely managed to save his own house by hosing it down himself. The Filipino houseman had taken off in Mr. Rosson's Cadillac. That really undid him. I returned to California to see him after we had moved back to New York in 1960. He was very taken with me because I was looking good in those days. He offered me some money which unfortunately I declined because I did not want him to feel he had to give me something just because I went to see him. As it turned out, that was the last time I ever saw him again. He went to live with his extremely avaricious sister who lived in Palm Beach in the winter and the South Shore of Long Island in the summer. Whether his decline was due to senility or drinking or whatever, there was no question that he was sedated at all times and also given powerful drugs. As I said before, I really liked Mr. Rosson, after the divorce. In fact you could say I eventually loved him too and therefore I was very upset when he was taken out of our lives like that. His sister wanted to inherit some of the De Mille millions. I did try to go and see him in Long Island and was given a terrible reception by the family. Poor Mr. Rosson seemed very drugged. I also tried to go and see him in South Palm Beach once when I was attending a seminar there, but the maid said I was, "persona non grata." They were obviously afraid he would give me some money. That would have been nice, but all I really wanted was to say hello just one more time, more than anything else.

87

The last time I had anything to do with the Rosson family was when Mr. Rosson died. And he was buried in the cemetery beside his sister and Cecil B. De Mille. Interestingly enough, it was a Masonic funeral, with the men wearing their aprons and everything. The fact that Mr. Rosson was a Mason prevented me from going to Catholic schools when we were in Beverly Hills. I would have been much happier, but that was not to be.

At his funeral there were some members of the second generation of the Rosson family. I think Arthur Rosson's son was there. In that family there was a marriage to the movie director, Victor Fleming, and to the actor Lee Bowman, but it seemed to me that nobody did anything interesting after Mr. Rosson died.

I was looking for suitable transportation to the funeral and burial for myself our son, Henry, then a fledgling movie producer on the West Coast, and so, after some research I found the MuMu Limousine Co. in San Fernando Valley. It was run by a couple of Pakistanis who sent their one and only white stretch limo to take us to the funeral held in a Masonic hall and then to the Hollywood entertainment industry's cemetery. Definitely a grade B movie scenario.

Mr. Rosson had an effect on my brother and me and our families for certain. It was this very connection with the movies that finally led me to this new amazing path, to the inspiration and beacon for my life—the personage known as Our Lady of Guadalupe which I will discuss in great detail later.

Somewhere in my past, maybe when I was four or so, when I had the imaginary friend who was my guardian angel, I decided that the only family I would ever really have was The Holy Family, as pictured on religious cards. So they welcomed me with open arms and adopted me. This is largely why I have always had a "coming home" feeling with regard to the Church.

CHAPTER ELEVEN

MY MOTHER'S DEATH

The pivotal day to end all pivotal days in my life came on September 29, 1955. It was the day my mother died: she was only 43 years old. I was only 24 and had four children under the age of four. To fully explain the grief and shock that day brought is near impossible. The only metaphor that comes to mind is the shocked reaction to the sinking of the Titanic. Nobody was expecting it and boom! "Husbands and wives, little children, lost their lives, when the big ship went down."

In 1992, the brilliant and respected movie commentator, Michael Medved, wrote a book entitled, *Hollywood*. Its basic premise is that there is a kind of madness or lack of rational thinking among the people who make decisions about what kind of "product" comes out of Hollywood. In other words, they seem to have lost their senses. But Medved didn't expand on the specific nature of this madness. He sees signs of hope for the future of Hollywood, and maybe he must, so he ends his book by quoting Winston Churchill, "could this be the end of the beginning?"

That's how it was for us when my mother died. At the ending of her life, precious to us all, a new life had to start, out of necessity. There was no way we could cope without her. To say she was the most charismatic woman that I, or my husband, or her mother, or my oldest daughter, or her three husbands and many lovers had ever known, was an understatement. Someone had taken the light out of our room: it was "the early rain", as spoken of by the Kansas City prophets. It was as if Tinker Bell's light had been permanently extinguished.

My Mother in 1948

My Mother

The end of the beginning started on September 29, 1955, the Feast of St. Michael the Archangel. That afternoon, I was just getting to the last assignment on my workaholic list of chores, cleaning up the house, which was the organizing of our collection of 78 RPM discs of classical music; French singers and folk songs. My husband and I had met at a Bach concert in Paris in 1950 and we have been avid music buffs ever since. We played our phonograph records a great deal in those days. We did not have a television set yet in those days, thank God!

Suddenly, I got a call from my grandmother, who was living with my mother at that apartment on Wilshire Boulevard in West Los Angeles. She said to me in a voice that sounded as if it had been knocked out of its voice box, "There is something wrong with your mother. She is on the kitchen floor and is not moving."

My heart started pounding and I knew something terrible had happened; something really too terrible, to which I did not want to give words. I called my husband at work for him to come home immediately so we could go over to my mother's apartment, since we had only one car.

When we got there, the paramedics were giving my mother CPR on the floor of the kitchen. My grandmother was sitting in a chair next to the window, facing the balcony on Wilshire Boulevard, rocking back and forth and rubbing her legs. Then the paramedic said that it was hopeless, she was dead. Somehow I found the strength to call Hal Rosson, who throughout his life, had loved her very much. No doubt he had married her not only for her amazing charisma, but also for the fact, as I found out many years later, that she was a dead ringer for the actress, Jean Harlow, who had been his first wife, except that my mother didn't dye her hair blonde.

I had a revulsion for my mother's third husband, who, because I held him responsible for some unspeakable acts of unkindness from the beginning of their marriage, I made no contact with him. I called my brother. I don't remember very much about what happened other than that I was sobbing and grabbing the outer door of the apartment for support. Shock was fast closing in around memory.

That evening, as I was putting our oldest child, our four-year-old daughter, Patricia, who worshipped my mother, to bed, tears came streaming down my face. I could not possibly tell her what had happened, about her grandmother's death earlier that evening. However, these are the events which flashed through my mind.

Sitting in that room in a phantasmagoric reverie, I saw my mother's face in the mirror of the closet door and she was in a great deal of pain. Then there was another face which I did not recognize so I asked, "Who are you?" and the reply was, "I am Guadalupe."

I did not know who that was, but I asked her, "whoever you are Guadalupe, please come to my aid." I had a horrible dream about my mother that night, so horrible that I cannot even put it down in this book. I pray for her always.

The next morning, two things happened. First, there was the sheriff at our front door saying he had been sent by my horrible second step-father to take back the paintings he had loaned my mother, who in turn had loaned them to us. My mother's body could not even have been cold yet, so who could have told him about her death so soon?

He was the only man I have ever met that I could say was an evil person (because I had never met people like Hitler or sadists and people like that). I have been thankfully sheltered from those things to a certain extent.

Some weird circumstances always made me wonder whether or not he had one of his girlfriends at the time, one of many, a real estate agent that my mother happened to visit the afternoon before she died, do something, something horrible. I imagined it must have been some kind of long-acting poison because this man, my horrible step-father, at that time was about to be made to pay my mother some serious alimony. He had every reason for wanting to get rid of her. Some years later, I noticed that this real estate girlfriend of his had opened her very own real estate office, a very fancy establishment, on South Robertson Boulevard in Los Angeles. But suspicious coincidental circumstances may or may not support serious allegations and I am not making any here.

The second thing that happened, two days after my mother's death, was that the door bell rang, in the very early hours, even before the daily struggle to give breakfast to my four babies, two of whom were still in diapers. On the steps, at the front door, was a very broad, not fat, but very broadly built woman of Mexican descent with severe acne on her face. "Who are you?" I asked her. "I am Juana Linn. The agency sent me." I was dumbfounded; she was the best present I could ever have received, coming exactly at this time of great need.

Some weeks before, out of sheer desperation, knowing that I needed help with my four little children, I called an agency to see if they had anyone who was willing to accept the low salary I could afford. They said that they didn't, but would keep my name on file. That was early August, 1955, six weeks before my mother died.

Juana Linn arrived on October 1, two days after my mother's death. No doubt she was accompanied by a choir of angels, since she was sent by the Queen of the Angels, La Senora de Los Angeles, after whom the city of Los Angeles was named, and the place where I was born. I didn't know it at the time, but that mysterious face I had seen in the mirror the night of my mother's death was indeed the Queen of the Angels.

Juana stayed with us for many years and literally saved the life of our young family. Already the strains were beginning to affect my constitution. I started to develop some serious medical problems, which culminated many years later in a hysterectomy in New York City. I was bleeding to death and had to stay in the hospital for a month.

Juana doted on our youngest child, an adorable and beautiful little baby who was given the name Elizabeth, which is on her birth certificate, but we changed it to Yvonne, my mother's name, right after my mother died, to honor her. Juana would take occasional trips to visit her family in Mexico. At these times, I had to resort to pinch-hitting. I had to make do with a few part-time baby sitters too.

After Juana left for good we were able to acquire Maureen Clegg, a young Anglo-Irish woman. I know my grandmother would have attributed her good qualities to the fact that she was of Irish extraction. Maureen was more than a nanny. She was a wonderful mother's help or as they say in French, "bonne à tous faire." Life was pretty hard in those days in California because a few years following my mother's death my oldest daughter developed health problems, which necessitated special care which I will discuss later. Anyway there we were with our first-born in a full body cast, three younger children, no parents, and no money. But somehow we all survived, thank God, with the aid of that young English woman. She helped me with everything—everything in the household, housework, the four children—everything!! and especially with our handicapped daughter.

I remember mainly just taking the children to school and back, figuring out their carpools from our place in Beverly Hills, and everything else—that took about half of my day. Thank God for this English girl. She tried to leave once but I blocked her at the pass!

My daughter in her full-bodied plaster cast and wheelchair became very attached to this young woman because she was such a good person and helped take such good care of her—did much of the primary care, really. I remember one afternoon in particular. My daughter was in her full-length cast and wheelchair and we were walking around Beverly Hills with the other children when a policeman stopped us and asked us why we were walking. That's a typical Beverly Hills joke, as people didn't walk much there. I guess now they're all jogging!

At that time television was just coming in and my husband wanted to get a set for the house. At first I resisted the idea because I didn't think it was good for the children. I wanted them to read. I myself was reading to them pretty regularly and was having a lot of fun doing it, especially doing Brer Rabbit in a southern accent. But eventually I relented. Harry said, "If you let me get a TV set, I'll let you get a drier." So for $100 each we bought a TV set and a drier in a compromise. The TV set turned out to be a good thing after all because, I guess, my whole life of fitness started a few days later when Jack Lalanne came on the screen.

95

He was so cheerful with his wife Elaine and with his dog, doing these exercises that he got me out of any depression I might have suffered.

I said to myself that this was good stuff and I was going to do it, and that is not even considering Captain Kangaroo, Mr. Green Jeans, Crabby Appleton and Manfred, the wonder dog for the children. Such non-violent and wonderful people in those innocent times! Where are you now?

It was November 4, 1956. Something happened that I remember vividly. The Soviet tanks rolled into Budapest and put down the brave Hungarians—the great Magyar race with whom I have a great affinity. (Remember Leslie Howard). Their rebellion was squelched brutally, very similarly to the more recent one in Tiannamen Square in June 1989. My children were in one of the small upstairs rooms, sleeping in bunk beds built by a kindly Norwegian carpenter who gave us a price break because we were poor, "Down and out in Beverly Hills". My little children and I said a daily rosary for the Hungarians for a whole week after that in their little attic room.

Almost two years thereafter on that fateful day in October 1958, over the radio comes the news that after a severe bout of hiccups, my great "Pope of My Youth," as characterized by the great Anglo-Irish writer, Aubrey Menen, Pope Pius XII, had expired. Perhaps if I had been blessed with the courage, commitment and health to continue saying the rosary with my brave little children, things might have been better.

We were lonely in Beverly Hills because we didn't know too many people. Those few friends that we had were mostly connected to my mother's lawyer, a Catholic, and then there were a few of my Catholic friends. However, since we weren't too far from UCLA (University of California at Los Angeles) I joined some of the University's committees as well as others so that I might meet local people. One of these committees was the Los Angeles World Affairs Council. I was the official French speaking chauffeur who handled the French speaking visitors of the Los Angeles

World Affairs Council—doing my duties in the most beaten down Dodge convertible you could ever care to see. So I would chauffeur these French-speaking Africans and all those other people who didn't speak any English, and that was pretty amusing. At least it got me out of the house and gave me a diversion.

I remember once driving down Olympic Boulevard in the convertible with all these Africans in the back seat, and by some incredible coincidence our gardener, who was Burmese (this was his neighborhood), was walking down the sidewalk. Anyway, here was this Burmese gardener looking at his employer driving along in her convertible with all these Africans. I smiled and said, "Why not!" As the thousand-year-old man said about the plastic bags, "That was good."

Little did I know it but my association with the World Affairs Council, not unlike many other events in my life, was preparing me for the time when I would be hosting conferences with distinguished guest speakers. Through my efforts at volunteering I met such famous world leaders as the German Chancellor, Konrad Adenauer, and Indian Prime Minister Jawaharlal Nehru.

I was present for the First International Music Festival in L.A. and met Bart Lytton, the Soviet composer Tikhon Kremnikov, as well as Lukas Foss. Dear, wonderful, Lukas Foss later became a member of my board when I started my own foundation. This was the first time I had heard this extraordinary man play the Bach *Brandenburg Concerto #5*, with the cadenza from the second movement.

I was also involved with the UCLA Art Gallery when, in 1960, the year Picasso turned sixty, Frederick Wight, the very brilliant and charismatic gallery director after whom the gallery was named, wished to give a show called, "Happy Birthday, Mr. Picasso." I had a beautiful Picasso, so he took a slide of it and sent it to the French Picasso expert who said that it was not "right," which in the art world means, not authentic. Wight thought it was too beautiful a picture not to be authentic, so he wrote to Picasso himself who told him that he did indeed paint it. In fact the lady in it, he said, is Jean Avril, a famous cabaret singer of the time. She was often painted by Toulouse-Lautrec. I sold that painting later, much too cheaply, to help support a relative who was in financial straits.

In 1961 I founded an organization, The Westside Association for Gifted Children, in an attempt to start a school for children who would not be intellectually challenged in the usual academic environment. This idea was the result of my realization that our second child, Henry, was unusually bright for his age and that whatever potential he had should be stimulated and developed in the right environment. I organized our first public meeting at which our guest speaker was Dr. John C. Gowan, a nationally known authority on the gifted child and then Professor of Education at the San Fernando Valley State College. Unfortunately, this idea never came to fruition because shortly after that meeting, my husband's business activities required us to move back East.

Life was a struggle in Los Angeles. My husband, being in the investment business which in those days was 90% New York, had some difficulty in establishing himself initially. Furthermore, he didn't like California. He was really like a fish out of water— an Easterner and moreover an Easterner who seemed quite British to the Californians with his reserved demeanor and accent.

Whether I liked it or not we were going to have to leave California since my husband had become an expert in foreign stock investments and needed to come back East to further his career. So after our thirteenth trip to Yosemite, where we brought all of our children to say goodbye, thanking the Almighty for our consolation, annual trips to one of the mightiest wonders of the natural world, we moved back East.

CHAPTER TWELVE

NATURAL DISASTERS

As a native of Southern California I grew up with earthquakes and fires which are endemic to the region. My first recollection was falling out of bed at midnight in 1938 for a 5.5 earthquake that rumbled through Brentwood, West Los Angeles, where my family lived.

Shortly after that, my stepfather, Hal Rosson, took me to the Riviera Country Club, a golf and polo club for movie stars and other assorted magnates at the time, to watch the whole mountain range behind us on fire. He said, "Don't worry Annabella, it won't harm us here. The Fire Department has hosed down everything between there and here."

But in the last days of December 1959, my husband's roommate from Princeton and his new bride of two years visited us in Beverly Hills for a New Year's holiday. We took a walk on the afternoon of December 31st, up Tower Grove Drive, past Walt Disney's house and the homes of other movie people, when we noticed a tendril of smoke rising in the distance. I said to myself, being a native Californian unlike the others, "That looks like the beginning of a fire." A few hours later, near our home, our own little mountain range above Benedict Canyon, which goes over the crest at Mulholland Drive, the road that runs along the tops of all the hills behind Hollywood, Beverly Hills, Belair and then down into Santa Monica, was all on fire!

Since it was New Year's Eve we wanted to take our Eastern guests to a party in one of the sprawling suburbs of this vast city, but we had four small children at home with our Anglo-Irish nanny, Maureen, and under the circumstances we couldn't go far, if at all. The Fire Department seemed to be very active, keeping things under control. So, instead of the fancy party miles away that we had planned to attend, we decided to make do with a quick trip to Ah Fong, the local Chinese restaurant, which was not only open, but the closest place to our house, only 10 minutes away. I remember vividly to this day going to Ah Fong's telephone booth every half hour to see if everything was OK at home. After our last fortune cookie, we rushed home where everyone was fine. The famous fire of January 1, 1960 was finally extinguished—maybe a week or so later.

These are extreme events which I remember vividly. In those days I didn't think much of it since in those days they were few and far between. But they may very well have been harbingers of future events.

Early in January 17, 1994, before the dawn broke, residents of Los Angeles and especially in this instance our older son, Henry, his wife and child, Alexandra—our granddaughter—were awakened by a deep rumbling. And then they felt it; the whole house was rumbling in a North-South motion instead of East-West which made this earthquake deadly different. Unfortunately for them all of their books were facing East-West and didn't fall out but all their china was facing North-South and took a direct hit. They were among the lucky ones though since there was only some structural damage to the house which was fixed in about two months' time.

Only recently I reviewed a documentary on this famous earthquake, one of many that have hit the Pacific region in recent years. The seismologist said there was no known fault, this was a new type of earthquake. It even took them at least 24 hours to determine where the epicenter was because it was not on a known fault. As we all found out later, it happened to be in Northridge in the San Fernando Valley. Seventeen people were crushed in an apartment building. You may remember pictures of that building in the newspapers.

It was brought to our attention only a month later in the Catholic and Evangelical press that Northridge happened to be the center, you could say the epicenter, of the production of most of the pornography in the world.

Back to Matthew 24 and those of us who read the Bible regularly, I guess we all said, "Wow, it's all coming to pass as predicted and prophesied."

Early in 1995, one of the great predictors of hurricanes said there were going to be more Atlantic hurricanes this year than in the last 50 years and they are going to be very strong. In the prophecies of Daniel in the Old Testament and in Matthew 24 and other places in the New Testament, there is reference to these events.

We have a house in St. Martin where I am writing this paper. As I descended the steps of the airplane and as I drove to my house in a rented convertible, not only was there real physical change with the smashed up boats and houses that were not repaired, but also the landscape looked almost lunar after the catastrophic, Category 5, Hurricane Luis.

Our place was relatively unscathed and we only lost one huge tree which was probably dying anyway. In its place, up popped seven or eight paw paw (papaya) trees, my favorite fruit. After the hurricane it was reported that the places that took the worst hit were the nude beach, and the Dutch side with its preponderance of casinos. I took a bold but controversial step as I felt it was part of the Northridge syndrome which is beginning to unfold as prophesied in Matthew 24.

God, the Father, has in His wisdom given us the beautiful island of St. Martin which He created. It is named after St. Martin of Tours, but I believe it harbors the spirit of St. Martin de Porres, the first Black saint to be canonized by Pope John Paul II, and in whose honor a shrine and hopefully a church will be built as soon as possible. A wake up call! But hopefully this wake up call will not be a repeat of the Scripture that was read at last Sunday's mass:

"But as the days of Noah were, so shall also the coming of the Son of man be. For as in the days that were before the flood they were eating and drinking, marrying and giving in marriage, until the day that Noah entered into the ark. And knew not until the flood came, and took them all away; so shall also the coming of the Son of man be. Then shall two be in the field; the one shall be taken, and the other left. Two women shall be grinding at the mill; the one shall be taken, and the other left. Watch therefore: for ye know not what hour your Lord doth come" (Matt: 24).

A Bronze statue of St. Martin de Porres in the rear of the Dominican church of St. Vincent Ferrer in New York City where Harry and I were married. It is similar to a statue of this beautiful Black saint given to St. Paul's church, Lyford Cay, Bahamas.

CHAPTER THIRTEEN

REMINISCENCES 1957-1971
BACK TO THE EAST COAST

This time we were not accompanied by hurricanes, in fact I don't even remember in any great detail how we moved back. After seven-and-a-half years in California, my husband's business activities necessitated a family move back to the East Coast. I set about selling the house and finally did, though not for a very good price, since the market wasn't very good then.

What I do remember is that the move was fairly arduous since I was pregnant and with the assistance of our wonderful mother's helper, Maureen Clegg, I had to do all the packing. It was November 1961 when we moved back to New York with all the antique furniture and all the paintings, and with our children's nanny. Quite Providentially, we were able to find a triplex for a reduced price, *mirable dictu*, but since it was not vacated we had to stay for a short while in a rather elegant hotel. This was a kind of exciting time for the children, though we had to economize; everybody had to share two breakfasts. Yet we managed; it was fun camping in a New York hotel, an Eloise kind of experience.

We moved to our triplex on 63rd Street where we had a wicker Eiffel Tower which I had bought on Little Santa Monica Boulevard, in Beverly Hills, in a shop owned by Peter Lawford's mother.

I think she must have been selling out her inventory because I managed to get it rather cheaply which was the hallmark for all my purchases in those days because of serious budget constraints. I was a little broke but did have enough money on the side to buy Yvonne her beloved Eiffel Tower (about which I will tell you later when describing us, Americans in Paris) which was really stunning, I must say.

Of course, we brought all our Eiffel Towers with us, large and small, when we moved to New York from California. We put the wicker one in one of the upstairs bedrooms facing South. At that time we had two cats, Boris and Igor, who somehow or other were named by osmosis, so to speak, no doubt influenced by my Russian ancestry. Boris and Igor liked to climb that wicker Tower to sharpen their claws.

There are synchronicities in the smallest details of our lives, positives and negatives, an undeniable order, a pattern. One day we came home after a short holiday away to a most dreadful smell. We thought maybe our sweet landlord (who had reduced the rent) had died while we were away. So on our return we anxiously pounded on the door, and when he answered it, quizzically, we embraced him. He had no clue what the commotion was all about. It turned out that a rat had died in the wall. In the words of the waggish wife of one of Harry's college friends, "Renoir on the wall, rat in the wall." It was a sign that it was time to move out.

But that short holiday away had been to visit with my husband's father and his wife who lived in a charming cottage in Tuxedo Park, New York called, "Glocamorra," from the Broadway show, Finian's Rainbow.

We had a fairly good time while we lived in that New York house. It was good for everybody except Patricia who had some terrible experiences due to her condition. She fell down the stairs leading to our "porch" one night, and I had to rush her to the Emergency Room to make sure that the rod, which Dr. Stinchfield had inserted in her leg, had not moved out of place. That was a very painful episode, one of the things that propelled our move to the country.

But the really intriguing thing about that triplex was our very special neighbors. Gypsy Rose Lee, the famous stripper and sister of June Havoc, lived on one side and down two houses lived Jock Whitney, the famous financier and publisher of the New York and Paris *Herald Tribune* newspapers. Both of their town houses took up the space of two regular town houses. Each had a courtyard. Jock Whitney had a beautiful forest of sorts on his rooftop.

I always liked to have an outdoor area, especially with four children and a new baby. We had this outdoor space, a deck of sorts, which was basically covered with asphalt. I installed one of those outdoor rubber swimming pools and a cupboard where I stored my cooking equipment, which included one of those forms for the famous French confections, Croquenbouche, which I'd used for one of our last dinner parties in Beverly Hills. That was when the fancy pyramid dessert? fell apart and with it—the cream puffs, comprising the pyramid, slid off the plate and almost fell on the floor. That was the dinner to which we had invited the Gettys, the Ahmansons and the Myers, all friends of my Irish Catholic friends, Marie Breslin Thorpe, married to Jack Thorpe, and Anne Breslin de Beixedon, now McGinley, two lovely and sweet girls.

We once visited the de Beixedons, Senior, in East Hampton, Long Island, where old Mr. de Beixedon had a most marvelous collection of antique cars. Besides those twelve meter boats which race in the America's Cup, I admire antique cars, especially the old Citröens which in French films they call, "noir."

Wending my way back to our triplex, in this cupboard on the makeshift deck, were all sorts of rather arcane cooking utensils that I didn't have a place for in my typically New York postage stamp sized kitchen. Nevertheless, I still liked giving dinner parties, at one of which I remember having Fred Gwynne, my favorite male friend with whom I had a marvelous relationship. Fred was an enormously entertaining and charming person of 6 feet 6 inches tall! I do not know why we got along so well. I do know that he liked women a lot. It was just something that I could not put my finger on. Maybe it was the human perspective of the other side of life. He and his wife lost a child who drowned in their pond. I think after that their marriage foundered and they divorced. At the table, one night at our New York triplex, was Fred sitting at my right, by design, of course. He was always very literary and witty. At this party we were talking about real phonies and phony phonies—something I had to make up to keep our conversation going. In those days I always pretended to know more than I really did and therefore was myself a phony!! But as we were talking about somebody I heard myself say, "That person is a real phony." Fred liked that.

CHAPTER FOURTEEN

WE MOVE FROM NEW YORK
TO CONNECTICUT

When we realized we couldn't live in New York City in a $700 a month triplex and pay for expensive schools for the children at the same time, we began to look for a suitable country location. As we deliberated our move we also prepared for the birth of our fifth child, Suzy, who arrived that August. Meanwhile, Patricia was away in Portugal where she spent a happy summer with my aunt and cousins.

As we considered our move, we were torn between Connecticut and New Jersey. Connecticut won out because the children didn't have any grandparents except for my husband's father who had remarried—and that wasn't the same thing as having my husband's mother, or my mother, alive and around for our children. I knew that with a handicapped daughter and four younger children, I would need the moral support of close friends. I had two friends, Nancy Pettee and Laurey Scott, who pulled out all the stops to ensure our move to Westport, Connecticut where they both lived.

Laurey lived in a hunting lodge situated in a beautiful park with her daughter Tatiana, who was beginning to develop symptoms of muscular dystrophy. Maybe it was too much for her husband, a very fine artist, who ran off to Japan and met a Japanese girl. Laurey divorced him and he married the Japanese girl. Despite her own troubles, Laurey was a second mother to my children. I knew that when my daughter was in the hospital in New Haven, that she probably wouldn't have made it but for Laurey's help. Her own daughter, Tatiana, was dying, but Tatiana held on to life until she was 21—very unusual for a girl with Duchennes Muscular Dystrophy to survive that long. It was really the tenacity of her mother's will that sustained Tatiana all those years, plus Tatiana's own indomitable spirit and personal holiness. Coincidentally it was the very same day that I had been scheduled to meet Mother Teresa at a reception in the White House, strange to say, that Tatiana had died.

I sat with Laurey for four days after Tatiana died in her bed. I knew that Tatiana's spirit had not left her body in that time, so we were keeping her company until she decided to move heavenwards on the fourth day.

My other friend in Connecticut, Nancy Pettee, and I were pregnant at the same time—she with her fourth pregnancy, and I with my sixth. That was in 1963. However, while Nancy was pregnant she discovered that she had breast cancer, something that happens to women who are genetically susceptible to the disease which pregnancy sometimes can bring on.

Nancy died leaving five children, including the twin boys who were born a couple of months after my own son, John. Her husband Michael, was fortunate in that he found a wonderful second wife, a real helpmeet, who actually looked like Nancy. They are a very warm and loving Catholic family.

When I was at Albertus Magnus, Michael was at Yale, and he and his Yale friends usually went out with a group of us from Albertus Magnus. We had a wonderful, crazy time that people had in college in those days. As far as I know, not one of us ever slept with those boys. In fact a few of those girls became nuns. That was one of the possibilities I held out for myself, but my mother would not hear of it. What I was not aware of at the time was that nuns didn't get much sleep and my usually precarious state of health required that I get a lot of sleep, or so I thought. Of course nobody ever mentioned to me that mothers of large families, especially where there was illness, didn't get much sleep either.

Finally after eight months in New York City we moved. Our move to Connecticut seemed to have been mapped out while I was at Albertus Magnus. I was awarded the leading rôle in a play by Paul Claudel, "L'annonce faite a Marie," or the Annunciation, and my leading man was Tom Tryon, who was then an actor in Yale Drama School. It was an extremely powerful play and I was excited about becoming an actress with Tom Tryon as my leading man. However God, or fate, had other plans for me and that seeming golden opportunity was scotched because, just at that same time, I became engaged and dropped out of school to get married.

One year after we were married and living in New York, Harry and I went to the Westport Country Playhouse to see a play with Jill Craft, an old friend from Hawthorne School in Beverly Hills, from the early 1940's and Tom Tryon who was her leading man! You can imagine how excited I was to be able to see Jill, my old chum from 20 years back, act in a play with Tom Tryon! It was a perfectly beautiful summer's day in Westport and we had such a wonderful time that I hoped that one day we could move to Westport and eventually we did in July 1962!

Patricia returned from France in November to join the rest of us in Connecticut.

Nothing particularly mystical happened to me during the 1960's. Those were the times of trial—of Patricia's first catatonic episode which lasted one whole week—hence her hospitalization at Yale, New Haven. That was the year of the big blackout. I was left wondering whether she would be okay since all the lights went out when we came home.

109

CHAPTER FIFTEEN

THE TRAUMA OF SUFFERING

Bibliotherapy was always my principal means of escape from troubling situations. For instance, I read *Mad Magazine* for the first time while Patricia was in the Children's Hospital taking tests to determine whether or not she had cancer. I purchased it from a corner drug store across the street from the hospital, on Sunset Boulevard. Years later at Yale, New Haven, where I was later to undergo the worst trauma of my life, unspeakable and unprintable, the few people to whom I blurted out my desperation from the depths of my weakness and passion responded by . . . well how can I say it? . . . . They just blanched. The only thing that got me through it was reading, *The Lord of the Rings*. I am writing this on December 12th, the feast of Our Lady of Guadalupe. It is fitting that on this occasion I have found "a spot," as described by Carlos Castaneda in his book, *Journey to Ixtlan*. Those of you who were reading books in the '60's and '70's, may recall that one of the great folk heroes of the day was the student character of Carlos Castaneda's books, who was Carlos himself. He had been given instructions by a Mexican shaman he referred to as Don Juan. Carlos was also a Mexican! A compatriot of Our Lady of Guadalupe. The teachings of this Mexican shaman in Castaneda's books are somewhat like a Western hemisphere version of feng shui, the Chinese art of positioning objects to obtain the maximum possible harmonic vibrations; the lesson was that it is very important to find your spot in life. Some previous spots I remember very clearly. For example, lying in a hospital room trying to overcome the effects of Demerol and all the other "poisons" that were needed to kill the pain following an emergency hysterectomy. This drastic measure was necessary to prevent me from bleeding to death during my menses. I now remember, after all these years, things that I had read in Carlos Castaneda's works. For 14 years Carlos had been writing about the four things Don Juan had told him: 1) that it was very important to find his spot, 2) that it would be very difficult indeed, but 3) he had to do it and 4) in any space there is always your spot.

Having found my spot, I now have the courage to delve into the early part of my life in order to speak and write about the life of my daughter, Patricia. The outlines of her horrific ordeal are laid out in a following chapter. However, it is only within the context of the apparitions of The Blessed Virgin Mary, especially Fatima, that the whole idea of suffering is beginning to make any sense to me, especially with regard to Patricia and also for the rest of us.

Patricia was the Great Sign to our family, of a major affliction to her as well as to the rest of the family—the hardship we would have to endure for years to come. Her cross gave us the shadows under which we stand and like the end times in whose glory we will also stand at the time of the coming of New Jerusalem; it is an illustration of the very present "mystery of iniquity" revealed to us only when we experience the resurrection of the body.

Patricia was very attached to my mother who died suddenly when Patricia was only four years old. Subsequently, Patricia developed cancer. The growth plate in her leg was removed to prevent the cancer from recurring. On moving to New York we visited an orthopedic surgeon who decided that an amputation was necessary so that Patricia could be fitted with a prosthesis which would aid her in walking.

What I am proposing is a symbolic synchronicity; just as according to John Haffert, Our Lady of Fatima had predicted the Great Sign of January 25 presaging the coming of the Second World War, Patricia, who was born of January 25, was the Great Sign for a major affliction affecting our family.

Patricia's presence was symbolic in other ways as well; she was present in the office of the great orthopedic surgeon at Columbia Presbyterian Hospital, Dr. Frank Stinchfield, who decided to put a rod in her leg to see if he could promote its growth.

While we were there, the eminent journalist, Lowell Thomas, came in to see Dr. Stinchfield. While coming down from the Himalayas, this aging man had suffered a broken back and had to be carried by porters the rest of the way down. Thomas had been given a message by the Dalai Lama of Tibet to warn the world of the invasion of that country by the Red Chinese, yet another move by "The Red Dragon" (communism) in the brutal and vehemently anti-religious takeover of the theocracy of Tibet.

Once again Patricia was linked with a great sign, Lowell Thomas, warning the West about the Red Dragon, this time China, while Patricia and Thomas were very coincidentally (?) in Stinchfield's office at the same time.

We were able to become patients of this remarkable surgeon, Dr. Frank Stinchfield, because the surgeon who operated on Patricia in California was Dr. Charles Lowman, President of the Orthopedic Hospital in Los Angeles, who had treated my stepfather for polio. As I have already said, Patricia's second operation was performed by Dr. Vernon Luck, President of the American Academy of Orthopedic Surgeons, an associate of Dr. Lowman, but who was a very cold and hard man who ordered a full body cast for our daughter for one-and-a-half years!

As a result of going to many physicians over the years, I have developed a very lively negative emotional reaction to such callous people as Dr. Luck, who had no thought of human suffering; he was technological, a scientist; by character, bloodless! I had a similar experience with Patricia's Yale psychiatrist that provoked in me great rancor against these kinds of doctors that lack empathy. For example the kinds of oncologists who automatically put all cancer patients through chemotherapy and exposure to radiation regardless of the suffering these treatments cause, suffering and other symptoms and disability which can be as bad as, if not worse, than the diseases they are intended to cure.

CHAPTER SIXTEEN

HOUSES & GHOSTS?

We had moved from California to New York in November, 1961, and then to Connecticut. I remember that because, on our arrival in New York it was already snowing and Maureen, our children's nanny, burnt out the transmission of our convertible when she got stuck in a deep snow drift.

The house to which we moved in Westport, Connecticut was, unfortunately, in some ways similar to that previous house in Wilton, Connecticut where we had lived when we first got married, the house my grandmother had called "the black hole of Calcutta." This house is now owned by the redoubtable Martha Stewart. It had been owned by an old Connecticut Nutmeg family that I had talked into giving us a low rent!

This Connecticut house was not insulated so we were all freezing to death that first winter. Patricia had to sleep downstairs because she was in a body cast. It was the yeoman, her sister, Yvonne, who helped her with a bed pan at night. Somehow we survived two difficult winters in that house. Henry slept in the library. The most pleasurable thing I can remember about that house is sitting cross-legged in front of the TV set in that library watching Sean Connery in *Henry IV, Parts I and II*. Those were the early glorious days of BBC programs shown on American television.

In that house, we developed a compassion for people undergoing suffering because our trials there were greater than they had ever been. So on May 28, 1963, even though I was eight months pregnant with our sixth child, John, I packed my bags to join the Civil Rights March on Washington with Martin Luther King, Jr. My husband actually barred the door, but I was ready. I could empathize with those who were in pain. I was suffering and so was our daughter and so, for that matter, was our whole family. Furthermore, I had begun to develop a relationship, if one can call it that, with the first canonized black saint, St. Martin de Porres, so I felt it imperative to march with Dr. King. But my husband as well as my friend Nancy finally dissuaded me from going.

On the third story of that house there was what I perceived as a friendly ghost in the smokehouse that was tucked into a corner of the third story attic, as was the custom in the 18th century. The vibrations up there were very good despite the very trying conditions below. I used to like to go up there and say to the spirit of the smokehouse, "What goes with you now?"

It was in this house that Patricia first got sick with a serious attack of catatonia which lasted almost a week. My husband was abroad in Japan. I didn't know what to do. I hadn't experienced mental illness in such a difficult form. We had a kindly neighbor who was afflicted with an abusive philandering husband and a dysfunctional adoptive child. She helped us get Patricia into Yale, New Haven after a few unsuccessful trips to the local hospital where there was a Roman Catholic priest, whose attitude was less than helpful.

At Yale, New Haven, Patricia was under the orthopaedic care of the illustrious and very well loved Dr. Wayne Southwick who, as I said before, was so caring and compassionate and did not charge us a cent. On the other hand, the psychiatrists did her more harm than good, as they were only interested in and capable of trying to pin "blame" on somebody. They put Patricia into wet sheets to restrain her! The sword that pierced Mary's heart, pierced my own heart as well. They also put her on huge amounts of ineffectual, toxic drugs and charged ludicrously large fees, insomuch that we had to take our two younger daughters out of private schools. My husband and I were in conflict about private vs. parochial schools. Alas, he won, of course.

Patricia's psychiatrist, a female, had the insensitivity to send Patricia a postcard from the top of an Alp, saying how she had literally schussed down these Alpine slopes and wasn't she lucky to have such good snow. She sent this to my poor daughter, who had just had her leg amputated and yet that psychiatrist said it had no connection with her emotional illness! Such cruel insensitivity! No wonder God will someday chastise this world! There are far too many people like her; insensitive and ungrateful for what they take for granted. The best help Patricia received was from that remarkable black aide named Harold, who gave our daughter the tender and wise encouragement to get out of her depression.

I made a lot of friends in Connecticut, mostly because I already had some friends there, particularly Nancy, my classmate from Albertus Magnus, and Laurey, my friend from California. That Westport house was old and rather cold at first so to keep our spirits up, we had a few parties, just as my family did while I was growing up. My family was always making occasions to celebrate something or other, and hosted a lot of parties. I guess this was a very French thing to do.

The house was old, dating from the early 1800's, and it was haunted. Really, there was a ghost in that house, up in the smokehouse in the third story attic. He was a happy ghost.

I think Martha should go up to that third story attic and have a talk with that ghost about any problems she might be having, notwithstanding her fame and fortune. I happen to admire Martha Stewart despite her occasional bad press. But who can say they have ever met a person without faults unless they are 2,000 years old!

The facts are that Martha has brought an enormous amount of joy, pleasure and sense of accomplishment to a lot of American women. She and I shared the same criticisms about our children's dentist because he kept them in braces for far too long. I remember sitting with Martha in the waiting room of our orthodontist who will mercifully, remain unnamed. There and then we both decided to get our children out of his clutches since he was torturing them with braces, prescribing that they wear them for more than five years, just for more fees, probably, or so we thought. I always did say that the reason doctors charge so much is because they have to pay for their kids' dental bills.

Someday I would like to say to Martha, "I'm not doing what you are doing, and you aren't doing what I'm doing, but maybe we could join forces." Who knows? I am after all among other things, a trained French chef; can still cook risotto and ratatouille; however only from vegetables just picked out of a garden. But I can't do all that other left brain stuff. Martha certainly knows how to make money for which I greatly admire her.

In 1965, we found another house, a very good house, through the kindly services of a Weston broker. It didn't cost us a fortune. It had been owned by a well-known Jewish stockbroker, a Mr. Newburger, whose wife had just died of cancer. This was another haunted house, though I didn't know it then, but this time by an unhappy ghost. The house had been part of the underground railroad during the Civil War, through which slaves could escape to the North. Maybe a slave had been killed by somebody in the house. Anyway, in part, through my psychical training, I could almost see Civil War veterans and women wearing great hoop skirts as were worn at the time. Everybody seemed to be wearing gray.

The broker really did a good job in selling it to us complete with Mr. Newburger's 15th century Spanish furniture, some of which were stacked away in the basement. Our daughter Suzy really appreciated this furniture: she does possess a rather eclectic taste in furnishings. That basement also became the domain of our son, Henry. That was where he entertained his gang of sycophantic friends and where he set up his racing car set as well as organizing a "jug band" very like Spike Jones (but worse!). Mr. Newburger had also put in a real blast shelter, at the height of the Cuban missile crisis, which you reached by going down many steps. But the thing was always full of water.

CHAPTER SEVENTEEN

PATRICIA'S ORDEALS

Patricia had her ups and downs in this Westport, Connecticut house. Maybe there were more downs than ups. This is perhaps because she wanted the attention of Henry's friends who only very infrequently paid her any attention, amputee that she was, and adolescents that they were. Once she threw herself down the cellar stairs because one of his friends did not pay more attention to her. We had a nurse named Goldie who could not deal with this situation too well but she was kind. We were pretty well drained and getting help for our situation was virtually impossible in those days.

After Patricia left Yale, New Haven in 1969 and came home, she was home-schooled. She had a wonderful teacher, Claire Gold, who subsequently became Superintendent of Schools in Westport, Connecticut. Patricia was actually able to get her GED. Ill-advisedly, I went away on a trip with my husband. I needed a break since I was on the verge of losing my sanity. In my absence, what with the yelling of the siblings at each other, Patricia went back into a catatonic episode. She became immobile and could not be moved for almost a month while the episode lasted.

As a result of this serious attack, Patricia was admitted into many hospitals other than Yale, in our attempt to find out about this conundrum of schizophrenia. It was only when she went to the Carrier Clinic in Belle Mead, New Jersey that I saw a glimmer of hope. There was one doctor there who deigned to use vitamins for schizophrenia. He was under the tutelage of the great Carl Pfeiffer, M.D, Ph.D, one of the chief pharmacologists in the U.S. Navy during the second World War. Then at a Monday night patients' meeting that I remember so well, the social worker there told us—parents, and relatives of the patients—that our loved ones would get better if we could just hang on and have faith. It was a social worker, and not a psychiatrist, who made the difference. "Don't give up hope. If you don't give up hope, your child will get better. " What words of encouragement!! At church the following Sunday, when we sang the hymn, "Faith of Our Fathers," I knew then that it was really God telling me that Patricia would eventually get better; I did not know how or when.

All through these years at different places, there were great crosses in our daughter's life and for us as well. It is not easy to recount these challenges, even now. I know Armando Valladares wrote about his years as a prisoner in Communist Cuba and how awful that was, and Jeremiah Denton wrote about his experiences as a Viet Cong prisoner in his book, *When Hell Was In Season*. I am not as brave as these men, nor can I write about my own terrible experiences as they did because right now I don't have that kind of anger, such as they were able to use to detonate their revulsion into words about the evils of Communism. Perhaps if I had to undergo anything as terrible as that, it might force me to express my deepest emotions regarding suffering. It is impossible to put into words.

Eventually I made a great leap of faith and put an ad in the paper for a couple to take her and help her get better. That was in 1977. I did this because my own health was being threatened by this tremendous strain; I was not able to take care of her and the big house and everything else in my life.

Patricia stayed with this couple for nine years and she did get better. She studied to be a nurse while living with them, but that was too physically challenging. They eventually became burned out and started to get mean to her, so she had to come home. In that year (1986), Patricia not only graduated from college, but also amazingly the same year we became seriously involved with the Shroud of Turin research that made such an impact on our lives, which I will explain in detail later. It seems that the great challenges of our lives also accompanied the Shroud research. This is what transforms our lives in conformity with the Passion of Jesus and God's will.

CHAPTER EIGHTEEN

REMINISCENCES OF TRAVELS ABROAD

Despite our constant trials at home, my husband and I have managed over the years to spend some time together, even while he was on business trips.

The Sacred and The Profane: The Sublime and The Ridiculous

On our trip to Europe in 1959—what a trip!—I persuaded my husband to join me on a pilgrimage to Foggia, Italy to see the famous Catholic mystic, Padre Pio, who lived in nearby San Giovanni del Rotundo. On this occasion, my husband remembered that he was supposed to have become a Roman Catholic after our marriage; it was part of the deal—our "pre-nuptial agreement".

Padre Pio had the same powers as St. Jean Vianney, the Curé d'Ars. He would read into one's soul during confession, displaying the *Siddhi* which is given supernaturally or naturally to people of sanctity and/or advanced psychic training. But Padre Pio also had this "thing" about women; he wouldn't hear their confessions because it was said that he thought women weren't bad enough sinners for him. Hey, that's good, I guess.

Padre Pio

Anyway, after getting up at four in the morning, which is standard practice for Roman Catholic clergy and religious, one reason I didn't become a nun, not good enough health, we pushed our way, absolutely de rigeur to the left side of the chapel so we could see Padre Pio say Mass with the stigmata on his hands, the blood was coming through his white gloves. The stigmata are the wounds of Christ becoming visible.

Sure enough, we saw them all right. After Mass, Padre Pio said, rather testily I thought, maybe due to his constant pain, "The men may come after Mass and have their holy objects blessed by me." These blessings took place in his antechamber. I had such ambivalent feelings, "Oh, phooey, why can't I go? After all it is my Franciscan cross he is going to bless."

Anyway, my husband dutifully took my very large and impressive Third Order of St. Francis cross to be blessed. Subsequently I gave that cross to my friend, Nancy, who had gone to Albertus Magnus with me, and who was dying of cancer. We were dismayed because we had a few children and life was hard. Her cancer was not helped by her pregnancy. But after her sons were born, she herself went downhill. When she went to Sloane Kettering, I gave her the cross blessed by Padre Pio, which her husband, Mike, returned after she died. I am sure this excellent woman went to Heaven.

Moving from the sublime experience of Padre Pio to the ridiculous, a Salvador Dali "extravaganza," made this 1959 European trip very memorable. I went to a "soirée" given at the "Bal des Petits Lits Blancs." In full regalia, I went with my very nice French uncle, the one who married my Aunt Suzanne. At the official entertainment, Salvador Dali, who was the Master of Ceremonies, decided this already decadent French crowd needed to see a rhinoceros in a cage. This enormous caged animal was suspended over the assembly of chic gawkers, bored by the lesser and more mundane pursuits of showgirls, transexuals and what have you that Paris dredges up, and has dredged up from time immemorial, especially after the wars of the 19th Century and before the French Revolution.

My husband and I sandwiched into our schedule both of these spectacular events before taking off for Venice for two or three magical days. However, while there I made the great error of drinking water from a tap at the lovely but not quite first-class Hotel Luna, and about a week later when we had returned to Paris, I came down with a 105 degree fever, chills, sweat, retching, etc. In other words, I was really sick. My urine was also dark and my stools were white.

On our return to Paris, our new nanny, Maureen Clegg, was still holding the fort with our four children. I was ill and had to seek medical treatment. The French doctor said, "Give her charbon (charcoal)." I asked, "Although I'm not a doctor, is it possible that I might have hepatitis?" They were ambivalent! Anyway I had to spend a few days in the clinic in Versailles, where my uncle's brother-in-law was a doctor at the same time as being a world-class tennis player. Better than his diagnostic skills, I hope!

While I was in the clinic, Harry was alone, in my deceased grandmother's apartment, for my family owned the building. Until that point in his life my husband was extremely skeptical about anything paranormal, but in my absence he had a very unusual experience. Now he can vouch for the fact that he has had the experience of the presence of a ghost. Maybe it was my grandmother who, by haunting him, was complaining in her own way that my husband wasn't treating me well enough . . . . . . a wife's interpretation.

Many years later another interesting phenomenon occurred while in that same apartment. I was looking at a photograph of Jesus on the wall and saw another photograph at the bottom in an upside down position!! I looked at it intently and mustered up the courage to turn that inset picture right side up. I was afraid to do so but I just had to. The face reminded me of what the Blessed Virgin had said to the visionaries in Medugorje, "I'm sorry to have to tell you this, but Satan exists." It looked like the face of Satan. There was never a 'rational' explanation for this, at least not yet, anyway.

On returning to California with our newly acquired English nanny, Maureen Clegg, and the four children, the doctor in Los Angeles gave me a blood test and said, "This is viral hepatitis, a bad case. Go to bed, avoid alcohol (and soireés with unlimited champagne featuring Salvador Dali entertainments) and call me in a few mornings."

Harry and I with Patricia in front of Harry's Bar in
Venice, Italy during one of our trips there.

The Scarlet Pimpernel

While on a trip to England in 1938, I have the memory of
seeing some voile curtains blowing in the soft breeze through a
window overlooking a garden, this in a very special room at
Claridges Hotel where I stayed with Mr. Rosson and my mother.
Why they brought me along, I don't know. Maybe it was for lack
of a babysitter.

Mr. Rosson was involved with the filming of the original version of, *Thief of Baghdad*, with Sabu, who later starred in films
based on Rudyard Kipling stories including *The Jungle Book*. I
remember very vividly being in that same bedroom with the white
curtains and receiving a book from my stepfather. He was about
to shoot a film based on it. The title of the book was, *The Scarlet
Pimpernel*. The copy my stepfather gave me bore an inscription
to me from the author, Baroness Emmuska Orczy!

I once mentioned the Scarlet Pimpernel to a young man, the
son of one of my daughter's companions. "What's that?" he asked,
somewhat mystified, whereupon I mused to myself that I was

after all old enough to be his grandmother and that of course he knew nothing whatever about the Scarlet Pimpernel. I realized that so much of this book is unknown to the younger generations and that my children and grandchildren wouldn't know anything about the Scarlet Pimpernel either, except recently for the Broadway play.

The Scarlet Pimpernel is a flower that grows in Europe, particularly in France and England. As the name implies, it is red in color and has a special configuration of its blossoms. This flower has a certain significance to it and it is quite rare. It was the heraldic emblem for an English aristocratic family, based on a true story, in Baroness Orczy's book. It had been in this family for years when a certain member began to covertly save French aristocrats from being executed under the guillotine during the French Revolution.

Leslie Howard as The Scarlet Pimpernel

Then I saw the film, *The Scarlet Pimpernel*. The actor who played the hero, the aristocratic Englishman, was Leslie Howard, who perished in an airplane crash, just as would Carole Lombard, during World War II. I fell deeply in love with Leslie Howard, as only an eight year old can. I said if ever I was to marry, I wanted someone as close to him as humanly possible. He was the epitome of the English gentleman, but in real life he was a Hungarian Jew. (My father, maybe, had some Hungarian Jewish blood which was unbeknownst to me at the time?)

When I was in France as a teenager, I visited American students who were living at the Circle Internationale, and met this wonderfully luminous international law student, an Oxonian named Herb Allen. Actually I fell in love with him, since he seemed to be a reincarnation of the Scarlet Pimpernel, or at least of Leslie Howard. I was too shy to tell him this, but once when we were walking home on a pleasant afternoon in Paris (you either walked or took a bus) he asked me if I loved him and I said, "Oh no." But of course I did. Shortly thereafter, maybe because of his ego, he got involved with an old lady of nineteen named Monique. That was the end of an affair we never had, much to my chagrin. I learned later that he ended his life leaping out of a window because of a failed romance. How very tragic!

I didn't realize that the man I was really to marry was the embodiment of the Scarlet Pimpernel as well. Maybe this is truer than ever. He is doing amazing things for the good of this world. Maybe just in the last year or so, who knows? There are very many similar characteristics; a gentle exterior, very aesthetic looks and a fire in the belly, just like Leslie Howard in *The Scarlet Pimpernel*.

So in 1993, when my Scarlet Pimpernel—my husband Harry—and I went to France on a business trip for his company, there was to be a director's meeting at the Crillon Hotel in Paris. We had exactly four days of vacation prior to that meeting and so we did exactly what we had done during another four-day trip in 1968, twenty-five years earlier. We had each taken out the Michelin Guide, the infallible French guide, and looked at it separately to see if by chance, any of our choices would match.

That's what we had done in 1968 and each of us had come up with the same place! That place then was Le Haut de Cagnes, an old medieval fortress town with a mini-chateau overlooking the Mediterranean. It was nearly impossible to get a reservation at the hotel, Le Cagnard, unless you reserved six months in advance. However, because of the now famous street fighting which was going on at that time in Paris in 1968, (my first cousin, Patrick was very amused to be near the barricades even while working for IBM in a shirt and tie), we managed to get a reservation.

It was very romantic, our room was in a tower overlooking the Mediterranean in the distance and in the Michelin Guide it had a one-star restaurant that had the best fish soup we were ever to have, and their famous loup à la fenouille (Monkfish with fennel). We were able to visit the Chapel in Vence, France where we saw the ineffable cut outs of Henri Matisse, as well as some other wonderful museums.

On the more recent occasion, twenty-five years later, we had some limitations in our choice of accommodation. Our chosen place had to be within fifty miles of the Charles de Gaulle Airport and the hotel had to have a swimming pool because in those days, even while travelling, I was swimming to help stay physically fit.

Gadzooks! (To use an expression of The Scarlet Pimpernel), Harry and I had inexplicably again independently chosen the same place out of the Michelin Guide. It was 50 miles from the airport, near Rheims, the home of the best champagne in the world, and the location of the oldest cathedral in France, the Church of St. Pierre, once presided over by King Clovis in the late fifth and early sixth centuries. Pope John Paul II visited this church a few years ago to try and get the French into some kind of national conversion, which they badly needed, I thought. This charming hotel had a lovely dining room, not quite one star but pleasantly French, with antiques, facing a riding ring which belonged to the riding school next door.

Two amazing things happened while we were there. The only

way I could get to church, the only one in five that was open on Sundays in that rural part of France, was by carpooling. That church was located in the next town. One of the ladies carpooling was an old woman who said, "Did you know that it is rumored there was once a cemetery next to the old Romanesque church near your hotel where there might be an unmarked gravestone of the Le Chevalier de L'oelliet Rouge?" "Sacre Bleu!" "Who's that?" I asked in disbelief. She replied, "It means the Cavalier of the Red Carnation. He was an English aristocrat who saved French aristocrats during the Terror at great personal risk, and they buried him in France, in the backyard of this hotel, unmarked, and well hidden, so the terrorists wouldn't desecrate his tomb." The old lady said that the place was run down and unkempt but that this was where they had buried him. Thus began our search for the burial place of the real Scarlet Pimpernel and there he was right in our backyard!

Harry and I spent two hours looking for it. It was overgrown with weeds since the Romanesque church had been there for centuries; their backyard had really been neglected. But when we cleared away the weeds, there was a stone that was unmarked. I called the old lady and told her we had found it. And so we came full circle, finding the final resting place of the real Scarlet Pimpernel close to the Church of St. Pierre, the Cathedral of Clovis, King of the Franks, the first Christian monarch of France. A 'spy-like' excursion!

The final resting place of the real Scarlet Pimpernel

Other Times in France

A significant trip to Paris was on the sad occasion of my grandmother's death in 1959. I must mention that on that trip my husband and I also made that trip to Italy while on a business trip to Europe. One of the things we did was to pick up our first long-term nanny. It was the first time we had ever had such a person to take care of our children, so finally we were able to leave them in her hands because they were also under the watchful eye of my aunt and her family.

This vignette reflects snatches of the memory of the high points of our happy but sad trip. It was happy because our children had never been to Paris before and sad because of my grandmother's passing. We did not make it to the funeral but came as soon as we could to console my aunt and put flowers on the family grave where my grandmother was buried. The family grave is in the Montparnasse cemetery on the Left Bank. It has the usual little "housette" with columns and a statue of a girl angel with wings and flowing robes and long flowing hair draped over the alcove. This angel represents my Aunt Denyse, my grandmother's youngest daughter who died young. My family dealt with death, dying and things of that nature in a very big symbolic way—something that I find very morbid. Moses said,

> "I call heaven and earth to record this day against you,
> that I have set before you life and death, blessing and
> cursing: therefore choose life that both thou and thy
> seed may live" (Deut. 30:19).

My family seems to put death almost on the same level with life, celebrating it in a very big way. I think it is so with Europeans because they have seen so much death—two world wars in addition to all the plagues and civil wars that they experienced before and since. Maybe the most memorable thing about this trip, for certain, was our then youngest daughter Yvonne's fascination with the Eiffel Tower. We went up to the second stage which was already quite a scary thing for me to do. After some of the traumas I had been through with my oldest daughter, Patricia, and my mother's death, I seemed to have lost my courage for things like sailing in small boats and certainly going to the very top of the Eiffel Tower which I had done a couple of times in my teens. So Harry took the children except Patricia who stayed with me. Yvonne was completely enthralled. You could say she fell in love with that monument. Her fascination was such that we started collecting Eiffel Towers for her after that. The Eiffel Tower even sent her some love postcards and letters after she returned home (my aunt and cousins, of course).

Years later, after we had moved from New York to Westport, Connecticut, we were able to take our three youngest children, Yvonne, Suzanne and John, back to France. We were rather cramped—all five of us traveling around in a small French car together with our luggage. Since my daughter Yvonne was a dancer in those days, she really watched what she ate while mother, Anne, was on a strict regime, both spiritual and physical. That was around 1979 when Yvonne and I would jog around the tracks at various French hotels where we stayed. We also had a memorable trip to Chartres where I remember fasting for the occasion. Foodies like myself always remember what we eat and also when we didn't eat! The formidable English guide at Chartres Cathedral was there. He was a famous fixture there and knew absolutely everything about its history including some very unusual facts brought out in the famous Henry Adams' book, *Mont St. Michel and Chartres* which he shared with us.

My husband, Harry, had written his senior thesis on Henry Adams who to this day is one of his favorites. There is also an occult-type book on the mysteries of the Cathedral at Chartres.

Another one of my husband's favorites was Leslie Caron whom I knew in Paris; her parents were friends of the family and owners of the Franco—American Caron drugstore—her mother was American and her father, French. At that time she was still a budding ballet dancer. All the men simply adored her. She was their favorite. She was lovely and delicate and had a toothy smile, plus a great deal of charm.

When I moved back to Beverly Hills in the 1950's Leslie Caron was at MGM and Harry and I had lunch with her in the commissary. At the time she was filming *Daddy Long Legs*, with Fred Astaire, and as dancers are always famished, it seems she ordered two steaks. When the bill came poor Harry did not have enough money to pay for her meal as well as ours, so she ended up buying us lunch instead. Harry was embarrassed. Later when MGM was auctioning off their properties as well as their back lots, I sent my friend Carole Bergerman to bid for her *Daddy Long Legs* Costume which I got for $200. It was a size 2! Judy Garland's ruby slippers went for about $15,000. Now they are worth about half a million dollars at least.

We invited Leslie Caron to our house and I made sure we had enough food so I ordered a whole rack of lamb. I believe at the time, George Hormel of the meat packing corporation, was her husband. My father-in-law was so taken with her that he saw, *Lili*, 13 times!! I think my husband was also taken with her. I believe she now runs a bed and breakfast in France.

During our aforementioned trip to France with our three younger children, I took a lot of photos of the children at museums, including the famous museum of Aimé Maeght who had an incredible gallery of Post Impressionist paintings of his clients— some of them friends of the family—and of the artist himself. One of the paintings in his stable, as it was called, was a fascinating and mysterious piece by our dear friend, Pierre Tal-coat, a unique Breton who used to mix his own paints because he believed that the colors were no good unless you mixed them yourself out of natural pigments made from earth stones and such. At his best he was totally brilliant. My first cousin Denyse (maid of honor in our wedding) was once married to Viscomte Christian who put on a show of his work at the Grand Palais—quite a coup that was! I must also mention that at Tal-Coat's worst some of the paints can liquefy and start to drip! We had one of those and up to this day I am not sure how to fix it!

That was a delightful family—Pierre, the great singer of songs, especially those from the Auvergne, and his wife and daughter, beloved by all of us. They were fine friends. They had this very comfortable country home in Dordogne, outside of Paris, where they had spectacular meals in the French style. They were always kind to Patricia—this I do remember. There is a kindness about the French, especially in the countryside, which is very special. I have never found anything like it in the U.S. There is something almost materialistic about Americans now. Kindness sometimes seems to be in short supply.

My cousin Denyse married again, an American from Virginia who bought a winery in the Var, not far from my aunt's home. My cousin was a very enterprising person, and with her husband's help was able to develop and market the first Cabernet from Provence. Quite a feat! It was called Chateau St. Jean, named after the saint, St. John the Baptist, by the man who was the head of the manor house (which my cousins purchased with the winery) two centuries ago.

Continuing the tradition of the noblemen of the villages, on the feast of St. Jean Baptiste on June 25, the head of the manor house would give a party for the whole village. This day happened to be the birthday of my cousin as well as that of our son, John. We went there for one of these memorable occasions. These are beautiful memories of which dreams are made and which may be retained for the rest of one's life—a respite from the more trying times. As years pass by people get older and then they die, of course. So when the time came for my beloved Uncle Robert, my Aunt Suzanne's husband, to die, she was absolutely devastated, but she is still hanging on with all her gifts and wit.

On my birthday, Aunt Suzanne calls me very dutifully, from the South of France, to wish me Happy Birthday. For her birthday, March 19, which is also the Feast of St. Joseph, very fortunately I was able to find a picture of St. Joseph with two angels, which I managed to send to her in time. I got this from my friend, Maureen Flynn of the *Signs of the Times*. She sells these beautiful pictures of the saints and angels, and magazines, as well as the latest *Catholic End Times News*.

*   *   *

My husband, Harry, and I were motoring into Le Drome from the superhighway that goes from Paris into the South, to a town called Dieulefit. This trip highlighted the ongoing struggle with our daughter's illnesses. Le Drome is in fact in the middle of France, a kind of geographic no-man's land, if you will, south of the beautiful wine country and north of Provence, which is in the South. Our daughter, Patricia, had started school there, this is before she went to live with Christine and David, the couple mentioned earlier, and we went to see how she was doing. Right before we were to visit her at the school, we stopped at an inn that was recommended in the Michelin Guide. For some reason what we had for dinner stuck in my mind. It was brains in a crust. Now imagine that! Only the French could pull that off.

The school had been founded many years ago by the Littlefields, an American couple who had become expatriates. They were willing to keep our daughter even though she had multiple problems even then. The struggle she had in France had a different quality to it. It was more desperate somehow. It would be good to get her home once again.

Newport, Rhode Island

Even today as I relate the story, our daughter Patricia is struggling with her multiple handicaps and we are struggling along with her. As I write this, the scenery is totally different. Here in this most glorious of American resorts, Newport, Rhode Island, there always seem to be a time when sailing puts on a special performance. We first came to Newport in 1973 when a very charming gentleman,

Barclay Douglas, took us out to watch the America's Cup on a chartered yacht. In spite of the fog, we were hooked. It was the most thrilling sporting event I had ever attended, even more thrilling than the horse-races which I loved at Ascot, Longchamps, or at Santa Anita, which I had attended as a teenager, shuttling as I did in those days, between California and Europe.

But the America's Cup, this was better. There was nothing like it and we started coming back to each of the America's Cup competitions. In fact it was just by chance I saw an advertisement for a one-week time share, as they are called, in the very same hotel where Barclay Douglas had put us up for the 1973 America's Cup race. It was then called the Old Shamrock Cliff, formerly one of Newport's great, although lesser, estates. It is now called Ocean Cliff and beside the hill which abuts the mansion of sorts, they had added a 5-unit house that has a reasonably picturesque Rhode Island look to it, later to be joined by a much larger and less attractive structure.

How best can I convey the vast difference, the dichotomy, between these ordinary although exciting and amazing day-to-day events, and the interior life which has produced so many amazing results, some of which can best be called synchronicities?

About Boats

My husband had bought a super powered formula boat around 1985, and it has become his favorite possession/toy, since he had to give up his motorcycle. In that respect we are complete opposites. He is a speed freak while I am becoming more of a slow freak. However, I have to admit that when we met in France in 1950, he took me on the back of his humongous motorcycle all over the Brittany coast, much to my grandmother's consternation.

This boat was and still is a very beautiful thing and very fast. Before telling of our next hurricane experience which involved that boat, I have to digress a little.

My husband and I have been very closely involved in the political process since 1979 when a friend of ours, Eben Graves, now deceased alas . . . talked us into giving a fundraiser for former Texas Governor, John Connally, a Republican primary candidate for the presidential election. That led to my being appointed to various health commissions (the last one being the National Council on Disability). My first appointment was by President Reagan, then by Secretary, Jack Kemp and finally by President George Bush to the NCD as it's called. It was under the tenure of George Bush that the American with Disabilities Act was signed into law.

We became friendly with the Bush family, so before going to our time-share in Newport, I said to Harry, "Why don't you bring the boat to Newport and you and Jay (the driver and our friend) can go up the coast to see George Bush at Kennebunkport (and maybe race)." I thought of this, since George also had a "cigarette boat." That was in 1991. I can't believe we ever had the energy or nerve to dream up such a thing.

Anyway, on the way up to Newport, Harry and Jay got lost in the fog. That was the same day our time-share became available. No sooner had they pulled into our little dock at our time-share than there were reports, not only of a fog, but also, yes, of a hurricane moving up the coast very fast. This time it was a hisocane called 'Bob.'

The next day Harry and Jay tried to tie the boat up before the onslaught but couldn't find a safe dock. In desperation they had to tie it finally to the flimsy dock at our time-share. Harry knows the story better than I. The next day there was no boat and no dock. The day after that, the boat turned up, by some miracle of a higher power; it slid up on the coast guard landing next door, injured but not terminally. The dock never did come back, alas.

The boat was saved and is still going strong, although too fast for me. So once I took the desperate measure of renting a sailboat with a skipper. It was docked in Stamford on a very nice condo harbor situated in a not too nice neighborhood and captained by a very engaging (very much the part!) woman, Eutha Brown. This adventure came about through an advertisement which went something like this: "Desperate housewife needs to go out on somebody's boat from time to time with skipper. Will pay a fee."

Australia

The first thing I remember about the Australians, with whom we became acquainted, was the arrival around 1977 of a rather heavy-set man coming to see us with his "secretary." This was Mr. Alan Bond. He was coming to promote some business with my husband, who was at that time beginning to take a look at the Australian stock market. I remember we had one of our famous bucolic lunches on a redwood table set under an enormous maple tree, reaching maybe 80 feet tall.

The occasion reminded me of a visit we once made to a German schloss where the trees were hundreds of years old and grandly majestic. Among my most enriching encounters with nature is to be dwarfed by magnificently tall old trees. It engenders the emotions expressed in a Robert Burns' poem which ends with the line "All's right with the world." Our fancy picnic table was half in the sun and half in the shade to accommodate everyone's taste. I remember that our Australian guest, Mr. Bond, was very impressed.

On a subsequent trip to Australia, we visited Mr. Bond and his family in Perth, where they lived in a very modern home. Mr. Bond's wife, Arlene, was a very gregarious woman and very hospitable to us. She and I had the same religious faith, which also created a bond.

Perth impressed me. It reminded me of southern California of 50 years ago, with its beautiful climate, no smog and with an irrepressible spirit, that of the frontier. In fact, all of Australia had a great deal of frontier spirit, but especially the western coast. You got the feeling that the boundaries were limitless, with the vineyards to the south and the beautiful Margaret Valley and the rich mineral deposits to the north. These may be reached in an aircraft called a "puddle jumper" which my husband took, of which even he was frightened. I would have simply passed out.

I always wanted to see Ayer's Rock. The attraction to this huge natural megalith held a strange and mysterious link to our ancient aboriginal past that attracted me. My life has been full of mysteries and I always put Ayer's Rock in that category. But alas, I never got there.

Australia is a land containing many mysteries. One Australian mystery that I became aware of was described in a film made by the noted Australian filmmaker, Peter Weir, in *Picnic at Hanging Rock*. This movie was about the unexplained disappearance of some adolescent girls.

But on one of my frequent visits to Ojai, California, to a health spa called the Oaks, where many synchronous events happened in my life (It's that kind of place) I saw another Australian movie, also directed by Peter Weir. This film, *The Last Wave*, was released two years earlier and was being shown in a cinema across the street from the health spa. Now I knew there was something synchronous about its being shown there at the time because whenever I was in Ojai, I was normally too tired to go out after a full day of exercise, and the cinema only played movies two nights a week. Therefore I usually never went to any movies while I was there, but this time something nudged me to go.

The Last Wave is by any measure one of the finest apocalyptic movies ever made. It's the story of a lawyer played by one of my favorite actors, Richard Chamberlain, who had been hired by the Aborigines to defend one of their men against a murder charge. During the course of the movie, which is a description of the events leading to the trial, mysterious and unexplainable events happen such as flooding and various events concerning inappropriately large amounts of water. The lawyer is in a car and had experienced a waking dream where the car was under water and bodies were floating by. On another occasion he comes home to discover water flowing down the staircase carrying debris. In the background a mysterious rumbling hum made by the sound of an Aboriginal musical instrument, the didgeridoo, intensifies the mystery that surrounds this closely guarded tribe of Aborigines. The lawyer's involvement with them eventually creates in him a sense of foreboding so that he decides that he must send his wife and daughter to the interior for a while.

The climactic ending begins when the Aborigines tell him that the answers are to be found if he goes deep into the sewers of the city, no doubt, Sydney. He does so and finds that the sewers lead to an ancient Aboriginal cave on which there are some pictographs. The Aborigines had told him that there had been a legend about the time of the ending of their civilization that a leader would come among them whose name was Pukaru. The lawyer read the pictograph and there was a stick figure larger than the others by himself and behind that figure, Pukaru, was a large wave.

Richard Chamberlain, as the lawyer, in a very dramatic moment says, "Am I Pukaru, the awaited one?" He clambers on up through the tunnel where the light of the sky becomes brighter and brighter and then we are shown a vast expanse of sand in the background. He then looks up and heading straight for him is a wave which visually appears to be about 500 feet tall. That was the end of the film. I was left stunned!

Being in a relatively high state of consciousness, due to the increased oxygen brought on by aerobic exercise, I felt I was becoming a Pukaru myself. Since a Pukaru is someone sent by God to warn the nation of some impending event, I felt as if I was sent by God to warn the people of the Fourth World civilization, as described by the Hopi Indians, that the end of their civilization was near.

Of course the Biblical account of Noah includes the promise that the world would not again be destroyed by flood waters. But this does not mean that God ever promised not to destroy the world by some other means. In the words of the author, James Baldwin, it would be "The fire next time."

Getting back to the Australians, our next experience with the Bond family was in Newport, Rhode Island, at the time of the 1983 America's Cup Trials. I remember going down to Bannister's Wharf with a large group of Australian women and I said, "Look, if you want to win, we should all start praying." We started praying and we started saying the Rosary right then and there.

We were the only Americans who knew the Bonds well enough to be on board their personal yacht, The Southern Star. And an extraordinary thing happened! The Australians were able to wrest the cup from the Americans! Perhaps due to the power of prayer?

During the many festivals, competitions, and events in Newport, for the America's Cup of 1983, there was a large loud speaker emanating either from a Coast Guard boat or one of the central docks. My husband and I smiled at each other knowingly when a voice came over the loud speaker, after the Australian's shattering victory saying, "Now, you Australians, behave yourselves!" to which came the immediate reply, "No wyyy!"

Another guest on the Southern Star was Anna Murdoch, then wife of the media tycoon, Rupert Murdoch (Bond had by then become a financial tycoon). We had met the Murdochs at a fundraising for the renovation of the Dominican church in New York City, St. Vincent Ferrer where both the Murdochs and my husband and I were married.

Interestingly enough, in the rear of the church is a statue of a black man—with one hand on his breast and the other outstretched—the Dominican friar and saint, St. Martin de Porres. It was a masterpiece but we did not realize it since it was in a poorly lit niche in that unrenovated church on that fateful day of April 14, 1951, when Anne Crellin and Harry Seggerman were married by three priests, my grandmother's three favorite cronies. Her cronies at the *New York Daily News* were all Irish, of course, and took pictures of us emerging from the church smiling rapturously as we came down the steps. The caption was and remains to this day, "East mates West." The time of St. Martin De Porres will re-emerge in this story later on and in increasingly important ways.

The fundraising for St. Vincent Ferrer was held in the Murdoch's apartment in New York where there was a speaker who told us about the importance of renovating this beautiful Gothic edifice. We met some interesting types there such as: the famous, or should I say infamous, Roy Cohn who had defended Richard Nixon and who had remained a stalwart conservative; Andy Warhol, the Polish Catholic who went on to paint soup cans and Marilyn Monroe; and Eleanor and Jack Howard, heir to the Scripps newspaper dynasty.

We had an amusing time with the Howards, which was repeated many years later in Newport, Rhode Island, when we graciously escorted them to their bed and breakfast after one of those illustrious parties thrown by Eileen Slocum, widow of the late, great John Slocum. This one was for the coming out of her granddaughter. That party was nothing but fun and laughs for us. I decided to push my table right in the way so people would have to go around it, and all sorts of amusing, talented, and sometimes well-known people would have to stop and say hello. A successful tactic since some of them would even sit down and stay awhile.

In 1973, an old schoolmate of mine had married a financier from Providence. She knew many people from Newport since our husbands were in the same business. They decided to ask us for one of the America's Cup week events and put us up in a charming antique called the Shamrock Cliff Hotel, which, nevertheless, had a breathtaking view of the entire Narragansett Bay. Our room was as large as a ballroom and maybe was three stories high; but two-thirds of our view was blocked by a chimney. This was typical Newport—absolutely wonderful—but yet there was something which was not working.

I was so enthralled by going out on a motor ship to try to find the America's Cup 12 Meters, which was an impossibility in the deep fog. Nevertheless, I was so charmed by the kind of people I met—so gracious and aristocratic—that I fell in love with this milieu immediately. In a way it reminded me of how I felt years before, on a couple of occasions coming back to the U.S. from France—reluctantly—it was as if I were almost seduced into not returning. I was leading a charmed intellectual and musical life, and in those days when I was much younger, it seemed to me that there were too many cowboys and Indians in the United States—a frontier kind of life that seemed increasingly anti-intellectual. But then in the words of St. Paul, I was only seeing as "through a glass darkly."

> "For now we see through a glass, darkly; but then face to face: now I know in part; but then shall I know even as also I am known" (I Cor. 13:12).

The Bonds fell on hard times and got a divorce. Anna Murdoch wrote a very good book and Rupert, as of today, had acquired the Los Angeles Dodgers; they also divorced.

But the Australian Connection of the "Real Reality" was spoken of by Thomas Merton in his book *Seeds of Contemplation* which is the spiritual reality of our existence and was not begun until 1996 with the mystic, Debra of Australia, in a later chapter.

Egypt

The most hilarious trip we ever took was in the early 80's, after Harry had gone to the Middle East on business. He had become friendly enough with the Egyptians that they told us about a travel agency in New Jersey that arranged trips to the Middle East. It could have been only within a year after the Camp David Accords or maybe less than that, when this travel agency had organized the first such trip that went to Egypt, then Jordan, then Israel, all in one fell swoop. Because of the wars in the Middle East, crossing the Allenby Bridge over the Jordan River was not possible until very recently.

We were very fortunate in that we were able to go with our daughter Patricia, her companions David and Christine and our three youngest children, Yvonne, Suzy and John. It was an all-in-one deal and so the group of us flew on the same airplane together to Cairo. I think we went by way of Milan. The tour group included one general—a General Guard (who was on TV recently, amazingly) and his wife, who were from southern California, one Jewish lady from New York and her husband, a father and son team (they were decorators, I think). The journey took no time at all to become very, very interesting and hilarious.

The general immediately started flirting with Patricia, which I thought was kind of cute and everybody was talking to each other in very loud voices over the din of the airplane.

We arrived very late at night at a hotel. This was in November and I was feeling so stressed out that I needed to go swimming and there was a swimming pool outside. I didn't ask about it: I just went in. I think when I came out I was kind of green. The water had been sitting there for a couple of months without any treatment.

We spent a couple of days in Cairo. I remember most the Cairo Museum. One went around in a kind of circle, more properly a rectangle, and tourists would go around counterclockwise. The first of three sides of the rectangle were devoted primarily to those famous stick figures of kings, of Pharaohnic and earlier times, where the form is very stylized and not at all true to life. And then follows the stunning surprise.

There, in the last hall of the rectangular Cairo Museum, is a picture of a man and a woman dressed in tunics, standing next to their cow. They seem to be some kind of farmers, but their depiction is very realistic. They could have been painted by Grant Wood or someone like that. I said, "What happened in that period, and in the succeeding centuries in Egyptian art to make them so different?" This picture was painted—and it is the only one extant—during the time of Cheops (Khufu); 2500 BC, who allegedly built the Great Pyramid of Giza.

Having labored in fields of esoteric studies, from association with Aldous Huxley and his followers, there was a period of my life that "pyramid power" came into being and everyone was studying pyramids, pyramidology, etc. and there were even pyramidologists. But whoever built that pyramid had the most profound understanding of universal arithmetic that has ever been displayed on the planet, before or since.

One writer, Scott Rogo, maintains that the Great Pyramid was built 25,000 years ago to withstand the great flood, since they had prophetic foreknowledge of that cataclysmic event. He makes a pretty good case for that, but then, people can make good cases for a lot of weird things if they are determined enough.

All I know is that on another trip when I actually clambered up to the king's chamber inside the Great Pyramid, a strenuous and hot ordeal that I barely survived, I took a picture of a guide in the very touted "King's Chamber;" there was a very strange light in the picture which was never explained. It is in my photo catalog under the "mysterious pictures" department, along with other alleged pictures of the Virgin Mary, crosses in the sky, etc.

After we had "done" Cairo, we embarked on the Nile Princess, one of the early paddle wheelers that took people from Cairo to Aswan by way of the Temples of Luxor. This was long before these paddle-wheelers were gussied up for the tourist trade. They were dank and rusty and all sorts of things happened to us on the boat, including the exploding lightbulb episode which almost electrocuted Dave and Christine in their tiny bathroom, which measured only about one by two feet.

The passengers in their own way were very funny, but the whole trip was hilarious because the Egyptians were very funny, charming and had a great sense of humor. I guess they have to be a little comical to put up with all the poverty. They are very graceful people: you can see vestiges of those ancient civilizations in their demeanor, unlike, in some ways, either the Romans or the Greeks. Maybe it's because so many of them are tall and thin and wear those white robes. We had a New Year's Eve party, right off shipboard, in the plaza of Luxor, during which time the escapades kept getting wilder all the time. Even the souvenir situation was a laugh, despite the peculiar pathos attached to it. Souvenirs were vended by very emaciated young men, wearing long pale gray robes and turbans around their heads, who would hawk artifacts thus; "authentic pieces of the temple dating back 3,000 years!" David, who is married to Christine, was completely convinced that he had purchased a genuine piece of the temple. I hope nobody ever disabuses him of this notion: he was so awed by it.

The Jewish lady, whom we all called "the bag-dragger", got that title because she literally dragged her bags full of souvenirs everywhere. The bag-dragger had bags full of not only pieces of temples, but everything else under the sun. I guess she figured correctly that she wouldn't be getting back to Egypt for a while and wanted to take it with her.

On that New Years Eve, that lady had a few proposals of marriage from the Egyptians, which made her husband, the jewelry dealer, furious. He thought they would actually marry his wife. I guess this was one way she could keep him interested.

The two men who were traveling together whom we were initially totally convinced were homosexuals because they were very effeminate and very caring toward each other, were indeed father and son. This only goes to show that my research on homosexuality, or perhaps just effeteness, has some examples tending to support the notion that there are a large segment of homosexuals that are truly genetic. I have seen instances of the very effeminate traits commonly associated with homosexuals in fathers and sons, including those two. Presumably no one offered them marriage proposals, but you never can tell.

My attractive daughters, Yvonne and Suzy, even as pre-teens, had all kinds of proposals and funny tales to tell. We all had a grand time, a great deal of slightly dangerous fun. We were, therefore, very glad to get back to our old sinking boat and make our way down the Nile, or more accurately, up the Nile to Aswan.

In some ways, at least 15 years ago anyway, Luxor was my favorite place on planet Earth, mainly because the Winter Palace Hotel had a balcony on the Nile, where we sat watching feluccas go by as the sun set over the Valley of the Kings.

My mystical life had already begun by that time, so it was with great interest that we descended into the tombs of Amenhoteph where I saw those little stick creatures with bulbous heads accompanying the souls and the bodies of the departed monarchs down into their Kingdom of Darkness. What is interesting about these stick figures is that there was one other occasion I recall seeing them, "dead ringers" one might say to the ET's in the last reel of *Close Encounters of the Third Kind* where the ET's descended very dramatically from their big spaceship. A discussion of psychotronic warfare, ET's, UFO's, and all that kind of phenomena will be taken up later in this book, since it has implications—political, transcendental and eschatological.

Me in Luxor with Howard Carter's guide who was with him in 1922 when he discovered the tomb of King Tut

147

My Shangri-La

As I have said before, my husband, Harry being an East-erner loves the Caribbean and in the early days of our marriage we would go island hopping. Eventually the Island of St. Martin in the French West Indies so captivated us that we decided to purchase a home there. St. Martin has a similar mythical quality to the Shangri-La created by James Hilton in his remarkable story, *Lost Horizon*.

Our house in St. Martin has a very special enchanting qual-ity to it. Besides the tremendous view we have from the deck, we also have a wide and unrestricted view of the northern end of the island: Pic Paradis, the highest point on the island with four views of the water. There is also Simpson's Bay with its proliferation of condos and boats that have a pleasing effect from a distance, and my very favorite view of all, the cliffs of Pt. Rouge. With the waves crashing below you can always tell how the surf is going to be by the force of the waves.

I remember one time we saw the surf as high as it has ever been. There had been a storm out at sea so we drove over to the Grand Case beach club at the end of the island which we would do from time-to-time, and had lunch. The waves were so rough we had to leave as the waves ended up crashing on the backyard of everybody who lived on the beach. Hurricane Luis was an-other matter; there was a total wipe out of much of the island for some time.

Our house also provided a western view that I liked, natu-rally. You could see the sunset, and I knew that if I could keep looking west long enough I would see California or Baja Califor-nia. One week while we were on the island, I asked God if I could have five rainbows that week as a consolation, and sure enough there were five rainbows exactly. On another trip, one rainbow actually moved and climbed over the neighboring hill (Stew Leonard's home is on top) and landed practically on our doorstep. Our caretaker, Kendall, is a witness to this unusual event. There is also that one night when the entire sky turned gold. I saw it but Harry did not see it. That never happened again, but there was a full eclipse of the moon a few years ago. It was awe-inspiring. Things like that are happening pretty regularly around here and thus give a magical quality to this island.

St. Martin definitely has enchantment to it. That is why I think I feel at home here. I know that, because of the special circumstances here—a relatively stress free lifestyle, thanks to the labor of other people—these pleasant experiences are mostly ephemeral.

What was it about the idea of Shangri-La that captured my imagination from the time I was a small child and even to the point when, as a college Freshman, I wrote about St. Thomas More's *Utopia*? I believe that over and above the fact that my mother's friend, Charles Bennett, who helped develop the script for the great movie classic based on James Hilton's book, *Lost Horizon,* told me that I would be a writer some day, I had a super-conscious store of information about future events that would be necessary for the establishment of the New Jerusalem as outlined in the remarkable *Kingdom of the Divine Will,* God's dictation to the bedridden Italian mystic, Luisa Picaretta.

CHAPTER NINETEEN

ANOTHER BASE—A NEW HOME

Finally my husband simply couldn't take the second Connecticut house any longer because it was too close to the thruway, as well as being haunted: he must have sensed this subconsciously. He has a sound amplification syndrome problem as I've said, the opposite of deafness, since he could even hear the Merritt Parkway from the back yard, miles away. So when I needed to remodel the kitchen which had literally become another "black hole of Calcutta", he said oh! oh! He was allergic to the word "remodeling," and so we finally moved.

My husband didn't want a commute that would have been too much longer so we started looking for another house that would not be much farther from New York. After seeing the first house, which was enormous and had a very high stone wall, a farm going back to the middle of the 19th century, I looked at about forty houses. But this first house was meant to be ours. It had been on an onion farm, like all the farms around here, since nearby Southport on Long Island Sound had been a world shipping capital for onions. This big farm house was close to the road so they could transport the onions to the ships for overseas destinations. Onions, like most spices, were highly prized in world trade since you couldn't grow them everywhere. That's why you see so much onion grass growing around here in Spring. The house, with the exception of not having a very convenient family room, was certainly perfect for us and the price was right, since it was owned by a bank for whom the previous owners had worked after the previous owners had sold it.

The previous owners couldn't maintain the place without help, so when the Brazilian couple who worked there left, I guess they had to leave too. They always had to have their guests or family help with the upkeep of the house, or so I was told. I had a similar problem in our previous house. I even had a painting party when we decided to paint the barn there, the one we had to sell because of my husband's sensitive hearing.

Roy Larsen, the owner of this once onion farm, prior to the people who couldn't keep it up, was the kind of person who could afford to live there. He was the Vice-Chairman and CEO of Time-Life Inc.. He brought the company from the red into the black after they got him back out of retirement to do that. He also had help for his four children. Apparently, his daughter, Ann, who was a gregarious child, had a very wild coming out party. This didn't phase me at all since this was part of my own background.

Roy's wife Margaret was a member of the well-known Zerbe family. One Zerbe was quite a good painter. I gave my sister-in-law one of my mother's Zerbes after she died.

Margaret had a very great interest in birds, which is why the Larsens gave one hundred and thirty-five acres to the Audubon Society as a wildlife sanctuary which adjoins our property. They have a hawk watching station; this is serious business. Every year for about five years, a serious looking young man with a beard and binoculars would watch for the hawks in season. But we didn't like the hawks. Our humorous Peruvian caretaker, Carlos, had these little chicken coops with each chicken's name on each coop. Yes, in fact he even gave the chickens names. Well, one day all of Carlos' chickens were done in by either pneumonia or the hawks. That was too bad because Carlos really loved his chickens.

So, after looking at 40 houses, we finally got back to this first one, the onion farm. There was a real synchronicity, in that on the very day we were supposed to sign the contract of purchase. On December 12, 1971, the feast day of Our Lady of Guadalupe, at about 6.30 a.m. we received a call from our neighbor, Ann Carter, that the house we were about to purchase was on fire and that we should come over. At that time we were still living in our haunted house which had still not been sold. The neighbors were very kind and took us in and consoled us. After the fire had been put out we tried to assess the damage which was contained in one wing, in an area over the boiler room. Apparently, for some reason or other, the hot water heater had ignited. The situation, to put it mildly was a mess. Of course we held off signing the contract because of the accident. Finally we did sign on December 12, 1972, and after some trials and tribulations, we did finally move in. This fire happened on the day that we received the prophetic letter from Dr. Krebs, discoverer of Laetrile as a control for cancer pain.

One reason I decided we should move into this house was that Richard Rodgers, the great composer, was a close neighbor. I loved the Rodgers & Hart partnership which preceded the musical collaboration of Rodgers & Hammerstein, because of the lyrics of Lorenz Hart, which were closer to my heart, no pun intended. I especially loved the piece called, "Lover." I would fantasize coming over to a tall hedge, as if in an English movie, which separated my property from Richard Rodgers' property. I would be playing an old Victrola and of course it would be playing "Lover" and then in the true Walter Mitty tradition, from an opening in a hedge, out would pop my beloved Richard Rodgers.

As it eventually happened, I gave a dinner party and sat between Roy Larsen and Richard Rodgers. It was the most awesome and thrilling responsibility I ever had as a hostess. By that time Richard Rodgers had lost his voice because of cancer and spoke through a new artificial voice box. The one time only that Richard Rodgers had written lyrics at all was for a musical *No Strings*, especially the ones for songs sung by Diahann Carroll.

My favorite tune of these is *The Sweetest Sounds*. I thought it might be a clue to the belovedness and grace of my hero, Richard Rodgers. His health declined from the beginning of our brief acquaintance. Once he asked us to play croquet, which I had declined to do because of my own poor health. We'll play croquet in Heaven, some day, I hope.

During one of my husband's business trips to Europe, I thought of Richard Rodgers, especially when I heard my favorite tune, *Edelweiss*, from Rodgers & Hammerstein's, *The Sound of Music*. The edelweiss is an Alpine flower which grows only at high altitudes. In a store window there was this card with a real, dried edelweiss on it, so I bought it for Mr. Rodgers, and put it in his mailbox on my return with a note telling him how much I loved him and his music. Alas, that was the very night he died. His widow, Dorothy, sent a very lovely reply.

The early years in our new home were difficult years due to lack of funds. We, like our immediate predecessors, also had a hard time keeping it up. It was a champagne house and we had a beer budget.

Once when my husband and I went to a monetary conference, we heard all these famous specialists in what can perhaps be called hard money finance and strategic politics. They seem to go together then as now. Arnaud de Borchgrave, Don McAlvany, Mike P. McKeever and the leading Soviet dissident of the day were present.

There was nothing I enjoyed more during the 80's than going to such conferences in New Orleans, where leading economists assembled. I especially loved those short breaks, hanging out at the swimming pool on top of the Royal Orleans Hotel with a view of St Louis Cathedral, watching and hearing a Mississippi riverboat carillon tinkling out its magical sounds. On the first such trip not long after we moved into the house in 1972, I wanted to meet the Nobel prize-winner, Frederick Hayek, who was a speaker. Now since I did not know much about economics, I figured I should start with the top guy and find out what he had to say. So I went up to him at the bar, where everybody was standing and asked, "Professor Hayek, what do you see for the future, in terms of economics?" and he simply said, "Barter, my dear young lady, Barter." I wondered what he meant. Eventually I found out and have been doing some bartering ever since. It has been the means of survival for managing our estate, which we bought for a very good price and at a low interest rate. However, bringing it up to snuff and keeping the place up was difficult, so I would barter; work in exchange for rent.

I can't remember all the caretakers we had, but there is one that I should mention. He was a young man with impeccable references from the Country Club of Fairfield (or so I thought), a very restricted club in Southport. I remember that letter of reference with an old-fashioned picture of a man bending over a golf tee with a ball, the emblem of the club on their stationery. So, on the basis of that recommendation alone, I hired him to be a part-time caretaker along with a couple of other people.

Soon after, we had our best friends over to see our new place. They were a young couple about 10 to 15 years younger than we; she was the younger sister of my best friend, Laurey, from grammar school days in Beverly Hills. Her husband, Emil, in addition to being very amusing and very handsome, was also a great decorator who subsequently became head of the American Division at Christies. He did the whole downstairs for us free of charge and it really hasn't changed much since. His wife was a wonderful cook and joined Martha Stewart's catering company for a while. These were absolutely delightful friends.

They first visited our new home shortly after we had had the grounds cleaned up, and they asked to be taken on an outdoor tour. So, we were strolling around the grounds, giving them an opportunity to check the place out for themselves. We took them to the greenhouse, which they particularly wanted to see. It was very tiny by Mrs. Marshall Fields' standards; that greenhouse which was only about three miles away was huge. The caretaker, the one with the fancy recommendation from the Country Club of

Fairfield, was supposedly growing tomatoes and seeing to things. So when my young friend, who was much more tuned into the "culture" of the day, and had circled the greenhouse more than once, turned to me and asked, "Do you know what these are?" I looked at the tall spindly plants and replied, with my rudimentary knowledge of horticulture as it then was, "I guess they are our tomatoes." He looked at me and said, "Baby, those are not tomatoes. That's marijuana." I said, "WHAT!?" Unfortunately he told my husband whose fury had no bounds. He ordered them to pull out all those plants immediately, and then he fired the entire staff. How was I to manage this huge place without any staff and at the same time look after six children as well as a disabled daughter? Life was difficult for me for a short while and that's putting it mildly. The caretaker left town quickly.

We have had a series of caretakers. Some were better than others. One of our prodigious ones was a refugee from the Communist invasion of Hungary in 1956, when as a little boy, he and his father literally walked out of their town and then the country, escaping Communism. He constructed a garage and then an apartment for himself, wife and their two children. He also built a chapel in record time since we were about to have our daughter Yvonne's wedding reception in the back yard. He put in wine grapes. He was an organic farmer, par excellence. There really was not anything that he could not do. His wife was very kind. She used to have me and my disabled daughter over for barbecues from time-to-time, and sometimes her kindly Hungarian parents would also be there.

The back of our property was overgrown with a vine like the morning glory or kudzu, growing as it does in Bermuda and other southern places where it takes over everything. We had this vine in our backyard which made me anxious because I feared it might climb up to us! (Too much science fiction.) So I hired four young men for a period of two weeks and got them literally to fill four train-car size dumpsters with this pernicious vine which reminded me of something out of *Suddenly Last Summer*, you know where Elizabeth Taylor is almost consumed by man eating plants in Montgomery Clift's greenhouse.

Since then, we have made gradual improvements on the garage and the barn that were already there and have put in a comet watching station. To liven things up around here we have had theme parties from time-to-time—about five of them so far. So when Halley's comet was visible in the Northern hemisphere, we decided to have a comet watching party. My husband, Harry, was dressed as Sir Edmund Halley and our daughter, Suzie, was dressed as the comet. We all went up to the second story of our tree house which was our point of observation, but could not see anything because there was too much light in Bridgeport. Later we had to dismantle that second story because it became too dangerous.

At another theme party I was dressed as the big pumpkin— my idea of emulating Charles Schultz who sometimes makes life worth living! We've had our ups and downs with this place but we are still here, many years later.

Harry and I at home

THE SCARLET PIMPERNEL (1)

They seek him here
They seek him there
Those Frenchies seek him everywhere
Is he in heaven?
Is he in hell?
That damned illusive Pimpernel.

THE SCARLET PIMPERNEL (2)

They seek it here
They seek it there
Those Yankees seek it everywhere.
Is it in heaven?
Is it in heck?
That damned illusive *Kohoutek.*

CHAPTER TWENTY

PARTIES—MY SPECIAL BIRTHDAY GIFTS

Concerning parties, I feel very much like the juggler of Notre Dame, that character in the story of the same name by Guy de Maupassant. In this story there was going to be an unveiling of the statue of the Virgin Mary, which inspired the wealthy and talented artisans of the town to bring their very special gifts such as gold and who knows, maybe frankincense, myrrh, and jewels. Whatever they had they were giving. The poor old juggler had nothing but his juggling act. So after everybody had left their gifts in front of the statue which was placed in the town square, and had gone away, the old juggler hesitatingly and timorously performed his juggling act in front of the statue. The Virgin Mary then comes down from her pedestal and blesses the juggler, and of course, in typical Maupassant fashion, the man dies from sheer joy.

Just like the poor juggler, I asked the Virgin Mary, "Please take my offering—my ability to give parties."

My offer must have been accepted because no sooner had we settled into our new house a number of causes for fundraising arose and I found myself volunteering to host these events at our home, despite the fact that it was in need of constant repair. I was born on May 13, the very day that Harry's Bar in Venice was opened—a place which is to this day a favorite watering hole for many. I also grew up in a tradition of parties. My French family were forever hosting parties for one reason or another, so it seemed like a natural thing for me to do. I try to be obedient and faithful to God, and He has been very good to me. Perhaps it will seem a little strange if I said that, to ease my burdens, God also provides parties for me—his special present for special occasions.

As my 50th birthday approached on May 13, 1981, I was feeling disconsolate because no one was going to give me a party, presents, or even flowers (this is pretty standard). In the mail that week was an invitation from the Secretary General of the Organization of American States, stating that Mrs. McConne requests the pleasure of my company at a dinner party and a CARE ball on Friday, May 13. Now I had never been a member of CARE. I had not been on their committee or anything like that, but here was an invitation to a party in Washington, and I knew that it had to be from God; how else do you explain it?

I needed a new outfit for the occasion, a dress that would be both decent looking and one that I could afford. Fortunately I was still a size 12, because when I went to the dress shop of Susan Shields, she could not immediately find anything appropriate but then she said, "Oh, yes. I remember, I have a dress here that I made especially for Cher." Cher had gorgeous clothes and this dress was too big for her (Cher was into fitness, lost weight and had been building muscle). It was the most exquisite gown I have ever seen, pale yellow chiffon with a little jacket with beautiful crystal beads, all hand made. I tried it on. It was a perfect fit. I felt like Cinderella and asked, "How much?" From the looks of it, the price could have been well over $1,000, but Susan Shields said, "For you, $400."

The party was largely made up of Ambassadors from various third world countries including Brazil since this was an OAS-type of function. The ball was held in the Brazilian Embassy. After a few glasses of good champagne, I was able to summon up the courage to announce that it was my 50th birthday and that I was also a devotee of Our Lady of Fatima who appeared on May 13 as well. I also said that I believed it was a gift from God that I was there and I wanted to thank them all very much, especially the Brazilians who have a Portuguese heritage. (Fatima is in Portugal.) There was a Black couple from Francophone Africa who were Christians, and they were very moved.

Ten years later, my 60th birthday rolled around. It wasn't quite as fancy as the CARE Ball, but it was kind of significant that I was invited to a function in Washington, DC which I was happy to attend with my son John, who is a wonderful escort. John has escorted me to many political affairs. I remember two occasions when John and I met with Charlton Heston. On one of those, we had our picture taken with the great man himself. Wisely, I usually try to stay out of pictures as much as possible with handsome males, such as those two.

I have not as yet turned 70, but the year I am writing this I turned 65 and didn't even consider if this might be an occasion for some miraculous gift, since this was the Medicare turning point when one is officially considered "old."

In April, I received a call from the Equestrian Order of the Knights and Ladies of the Holy Sepulchre and learned that I was just elevated to Commander. I had only been to one function at Sacred Heart University, wearing my Sepulchre Robe, with the Cross of Jerusalem. Malcolm Forbes, Jr. received an honorary degree in Humane Letters from Sacred Heart University, just as I had many years earlier. I wondered, "Why in the world would they make me Commander of the Holy Sepulchre unless they knew about the Shroud work? What does it mean?" (other than the fact that it looks good on the resumé?) My grandmother was awarded the Legion of Honor for her work during World War I, for which of my works was I being rewarded? Putting aside the 'whys' and 'hows', I believe it was one of those miraculous birthday presents.

It turned out that I was recommended for the post by my dear, beloved Bishop, Edward Egan, Bishop of the Roman Catholic Diocese of Bridgeport, Connecticut. So I wrote him a thank-you letter.

I hope that I am around for my 70th birthday. I can hardly wait.

PART II

PART II

CHAPTER TWENTY-ONE

FATEFUL ENCOUNTERS

F ateful encounters became a part of a pattern signaling major shifts in my life. These encounters led to the establishment of the Connecticut Chapter of the Huxley Institute, the first such chapter of what was previously known as the American Schizophrenia Association. This became the springboard that eventually led to the creation of the Fourth World Foundation and later to my Presidential appointments in the 1980's.

The prolific writer, Aldous Huxley, was considered one of the gurus of the New Age and is now emerging from the shadows of the past as a great visionary. The motto of the Huxley Institute was a phrase which Aldous often used, "a sane mind in a sound body". During the early stages of his cancer, Aldous had been drawn to an assembly of scientists who wanted to know what this great thinker had to tell them. He said, "Be a little kinder." As he lay dying, Aldous' last words to his wife Laura were, "God is Love."

I was to meet Laura and many other like-minded persons in her milieu through a set of coincidental circumstances. But these occurred only after another fateful encounter with my sub-conscious through a workshop I attended. This was in early 1971. José Silva, the founder of the system he called Silva Mind Control, like the founders of similar movements, came to his understanding through a revelation from God. He was required to share his insight with others for the betterment of mankind, no doubt because we are all on the eve of the most significant period of human history, the 3rd fiat of God as revealed to the mystic, Luisa Piccaretta. Evangelicals and Protestants sometimes term these times in which we now live the "Latter Rain," which could signify the beginning of the chastisement of the latter days.

I suppose José Silva was chosen for his mission since he began as a humble Mexican American living in the Southwest. His first inspired experiment involved a group of children in New Mexico. He trained them to scan a map, using only their minds, to determine where petroleum deposits could be found. Their uncanny success in doing so astounded a group of Texas oil men who were involved. This first successful demonstration helped launch José's system of Mind Control training.

I was introduced to the Silva Mind Control training through Mary Shadow Hill, a marvelous Tennessee woman, the mother of seven children, the oldest of whom had the metabolic dysperception known as schizophrenia, as did our daughter. Mary, who was the youngest woman ever elected to the Tennessee legislature and gifted with many other accomplishments, went on to become my great female mentor and a reliable guidepost for most of my subsequent actions concerning my family's health. When Mary announced that she had just finished this mind training in trying to solve the riddle of schizophrenia, I decided that I would try it too. I was very fortunate to be able to get instruction from the original trainers taught by José Silva.

On that propitious occasion in 1971, the group held its workshop in a room above the Howard Johnson Motel in nearby Darien, Connecticut. The first course was an "intensive," structured over a period of four days and led by Chris Jensen, a former racing car driver. At the first session, we were shown how to go into a deep meditative or trance-like state that they called your "level." After training our minds to explore everything around us, including going into objects made of metal, no less, which was indescribable when we really achieved this, we were ready for the fourth and final day. On that day we were able to go to our deepest level and receive there whatever would be meaningful to us, presumably, for the rest of our lives.

When I went to my deepest level—since this was basically a guided hypnosis and more—climbing down a long staircase, I saw a beautifully upholstered chair in the 18th century French style and next to it a tall narrow chest of very small drawers. There might have been forty of them. I didn't know what that meant, but later on I found out that in the 18th Century, French herbologists stored their herbs in furniture of a similar kind. I thought that some day I would perhaps work with herbs or might even become a herbologist myself, and that may only now begin to come true in preparing for Y2K and beyond. I must say that our daughter, Patricia's Herb Book, which was her senior project for her double major of Art and Biology, is quite a masterpiece. In it she describes the medicinal properties of most of the major herbs exquisitely hand illustrated, very much like a 19th Century herbal anthology, as good now as ever.

Patricia is recovering through the use of vitamins, a new medication and also through the use of herbs. One of the things which, essentially, has helped to keep my husband alive is an herb which is given intravenously in Germany, since the Germans are so much more advanced in herbology than Americans. In fact the whole world is more advanced than Americans in the use of herbs. This is changing only now as the clenched fist grip of domination by big drug companies and their henchmen, some of the old school of "orthodox" drug oriented practitioners, loosens its hold on American public opinion regarding healthcare.

While the Silva Mind Control course provided the know-how to such unusual skills like entering metal, its major dictum was based on Jesus' message to avoid condemning our fellow man (Matt. 7: 1-5). The Silva dictum urged us to avoid thinking or speaking anything negative. Our formula for perfection was a well repeated phrase, "Cancel, cancel the negative thoughts."

I think I was the second best student of that Silva Mind Control group. The best student was a Steven Barham of Rhode Island who really picked up the whole thing dazzlingly. He was very right-brained like me and went on to become an Archimandrite priest, the Archimandrites being an obscure off-shoot of Roman Catholicism. He is a marvelous lecturer and brings comic relief to large gatherings where many Roman Catholic mystics are featured, whose messages are definitely on the serious side. I saw him at a gathering in Pittsburgh a few years ago. At the same meeting were a seer from Medjugorje, a mystic, Christine Gallagher from Ireland and the Greek Orthodox mystic, Vassula Ryden, who speaks seven languages and eventually came to our home, which will be described later.

IN MEMORY OF MARY HILL

(Adapted from Shelley's Elegy in memory of Keats)

How can I speak when there are no words.
How can I express our loss and our love.

Recently I was praying to God for the name of our chapel and He said it will be called The Chapel of Adonai, which is to say, the Lord.

And therefore the elegy of Adonais was given to me as a panegyric for the loss of our beloved Mary Hill.

I weep for Adonais—he is dead:
Oh, weep for Adonais: though our tears
Thaw not the frost which binds so dear a head:
And thou, sad Hour, selected from all years
Mourn our loss, rouse thy obscure compeers,
And teach them thine own sorrow: Say:
'With me Died Adonais; till.the Future dares
Forget the Past, his fate and fame shall be
An echo and a light unto eternity:

Weep not for Mary Hill.
She lives. In the words of the Evangelist, St. John,

Jesus says: Nevertheless I tell you the truth;
it is expedient for you that I go away:
for if I go not away, the comforter will not come unto you:
but if I depart, I will send him unto you.
And so it is for the departed Christian,
her spirit will remain with us in a new more powerful way.

We speak of the American woman wearing many hats.
Of no other woman I have known can it be said this and yet—
like Madam Gracci said of her sons who were founders of the
    Roman Republic
Mary unfailingly said of her children, "These are my jewels."
Her final hat is a crown of glory.

And St. Paul tells us—
For I am now ready to be offered,
and the time of my departure is at hand.

I have fought a good fight,
I have finished my course,
I have kept the faith:

That Light whose smile kindles the Universe,
That Beauty in which all things work and move,
That Benediction which the eclipsing Curse
Of birth can quench not, that sustaining Love
Which through the web of being blindly wove
By man and beast and earth and air and sea,
Burns bright or dim, as each are mirrors of
The fire for which all thirst, now beams on me,
Consuming the last clouds of cold mortality.

Henceforth there is laid up for me a crown of riqhteousness,
which the Lord, the Righteous Judge,
shall give me at that day: and not to me only,
but unto all them also that love his appearing.

Adonai the Father blesses Mary's Crown of Jewels,
her children and grandchildren.
She has passed on to them everything that she was
and everything that she did; they will carry on her torch.

CHAPTER TWENTY-TWO

MAKING THE HUXLEY CONNECTION

It was in 1972, shortly after we moved to our new home in Greenfield Hill, Connecticut that my husband and I visited the Island of St. Martin for the first time. Harry, being from the East Coast, loved the Caribbean and liked to go island hopping, following in the footsteps of John Adams, the esteemed father of one of the great influences in my husband's life, Henry Adams, on whose work my husband had written while in college. In one of his letters, John Adams had said that the colonies needed the Caribbean islands as much as the islands needed the colonies. We were fortunate enough to visit most of the Caribbean islands, vacationing from one to another of them with our growing number of children.

We were favorably impressed with St. Martin because of its dry weather and its international flair, the island being half-French and half-Dutch. The accommodations were mediocre, especially if you were on a budget, as we were in those days. At first we went to a really seedy place, The Grand Hotel St. Martin, complete with cockroaches and faulty plumbing. (It has now been done over.) We stayed there one night and headed instead to the Caravanserai Hotel (Dutch for caravan) on the Dutch part of the island, probably the best hotel the island had at the time.

The first evening as we sat in the dining room, an extremely romantic place, with the tables lit by candles, we noticed another couple sitting across the room. They were by comparison older than we were and smiled at us graciously.

The following day we felt like inspecting the new Concord Hotel which was under construction across the adjacent beach, whose major attraction (for thrill seekers?) were the airplanes landing, seemingly just about 50 feet over our heads since the beach was almost part of the runway. As we made our way across the beach whom did we come across but the couple we saw the previous evening. They introduced themselves graciously as Jane and Henry Adams Ashforth of the well-known New York real estate company. Jane was his second wife. Distinguished Mr. Henry Adams Ashforth, real estate agent that he was, was pulling out drawers, opening closets and checking on the construction, no doubt trying to ascertain that the Concord was indeed going to be well appointed. "Not bad," he would say. This hotel would go on to become Maho Beach years later.

They were also staying at the Caravanserai so we had dinner with them that evening. Over dinner it turned out that we shared a great deal in common since Jane Ashforth's son from a previous marriage, and our daughter Patricia, both suffered from schizophrenia, that terrible disease. While Patricia had been hospitalized in Yale, New Haven, in Tompkins I, the in-patient psychiatric unit where it seemed she was getting worse, not better, I had the good fortune, after much seeking, to read about the Canadian Schizophrenia Association. It had just moved from Toronto, Canada to Ann Arbor, Michigan, and then to New York City, changing its name to the American Schizophrenia Foundation, a fairly new national organization devoted to finding the causes of, and promulgating information about complementary/alternative treatments for major mental illnesses, including schizophrenia.

This was in 1972 when synchronicities began to happen.

The Adams Ashworths turned out to be great contributors to this fledgling organization and they asked us to be guests at their table at the next meeting where the keynote speaker was to be Dr. Linus Pauling, a figure from my long ago past.

This meeting, preceding the fundraising dinner to which we

had been invited, was held at the Hilton Hotel on 6th Avenue in New York. At that meeting, which was called "The First Conference on Aging," we sat virtually at the feet of Dr. Linus Pauling who spoke about the pioneering work of Dr. Irving Stone on Vitamin C. This was indeed heady stuff for me. Dr. Pauling said that studies showed that primates had lost their capability to metabolize their own Vitamin C, resulting in something called human hypoascorbemia. He was also beginning to use the results of this work in his own Institute for Science and Medicine, and indeed wrote a seminal paper on this general topic in the magazine *Science* in 1968, entitled, "Orthomolecular Psychiatry."

Many famous scientists and physicians sat on the dais besides Linus Pauling, the only man then alive ever to win both the Nobel Peace Prize and the Nobel Prize for Chemistry. Dr. Pauling was considered by some to be the father of modern chemistry. Also present were Dr. Stone, who did the original research on Vitamin C, of whose work Pauling had spoken and on which he based much of his own work, and Dr. Roger J. Williams, Director of the Clayton Institute at the University of Texas in Austin, a great medical center. Dr. Williams was the man credited with the discovery of the vitamin, pantothenic acid, and author of many books including the fascinating *Biochemical Individuality*, something modern medicine does not always take into consideration.

After Dr. Pauling spoke, I went up to shake his hand, asking him if he remembered me. This was merely a gesture to break any ice as I had not seen him since I was four years old in my grandfather's backyard back in Pasadena. How could he possibly remember me? But as I've already said, Dr. Pauling earned his Ph.D from California Institute of Technology, under my grandfather Crellin's inspiration and subsequently Dr. Pauling named his youngest son Crellin, after my grandfather who had donated the Chemistry laboratory to Cal Tech, instead of leaving anything to me or my brother in his will. No doubt this was part of God's plan; it made me work harder all my life.

Dr. Pauling replied, "Oh, yes, nice to see you, but do see my wife." Ava Pauling was a tremendous help in her husband's life, as is the case with many famous men and therefore her influence was probably more than I shall ever really know. However, I do know that during my visit to them at their home in Portola, California, outside of San Francisco in the Valley, when I brought up the subject of religion, they showed me a copy of *The Urantia Book* which is something like *A Course in Miracles*, but much stronger, and much more intensely arcane!

On the dais, along with Dr. Pauling sat Laura Huxley (widow of Aldous Huxley). I went up to Laura, timorously as always, but since she was Italian and spoke French, of course, like all educated Italians of her generation, I started speaking to her in French. She liked that. She liked my dress too.

At the time, I always considered myself an okay looking housewife who still managed to get into a very beautiful couturier size 10 dress, which my mother had had made for me in Paris before I was married. At least I didn't look like a dowdy housewife.

It was the same dress that I had worn to a special party shortly after we moved to California in 1954. My husband and I crashed a party at Mary Pickford's Estate on Tower Drive, which was announced in the *Los Angeles Times* the day before. It was very close to my mother's house on Chevy Chase Drive to which we had just moved. We arrived in my stepfather's Jaguar which I had borrowed, and I was wearing that same dress. I had the courage to say to the doorman, "I am a friend of Dolores Costello (which in fact I was) and I am sure she will be here," to which he replied with a flourish, "Oh, yes. Please come in, Madam." Buddy Rogers, her then husband, (who only recently died, some 40 years later as I write this book!) was there greeting the guests, who were for the most part movie stars from the silent movie era. Later, old Mary Pickford, who was already ailing, sat in a back room and one by one we went in to see her.

Laura invited me to speak privately with her in her hotel room. I was overwhelmed to be so honored—the widow of the late Aldous Huxley asking me up to her room!! At the end of our later tête à tête, she suggested that I show up for the Board of Directors meeting of the newly formed Huxley Institute which would take place the next day in the same hotel. So, the American Schizophrenia Association was indeed about to change its name to the Huxley Institute. One reason for the change of name was that there was a stigma attached to the word schizophrenia, and secondly, attaching the Huxley name to the organization would associate it with the scientific renown of the Huxley family. Aldous had wanted to be a doctor, but couldn't achieve this aim because of his poor eyesight. Sir Julian Huxley had studied genetics and schizophrenia and his work was considered a definite influence on the work of the organization.

Dr. Humphrey Osmond, co-discoverer with fellow Canadian, Abram Hoffer, M.D. Ph.D, of the megavitamin treatment for mental illness, had been a major disciple of Aldous Huxley as well as his personal physician. Dr. Osmond had been a founding member of the association in Canada and of a system of treatment now sometimes referred to as Orthomolecular Medicine or Complementary Medicine, as termed by Dr. Pauling's protégé, Dr. Jeff Bland.

So, lo and behold, the day after that conference at the Hilton, I was at the board meeting of the renamed Huxley Institute, quaking in my new shoes with my head bowed the whole time. They voted *me* in as a member!! I guess they thought I had a lot of money. I was awestruck by all of these famous people and asked myself, "What am I doing here?" I must have looked good though since a board member, the well-known Canadian financier, Donald Webster, invited me out to lunch the next day. That sort of clinched the deal. He thought that besides my having that very nice dress that my husband might have some money to help support the Institute, which the Board members were supposed to do anyway. (At that time, he didn't!)

After that board meeting it occurred to me that in order to get anything done I needed to start at the local level so I decided to give a fundraising party in support of the Huxley Institute. That was to be my first Huxley initiative so in order to garner publicity I fooled the local press into thinking it was going to be something glamorous and not the serious event that it really was, but that was to happen months later.

175

CHAPTER TWENTY-THREE

ENCOUNTERING NEW VIEWS: NEW AGE, NEW SCIENCE

Right after that first meeting of the Huxley Institute in New York City at the Hilton Hotel, Jeanette Rockefeller financed the party for the "heavy hitters" which, with so much promise and fanfare, gave the Huxley Institute its first great impetus in the early 70's.

Carole Bergerman, my old childhood friend from California, and granddaughter of the movie industry pioneer, Carl Laemmle, was with me for the event since she loved parties, had never married, and we were still, as always when we were together, the giggling teenagers. We were sitting in a booth in a room next to the bar at the Hilton after the grand dinner. I was sitting next to Dr. Edwin Boyle, director of the Miami Heart Institute, a founding member of Huxley and a very dashing man; next to him sat Laura Huxley. Laura was flirting with him, a de rigeur thing to do, since she considered herself one of the "grandes amoureuses", as they are called in French—beautiful and fascinating women who purportedly have many lovers and admirers. You could say that my mother was one of those, also. Laura, as I recall, also prided herself on the devotion of her lovers (and many fans) she had had in her life including, of course, her late husband, Aldous. She was definitely right out of the screenplay of *8 & 1/2* by Frederico Fellini, or so I thought, an anti-clerical artistic intellectual Italian, but with a difference; Laura was kind, brilliant and a great leader.

So there I was at the Hilton bar with Carole, my sister Californian and trusted friend, Laura, the flamboyant Italian intellectual, and the distinguished cardiologist, Dr. Ed. Boyle. Good little Irish Catholic Anne wouldn't dream of flirting with anyone after her marriage, but I was fascinated with what Dr. Boyle had to say. Since these were holistic physicians, a great deal of the new wave thinking crept in. He was talking about his experience in age regressing his patients to a previous "life," one of the things he did as a hobby, aside from taking care of his heart patients. I remembered Dr. Boyle speaking particularly about one young woman whose case was similar to that of Virginia Tighe, who under hypnosis had remembered her previous life in Ireland as Bridey Murphy. Dr. Boyle had observed in his many age regressed patients, that there seemed to be a consistent hiatus of around six years between their present life and their previous life. This had some significance later when I was about to start my own foundation.

David Smith of Earth House

Here I must recount my meeting with David Smith, the Yoga instructor at the holistic half-way house for the mentally ill, Earth House, in Millstone, New Jersey, a paragon for half-way houses in the U.S. We arrived at our meeting place only to discover that we were carrying the same book by Rudolf Steiner , *Egyptian Myths and Mysteries*. That incident launched me into my study of Rudolf

Steiner. It was at that time that I came upon the logo of one of Steiner's works, *Towards a World Economy*, and to my utter surprise discovered that it was almost identical to the logo for the Fourth World Foundation I was to launch later. The only difference was that my foundation's logo has the paraclete descending on the globe. I am now sure of the fact that that design was given to me by divine inspiration, though I was not aware of it at the time.

In his aforementioned book, *Egyptian Myths and Mysteries*, Rudolf Steiner made a profound statement, with the precision and severity of the blow of the guillotine, refuting the general premise of all of the so-called New Age persons, that we could all become "gods." Steiner stated unequivocally that the most important event in the history of the universe was the incarnation of Jesus Christ. There is no Christian who could argue with such a pronouncement, except those who in that same book, have adopted "Modernism," one way or another.

Steiner had been a disciple of the Theosophists who were basically a cult of the ilk of such people as Madame Helena Blavatsky. He also received instruction about the mysteries of the universe, by someone whom you might call a Shaman, or the old man of the woods, according to Austrian lore. It was this Shaman who showed him the importance of this knowledge of religious science, which he took with him when he left the Theosophists and started his own "science," entitled, Anthroposophy, or the study of man. He had a special connection with nature and was one of the few people who manifested metaphysical energy. He was a disciple of the great German poet, Goethe and went on to found schools of dance called eurythmics, which I believe was the foundation for the choreography of Martha Graham, and certainly Meredith Monk. Steiner also founded the Waldorf schools which were precursors of Maria Montessori, of which I had the benefit during my early years in a similar school setting in Brentwood, the famous Town and Country School. Steiner also introduced bio-dynamic gardening in which every inch of soil is sown in the rhythms of our own solar system and also by using the raised bed technique.

The Spanish Cathedral, La Famalia Sagrada, designed
by Antonio Gaudi at night

Rudolf Steiner

There are two synchronicities linking me with Rudolf Steiner. The first was in my choice of the logo for my foundation, which I have already mentioned. The second is that I was born six years after his death as per the research of the late Dr. Edwin Boyle.

A couple of years later, I had a meeting with the charismatic, Jewish and kindred spirit, Judy Skutch, whose daughter-in-law, Helen Bluckman, received information, channelled to her which led to her writing, *The Book of Miracles.* Judy told me—as recounted to her by her daughter-in-law—that reincarnation is only the genetic memory in the mitochondria of our cells. Everything genetic that we have is in our cells. (There is a *New York Times* article of ten years ago which stated that there had been studies on this subject.) So, if you think there was a Rudolf Steiner or Cleopatra for that matter, in your family, then you may have such genetic memory of them in your cells.

Rudolf Steiner's Headquarters, his Goethenaum

I'm doing a lot of the things Steiner did, some of it is almost identical; I have the same kind of workaholic, incredibly eclectic lifestyle. I had been working myself to death the way he did, though

I'm trying to change that. Also, I have fought the Red Dragon and continue to do so and am now fighting the Black Panther just as he did. Notwithstanding these facts, I'm not the reincarnation of Rudolf Steiner. I am just related to him, that's all. No big deal!

Steiner's headquarters were at the junction of Switzerland, Germany and Austria. His architecture for his headquarters was reminiscent of the Spanish Cathedral, La Famalia Sagrada, designed by Antonio Gaudi (where the word gaudy comes from). This was definitely right brain architecture. One was always worried that if the sun got any hotter it would melt. The same could be said of Steiner's Goetheanum. I went to visit the place where there is a picture of Steiner with two statues—one of which was the Red Dragon and the other was of the Black Panther. Steiner maintained throughout his life that these images represented the two faces of Satan—Lucifer (the Red Dragon) which in our times is dialectical Communism, and Ahriman (the Black Panther) which is secular humanism in all its forms (including the so-called Illuminati or the New World Order).

Steiner foresaw the danger that Hitler would present to the world ten years before it became apparent to the rest of the world, since he died in 1925. I was born six years after that.

Judy Skutch and I first met at the time of the Camp David Accord and on the cover of *Time Magazine* there was a map of the Middle East with a rainbow between Israel and Jordan and a dove flying over the rainbow. I brought along a copy of this magazine cover when I visited Judy in her apartment in Arlington and we both understood that the rainbow and the dove symbolized our relationship so she joined the board of the Fourth World Foundation at that time. Judy had especially chosen this apartment overlooking the Potomac River and all of Washington to beam her considerable light energy in the direction of Washington, DC!

A couple of years later we again met but this time it was at a party in her apartment in New York overlooking Central Park; and who was there but my old mind control teacher, Chris Jensen! I remember his response to my question, "What are you doing now, Chris?" He replied immediately, "Vibrations. Everything is vibrations." I was kind of taken aback since I had never heard anything like that but now, many, many years later, I find that there is much truth to this. Nevertheless, this kind of thinking is not for everybody. This is something you obviously could not do if you were on the floor of the stock market or managing other people's millions of dollars, or if you were a trial lawyer. However, you do pick up vibrations. I sense vibrations when I am tuned in, so to speak; upon entering a room I can pick up its vibrations generally and also one on one I sense other people's feelings, especially their feelings about me (which is sometimes unfortunate!).

I remember when I went by to see Laura for the first time at the aerie she had shared with Aldous, I stopped to get her some flowers at a gas station in Hollywood, a most unlikely place, but the only place I could obtain flowers on that Sunday upon my arrival at the airport. When the garage attendant, who was also the flower salesman, found out where I was going, he insisted on giving me the flowers with a great flourish, practically genuflecting. He was so grateful to have his flowers brought to the abode of the late great guru, Aldous Huxley, and guruess of the New Age, Laura.

Laura Huxley

It was on this occasion that I was to have one of the peak experiences of my life, characterized by the great psychologist, Abraham Maslow as, a "peak experience," or a life changing event. My credentials and persona had, for a second time, passed muster with Laura, whereupon she took me into her exercise room where she had a contraption which turned the body upside down, so as to hang by the feet. These were many of the new fads of the 70's. She also showed me her garbage artwork which consisted of her composted vegetables suspended in colored water in some kind of glass vases in the same shape as the containers used for ant farms. The background for all this was seen through her kitchen windows which faced the Hollywood hills with no homes on them at all! Amazingly stretched out across the hills for the whole world to see was the great white sign, "Hollywoodland," later changed to "Hollywood."

Laura also showed me her collection of almonds, whose pits contained Laetrile, one of the great panaceas for pain in cancer. She took one every day because she was afraid of getting cancer, of which both Aldous and his first wife had died, and she wasn't taking any chances.

In 1950, Dr. Ernst Krebs Jr. had discovered Laetrile, a type of Glucoside, also known as Vitamin B17, found in the seeds, stones or kernels of most members of the rose family (rosaceae) as well as the seeds of many fruit varieties, especially almonds. There is a link between the uncontrolled growth of cancer cells and a substance found in the placenta. Laetrile was demonstrated to have a dampening effect on the uncontrolled growth of cancer cells as well as a frequent panacea for cancer pain.

I have a letter from Dr. Krebs about our daughter, Patricia, which became an early harbinger both for suffering and for hope which is dealt with at the end of this chapter.

Laura, being a New Age advocate, decided to "tune me in," so to speak. She put a Tibetan tuning fork on my head. Having been a recent graduate and even a star performer of the Silva Mind Control Workshop given in Darien, Connecticut, this meant that it would be able to elicit a response from me, no doubt. Therefore, when Laura put the Tibetan tuning fork on my head, something was supposed to happen; it did! Without even trying, I went into as deep a trance state as I have ever been, and then Laura led me into yet another room across from an empty rocking chair where I rested peacefully for, in Laura's words, "a timeless moment," (from her book of the same name). Slowly, very slowly, I came out of the trance. Laura asked me what I had experienced and I said to her, almost in amazement, "Well, as a matter of fact, I saw your late husband sitting in his chair smoking his pipe with a seraphic smile on his face. He didn't say anything, but he was smiling as if looking right through me," similar to the smile and look I experienced years later in an encounter with St. Michael the Archangel.

At this point I must recount that the second encounter with a discarnate being occurred on May 18, 1978, the day that I had attended a fundraising for my old boarding school, Ethel Walker's. We were doing a phonathon—volunteers phoning alumnae to donate to the annual giving fund. Afterwards, I had dinner with an old school mate, Arden Bondy Sperry and her husband. I was feeling terrific. It had been a wonderful evening. It was about 11.00—11.30 p.m. when I set out for home in my convertible with the top down. In those days I used to drive alone at night. No problem. As I approached the toll booth separating Manhattan from the Bronx on the way home to Connecticut, with one hand on the steering wheel, and the other groping for change, I looked up and saw something which is very hard to describe. Instead of the usual man in the toll booth, there was a being full of light, much larger than the toll booth. He had very brilliant blue eyes that looked right through my body and into my soul, and smiled at me with an indescribable loving and tender smile. He was wearing a white shirt with long sleeves under pale blue overalls. He also had curly red hair. I was transfixed! I was ecstatic! I cannot remember whether this being had wings. I have no idea what I did next, certainly not paying the toll. I crawled through the toll booth and pulled over to the side. I asked my-self, "What or who was that?" and the telepathic(?) answer came that it was St. Michael, the archangel, my own guardian angel. I was so over-awed that I thought it best to drive in the slow lane. I wondered why I should see my guardian angel in a toll booth leaving New York City. I still don't know. God will reveal this in His time. The confirmation of St. Michael's likeness came years later in a mosaic in the apse of the Church of Santa Sofia in Istanbul, Turkey, which will be explained later with confirma-tions of other mystical experiences.

Back to Laura: When I told her that I had seen her husband in my trance state, she replied, "Oh yes, that was Aldous' favor-ite chair; he always sat there. This was his study." It seemed similar to the apparition of the Madonna standing on top of the church in Zeitoun (Heliopolis), Egypt, not saying anything to the millions of people who came to see her there in her transfigured body. She was just smiling. At that time I had a synchronistic coincidence connected with the apparition of Zeitoun, the mod-ern name for Heliopolis, the city to which the Holy Family fled to escape Herod's slaughter of the newborn males after the birth of Jesus. When I had arrived at the Cairo airport, the tax-free counter (yes, they even had tax-free counters in Egypt in the 1970's) had a new French perfume I had eagerly awaited called "Silences." Later that day, as my husband and I were having lunch, I heard the song, *The Sounds of Silence*, which they were playing in this out of the way cafe. I knew that Our Lady, or "The Lady of Si-lence," without further synchronicities, was making the same kind of nonverbal communication that I received from Aldous Huxley on that fateful day at Laura's in 1972.

Just recently, as a matter of fact, I went to see Laura for the first time in many years at a conference she gave entitled, "Chil-dren: Our Ultimate Investment," something she had wanted to do for a long time. It was about conscious conception and con-scious parenting, which might now be called intentional conception and parenting.

Laura never had any children of her own, but had adopted a little baby girl. While she lavished all of her affection on this child, whom she brought up as her own daughter, Laura also was very close to the baby's young mother who was unable to care for the child at that time. I remember Laura spoon-feeding raw liver to the little girl (not as bad as it sounds), who apparently enjoyed it, and she has since grown up to be Laura's pride and joy.

Laura really cared about children. At another time, Laura was planning an organization where grandmothers would take care of babies while their mothers worked. Laura called that initiative, "Project Caress." Her other non-profit organization followed the name of the conference she gave, "Children: Our Ultimate Investment," which was more ambitious, and whose objective was to get people to live in such a way that they would have healthy babies—a kind of preventive medicine before conception. This conference in California that I attended more recently was to bring awareness to these issues. Her keynote speaker was the dropout, if you will, from the heirdom of the Baskin-Robbins ice cream chain fortune, John Robbins, a well-known speaker and author of many books advocating vegetarianism and other healthy modes of living, including *Diet for a New America*. I remember that conference very well. Laura let me speak to the conference (shortly) about our Huxley Institute Connecticut Chapter, one of only two left in the world, I think, the other one being run by stalwart, Elizabeth Plante, of Eastchester, New York, whose late husband had been schizophrenic. As I spoke before John Robbins was to speak, I remember saying, "This is going to be a hard act to precede," and indeed it was since he gave a great speech.

My son, Henry, was there since he was a filmmaker at the time and I was trying to get him interested in the script for *Island*, (Aldous's last novel), but the rights had been sold to someone who was sitting on the project. Too bad! It would have made a great movie.

One of Laura's many friends was the New Age guru, Richard

Alpert, who became Baba Ram Dass. He and his colleague Timothy Leary were both professors at Harvard University when they decided it was time to "tune in, turn on and drop out." This led me to speculate as to why people dropped out in droves in the 60's.

Those drop-outs of the 60's were known as the "Hippies." It is true that they were much maligned with good reason. They smoked marijuana; they didn't shave or take regular baths; they made a lot of trouble for their parents, their teachers and everyone else. But there is something more profound here than a generation of under-washed rebels. They were honest enough to reflect on the malaise of their generation and to react to a situation that mankind was facing for the first time in history—a situation that produced this new strange behavior. Why would they do this? What were they reflecting? How did it start?

I had a talk with author Will Brownell, who originally was to be a co-author of this book. We agreed that my experiences, as well as the world changes were brought about by a shift of consciousness or the so-called paradigm shift. We kept going back in time to find out what caused the great shift which began a long time ago, e.g. when man stopped building cathedrals and began building castles. Since the 13th century, mankind has begun to slide downhill. The shift of the 20th century was manifested in the Beat Generation of the 1950's, the Hippies of the 1960's and Woodstock.

I believe this shift may be due to the fault of kinship with people who are today in their 40's and 50's who were trying to escape materialism. Will Brownell and I asked each other what caused the Hippie culture. I believe it started with Jack Kerouac, the Dharma Bum of the 50's Beat Generation, who was "on the road," and wrote a book, *On The Road*, which was about escaping the mechanistic technological fall-out of the developed nations. Jack Kerouac was a French Canadian who rebelled against his traditional roots. He was the first of the Beatniks as well as being "King of the Road." He was the first rebel after the war. What was it that caused him to rebel and indeed lead a whole generation to rebel?

The answer to that, I believe, was to be seen on the fuselage of the airplane called Enola Gay, a name seared forever in human history. On the morning of August 6, 1945 that airplane, Enola Gay, took off on a mission which would cause the turning point, as well as the end, of World War II. It was also the turning point in humanitarian history where mankind had progressed from destroying its enemies with clubs (like Fred Flintstone?) or with bows and arrows like Robin Hood, to the final act of dropping an atomic bomb on Hiroshima. The symbol for this destruction is the mushroom cloud and it is in the subconscious of everyone who knows about it, like it or not. This is the event that produced people like Jack Kerouac. Not all of them would remain dropouts. One group, for instance, had met once on a beach in the Yucatan Peninsula in the early 60's and a voice from God told them to start an organization called the Foundation Faith of God. Over the years they had become a national organization of people with headquarters in Reno, Nevada, taking care of terminally ill children by sending in clowns in hospitals, trying to prevent cruelty to animals in drug and chemical testing, and 101 other worthy causes to reduce suffering on the planet.

Harvard professor Richard Alpert, who became Guru Baba RamDass, was also in this category. His Hanuman Foundation was born after he found himself doing more and more for the needs of prisoners and now he spends his life exhorting people to do the same. Indeed one of his books, entitled, *How Can I Help?* says it all. From that generation of drop-outs came some amazing new discoveries from those who did not drop out.

One of the several authors of that time was Ken Kesey, who wrote the powerful book, *One Flew Over The Cuckoo's Nest*, from which the Academy Award winning film was made. Another was Ken Keyes Jr. who wrote a book entitled, *The Hundredth Monkey*; this is the story:

The Japanese monkey, Macaca fuscata, had been observed in the wild for a period of over 30 years. In 1952, on the island of Koshima, scientists were providing monkeys with sweet potatoes dropped in the sand. The monkeys liked the taste of the raw sweet potatoes, but they found the dirt unpleasant. An 18-month-old female named Imo found she could solve the problem by washing the potatoes in a nearby stream. She taught this trick to her mother. Her playmates also learned this new way and they taught their mothers too. This cultural innovation was gradually picked up by various monkeys before the eyes of the scientists. Between 1952 and 1958 all the young monkeys learned to wash the sandy sweet potatoes to make them more palatable. Only the adults who imitated their children learned this social improvement. Other adults kept eating the dirty sweet potatoes. Then something startling took place. In the autumn of 1958, a certain number of Koshima monkeys were washing sweet potatoes—the exact number is not known. Let us suppose that when the sun rose one morning there were 99 monkeys on Koshima Island who had learned to wash their sweet potatoes. Let's further suppose that later that morning, the hundredth monkey learned to wash potatoes. THEN IT HAPPENED! By that evening almost everyone in the tribe was washing sweet potatoes before eating them. The added energy of this hundredth monkey somehow created an ideological breakthrough!

This phenomenon was not dependent on any of the five senses as we know them. It was clearly evidence of intra-species communication about which British scientist, Rupert Sheldrake, wrote in his seminal ground-breaking book, *The New Science of Life*, which describes what he calls, "morphic resonance." Sheldrake posits that there must be a similar form of communication among humans but so far this has not been proved. He alleges that this communication truly exists and is the causative factor, invisible to the human eye and other senses, which is responsible for the conduit of information among members of the same species. In some remarkable experiments he demonstrated the effect of "thought waves" on humans and other entities. This gives rise to the concept that "thoughts are things." This basically, is the message from the "heavenlies," that prayer can change the world, can mitigate the prophesied chastisements from a just God to a sinful and sorrowful mankind.

Another outstanding practitioner of this "new science," the esoteric science of this period, was Dutch philosopher / practitioner, Jack Schwartz, who, during the Nazi occupation of the Netherlands, was made to wear a black arm band because he was a Jew and was eventually thrown into prison at the age of 17.

After having been severely beaten by his jailer, Jack experienced a visitation from Jesus who told him, "Forgive your jailer and tell him I forgive him too." Jack did just that at which point the jailer broke down weeping and let him go free.

Since Schwartz's arrival in the United States, he has been a leader of a unique movement of western gurumanship, if you can call it that, and has conducted workshops on techniques which enabled him to develop the capability of making changes in the autonomic nervous system, heretofore not accomplished by Westerners, but only by Eastern masters; e.g. he could reduce or raise his blood pressure and temperature at will. He also effected a lifestyle requiring an intake of about only 400 calories of food and four hours of sleep per night. We read about Dick Gregory's espousal of breatharianism and other wonders brought about by very advanced techniques known to the Indian yogis for millennia.

In a book by Joan Carroll Cruz entitled, *The Incorruptibles* she demonstrates that many Christian saints' bodies have remained incorrupt over the years and in some cases centuries. There were also instances where the bodies of well-known Indian holy men have remained incorrupt as well, through the same ascetic practices employed by the Christian saints.

I believe Schwartz, who wrote many books on the subject, has been teaching people how to achieve wholeness on the way to holiness! This wholeness is manifested in the control of one's autonomic nervous system which is a great tool for expanding one's awareness and hence compassion. At one health resort in California, I did learn how to change my body temperature at will, but it took a lot of practice!

Interestingly enough, Jack Schwartz was the first of the "New Age" holy men to make a trip to Medjugorje, Yugoslavia, the site of the very famous Marian apparitions.

Another paragon of the 70's was an Indian holy man whose name was Gopi Krishna. He wrote several books, two of which are: *The Biological Basis of Religion and Genius,* and his last book, *The Shape of Things To Come,* which was the sign of the times to come. On its cover is the picture of Jesus on the Cross, and it dealt with Christian descriptions of the chastisements to come. The entire book was written in very beautiful poetry. However, Krishna called himself a pandit which means teacher in Sanskrit; he wanted to be sure we, the audience, did not consider him a guru. What he was teaching fundamentally was the science behind an energy known as Kundalini.

Gopi was a celibate pandit who had successfully sublimated his sexual energy. One morning as he was meditating and praying as he sat cross-legged in front of his window in the early dawn, he experienced a rush of energy from the base of his spine to the top of his head. This was the so-called Kundalini energy which is basically one name for energy known as Chi to the Chinese and Prana to the Indians. It is the energy (of the universe, or at least of the planet earth, and our atmosphere) that resides first of all in the lower chakras which are the points of energy in the human organism. The sublimation of that energy, raising it, so to speak, to the highest level, is accomplished through prayer, meditation and yogic breathing. Gupi practiced Kundalini yoga, which I actually experienced on a trip to the camp in Arizona run by the Sikhs. It constitutes very strenuous yoga positions second only in difficulty in my experience in trying to learn ballet. I often wondered if it would not be a good idea to teach Kundalini yoga exercises to celibate Catholic priests. It might make life easier.

Yet another one of these remarkable men is Peter Russell, whose books include *The Global Brain* and *The White Hole in Space*. In the first book, Russell maintains that the earth's rhythm is at 8-12 megahertz similar to our own human alpha state. When the population on the planet becomes 10 billion, somehow or another we need to be in the alpha state to sustain life on Mother Earth. That makes a lot of sense. Peter Russell is an engaging and charismatic Englishman, very much like the ones I met when I was hobnobbing with the Australian, Michael Riddell. Of course, their hypotheses and discoveries are delivered to the few, not the many.

During that amazing week, the third week in May 1978, I experienced a time warp visiting my older son, Henry, in the basement of the Hilton Hotel in New York City. Only a week later, by some extraordinary coincidence, I signed up for a workshop with the author of the book, *Stalking the Wild Pendulum*, Iztak Bentov, who for the workshop that day was teaching us how to achieve a time warp (the ability to "create" extra time). Strangely enough, later that year Bentov, while on his way to a book fair in Chicago, was on an airplane that crashed and amongst the passengers were many distinguished authors, such as the esteemed Henry Regnery. I always wondered whether Bentov's strange experiments had anything to do with it.

Richard Alpert, the aforementioned Harvard professor who became Baba Ram Dass, was a friend of Laura's and she introduced me to him at a party in Beverly Hills. He was sitting on the floor—Buddha style: he was also quite large—also Buddha style. Years later my husband escorted me to meet him—an unusual event. In those days my husband sometimes accompanied me on my more particularly interesting trips. As we were ushered in to his apartment on or near Riverside Dr. on the West side of New York City, a girl with long, thin, straight hair handed the guru a single beautiful flower as she departed. I believe she even genuflected or bowed deeply in front of him. You get the picture, I am sure. But you won't believe what I am now about to say. This man, now the world renowned guru, Baba Ram Dass, founder of the Hanuman Foundation, a fine prison ministry, was viewed as a prophet, but to my husband as some kind of (wierdo?) fortune teller. So, on being introduced to him my husband said, "What do you think gold is going to do?" Instantly there was a kind of quiet. Ram Dass muttered something, some kind of non sequitur—I felt like sinking through the floor like Rumpelstiltskin.

On another evening Laura took me to meet some of her friends of the Order of St. John of Jerusalem—the New Age version of the Knights and Dames of Malta (of which I was eventually to became a member). At that gathering was Elizabeth Kubler Ross who started the hospice movement for the compassionate and humane care of dying cancer patients. Werner Erhard, the founder of *EST*, was there, too. He also started the Break Through Foundation, with which we became connected many years later in our efforts to help the inner city of Bridgeport, Connecticut. Buckminster Fuller was also there. He was very old, in fact he died shortly after that; sensing that, I did not ask him to join my foundation. There were some other dignitaries, and of course, Ram Dass. There he was on the floor.

It was always exciting to be with Laura. She was a very remarkable person, in some ways (except the age), like the High Lama of *Lost Horizon*, with an agelessness and wisdom beyond reckoning.

During those days when I was being introduced to the leaders of the New Age movement, in the good sense of the word, I had another encounter with the nephew of Laura Huxley, Piero Asseogoli, with whom I took a really extraordinary workshop in the basement of a bank in White Plains and who brought into being the science known as psychosynthesis, meaning, getting it together. We sat around in a circle and with our minds and bodies working in harmony, were able to send very palpable energy in the direction to which Piero instructed us; in fact the 30 or so participants sitting in a circle, swayed left spontaneously just by our collective thought to do so. Martial arts—the oriental getting it together par excellence—has demonstrated that a man can chop a phone book in half with his hand. I actually saw this during a demonstration of Tai-chi at the mountain top aerie of one of my mentors, Greta Woodrew, who wrote, *On a Slide of Light*. It was her brother who performed an awe inspiring Tai-chi demonstration which concluded with the chopping of a book in half with his hands, which demonstrated that he had obviously gotten it together, "it," being body, mind and spirit.

Piero's demonstration involved more mind than body. He spoke about achieving metaphysical energy, sometimes demonstrated in physical feats and sometimes in sheer volume as practiced by Sri Chinmoy, the Indian guru (for the U.N!).

Sri Chinmoy flanked by John McLaughlin (left) and
Carlos Santana (right) from the cover of their album
Love Devotion Surrender

In that period I also met Gay Mehegan, the wife of jazz musician John Mehegan, the music teacher of the sons of Dave Brubeck. I also encountered other jazz musicians who were protégés of Sri Chinmoy, and also friends of the world renowned guitarists, John McLaughlin and Carlos Santana; they ran a restaurant in Greenwich called "Love & Serve." Actually John McLaughlin, very kindly in a beautiful letter, made it known that he wanted to do a fundraiser for Huxley, but alas that was not to be! Dear Dave Brubeck actually did a fundraiser for us in 1983 at the Klein Memorial Auditorium in downtown Bridgeport.

It was during the summer of 1974 that many of these musicians would come to my home and play beautiful jazz music, extemporaneously composed by Gay Mehegan, John's wife. One afternoon while my husband was away in Japan on business, I acquired a lucite pyramid (remember the pyramids?) and had it erected just behind our historic pool house. I am certain my husband would not totally have approved of this. (This is an understatement.) This poolhouse was on the historic register in the Fairfield Town Hall since it was designed by the famous and distinguished Fairfield architect, Cameron Clark, and was used by Burt Lancaster in the film, *The Swimmer*. That film featured our pool, the first pool he used, where he picked up the babysitter on his way home, swimming across pools in Fairfield County. This film has become a cult classsic since it proved, sadly, that you can't go home again, even swimming your way home with a beautiful young girl. I had all these musician disciples of Sri Chinmoy sitting under the pyramid before playing Gay's compositions. One in particular was extraordinarily haunting—perhaps as beautiful a tape I have ever heard.

There is no doubt at all that Sri Chinmoy had metaphysical energy. He allegedly wrote 100,000 songs and 1,000 poems and required only two hours' sleep a night. In one of his books, entitled, *Transcendence*, Sri Chinmoy makes the point that when one is on the spiritual path, one must always return to one's roots.

Since I had been messing about with all sorts of teachings it was time for me to sign off as a plain old psychic. Because of the work I had done in brain research, including the extraordinary seminars on human consciousness by Robert Ornstein, usually held in San Francisco, and all the seminars on brain functions I had attended, including the so-called mind control workshop, I picked up the ability, when in the right state of mind, to visualize certain events of a person's future as well as some of the problems they were having, and also how to guide them safely to their best goals. I remember during the times I used to visit my renowned spa, where I went to keep my weight down (and also just to stay alive!), sometimes people would line up (always free of charge) to get a reading from me which usually turned out to be pretty accurate.

Sri Chinmoy was truly a holy man. Taking his advice about returning to one's roots, I knew it was time to quit that kind of thing and progress to Catholic mysticism, even though at that time I had not received the charism of the Holy Spirit. That came gradually over a period of time. Nevertheless, in that decade of the 1970's I had many so-called mystical experiences—synchronicities and words of knowledge coming my way.

CHAPTER TWENTY-FOUR

INTERVAL: MEMORIES OF CAROLE

"She was somewhere else. She wasn't on any West 12th Street." Bob Beattie, the driver, exhaled more smoke from his Muriel cigar. He was telling about this chick who was on a bad trip in the village last night; how she was staring at him and not seeing him, crooking her wrist in front of her face and hiding behind the telephone booth.

There were a lot of trips today; Bob Beattie was driving me to New Haven alone in our newly washed and vacuumed nine-passenger station wagon, spruced up for the doctors that didn't make this trip. They were in our blue and white Buick convertible, all squeezed together, talking about their various shops, acetylcholine production, hypocerbaric oxygen chambers, controlled fasting and maybe bad LSD trips. I was a little sad because "we had established rapport".

That was last November at the last meeting, where a Mrs. Rockefeller, living well enough on alimony, had underwritten an expensive dinner, including two wines and a pretentious but soggy Beef Wellington. I don't really remember why she did this, but in any case we never saw her again. What I do remember is DB, gawking slightly at his effortless speechmaking, not saying a word. Then Carole Bergerman, my bleached blonde friend from California, after it was all over, went to the Hilton bar, for a final orange juice—(don't ask me why? Maybe to nurse an incipient hangover) and there he appears from nowhere and orders an orange juice. Three O.J's at the Hilton bar. And then the séance.

We have established rapport.

Bob Beattie asks me, "Will you be real late?" "Yes, (tritely) that's the story of my life. Real late." We had just switched from the Merritt Parkway on a lazy autumn day to the Connecticut Turnpike. There was at that moment a train gliding behind the no longer brilliant, but still noble coloring of browns, reds, and ochre shades of the trees on the bank of a river (the Housatonic?). It was a strange impression, like a thief in a James Thurber fairy tale.

We are at the West Haven tolls. All bodes well for us. We shall be at the watering place made famous by Cole Porter in five minutes.

CHAPTER TWENTY-FIVE

THE HUXLEY INSTITUTE
TAKES SHAPE

The following occurred after that extraordinary encounter with the discarnate Aldous Huxley when we were living in our haunted house # 2. A vivacious Hungarian woman, Josie, friend of my buddy Nancy Pettee, godmother to our daughter, Marianne, and one of the reasons why we moved to Connecticut, called me up. Josie wanted to know, since we had a really nice old house, if I would consider giving a party for the Connecticut Heart Association of which she was chairman.

She was a very nice and engaging entrepreneur, as are many Hungarians, and ran a boutique for brides and bridesmaids in Westport, Connecticut—still in business in 1999! This proposal sounded like fun and I liked giving parties, it was in our family tradition so I said yes. I realized that in order to make a real go of it, I would try to get some of my celebrity friends to attract the local newspaper which liked to cover special events, always so popular with the local citizenry. And so, among other glamorous socialite friends, I asked my good friend, Fred Gwynne, whose wife, Foxie, had grown up in Tuxedo Park with my husband, Harry, during his late teenage years.

Fred had also been an outstanding actor in the Harvard Hasty Pudding Club before embarking on his successful professional acting career. When we were first married, we saw him as a comical gangster in *Mrs. McThing* with Helen Hayes, a charming play. Most people remember Fred as Herman Munster, but I remember him fondly as Francis Muldoon, the Cop in the television series, *Car 54 Where Are You?*. Do you remember that episode where Francis is kind of bordering on the grotesque and has to go on a date? He has to psych himself up in order to make himself handsome. I thought it was one of Fred's finest performances. Well, by golly, for at least ten minutes on the TV screen, he really did become Francis, the handsome cop. Whenever I feel down or in desperate need to fix myself up for a party, I recall that segment and think that if Francis can do it, I can do it. Sometimes I do and sometimes I don't.

The party was a success and thereafter many people would ask me to give parties for them. Then it came to my attention that on the day I was born, May 13, 1931, two other things happened. First, on that precise date, the country of Portugal was dedicated to the Immaculate Heart of Mary; that synchronicity has yet to be completed. Second, that was also the day that Arrigo Cipriani gave birth to his famous restaurant, Harry's Bar, on the Venetian lagoon; it is still, in some ways, quite wonderful.

So, after the Heart Fund party, I thought, "Hey, why don't I give a party for the Save Venice Committee?" I called Harry Grey, head of the Save Venice Committee in New York. He lived in the Gramercy Park Hotel, where my friend Kay Fryer also lived (this woman really helped save our daughter, Patricia's life after she had become ill in the sixties). Kay's own daughter had taken her life because of schizophrenia, so to help others, Kay started the Fryer Clinic in New York City which is run by her daughter, Cathy Fryer, and is still going strong and helping thousands. Kay's other daughter, Sara Fryer Leibowitz, is a distinguished researcher at Rockefeller University. Shortly before Kay's passing, she told me that she thought her daughter should be a candidate for the Nobel Prize if she succeeded in her research on why neuroleptics cause obesity. That Gramercy Arts Club had some wonderful tenants.

I phoned Harry Grey who gave me the OK. I gave the first of two Save Venice parties. This was during the last years we lived in our haunted house, and I had just become a member of the National Committee of the Huxley Institute in New York City. I knew then that the real work had to be done at the grass roots level where the schizophrenics, manic depressives and others afflicted with disorders of the central nervous system, such as learning disabilities and senile psychosis, and their families lived.

One year after my first Save Venice party, I decided to continue in this role of giving good parties to attract the press. I simply put an announcement in the paper that the First Chapter of the International Huxley Institute was to be launched in Fairfield County, Connecticut and invited the press to attend.

They were somewhat surprised because this was not a glamorous celebrity studded party. However, some stalwart, interested souls saw my newspaper article about this first meeting and responded. This revolution was rather slow-moving in the beginning (I didn't forget that Connecticut is the nutmeg state). It took some time for people to realize that Complementary Alternative Medicine is not just for people with central nervous system disorders, but for all human disorders.

Some of those early stalwarts were: Dr. Richard Brodie, who is still president of the Fairfield County Huxley Institute after all these years; Dr. Fred Esposito of the University of Bridgeport; the distinguished dentist, Dr. Robert Friedman and my two stellar ladies, both of whom helped greatly to make the Huxley Institute happen—Lola Leeming, who was head of the Fairfield Chapter of the Connecticut Association of Children with Learning Disabilities, and the redoubtable wizard, Adele Behar, an incredible interior decorator, or should I say, space manager; she was always proud to say that she had earned a living since she was twelve. The Huxley Institute couldn't have gotten off the ground without the enormous efforts of Adele Behar, since being so right-brained, I didn't know what I was doing half the time.

Our first meeting, held at the Bedford Junior High School on Riverside Avenue in Westport, attracted five hundred people. The speaker was Gena Larsen, the educator and nutritionist, who for over a period of one year had demonstrated success in her methods for students who improved both academically and physically in sports, with a tenth grade high school class in California. It was noted that these results were due to an improvement in the standard of food made available to the students. Gone were the junk foods which usually appeared on cafeteria menus. Instead were the healthful and tasty foods that the students largely prepared themselves in their Home Economics Class supervised by Gena Larsen.

Could you imagine what would have happened if all the American people had been privy to this information and acted on it?

For instance, we might never have elected such a terrible President. But a generation of Americans, most of them addicted to junk food, could only have produced what the redoubtable William Buckley has often characterized as junk thought, resulting in our current disaster.

Statistics and demographics point to the deteriorating health of American children. SAT scores have declined precipitously and morbidity and mortality have increased dramatically. Obesity is endemic in middle and working-class America. One only needs to go to the resorts of Disney World and Six Flags, etc. for a look at contemporary Americans. Half the people are waddling! This sorry and deplorable condition is the direct result of AKD, otherwise known as The American Killer Diet—calories but no nutrition. Ray Krok's ghost, take heed.

The Huxley Institute needed a board and I think that we had to have some famous names attached to it. The fact is that since nobody had heard of us, we needed the credibility and weight of well-known people to launch our ideas. Quite definitely we were an idea whose time, if it had not come yet, was destined to come sooner or later. And so, through the help of what could only be called my higher power, working on the consciousness of those who were called, we assembled a stellar cast of marvelous and talented individuals. Sometimes it was my secretary who knew somebody who knew somebody. God Bless them. What could I have done without such a stellar cast of secretaries over the years? They literally saved my life as well as made the formation of the Huxley Institute Chapter in Connecticut possible.

The Huxley Institute began to give conferences and seminars at Fairfield University since they seemed to be available for this activity—thanks to their heads of events, including my dear and talented friend, Audrey Thompson, and the great food manager, Jim Fitzgerald, who at last count is still there—and also because they were amenable to giving interesting conferences. This is partly because the head of the Department of Biology, Dr. Don Ross, was a member of our board and someone who was researching issues which are only now catching on. At that time he had just co-authored a book with the late eminent cardiologist, Dr. Kurt Oster, outlining the dangers of homogenized milk for heart patients and the efficacy of folic acid in preventing heart disease. These were pioneers who were practically ignored at the time, but now accepted universally. According to the dictum of Dr. Humphrey Osmond, any new idea will be reviled at first and then grudgingly accepted and finally it will be seen as "old hat." That seems to be true now with the role of folic acid in the treatment of many diseases, especially heart disease.

Another local pioneer was Dr. William Kaufman, who wrote two major scientific volumes on the efficacy of niacinamide in the treatment of arthritis. I even took a course in Human Biochemistry at Fairfield University with Dr. Ross and I learned how essential all these co-enzymes are for the maintenance of human health, as outlined by Dr. Linus Pauling in his seminal paper, "Ortho-Molecular Psychiatry", in *Science Magazine* of 1968.

The public and the media are only now catching up to these basic fundamental truths of science and human nutrition; truths which were kept from us through the collusion of the American Medical Association, the American Psychological Association, the Food and Drug Administration, drug companies et al. These are the usual cast of suspects all harnessed together by a strong rope called ignorance, perpetuated by greed. That conference of the Huxley Institute was held at Fairfield University.

How could it be that a Franciscan (at the time I attended a Franciscan chapter of St. Maximillan Kolbe in Bridgeport, Connecticut) who attended a Dominican school (Albertus Magnus) was running her first public conference at a Jesuit institution? Well it must have been the Holy Spirit, I guess. These were all Catholic institutions, of course, though each had a somewhat different emphasis. But the conference worked because we had a very good crowd. Our sign-up sheet was the key to our early membership. Subsequently, I had a lot of fun designing the DNA logo for the conference with the eminent Dr. Carl Pfeiffer, formerly one of the heads of the Department of Pharmacology for the U.S. Navy during World War II, and the pioneer in the CAM (Complementary Alternative Medicine) treatment of mental disorders. We had yet another striking poster.

Our second speaker was Dr. Jack Cooper, winner of the Psychiatrist of the Year award for his work in improving prisoners' nutrition by way of his famous Cooper cocktail, a blend of various vitamins in apple sauce. Dr. Cooper claimed this nutritional change had improved behavior. However, there have not been enough studies conducted to support this claim. This is an area of study that should interest managers of prison systems as well as members of the medical profession. There is now increasing evidence that nutrition does influence behavior, especially in persons who are genetically inclined to violent or aberrant behavior.

A year after the conference with prison psychiatrist, Jack Cooper, we held our third conference which dealt with alcoholism. This conference featured many professionals working in that field, notably Dr. Russell Smith, who headed a 5,000-bed hospital of alcoholic Navy veterans and gave them all vitamins with good results. Dr. Smith had been a friend of Drs. Hoffer and Osmond, as well as of Bill W., founder of Alcoholics Anonymous, himself the author of three papers advocating the efficacy of the vitamin treatment for alcoholism, especially Vitamin B3,—which were captioned, "To the Doctors I, II and III."

Bill W. died too soon for this discovery to catch on. There

are a few exceptions to this ignorance of these amazing treatises of Bill W, notably Dr. Ken Blum of the University of Texas who has devised a formula specially for alcoholics, which he calls SAAVE, composed of vitamins (co-enzymes) and amino acids, as described in his groundbreaking primer, *Alcohol and the Addictive Brain*.

In organizing this conference I had the privilege of befriending the remarkable and astoundingly gracious Lois Wilson, Bill W's widow. Her book, fittingly enough is, *Lois Remembers*. I asked her to join the board of the Huxley Institute, the only person outside of Connecticut to do so.

When we attended Lois' annual New Year's Eve party at their famous home, "Stepping Stones," in Westchester County, New York, she took my husband and me upstairs to her late husband's study (shades of Aldous Huxley!) and showed us this extraordinary letter to him from the great Swiss psychiatrist, Carl Gustave Jung.

Another supporter of the Huxley at that time was Rufus Jarman, who had previously worked with radio personality, Arthur Godfrey. Over the course of the years, he had become an alcoholic and came across the work of Bill W. Rufus wrote a very nice article about the Huxley in the newspaper. He also told me about a friend of his, a psychic/medium by the name of Mrs. Ethel Myers of Pownal Center, Vermont. He told me some amazing stories about her, and since I owed him a debt of gratitude, I let him bring her to our house for a "reading." She gave me the usual psychic stuff about my having been in Atlantis and Egypt. She also said, "I see a man here; he is very close to you and he is wearing a goatee." I said, "Good grief! My godfather wore a goatee." I took her upstairs where she saw a wedding picture of us coming down the steps of St. Vincent's Church (the famous *Daily News* photograph with the caption, "East Mates West."). The other picture was of me and my godfather who gave me away in marriage. Mrs. Myers entoned gravely, "That is the same man I saw in your living room." Well, maybe this is some proof that my godfather is still close to me. I actually feel close to many discarnate souls. Years later, Mrs. Myers told me that I should see Guy Levrier, a friend from a distant past. That has not yet happened.

Pascal Bonetti, my godfather, the only real father I ever had, was of Corsican descent. Perhaps born there. Had been secretary to my grandfather, Alfred Gosling LaGrave, and was later the unofficial poet laureate of France, President of the Society of French Poets and a minister of Education in France during the 1930's. He was the man ho gave me away in marriage.

Our second to last conference in that glorious Oak Room at Fairfield University, now the Student Center, featured the aforementioned Dr. Carl Pfeiffer, Michael Schachter who still runs one of the top orthomolecular clinics in the U.S., and Dr. Eleanor Alexander Jackson, biochemist. The most interesting thing about this conference was Dr. Jackson's presentation, wherein she described the work of her father, Dr. Alexander, the eminent neuroanatomist from the University of Buffalo, the first doctor of his generation to autopsy the brains of schizophrenics. In 100% of his autopsies, no less, he found a mysterious lesion obviously caused by some pathogen, which he called progenitor cryptocides, which means something hidden. This study indicates that there is a bacterium involved in the development of schizophrenia. I am hoping this research will continue at the well-funded NARSAD (National Association for Research In Schizophrenia and Depression).

Our last conference at Fairfield University concluded some really productive, interesting years, ending not with a whimper, but a bang. Our keynote speaker on that occasion was Gloria Swanson, who brought along her husband (her fifth), William Dufty, author of the popular best seller, *Sugar Blues*. Among other things, Gloria may have married Bill so that she could have somebody to carry around her health foods in her portable refrigerator. Bill followed Gloria around with it like a puppy dog—which was actually very sweet. But Gloria had earlier saved his life by showing him how to lose, what was it—100 lbs? So he was merely reciprocating her goodness to him.

Gloria was a very formidable woman. Besides being Joe Kennedy's girlfriend, she strove for many years, with her charm, intelligence, and chutzpah (see *Sunset Boulevard*), in 1958 to persuade Congress, via Congressman Joe Delaney, to pass a law, the Delaney Amendment, to make it mandatory for food manufacturers to declare the ingredients of foodstuffs, whether canned or packaged, on labels. This one act certainly has not only saved many American lives, but has definitely improved the quality of American health since it was put into law. Do you read the labels of food stuffs sold in supermarkets? As explained in the book, *The Chemical Feast*, a large proportion of American canned or packaged foods is full of chemicals. Combined with other factors, the awareness of the chemical contamination of common foodstuffs is responsible for the upsurge in the do-it-yourself health food movement. Human beings are supposed to eat food, not chemicals. Thank you, Gloria and Congressman Delaney. May you both rest in peace.

Gloria Swanson and William Dufty

I was able to get Gloria Swanson to address our conference due to meeting her backstage at the Westport Country Playhouse, a place that drew me to Connecticut in the first place, after a play in which she was appearing. I introduced myself and told her that I had been raised in and around the movie industry and was a friend of Dolores Costello. I also told her I was a great fan of hers, both professionally and for her work as a champion for the consumer in promoting healthy food. So when I asked her to be my keynote speaker, she accepted.

Gloria Swanson was a hard act to follow, for sure. I think at that moment, the Paraclete was nudging me into another direction since we (the Huxley Institute) were not able to start the clinic which we so badly wanted to do. At the time, the Huxley Institute offices were located at the University of Bridgeport. That fateful collaboration resulted in a now celebrated Department of Nutrition at Bridgeport University, which was expanded to include Chiropractic and Naturopathy. Hallelujah! After the Gloria Swanson conference, the Huxley Institute, in conjunction with the University of Bridgeport, hosted a conference which was organized by my successors, Jerry Kosting and Donna Barry—a wonderful team, who had taken over from me, thank God. There was this other idea which was turning me in another direction.

So, I left the Huxley Institute just as I was at the threshold of the formation of this new Foundation. I left behind a strong leadership team consisting of Gerry Kosting, who had an ill son and was therefore very motivated, and Donna Barry, who had been fighting addiction problems and succeeded, thanks to the aid of orthomolecular medicine and Alcoholics Anonymous. Bill W.— the founder of Alcoholics Anonymous, had finally addressed the importance of the B vitamins in the treatment of alcoholism just before he died. Also in the addiction field, Vic Powlak, head of the "Do It Now Foundation" in Arizona, promoted the use of vitamins for the treatment of narcotic addictions of all kinds. Obviously, one of the premises is that if you feel well enough, you would not ingest a substance which makes you feel worse. But, of course, it's more complicated than that. Genes and environment play their part.

The team of Gerry Kosting and Donna Barry had moved the office of Huxley Institute from my backyard to an old Victorian house on the campus of the University of Bridgeport, since among other things, Dr. Fred Esposito was one of their professors. The leadership there was intrigued by these new ideas, although I must report that the very morning after Gerry had moved everything in, two typewriters had already been stolen. So, we had to bolt the remaining typewriters to the desk. That's the old Bridgeport for you. I am hoping a "new" Bridgeport will emerge, beginning with the redoubtable and ferocious (I hope) baseball team, our own Bridgeport Bluefish.

Gerry and Donna gave a very fine conference which eventually led, as I mentioned, to the establishment of the University of Bridgeport's Department of Nutrition, famous now on the East Coast and drawing students from everywhere.

Just as Huxley was ending events in my life that seemed to be moving at warp speed, there emerged a necessity to investigate what was known originally to New Agers as the paradigm shift. I happened to appear on a local TV show talking about vitamins for about 20 minutes because I was the Huxley "vitamin lady." In the usual synchronous fashion, the other 20 minutes were taken up by a Paul Solomon, a professional psychic from

Virginia, who announced he was a successor to Edgar Cayce and that he had been given messages similar to Cayce's about diagnoses and illnesses, but particularly in terms of what was presented on this TV program, "Earth Changes."

Thereafter he had been put in touch with many people in the same field, including one author, Jeffrey Goodman, who wrote the book entitled *We Are The Earthquake Generation*. The premise of the book was at the same time exciting and frightening with projections of how earthquakes actually would be increasing at a very exponential rate and that there would be accompanying earth changes. This book is written in a quasi-scientific fashion, but scientific enough to satisfy quasi-scientific types like myself. I knew strange things were happening in my life, and I really could not explain them, but I was really going into a very fast change in consciousness that Marilyn Ferguson describes in her book, *The Aquarian Conspiracy*. I tried to convey this to my skeptical husband that the planet was going into some major changes as well.

He is truly a skeptic which accounts in part for his being so good an investment manager. Also, as I said to him, "What has to happen for you to believe in some of this stuff?" He said, "Hmm! How about an earthquake (since I was reading that book). The only thing is, it cannot be in California and it has to be more than seven points on the Richter scale." I said, "Okay," and then said, "God, I'm sorry to say, Harry needs an earthquake. I'm sorry it has to be an earthquake more than seven points on the Richter scale and not in California." That seemed like a tall order, but there it was.

This was the first time in our lives when we had a truly empty nest. Our youngest child, John, had just gone off for the first time to prep school, Taft, in Watertown, Connecticut. I suppose this is one reason I started getting very busy in all of these situations that seemed to be thrust at me.

It was the first week in October of 1977 when I made the deal with my husband. I had forgotten about it until a hurricane began to come up the coast. So I went to my husband and asked, "How about a hurricane?" and he said, "No, no; it has to be an earthquake." Our deal would be up on Monday at 8.00 p.m. since Harry had allowed me (and God) one week.

Here we were, alone in our big house, rocking in our rockers that I got at Bloomingdale's seventh floor discount section, with a large couch to match. We still have them. We used to listen, in the wonderful rockers, to our favorite program station, the classical music station WNCN from New York City. WNCN was a very straight classical station which was terrific for me, with a great emphasis on Baroque and Johann Sebastian Bach. They were definitely not an AM station in any way, shape, or form. They would never break into the programming and say anything unless someone was just assassinated, or in the case of this announcement at 7.50 p.m. at the end of the famous week . . . ."I am sorry to interrupt the music, but I have an important announcement to make; there has been an earthquake in Swabia, measuring 7.5 on the Richter scale." Swabia happens to be, among other things, the region in Germany where the Seggermans come from. I hoped at least there were no casualties. I started laughing. "Well, God, you have a great sense of humor."

The few times I have been to Germany I did ask everybody I could find to tell me about the Swabian earthquake of 1977, the biggest they had ever had. They would say a lot of damage was done. No one told me about the casualties, I really didn't want to know, anyway. For a time, at least, my husband allowed that something was going on.

CHAPTER TWENTY-SIX

BRAIN RESEARCH

Out of my association with The Huxley Institute I wanted to understand the mechanisms of the brain; the most current and strongest paradigm for interpreting how we receive information as human beings.

Fifteen years ago or so, I heard of a man with the mid-section of his brain having been injured. The doctors had to operate. They deduced that there could be no communication between the left and right hemispheres of the man's brain, since the corpus collosum, the canal which separates the hemispheres, had been severed.

The brain is sort of heart-shaped; the two sections of the brain are the right and left hemispheres or more simply the right and left brains. It was noted at that time, that in an effort to restore some kind of function for accident victims of this kind, that information would be gathered quite differently. A person who didn't have a left-brained communication saw things very differently and couldn't relate facts in the same way that a left brained person could.

Out of these physiological experiments in the laboratory and in vivo, it came out that the right brain contained the spatial, metaphysical, poetic and intuitive functions, while the left brain held the rational, mathematical, language arts and scientific reasoning functions.

Our present day society is basically a left-brained society; a technological society. Primitive societies by comparison are right-brained societies. It's absolutely a new world for someone from a primitive society to understand for the first time how we human beings in technological society function and vice versa. It can often be a shattering experience, especially for the primitive person, such as, for example, our own first Americans, the native Americans. They sometimes found it very difficult to cope in a Western society but now are excelling in the establishment of gambling casinos! They are no doubt getting outside help. Don't ask, don't tell!

A body of knowledge has grown with organizations devoted solely to the understanding of the left and the right brains. I've been to many conferences and I've read dozens of books. I can now lecture on left and right brain modalities, albeit my bibliography would have to be a little more scientific to gain credibility among the left-brained. I can say that I am basically a right-brained person. I found that a book by Assistant Princeton University professor, Julian Jaynes (he wanted to be an assistant professor so that he could write his book), held some great theories. A very exciting and unique one concerned the survivors of the Great Flood, which probably destroyed the ancient civilization of Atlantis and Lemuria and the whole planet except for the ark. (as declared in the revealed literature of the great archival library of Alexandria, Egypt before it was burned down). There were probably some other survivors, but we don't know the facts exactly, because that information was destroyed with that great library. What we do know is that a boat of some kind—perhaps it is the ark, has been found on Mt. Ararat, which, according to the Bible, is where the ark finally came to rest as the waters of the flood subsided (Gen. 8:4). As usual, I had a synchronicity when I sat next to an Armenian monk, who claimed to have seen the ark from an airplane and actually showed me photographs of it which were taken before the Soviet Union banned such flights.

Some of the descendants of these survivors of the Great Flood went to Egypt while others became the tribes of the Hebrews.

On a trip to Greece that Harry and I took with our daughter, Yvonne, and her friend from school, some time in the '70's, we of course went to Delphi for a day. After experiencing that unmatched and unique city and one of the great pantheons of the great gods and goddesses, Harry postulated, on going up to the top of the hill overlooking Delphi, that the Greeks in power must have spent their entire treasuries on the Delphic temples and statues, since the remnants of statues now found in museums and elsewhere indicate that they must have been once rather magnificent. Those Greeks of that period before Socrates must also have had a bicameral mind since the gods were so important to them, thought my brilliant spouse.

Before the Great Flood, Jaynes postulates that people spoke directly to God; that they got all their divine instruction directly through their right brain and left brain. He elaborates on the left brain/right brain theory. After the Great Flood people could no longer cope in ways they had known before. Things were so difficult that they could no longer speak directly to God; they found they had lost their ability to get all their information and directions directly from God and therefore they had to start using their left brain only.

But one still sees remnants of ancient societies where people spoke to and heard directly from God; the refugees of these societies were the prophets of Israel and the early Egyptians who were also metaphysically oriented. One has only to go visit the tombs in the Valley of the Kings to know this. It's an interesting theory. I've been fortunate enough to have traveled a great deal and I think a lot of it makes sense. Certainly it's only one man's interpretation of brain function, but I think there's enough in it to give one serious pause. Nevertheless, Marshall McLuhan, as might be predicted, didn't think much about Professor Jaynes' book (professional jealousy?). He said while he thought the work of Dr. Julian Jaynes was fascinating, there were too many metaphrands. He went on to say that Jaynes did not understand the nature of the alphabet or writing because of his assertion that

the breakdown of the bi-cameral mind occurred with the introduction of writing, which was wrong. McLuhan asserted that the
breakdown occurred with the appearance of the phonetic alphabet.

However, some years later, Professor Jaynes gave a conference at Princeton University entitled, "The Return of the
Bicameral Mind," which very regretfully I couldn't attend. Today's
events together with my own and the mystical experiences of
others, certainly corroborate this thesis since, among other things,
Biblical prophecy is demonstrated by the prophet Joel;

> "And it shall come to pass afterward, that I will pour out
> my spirit upon all flesh; and your sons and your daugh-
> ters shall prophesy, your old men shall dream dreams,
> your young men shall see visions" (Joel 2:28).

Another factor throughout my whole life is synchronicity. As
described by Carl Gustav Jung, synchronicity is basically understanding enough about how the universe works that somehow your
right brain puts you in the right place at the right time and you have
synchronized experiences as a result. Synchronicities serve very
well to illustrate there is something beyond which most people see
most of their waking hours. The invisible world becomes visible.
One of the results of opening to right-brain information was that I
began to receive direction from synchronicities.

With hindsight, I would say that I had a synchronized experience once when I was in Florida. I happened to read an old
issue of *Time Magazine*. I never read *Time* and I'm hardly ever in
Florida, but in it was an article about Julian Jaynes' book. The
book was also recommended to me by Avery Dulles, S. J. and
that was also a synchronized experience. The article said if one
had an imaginary friend and had schizophrenia in the family,
then one probably had a bicameral mind, which means one had
a right brain tendency to speak directly to the Universal Unconsciousness or It, to you—God—to dialogue.

Of course, I did have an imaginary friend as a child and I have schizophrenia in the family. Well, I thought, "Good! I guess this explains why I've always had a communication with the Universal Unconsciousness, or God, or the Saints and I still do." I had really kind of lost it in the "left brained" environment at Ethel Walker's and maybe also a little bit at Albertus Magnus. I was trying to cope. I had a lot of trouble coping because right brain people cope very poorly in a technological society. Most people use their left brain in their average working state, crossing the street without getting hit by a bus. (I have trouble with this sometimes. I almost got run over by a double-decker bus in London. I was looking the wrong way!!) To this day I can't work machines; my sense of direction is wacky. But when it comes to right brained material, I've had a lot of practice. I think being right brained is valuable to me now for the kind of work I'm doing.

Finding applications and examples of the bicameral mind, right and left brained theories of Professor Jaynes has been an absorbing interest of mine for many years now; a continuing study. According to Professor McLuhan one must be able to move effectively between right and left hemispheres, and that the best training for the western mind in right hemisphere thinking is through the works of James Joyce, T.S. Eliot and Ezra Pound.

I perceive myself as so right brained that I just do what I'm told. I'm just like the survivor of the Great Flood. I am used to being told to do what God tells me to do. I check in for instructions every morning (when I remember). I get them and I do what I'm told some of the time, usually if I'm granted the strength or the will and the wisdom to do them.

Today, raising consciousness has a great deal to do with physical health because we are body, mind and spirit and if the physical body is not in good shape, the rest isn't going to be working too well, either, most times—unless you are a saint, of course. If one is spreading the Gospel, one first has to feed people; to improve their physical health. One must look after or heal the sick. There's a lot of good advice in the Bible and we should think about these things. Much of it would be inherited from what Professor Jaynes would doubtless describe as a more right brained society.

CHAPTER TWENTY-SEVEN

FUNNY AND FUN:
STAFF AND FRIENDS

During those days in the 70's there were many wonderfully funny and great people who came into our lives. Maybe I could start with E.J. But before describing E.J., I'd better go back in time to our old house, the "haunted house." Actually both Connecticut houses we lived in, after moving East from California were haunted, so this was during our sojourn in the second haunted house, the one with bad vibes. There, my first secretary, Joy Dunlop, was hired. My good friend, Carole Bergerman, once said to me, "Annie, why are you going around with all those papers under your arms? What you need—desperately—is a secretary!" So I hired Joy. I started after my husband could no longer afford the time to take care of domestic matters once we moved to Connecticut. He had a two-hour commute each way and there was simply no way he could physically attend to all those bills any more.

Joy and I liked to lie on the blanket in my backyard. I would lie on my back so I could dictate and she would lie on her stomach taking dictation. As it happened, her mother had a small Catholic foundation, which was the first miraculous donor to our Chapter of the Huxley Institute.

I was on a very strict budget since we had six children—one being dually disabled—and, as we used to say in those days, "Harry's junk had not come in." This metaphor was reflected on the wallpaper along the staircase walls (the only area I could afford to wallpaper in those days since it required only four yards) which depicted Chinese junks. It would be that Harry's junk would come in some day. But at that time Harry's junk was still at sea and I had my first early directive to do something about the catastrophic disease, which afflicted our daughter, Patricia, and thus our whole family.

That's what drove me to start the Huxley Institute Chapter in Connecticut. Thanks to Joy for her help, Joy's mother, and Mel Seiden, a financier friend of ours, who sent me the second donation. Thanks also to a Mr. Mann of the IRS in Hartford, who helped me obtain the correct incorporation papers after hearing of my plight. (I couldn't afford a lawyer. I was able, lawyerless, to get my 501–C3 in six weeks! Does the IRS still do these things I wonder?) And eventually thanks to Joanne Woodward and Paul Newman, who sent me another donation, all of which kept the Chapter going. I took a workshop at the Wharton School of Economics—a short intensive course in entrepreneurship and fundraising. What I got out of it included the confidence to write a letter with the expectation that some-body would send money. That's the kind of letter I wrote to the "Nosuch Fundation" (The Newmans) and God bless them, they did give me some money.

We finally moved from the house that was haunted, at least that was the reputation it had, although the real estate agent didn't bother to tell us of course, they never do, until after we had moved out. I had just come back from taking that course in Silva Mind Control, which convinced me that there was a ghost in the stairway. It was possibly that of a former slave who had been fleeing north and was thrust down the stairs through a trap door that had been at the bottom of the staircase which led into the basement. This house was part of the famous "underground railroad," an escape route for slaves fleeing the south. I thought I saw that ghost one night, but it turned out to be some light reflecting through a loudspeaker which was in the wall.

Ghost or no ghost, there were definitely negative vibrations in that house, since the wife of the former owner died of cancer there and frankly speaking, our daughter got sick in that house too.

It wasn't all sadness at this time because we did manage to host a few parties to which I always invited my California girlfriends— Laurey Scott, her younger sister, Sunny and sometimes Meg Whitcomb who is now Aunt Meg, and my beloved and departed friend, Carole Bergerman who came East all the time. We always had a good time together. One of the popular tunes at that time, which was also my favorite, was "California Girl" by the Beach Boys, which we played at those parties. Those occasions were special.

E.J. Russo was my first secretary in our present home. E.J. had been a secretary and friend to A. E. Hotchner, author of many books including *King of the Hill,* and he was also Paul Newman's great friend. Like Paul Newman, he is also a fine person. His wife, Ursula, is a very charming person whom regretfully I have not seen for years. She was always very sympathetic to the cause of the Huxley Institute.

Now E. J. was really fun and very humorous, probably fortyish (sorry, E.J.) when she worked for me. She always thought of herself as a perpetual ingenue and she wore ingenue clothing with a flair that would be entertaining to any writer, myself included. She wore high-heeled boots, had short blond hair and wore rather thick glasses. She was the best secretary I ever had which says something. She was terrific. Her famous phrase was, "May I go to the bathroom now?" After that, no secretary had to ask permission to go to the bathroom again. I have missed E. J. all these years.

Here's another story. It involves the Newmans. Joanne had taken on as a protégé a young talented dancer, Dennis Wayne, who had a ballet company. Joanne had been a ballet dancer herself, as well as having been Miss North Carolina. Joanne called me to see if I could do anything to help her mother who was dying from Alzheimers disease. She thoroughly believed in the efforts of the Huxley Institute and all that goes with it, which is why she joined and brought her husband in as well. Unfortunately, I couldn't help her then because there wasn't the data bank that exists now, including the internet, and I only had one secretary. There is quite a lot you can do for Alzheimers' today, including alternative methods.

Joanne had Dennis Wayne's ballet company as her main interest. She invited me and hundreds of others to her fundraiser for that company which was to be held at Studio 54 in New York, then in its hey day. This invitation was irresistible. I just had to go.

My daughter Patricia, David and Christine, the couple Patricia was living with at the time, and I think my son Henry and his new wife Vera were there. We sat at this big round table to watch the parade going on around us.

I remember wearing an angel costume in pale blue rayon. It was pretty authentic looking, since it had gauze wings and my halo was a tiny gold frame. It was sublime and idiotic at the same time, which is sometimes my style. It was a good move however. Alexis Smith, who was one of the celebrities of honor, came over to our table and said to me, "You have the best costume here." I said, "Thank you, Alexis, I agree." It was a costume party as well and the best one was going to get a prize.

Prior to the prize giving, Studio 54 put on their famous strobe lights of which they were the pioneers and which brought them into the world of rock and roll and disco. The late Steve Rubell was definitely a genius in entertainment. He was also one of the people apparently who helped in the redevelopment of Norwich, Connecticut, the old mill town on the banks of the Thames River, one of my favorite spots.

Patricia wore a Moroccan caftan and as we got up to dance, would you believe it, the Smothers Brothers, also dressed in Moroccan caftans, came up to us and danced with us. It was a thoroughly wonderful evening up to this point. Then came the prize giving.

First prize went to a cross-dresser with very hairy legs, wearing a tutu. I found this a very distressing sign of the times.

A Huxley Institute Fundraising Letter . . . .

Dear Friend of the Fairfield County Chapter of Huxley Institute;

As I write this letter to you there is a picture that I cannot get out of my mind: a long line of formless creatures with shapeless gowns, shuffling single file with zombie-like expressions to receive a meal of nutritionless tepid soup and tasteless "stew. " This is not a made-up story; this is the scene that I personally have seen many times in a nearby state mental hospital. I call them creatures because years of large doses of tranquillizers, indifference, neglect and cruelty have robbed these unfortunate human beings of their humanity. It is not unrealistic to imagine that this scene is repeated everywhere there is schizophrenia which continues to affect humanity. This disease has done so throughout history in every nation, race, period of time and economic level.

Another scene we have all witnessed is the huddled figure of a man or woman in a dirty street corner, the miserable outcast whose addiction to alcohol has turned him into a derelict. These scenes, which artists and poets can depict so well in paintings and movies like "The Snake Pit" and "The Lost Weekend" are what human suffering look like.

The Huxley Institute also cares for the children . . . and their families . . . with learning disabilities, behavior problems and drug addiction; the aging person whose senility makes him a burden on his family and society and his last years without hope or dignity.

The time has come when this waste of human lives can be changed. Alleviation of this suffering is now possible with the treatment of the doctors associated with the Huxley Institute. This treatment is called orthomolecular medicine, which means to restore biochemical balance by means of diet and vitamins, as well as by other therapies. THIS TREATMENT NOT ONLY RESTORES HEALTH TO THE SICK BUT PREVENTS DISEASE IN THE HEALTHY.

Legislation has been passed in California promoting this new, promising, humane treatment. We are now working to make this a reality in Connecticut, as evidenced in the enclosures.

The Fairfield Chapter of the Huxley Institute has never before sought funds. Up to now we have educated thousands of people and through education and doctor referral restored health and hope to countless families. But to continue our work of education, legislation and the establishment of a preventive medical clinic, we need money. OUR WORK SAVES LIVES, BUT IT REALLY NEEDS YOUR FINANCIAL HELP NOW, URGENTLY.

Won't you please join me in helping continue this important work? Please make your check payable to the HUXLEY INSTITUTE for Biosocial Research of Fairfield County, and mail it to me in the attached envelope. It is all tax deductible.

Many thanks.
Anne Crellin Seggerman

CHAPTER TWENTY-EIGHT

THE MAKING OF THE FOURTH WORLD FOUNDATION

Before leaving Huxley, I thought it might be a good idea to have a conference at Yale with Linus Pauling as our keynote speaker, on the question as to what America should do about starvation in Africa. I finally got hold of the head of the Biology Department at Yale University who was intrigued with the idea. However, my own health was beginning to deteriorate so I couldn't go through with it.

It was at that time that I came across what seemed to be the premier international body of science, philosophy and men of many disciplines addressing many planetary problems. This entity was called, The Club of Rome (now defunct). After reading their second report entitled, "Rio," I made an observation that amazed me: it seemed that the first and third worlds were cooperating in solving some global problems, but the second world, i.e. the Centrist or Communist states of the Soviet Union and Eastern Europe, not only were not cooperating, but they did not even send observers to the meetings of The Club of Rome. It seemed that the human race and the planet itself were in serious trouble and over and above everything else, I had a desire to address this problem which in fact spawned the Fourth World Foundation.

I always wanted to start an ortho-molecular clinic but I had experienced much resistance to the idea from the establishment, and not enough support from our own doctors. I guess that was because their lives were too tough already. One of the doctors, a Canadian, who had studied under Linus Pauling, and now treats Lyme Disease, was thrown off the staff of a local hospital for using vitamins! The hospital shall mercifully remain unnamed. Do you see why Connecticut is called the "Nutmeg State," and "hard-headed," to the point of being obtunded?

I needed to start my own foundation to address some global problems by using in part the medical model of holistic health. In the beginning, as in a waking dream, I was given a picture of the planet and the dove. I knew immediately that its symbol, its logo, had to be a globe with a grid on it and a dove representing the paraclete descending upon it. Since I didn't know how to draw a bird descending, I decided to use as my model the cover illustration of the book, *Jonathan Livingston Seagull*. So, one day when Patricia and her companion Christine were at home, I asked them to find that book for me. I didn't know what it meant then. It was a symbol in search of a meaning.

All I knew was that I wanted my own foundation, one that could address the problems of the planet. When I drafted the logo I knew there and then that my foundation had to be called "The Fourth World Foundation", even though I hadn't any idea why it should be so called. The figure of a dove descending upon the planet seemed to symbolize the interaction between the planet earth and the Holy Spirit. Eventually, the symbol of the dove took form and its meaning became clear.

When you draw a three-dimensional object, whether it's a globe or a cone or a rectangle, there will be gradations of light and dark to signify the variations in light that reflect from the three-dimensional object. Just so, the Fourth World Foundation has many meanings, nevertheless all coming forth from a unified whole.

So whenever we had a new board member, we asked what the Fourth World Foundation meant. We gave it our meaning, as a unified theory: "It is the world of the Spirit."

The only experience I had in the non-profit sector was start-ing a Chapter of the Huxley Institute which was already a known entity with headquarters in New York City. Starting one's own foundation involved much more. I knew that I would need a law-yer and the only close friend I had who was a lawyer was John Brosnan, brother of an old friend of the family, Mary Ellen, pre-viously mentioned in "Summer of 1948," with whom I enjoyed wonderful intellectual conversations and who wrote fine poetry. His father was the head of the Board of Regents for New York and a very distinguished lawyer. John himself had been involved with the Columbia Law Review Journal and his uncle was Head of Catholic Charities and one of the three priests officiating at our wedding ceremony.

John said he knew someone who could help me. Her name was Gilberte Driscoll; she had gone to school with him at Colum-bia. He said she was very competent and probably would not charge me too much. Gilberte took me on, although she realized I was a bit on the flaky side and really didn't know yet what I was doing. As a child in Belgium, she had seen box cars of Jews being sent to extermination camps which gave her the impetus to make a difference in the world for the better, like her compatriot, Elizabeth Kubler Ross, who started the Hospice movement. Gilberte was a lawyer with a difference who helped people, and tried to do good things. I had trouble explaining to her what the Fourth World Foundation was about, partly because of the im-pingement of the mystical dimension. I knew I had to start this foundation (to save the world)! And my other life's work was to make a movie about the Virgin of Guadalupe, but I neither knew how to start a Foundation nor to raise money for a movie. Never-theless, I had the notion that the Foundation would serve both purposes, in that while the movie was being made, people would make donations to the Fourth World Foundation to help finance it in the early stages. Eventually it became clear that two sepa-rate entities were needed and the Fourth World Foundation was launched exclusively as a vehicle for social and religious projects.

I needed to get some board members quickly and that was an adventure. I started with my friend, Dr. David Sheinkin, my best friend, and family physician, the only one who had given our daughter, Patricia, a good prognosis. Dr. Sheinkin was tragically killed in an airplane crash in March of 1983. He lived dangerously and unfortunately the crash also brought down with him his sister-in-law, a niece, nephews and his mother! That was such a tragedy for everybody who knew him, as you can imagine. After he died I couldn't even set foot in his office for six years!

However, just before his death he shared with me some stupefying research he had just embarked on in the Old Testament in which he had discovered a code with discernible messages for mankind. Twenty-five years later, we now have *The Bible Code* and researchers are studying the same phenomenon that fascinated my beloved friend, Dr. Sheinkin. Interestingly enough, some of the messages are eschatological in nature.

Another board member was my colleague in holistic medicine, and an interesting athlete, David Smith, author of the *East West Exercise Book*, and the yoga therapist at Earth House, in New Jersey, a half-way house for the mentally ill and a paragon for half-way houses in the US. He also took students (as the patients there are called) on camping trips which was very therapeutic. The very eminent Dr. Carl Pfeiffer, deceased, who headed the Brain Bio-Center, the number one out-patient treatment center for schizophrenia and related diseases in the United States, also supported and gave medical advice to this establishment.

David Smith was a Californian like myself. He was from Northern California and was pretty exuberant in a typical right-brained fashion. He was also much taken to a lot of derring-do, as is the wont of world-class athletes, like swimming across the Straits of Gibraltar, and things like that, but not quite as remarkable as Jack La Lanne's (my first exercise mentor on TV) dragging a row boat with his teeth, with one hand tied behind his back, from

Long Beach to Catalina Island, near L.A. for his 60th birthday celebration. But his accomplishments were still pretty good. I remember what David told me when I was visiting him in New York—the best piece of advice he ever gave me since I was always battling health problems including my weight. He said, "Keep moving." That's all.

I also contacted Virginia Fitzgerald, an early advocate of futuristic holistic thinking, and my friend, Laura Huxley, to become board members. Thus the early years of the Fourth World Foundation were heavily influenced by the Huxley Institute experiences.

At that time, David Smith introduced Michael Riddell, an Australian to me. He was not a candidate for my board, but was very well connected, and was what my husband would have considered a hustler.

Michael Riddell started us off by producing a documentary in England entitled *The Children of Hope*. The film was David Smith's idea. It was not a financial success though it addressed the plight of children who were refugees from war. It was about that time when I was visiting Britain that Michael introduced me to Trevor Ravenscroft, who wrote the *Spear of Destiny*, an almost stupefying tale which describes his experiences as a prisoner during WWII, when he was incarcerated with Walter Johannes Stein. Stein knew Adolph Hitler during their youth and eventually got to know him quite well as an adult. Much to his dismay he discovered that Hitler was not only mediocre but crazy. He found out that Hitler acquired some knowledge of the supernatural, particularly Satanic power, after visits to the museum in Vienna where the famous Spear of Longinus, which allegedly pierced the side of Christ, was on display.

According to Stein, Hitler, by becoming a member of a Satanic cult, had sold his soul to Satan in exchange for his otherwise unexplained meteoric rise to power—very much as Marx had sold his soul to Satan, as outlined in the books, *Was Marx a Satanist?* and *Marx and Satan*, by Richard Wurmbrand, the

Lutheran Jewish pastor incarcerated for many years by the Communists. These two, Hitler and Marx, obviously were to become the two major anti-Christs of our time. It wouldn't come as much of a surprise to know that Lenin, Stalin, Mao, Pol Pot, Saddam Hussein and others may have made the same diabolical deal.

Trevor was somewhat Orson Wellian, maybe like Rochester in Jane Eyre. He was tall, large and had taken to wearing capes. I was absolutely awestruck at the idea of meeting him. I sat in the living room of his London townhouse, with the shades drawn which made it even spookier, waiting to meet him. Suddenly he strode in and as I fearfully mumbled something about my trying to make a film about Our Lady of Guadalupe, a project given to me by the distinguished Henry King of "Song of Bernadette" fame, he looked at me intently and said, "Yes, the Woman is very powerful." He strode out of the room and out of my life for several years only to re-emerge in an amazing fashion years later in Ventura County, California. At that time he was visiting his daughter who was a shepherdess living in the Channel Islands, and I was in residence at my health club in Ojai. In addition to his other pursuits, he wrote about mysterious things like the great cathedrals of Europe, which, when lain out on a map, conform to the constellation of Venus.

On this visit to England I also came across Joyce Petschek, Yuri Geller's former girlfriend. She allegedly could turn door knobs into gold, or things like that. Joyce Petschek told me about Tom Bearden, a nuclear physicist in Huntsville, Alabama who was researching psychotronic warfare, the effectiveness of which the Russians had been investigating since the 1920's. They were using the works of Nicolas Tesla, an eccentric Yugoslav genius who went on to conduct his own electrical experiments in the Flat Iron Building in New York City. The building allegedly rocked during his experiments. Eventually America woke up and we are now conducting our own experiments in psychotronic warfare— warfare by means of thought control and that could be the subject of a whole book by itself.

On this same trip to the legendary Glastonbury, near Stonehenge, Michael and his entourage took me to meet a large mysterious male who had been bedridden for many years. They ushered me into the presence of a man who looked like Sidney Greenstreet, who announced solemnly to our group that he was the Karma of England and descended from the Order of Priests of Melchisedeck! This was typical of Michael's acts of derring-do, not to say, hocus pocus. This was the kind of stuff that I was doing in those days in a Candide kind of style. I did not know what was really going on in those days. Things just happened. It seemed, in a strange sort of way, that the Fourth World Foundation was beginning to break through.

Another Michael Riddell adventure involved my meeting with Ruth Carter Stapleton, a bona fide healer who had an impressive track record. She made it known that when confronted with difficult cases of inner healing, she called on the Virgin Mary for help, which is probably one reason why I worked to support Jimmy Carter, her brother.

It was in these interesting times at the beginning of the 80's, that we had some very unusual experiences. During this time I took my daughter, Suzanne, for the first time to Kenyon College, Gambier, Ohio where she was an English Literature major with a minor in Religion. At that time *The Kenyon Review* was one of the finest college publications, which influenced her in going to that beautiful campus, which was initially set up for the education of Episcopalian Bishops. After settling her in I remember rushing back to the airport and making the flight by one minute, after having to contend with potholes, road construction and even a flat tire. It was all in an effort to get back home in time for a mini conference being held in our home under the auspices of the Huxley Institute. Our keynote speaker was Dr. Ray Brown, an extraordinary man.

Everything concerning this man had a dream-like quality. Even as I look back, I wonder if it really happened. In a felicitous part of my life in the late 1970's I made frequent visits to the health clinic, the Golden Door, where the young woman, who at that time did the facials, told me of her experience while she attended a lecture by the homeopath, Ray Brown, in nearby San Diego where he also practiced. This young woman was a self-proclaimed psychic and the two of us used to read each other's minds, so she was quite adept at making that mental connection with some people. She said that she experienced that same kind of connection with Dr. Brown as she had with me, but much more so. In his case she said that the connection was in the form of a blue ray of light connecting them, which both of them, and I suppose people in the audience as well, could see. Whether true or untrue, his story was fantastic.

Dr. Ray Brown was a man of many parts. Not only was he a homeopathic doctor, but also a computer expert. He built his own computers long before the hackers of today were smart enough to do so. He was also a deep-sea diver and during one of his dives off the Coast of Bimini, he went into a cave where he found a crystal which he thought had extraordinary qualities; so he brought it up. He began giving lectures on it saying it was *a*, if not, *the* crystal of Atlantis, that it must have been a source of power for that great sunken civilization and no doubt there were other crystals like it yet to be found. He was sure that crystals gave power to great civilizations like Atlantis sunk under the ocean 10,000 years ago. It is a fact that crystals are crucial to our computer technology, the internet, and solar energy cells. Therefore, it is plausible that the use of crystals was a factor in the advancement of those great civilizations in the times of Noah, which, according to the Bible, were destroyed because of their sinfulness.

In any event, as the saying goes, when it rains, it pours. On that day, according to my calendar, not only had I to take my daughter to college that weekend, but I also had to get back in time for the Ray Brown lecture. Needless to say, my husband was extremely skeptical, and I must confess, I was a bit confused. But Dr. Brown was surely interesting.

Dr. Brown was somewhat like the great Tai Chi practitioner, Al Huang, a great friend of Laura Huxley. We met Al on one of our trips to Los Angeles. I don't remember the exact occasion but I do remember that Al, considered one of, if not, the most famous and versatile Tai Chi master in the Western world, was giving a "workshop" for everybody whether or not they had ever taken Tai Chi. I think Laura had gathered some people there for something else as well.

Anyway, there was this gathering of about 100 people—everyone from hippies to professors, to people like my husband wearing business suits—sitting in the auditorium of the Masonic Temple on Wilshire Boulevard in Los Angeles, when Al said, in his wonderful voice, "All right everybody. Now you all get up on the stage." Then Al, in his inimitable fashion, put on some marvelous music—classical, of course and said, "Now start dancing. Just let your body move the way the music tells you." And there they were, my husband included, doing what my husband would call, "snoopy" dancing, of which he used to accuse me, which is true especially to those tunes from "Saturday Night Fever." Charles Schultz fans will immediately know what snoopy dancing is. The strange thing about this was that on the balustrade of that Masonic Temple was an inscription, "Manu of Lemuria," which stood out to me in a blaze of mystery.

On a trip to Hawaii, which we took sometime in the 70's with our three younger children, Harry took Yvonne to Hana Maui and they saw, of course, the double rainbow. But the thing that sticks in my mind was that while we were at the Royal Hawaiian Hotel, where we stayed for one night, I visited the gift shop where I came across a map of a place called Gonawanaland which was a civilization in the Pacific Ocean which allegedly sunk about the same time as the great civilization of Atlantis in the Atlantic Ocean. Like Atlantis, Gowanaland was legendary and also known as Lemuria which supposedly had a great leader by the name of Manu, sometimes known as Mu.

Without thinking too much about this, I thought, "How strange that my husband became an Orientophile really by chance and it has continued through his business career to this very day." It first began with Chinese calligraphy, then the Japan fund which led to Japan investments for Fidelity, Inc. and now, finally, Korea. Was the connection between these occurrences brought about by some strange synchronicity?

I haven't the foggiest idea, but I do remember that Mrs. Myers, the psychic, said that I had been in Atlantis and the caption under our wedding picture was "East mates West."

During this time in the 1970's I was very active in promoting health care for central nervous system disorders in the Huxley Institute, and Jimmy Carter was running for President. It was known that his wife, Rosalynn, was very interested in setting up a committee for studies in mental health and mental illness, an area that had been sadly neglected by the public sector. I was interested in Jimmy Carter because he was a born-again Christian and I felt that he might bring some sanity and ethics to the White House. My husband even made a donation to the party. Since I was a registered Independent at that time I decided to go to Washington to talk to Carter's people, not knowing that nothing would come of it. I took Denny Brown, my staff person with me. Denny was a kindred spirit from Southern California.

We were met at the East Gate by the most cavalier young man I have ever encountered. He was tall, had red hair and looked like a beach boy. He seemed to know nothing about anything. (Was that symptomatic of the Carter Administration?) I undertook this trip during the week of May 15, 1978, the most unusual week of my life. Denny and I flew back to White Plains Airport in a small airplane. As we descended the steps from the plane we had the most amazing experience. There was the famous quadruple rainbow of Westport, Connecticut, that actually made the front page of all the local papers, which is very unusual itself. This was a sign which I did not really figure out. I know that the rainbow is a sign of God's favor.

That same week, incidentally, I "saw" St. Michael the Archangel and experienced a bona fide time warp in meeting with my son, Henry, in New York City.

Likewise, it seems as if my trips to Great Britain were both unusual and instrumental in the development of my budding Foundation because on my next trip there, I met Lady Collins, head of that great British publishing house, Collins, which subsequently became Harper Collins, publishers of "Something Beautiful for God," by Malcolm Muggeridge. This book told of the author's first encounter with Mother Teresa of Calcutta. This led me to get in touch with him.

I remember my communication with Malcolm Muggeridge very well. I was staying at an inexpensive hotel, one of those innumerable hotels in London where there are no phones in the rooms and where one has to make calls from a pay phone downstairs. I went downstairs and called Malcolm Muggeridge at his home in Sussex and asked him about becoming a member of my board. I told him about the Fourth World Foundation and its goals and I mentioned that Laura Huxley was on it and that we would be most honored if he could join us. If you have ever heard his voice you could imagine him saying, "My dear girl, I think it is a very splendid idea. I think I shall be pleased to join your board. Please send me your literature." Dear Malcolm Muggeridge in those instances was like me, on fire for the Lord.

Marshall McLuhan was a good friend of Malcolm Muggeridge. So, one year later, I decided to ask him to join my board. I told him that Malcolm Muggeridge, a good friend and somewhat of a colleague and fellow writer of his, had joined. He wanted to know about the Fourth World Foundation, but before I could answer he said something which I didn't quite get at the time. He said, "Oh, Annie, of course I'll join. And this is what the Fourth World is: the electronic circuitry of the globe." I can't argue now since the internet has become the major means of transporting our information. His prediction was universal, clear and self-fulfilled.

Professor McLuhan, who I think was the most right-brained white person I have ever met, a mega-visionary if ever there was one, said to me when I went to see him at his headquarters in the Math Building at the University of Toronto, "Annie, you know that the people with dark skin are all right-brained."

In the transition period between running the Huxley Institute and launching the Fourth World Foundation I had some extraordinary experiences, one of which started in 1979 when I was at my health farm in the swimming pool doing some water exercises and met a very special and interesting woman by the name of Frances Alsup. Jimmy Carter was still President and we were talking about politics. I had voted for Carter and Frances told me that she would never have voted for him because she noticed that Rosalynn Carter was always a few steps behind her husband. Frankly I had not noticed this, and what's more, I didn't really care but Frances was quite upset about this.

From this point we struck up a relationship which led thereafter to a friendship which usually happens at this health farm; there is an atmosphere of camaraderie there which leads to the finding of kindred spirits. Frances was a kindred spirit.

Unbeknownst to me at that time, Frances was the mother of Gary Kurtz's wife, Meredith. Gary Kurtz was the producer of the first Star Wars movie and a colleague of George Lucas, with whom he attended film school at the University of Southern California. Frances said she was the unofficial den mother of those film students because she was involved with the so-called Great White Brotherhood from which they gained their basic idea of the Star Wars trilogy. Frankly, let's face it, the real battle is not between good and evil in armor plate and strange disguises. The struggle has always been between Jesus Christ and His Adversary, Satan.

Nevertheless, it was lots of fun visiting the Kurtz' in their mountain top aerie in the Hollywood Hills, the front door of which you could reach only by way of a precipitous driveway—appropriately enough, I thought. They were kind enough to ask me to the Hollywood premiere of *The Empire Strikes Back*.

Later that year, I went to England for the purpose of visiting Meredith Kurtz, who lived outside of London. I was staying in

London at the St. James' Hotel. On returning home from dinner with friends I was listening to a music program on the radio when I heard a voice break in and say, "We are your brothers stopping by to say hello. We are from the galaxy of Andromeda." Oh, well.

In that vein maybe the most extraordinary piece of information would come to me by way of Dr. Roman Chrucky, a Ukrainian physician who practiced holistic medicine with a special emphasis on electro-magnetic fields and those disciplines that came out of Eastern Europe, including Russia, home of Kirlian photography, which is capable of registering auras.

Dr. Chrucky was the only person that I knew who was involved in both holistic medicine and the apparitions of Mary. Anyway, just as I was about to launch the Fourth World Foundation, I remember taking him upstairs to my Huxley office which we also call the Sunshine Office, since it has an unobstructed southern exposure. As I showed him the fledgling collection of literature on the Fourth World Foundation, including Marian apparitions, he said to me, "Annie, I think I have a story to tell you. Please sit down." So we sat at the two desks in that office.

He continued, "You may have wondered how I became a holistic physician. It happened when I was a student at the University of Salamanca in Spain in the early '60's. I had a rash of warts and my fellow Spanish students told me the best way to get rid of them was by taking high doses of Vitamin B6. Well, I took this advice and sure enough my warts went away. This convinced me that what we now call orthomolecular medicine was the only way to go as a medical doctor.

In those days also there were reports that Mary was appearing at the top of a mountain not so far from Santander where the university was located, in a village called Garabandal. So together with a fellow medical student, who was also a Roman Catholic, I set out on foot for that mountain top village and on the way we had some extraordinary experiences, such as being attacked by demons. While we were still making our ascent my colleague and I decided to say the rosary as a means of defense.

We observed that the demons would leave us while we prayed, so because we were medical students, we decided right there and then to conduct an experiment. We observed that when we stopped saying the rosary the demons returned. In this instance, it seemed as if the rosary was our sole protection against the evil one.

After spending a few days in Garabandal and getting to know the visionaries, I became friendly with one of them, Conchita, the oldest of the five. Conchita said something to me which may be the most extraordinary revelation of my life. She took me aside one day and said, "Roman, I must share with you something the Blessed Mother told us and it is a secret. It is only for you and for those to whom you tell it. When you consider what's going on these days, it hardly seems strange, does it? The Blessed Mother told us that this is the fallen planet."

Well Andromeda or no Andromeda I nearly fell out of my chair and immediately started asking around if anybody ever heard such a thing and there was one person, a great Christian writer, who guessed as much. His name was C.S. Lewis and he wrote about this fallen planet in his *Space Trilogy*. The books of this trilogy are *Out of the Silent Planet* (that's Earth), *Perelandra* (that's Venus) and *That Hideous Strength* (a climactic battle between the forces of good and evil, right here on Earth).

CHAPTER TWENTY-NINE

THE FOURTH WORLD AND
HARMONIC CONVERGENCE

At the beginning of 1977 I had no idea exactly how the Fourth World Foundation would take shape. I knew that the Fourth World was obviously of the spiritual world, but I didn't know that our present technological, left-brained, mechanistic, materialistic, "Piscean" civilization or their Fourth World, was about to end again according to the Hopi Indians. When I did learn this in 1979, I realized that the great traditions of the Native Americans of the Western Hemisphere, including the Mayans, had similar legends. The Mayan "long count", the longest time period in their calendar, comes to an end in 2012.

In a book entitled *The Mayan Factor*, written by Professor José Arguelles of the University of New Mexico, he states that there will come a time when the uncreated total power will send a beam of light through space. If the planet earth doesn't enter the beam of light at the appointed time, in this case the year 2012, then the planet earth will be cast out again into darkness to the void before present creation. In other words, the earth will be destroyed. The beam of light represents the light from the uncreated One of Love and Energy by which and through which harmonic goals for this planet could be achieved. Does this sound vaguely familiar?

While I was still active in the Huxley Institute, my adopted guru, Sri Chinmoy, showed me that my spiritual path was Roman Catholic and not Native American, or perhaps Roman Catholic including Native American. Nevertheless, just for the heck of it, I threw for my New Age type friends (and a few others) a Harmonic Convergence party. Looking back on this, I wonder now how in the world my husband ever went along with this.

The party was a great success, as parties go. There were candles on the tables outside under a tent. The candles were in little containers flickering in the soft evening light and gave our gathering a serene aura. The newspapers liked this kind of stuff at the time and we had a very good article written about it in *Spotlight Magazine*. I now think back and wonder what people might have thought of such a person, a Roman Catholic, in good standing, also espousing Mayan legends?

Certainly, there is a consensus among right-brained people across the planet that there are planetary changes due any day now that have already begun and that, in the words of my visionary friend, Greta Woodrew, it was "nature's plan, and also because of man's inhumanity to man."

I owe a debt of gratitude to Greta Woodrew whom I met coincidentally at my friend Adele Behar's house. If you remember, Adele was one of those who helped me get the Huxley Institute chapter off the ground. This was actually the last day that Greta Woodrew would be in Westport, Connecticut, an incredible synchronicity if ever there was one. She was moving to an aerie with her husband, Dick, at the confluence of the Great Smoky and Shenandoah Mountains, near the great Biltmore in Asheville, North Carolina. I visited her at this magnificent place only once, regretfully, to attend a workshop at her then bi-annual conference, and learned to become a bona fide dowser. It helped me a great deal in putting in septic systems for instance, because if I could find where the water was, and I did, then conversely, I would know where the water was not. So instead of the professionals putting in useless and expensive holes all over the place, you simply dowse for water and there it is.

At Greta's place I also remember her brother putting on a performance of various martial arts that rivaled anything Mikhail Baryshnikov could perform. Really! He was also a healer.

This consensus in the prediction of coming disaster was covered by a rather comprehensive two-part television documentary entitled *Ancient Prophecies*, which featured everyone from Edgar Cayce to Marian apparitions. The message is always the same; that time is running out for mankind to return to Godly ways before an impending chastisement. One of many intriguing book titles is, *The Day of the Great Purification* by Ken Carey, which in Biblical terms would be the Great and Terrible day of the Lord.

The same theme was reiterated some years ago by some Andean Indians who approached the leading television production company in the world, the BBC. They were of a primitive tribe living high in the Andes who had been undisturbed by the outside world for centuries. These Aborigines of South America wore white robes and had no crime and virtually none of the civilized world's diseases and afflictions. Something terrible had to have happened for them to have come down from the mountains for the first time in their history. They call themselves the "Elder Brothers," and their goal was to seek only a younger brother, someone from the outside world, who would have the best connections to deliver their message to the rest of the world.

One Elder Brother eventually made his way down to a television producer in Brazil who had worked for the BBC, arguably the best television our planet has, and hence having the capability of delivering their message, although unfortunately it didn't turn out this way. From this meeting came undoubtedly one of the finest and most powerful documentaries ever made, *The Elder Brothers Speak to the Younger Brothers of the World*, which unfortunately was seen only by the few, not the many, engrossed as they are with mindless "entertainment."

The startling event that these harmonious peaceful people had come down to reveal was this: that plants on the top of the mountains were drying out for the first time ever. Eventually, this will require research by environmental and plant scientists, but it seems to be a harbinger of the global warming underway and its accompanying droughts and floods worldwide. This message was given long before global warming was universally "accepted."

CHAPTER THIRTY

THE SPANELS

Looking back on my relationship with Peggy and Abe Spanel, which lasted a few years, I now realize that it was very important to me for a variety of reasons. I can say with some certainty that that relationship was orchestrated by a higher power! Abe Spanel was a Russian Jew who had come to America with the typical immigrant's story—penniless but with a fine mind, genius I.Q., great aspirations and the desire to succeed. He invented latex and was a brilliant success over the course of his life. Mr. Spanel was a charming and conservative man who fully realized the dangers of the Soviet Empire from its inception.

The Spanels lived in Princeton, New Jersey, and later they moved to a smaller house. After her husband died, Mrs. Spanel moved from Princeton to Vermont where she built a house which had French doors with skylights above them. This design impressed me very much as her exquisite taste had been reflected in the architecture of their Princeton home as well.

Some time in the Fall of 1975, I received a phone call from Peggy Spanel. I'm not sure why Mrs. Spanel called me, but she viewed me as an expert on the treatment of schizophrenia and wanted help for her then ill daughter who was living in New York City. I believe I recommended that the Spanels go to a conference in Princeton, where the eminent physician and researcher, Dr. Carl Pfeiffer, was to give a talk about his treatment for schizophrenia, and that they try to get their daughter on his program. Whatever I recommended, it seemed to have worked over the years. My husband and I also attended that conference where we met with the Spanels.

My husband, when he was able to be present, and I, built up a good relationship with the Spanels which was bonded not only by our shared experience with schizophrenia but by a great love of music, and in our case, especially that of J.S. Bach. Mrs. Spanel was on the Board of the Marlboro Music Festival which we used to attend during those years when they still played a certain amount of Bach. Our relationship was also bonded by the fact that both of our husbands were avid conservatives.

Being with the Spanels was like "magic" for me, if I could use that word. Both of them were kind and generous. Mrs. Spanel put me into the hands of maybe the most competent female gynecologist in New York, when I was literally bleeding to death from "female" problems brought on by stress over the years. She performed an operation as well as a hysterectomy which saved my life. I had to remain in Columbia Presbyterian Hospital for one month (where I read Carlos Castenada, thank God!).

Mrs. Spanel liked to give tea parties and soirées. I remember one occasion when I attended a tea party at their home while they were still living in Princeton. Since she loved music, it was not uncommon for her to have someone perform during her gatherings. Fernando Valenti, the harpsichordist, once played for a few of her friends in her living room. This included an excruciatingly exquisite rendering of Scarlatti and Padre Soler.

At another tea party I met the son of William Scheide, the impresario for the Bach Aria group that Harry and I used to attend at Town Hall in New York City even before we were married. The son was nothing like his father. In fact he was illustrative of the observation made by some professors, which is, that in families where there is mental imbalance or even mental illness, there is often a member with great talent or even genius. In the famous Huxley family, which could be traced back to Thomas Henry Huxley, the head of that great 19th century family, there was the well-known and accomplished Aldous, an older brother, Julian, and Trevellian, the younger brother, a schizophrenic who eventually committed suicide. As soon as I started talking with William Scheide's son, it became obvious to me that he might be schizophrenic. He told me that he thought he had uncovered the secret of anti-matter and began to describe it to me as a series of black holes winding down into very small concentric circles ending in a point. Two nights previously I had that same nightmarish? image in a dream, but didn't know what to make of it. If ever I get a chance to develop my hypothesis on the nature of the universe, I'd like to address some of those theories concerning black holes, mole holes in space, and the string theory of ten. (Maybe in another incarnation! Don't worry—just kidding!) These are right-brain concepts in sub-atomic physics. Whether there is some orchestration of the higher or lower power, I don't know but we will see.

I had some wonderful times in California with Peggy Spanel and Dr. Mike Lesser, President of the California Orthomolecular Society which is located in Berkeley. On one occasion Peggy had asked me to join her at the Huntington Hotel in San Francisco on a trip to meet Dr. Linus Pauling, because her husband had given Pauling some money for his institute. We were given the O.K. to see Dr. Pauling and we brought Dr. Lesser along since they were colleagues in orthomolecular medicine. Dr. Lesser was one of my Jewish cronies along with Dr. David Sheinkin. I considered them among my closest friends. We shared the same kind of humor and both of these doctors had an interest in schizophrenia. Dr. Sheinkin was the son of a Rabbi, and the holistic physician for our family. Dr. Lesser had a brother who was a Rabbi and he also had a schizophrenic brother. He was wonderful. If he hadn't been on the West Coast he would have been our doctor.

We were invited into Dr. Pauling's inner sanctum and permitted to look at his marvelous research papers. We even had the opportunity to see Dr. Frank Catchpool who was currently the clinical head of Pauling's Institute of Medicine and formerly head of the Albert Schweitzer Clinic in Africa for many years. Dr. Pauling's clinic was very advanced. At the end of our meeting, Mike and I decided to copy some of these papers, one of which was written by Dr. Wilfrid van Dusen, a disciple of Emmanuel Swedenborg, from whom he extrapolated his thesis, "The Presence of Spirits in Madness." I decided to copy this paper, but couldn't get a copy of it because it came out all black! There was a deus ex machina there for sure. Mike and I didn't have time then to ponder this imponderable. The same thing happened with my mother's helper, Kim di Quattro, an amazing baby sitter, a descendant of the di Quattros of 19th century Italy, of Count Cavour fame. Well, one day I asked Kim to make copies of a document for me and all she could get was a set of stripes, until the repairman came in to fix the copier. The Scriptural reading for that day was, " . . . . . . with his stripes we are healed" (Isa. 53:5).

CHAPTER THIRTY-ONE

THE WIDE OUTREACH OF HUXLEY

During my many years serving as the President of the Connecticut Chapter of the Huxley Institute, I made quite a large number of friends in the medical field and its periphery. One of these people was Barbara Levine, who had a terminal brain tumor and who cured herself with holistic medicine and prayer. She and I had become good friends and had a strong bond.

It was early in 1985 that Barbara called me up and said, "I have a friend, this wonderful doctor from St. Vincent's Hospital, Marty Reichgut. Marty has been involved with the inner city of Bridgeport, and we both became attached to the program started by Werner Erhard in the 60's as a consequence of EST training." After training in EST, presumably one can go on to save the world more effectively, or in the case of the majority of the EST graduates, at least one can save oneself. This program, which I must admit was brilliantly conceived was called The Breakthrough Foundation, teamed up later with Youth at Risk, which had already been established, identifying the youth at risk in the inner city.

The concept was simplicity itself, to adopt one young person and to take them for ten days on an Outward Bound type of experience with other youths from the inner city. This was supposed to be a transforming experience just as it is with the adults who have gone through the Outward Bound program. The tremendous challenges presented by this program, when overcome, enable a person to overcome his fears and certainly boost his self-esteem.

The youth would then return, a reformed person, to the dysfunctional environment from which he came, in order to share his new vision with his family or whomever he lives with. In addition, he would also have the ongoing support of his adopted family, supplied by his own community. This program, I am told, had done well in Detroit and also in San Francisco.

A few years after we launched it, the program faltered after an auspicious beginning. It faltered because of the nature of the inner city of Bridgeport, Connecticut, whose main problem, like that of a Banana Republic, was an endemic corruption from top to bottom, combined with an endemic apathy from the outlying suburbs. This has begun to change only recently.

So Marty and Barbara talked me into having a fundraiser to launch the Youth At Risk program. They didn't have to twist my arm too much since my backyard has been the site for many other such launches, political gatherings, weddings, flower shows and practically anything you can think of, even steel bands! The scheduled date for this event was precisely September 24, 1985.

What we didn't count on however was a little lady, a hurricane by the name of Gloria, who came up very fast, crossing Long Island September 23, 1985 and racing her way through Connecticut and Rhode Island in short order, leaving much damage in her wake. So here she was, Hurricane Gloria, on the eve of this important gathering for a very good cause, at which our favorite jazz musician and friend, Gay Mehegan, was scheduled to appear and perform.

We had originally scheduled another musician, Matthew Quinn, a junior type Brubeck, you might say, because while in Rhode Island, we had heard him play his blues and jazz piano improvisations and were very impressed, but he couldn't get down here from Rhode Island because of the storm.

After the hurricane everything was a mess, but the higher power as is His wont, smiled on us magnificently. The barter gardener couple on our property completely cleaned up the place by the time September 24 at 11 a.m. rolled around. That was the scheduled time of the fundraiser.

We didn't have electricity, a condition that would last for nine whole days. I dispatched our faithful and sometimes comical Peruvian born caretaker, Carlos, to quickly buy a generator so that Gay could play her electric organ on time. There was only one generator left at Sears Roebuck; it was so loud that we had to put it in the front yard and hook her piano through our house to the generator so it didn't drown out her music.

The star for the event was a basketball player named Meadowlark Lemon, a Bridgeport native, who had also become a Christian. He had been a Harlem Globetrotter. He was maybe one of the shortest, sweetest basketball players I ever met. Somehow we pulled it off.

In 1995 I tried to revive the Youth at Risk Program but just didn't have the resources to do it. I have to say that Marty Reichgut's first crew of volunteers were the most dedicated I have ever experienced in my long life of working with volunteers. Thank you forever, dear friends, wherever you are now.

CHAPTER THIRTY-TWO

THE MEANING OF *FOURTH*

It would be a good idea here to explain the meaning of "fourth" in the Fourth World which became clear after various encounters with Native Americans and their culture including, of course, that of the man whom I will now call my foster father who was half Oglala Sioux.

Denny Brown, my redoubtable staff person, conducted the research on my foster father which revealed that Curtis Crellin, had indeed been born in Marshalltown, Iowa, just a stone's throw from the Rosebud Reservation of the Oglala Sioux.

She did the best work ever done by anyone who had worked for me, partly because she was a very serious and motivated feminist and I seemed to have propelled her into the field of promoting a more mystical female consciousness.

Two semi-mystical synchronicities and confirmations followed the disclosure of information regarding the origins of my putative father. One is that the issue of Ms. Crellin and the unknown brave, bore a remarkable resemblance to the man on the cover of the book, *Black Elk Speaks*, the Holy Man of the Sioux Indians made popular by the narratives taken down by John Neihardt.

The second came during an airplane trip, the locus of many synchronicities. Usually they occur with me during flights from coast-to-coast. This time it was connected with a mini-documentary announcing the arrival of the great film *Dances with Wolves*, starring Kevin Costner. He was being asked what in the world inspired him to make such a great film, and a great film it was, long overdue, too. He replied, looking straight into the camera (and I thought looking straight at me),"This lady here was the inspiration for this film." As Kevin Costner looked down at her, almost tenderly, she said, "Yes, I am from the Rosebud Reservation of the Oglala Sioux, and I was mandated by the Great White Spirit to make sure that this film be made." (She was the technical advisor, too.)

The most prophetic of the Indian nations was that of the Hopi and, after reading the prophecies of the Hopi, I unwittingly realized that the meaning of "fourth" in the Fourth World was given to me concerning the Hopi Prophecy. The Hopi world view is epochal, similar to that of other groups or individuals who are given the epochal theories of history, such as Rudolf Steiner's "Sixth Epoch". According to the Hopi, the history of the universe and of our planet in particular, is divided into their "worlds", each of which was handed down from the elders as long as the Hopi could remember. That sequence of "worlds" dates back from the time their ancestors crossed the Bering Strait from Asia to populate the Western Hemisphere.

The cosmology of the Hopi consists of six worlds, and we are now living in the fourth world. The three worlds that preceded this one had been given the great powers of a successful and harmonic culture by the Great Spirit. However, through their sinfulness and by not obeying the dicta given to them by the Great Spirit, the previous worlds were destroyed. This sequence happened for all three worlds preceding this, the fourth world, and the prophecy was made that the fourth world in turn would soon be destroyed for the same reasons.

> The name of this Fourth World is Tuwaqachi, World
> Complete. You will find out why. It is not all beautiful
> and easy like the Previous ones. It has height and depth,

> heat and cold, beauty and barrenness; it has everything
> for you to choose from. What you choose will determine
> if this time you can carry out the plan of Creation on it or
> whether it must in time be destroyed too.
>
> From the *Book of Hopi* by Frank Walters

The American Indian connection has always been strong because of my foster father's strong ties with the Oglala tribe. I must say that over the years, especially in the late 70's, early 80's during the early days of the Fourth World Foundation, some amazing things happened to me while working with Native Americans, and also in part while I was involved in movie making at that time.

A friend of my sister-in-law's, a fellow actress whose name was Cheyenne Crane, was a half-blood Cheyenne, had written a script about a half-Native American, half-African American sheriff of the town in Oklahoma where she grew up. Cheyenne was not able to make her film but nevertheless involved herself in many activities helpful to her Native American brothers and sisters. More recently, I introduced her to the General Manager of the Norwich Inn who was also half-Native American/African American, to see if, by any chance, his by now wealthy tribe, the Mashantucket Pequots, would be able to finance some of the poor members of the Cheyenne nation.

The story of great interest at the time Cheyenne came to share with the Mashantucket Pequots, surrounds the great prophecy of the white buffalo calf which was born the year before her trip East. It was a sign to the Native Americans of the beginning of the end times. In that vein, I must point out that much attention was also given to the birth of the red heifer across the ocean in Israel, at precisely the same time. The birth of the red heifer is being hailed by religious Jews as a sign from God that work can soon begin on building the third temple in Jerusalem, and Christians view the rebuilding of the temple as an important sign of the return of the Messiah.

Being the eschatologist that I am, I recognize that these are important signs to watch, very similar, you might say, to the message from the elder brothers to the younger brothers of the world concerning the global drought that has been prophesized and is now coming to us as I write this in the year 1999.

The major Christian typography of the time when this destruction would occur was given to the Italian mystic, Luisa Piccarreta, in the 30's. After a brief illness, she remained in bed for the rest of her life, receiving messages from God and recording them, similar to other mystics who became bedridden for this sole purpose, such as the 19th century German nun, Katherine Emmerich and the Italian mystic of the 20th century, Maria Valtorta.

God revealed to Luisa what I consider the most powerful mystical message of its kind ever given: God has ordained that there be three fiats: the first one being of Creation; the second fiat was the incarnation and subsequent life and message of Jesus Christ, the Son of God and the Son of Man; the third fiat from God is the time in which we are now living. It affirms that we are on the eve of the transformation of the planet like the paradise prior to the fall, the time that "God's will be done on earth as it is in Heaven." It is only in espousing this divine fiat that we will have the opportunity of seeing Heaven on earth, which is the culmination of the expectation of Utopia or the New Jerusalem (Shangri-la?). This has been the salient theme of my life.

In order for the third fiat to take place, there must be no sin or darkness anywhere because Jesus said, "Will there be any faith left (on my return)?" This means that only when there is complete faith on earth can Jesus return in His glory. Furthermore, this explains, of course, the growing movement of the healing of the family tree and the deliverance of the discarnate family members, which means all the discarnate souls since the creation, the mystical body of Christ, must also be given over to perfection. We must therefore expect a tremendous cleaning up,

Hopi style, as well as the return to God by all of our undelivered ancestors. At least this is what I think.

The subconscious awareness of the imminence of this transformation was one reason for the popularity of the book by Dr. José Arguelles on the Harmonic Convergence, the prophecy of the Maya . As previously mentioned, the Maya maintain that this planet would be given one last chance to enter into the beam (the ray of light from God's perfection) sometime before the year 2012 AD. If we don't make it, according to the Maya, we shall be thrust forever into the outer darkness of the universe; the void from which creation came.

The only knowledge that the Maya didn't possess was the news of the incarnation of God as Man and the mercy and mankind's subsequent salvation, or as Steiner said, the most important event in the history of the Universe is the incarnation of Jesus, the Christ, born of the woman in Revelation:

> "And there appeared a great wonder in heaven; a woman clothed with the sun, and the moon under her feet, and upon her head a crown of twelve stars: And she being with child cried, travailing in birth, and pained to be delivered. And there appeared another wonder in heaven; and behold a great red dragon, having seven heads and ten horns, and seven crowns upon his heads . . . . And she brought forth a man child, who was to rule all nations with a rod of iron: and her child was caught up unto God, and to his throne" (Rev. 12: 1-3 & 5).

CHAPTER THIRTY-THREE

SEEKING AND FINDING
ANOTHER LEVEL

Albert Einstein is reputed to have said that the level at which problems are created is not the level at which they will be solved. They can only be solved in the non-material world, the world of Spirit, of the heart, the world of Love.

The global definition of "worlds" includes a fourth world, the world of the poorest of the poor. This includes nations, and even communities within nations that are not even in a development stage such as Bangladesh, Haiti, as well as the shanty towns and slums in economically thriving societies, such as Calcutta, where Mother Teresa worked and led us to look. While she worked in the streets of Calcutta, she constantly looked to that world of Spirit to find solutions to their problems.

I knew I had to continue to seek out this level, the world of the Spirit, when I invited Dean Ernest Gordon, to become a member of the board and he asked me to describe the foundation's goals. He had been Dean of the chapel of Princeton University for 35 years and had also been a survivor of Japanese internment at the same camp featured in *Bridge Over the River Kwai*. He described the real story in detail in his book *Miracle on the River Kwai*. I met Dean Gordon on the occasion of my husband's

25th Princeton reunion, the very year he was retiring. When I told him of the goals of my foundation and asked him to become a member of my board, he said, "Oh, you must be an eschatologist." That word is derived from the Greek, Eschaton, which means "the end times." I pondered to myself, "What is that?" but said aloud, "Oh." The good Dean then said to me, "May I tell you what that means? It means to be a student of the end times." "Well, thank you, Dean. You are right."

Being a devout Presbyterian, which of course presupposes all the attributes of a born again Christian, along with the holiness and gifts of the Holy Spirit, Dean Gordon was also fervent in addressing global problems with an end times perspective. He was sending Bibles behind the Iron Curtain, which was at that time opened for a temporary window of opportunity for conversion activity, but for how long we do not know.

Investigating this world of the Spirit seemed to be a continuation of the work I was doing for the Huxley Institute and for PCMR (President's Committee on Mental Retardation), President Reagan's Committee for the mentally retarded. There were the needs of yet another group that comprised the fourth world—the Hopi Indian. Indeed, the fourth world of the Hopi is the civilization in which we now find ourselves and, which according to their lore, is destined for an imminent collapse. Something needed to be done fast because time was short. That something had to be spiritual.

At just about this time, as I began to organize my Foundation on the East Coast, an interesting development was taking place in California. By very unusual circumstances, my sister-in-law was approached by a film director, Henry King, who was interested in possibly funding a film on "Our Lady of Guadalupe." My sister-in-law's father had a friend who was a friend of Henry King. Well known for his direction of *"The Song of Bernadette,"* which, in my opinion, was one of the two best religious films ever made and which won so many academy awards that 20th Century Fox was brought from red ink into black. After he left

20thCentury Fox, Mr. King owned his own production company, and obtained permission from Mexico's Portillo government to film in Mexico. He was interested in directing this film which would both edify the public about Our Lady and feed the spiritual void rampant in society.

Just prior to visiting California, I happened to glimpse a note to call my sister-in-law about a film. Forgetting to act on the message, one morning I happened to open a drawer in a piece of my mother's furniture, which I never use. Inside the drawer was a postcard of the miraculous image of Juan Diego in the eye of Our Lady of Guadalupe, which I had lost four years earlier in another house. Such messages, which seem to come from Our Lady, have been occurring with frequent regularity. I interpreted this as a sign, and so, off to California again, literally clutching that postcard of the Guadalupe image, I joined my sister-in-law for the meeting with the venerable, distinguished and world famous motion picture director, Henry King.

We conversed at length about his tremendous movie background and his passion to make this movie, and all the disappointments and accidents that happened to prevent his making it to date.

Henry King was primarily famous for swashbuckling dramas, including *The Captain from Castille, The Sun Also Rises.* I happened to be in Paris once when they were having a Henry King retrospective. The French are very appreciative of great Hollywood movie directors. At some point in time, Henry King converted to Roman Catholicism. I do not know much about that, but I do know that when Sam Peckinpah became director under the new order at 20th Century Fox, he began making many violent films that to this day nobody has made more violent films than he.

Henry King was getting on in years and he knew that his kind of movies were no longer popular, so he did not have much of a future with 20th Century Fox. This was in the late 1960's when there was a great shift of consciousness, "Make love not war," "Tune in and drop out," Woodstock, Vietnam, riots on college campuses etc. This was the beginning of the final unleashing of the famous last half of the decade given to the negative forces for one last final battle before the big blow-up.

Henry King wanted to get out on the good side, so after 35 years at 20th Century Fox he left to form his own production company. Because of his conversion and the success of *Song of Bernadette*, and especially because of the power of that Lady who is called, "The Woman," in the Apocalypse, Henry King decided, as his last great final masterpiece, to make a movie of Our Lady of Guadalupe.

My sister-in-law informed me that she thought I could probably raise funds for Henry King since I had a non-profit organization, so could I please come out and meet him. Wow! This was a challenge. I had done a lot of interesting things in my life, but raising money to make a film? I could not even balance my checkbook, but when that Lady calls, you have got to go. So I went to California and stayed with my sister-in-law. I remember both of us timorously entering Mr. King's lovely ranch house which I believe was on Toluca Lake in San Fernando Valley. It had the kind of furnishings and atmosphere to which I had been exposed so often as I was growing up amidst the movie industry. It was the kind of feeling unlike any other. On the wall there were books and pictures of movie stars, an untold number of awards and accomplishments etc. There was a kind of pseudo sporty look in the lamps, maybe even a moose or something. Henry King might have been a golfer and I remember a few golf-related things here and there (not strewn about). I think the house might even have been on a golf course. The furniture in those homes was always comfortable, leather and down-filled chairs, thick rugs etc.—you get the picture. Above and beyond that, there is this Hollywood feeling that you do not get in any other place in the world. Heaven knows, Paris also has its feeling which is so very pronounced, so intrinsic, being there also gives one a special feeling.

We were ushered into his study and sat down in some wonderfully comfortable leather sofas and I had time to carefully read all his awards and honors, framed on his wall as in a particularly distinguished and busy doctor's office. Before I could get half-way through, since there were so many, in came Mr. King, accompanied by his charming second wife, Ida.

Lili and I were sitting on a very comfortable couch waiting for Mr. King, who shook Lili's hand first because they had met before and she introduced me to him. He was at the same time warm but reserved. How could this aging but world-class movie director, having worked with the greats, as they were then called, shake hands with a fast becoming middle-aged housewife, who had trouble balancing her checkbook and who had all the responsibilities of a home? How indeed? He and I were both aware that this was not really our doing. We were not exactly puppets because we had free will, but we were certainly taking orders from higher powers.

I told him about the impact that movie, *The Song of Bernadette*, had on me when I saw it during those dark, dreary days following the German invasion of France. I remember my mother and grandmother weeping profuse tears with many others in the cinema, when they played the Marseilleise in "Casablanca," a film shot the same year. This was the year before the U.S. joined in the war. It was a time when there were so many good films on release.

On my return home to my lonely room at 911 N. Rexford Drive, after seeing that film, I remember praying to the Blessed Virgin in a corner of my room, saying that if she wanted to conscript me into her service, then I would be hers.

Henry King was very pleased to hear this and so, through some absolutely remarkable circumstances, he enlisted me as the person to raise the money to make what he hoped to be his final great masterpiece, *The Story of Guadalupe*. That was in 1977.

Later, Carole, my Beverly Hills chum, was with me on a trip to California when I tried to get a screenwriter for the screen play about Our Lady of Guadalupe. On another visit to California, I met Terry Moore, the actress, through my niece, Christa, my sister-in-law Lili's daughter. I needed to go see her because she knew someone in Malibu by the name of Jess Stearn, a writer. He had authored books on Edgar Cayce. I really wanted to see him, so Carole first drove me to Terry Moore's, so she could pave the way, but when we got there the doors were locked and she didn't even answer her door. So I went to the back of the house and could see she was in bed with her manager and current boyfriend. I knocked on the window and finally her friend came to the door to say that Terry was very sick with a cold. I felt compelled to make Terry some chicken soup (even before I knew I was Jewish) and would want to ask her to call her friend, Jess Stearn, to make an appointment for that very same day.

There was a chicken in the refrigerator and some vegetables. It was good soup: I love to cook when I have time and the right ingredients. An hour later after the soup, feeling that certainly she must be better now, I then asked Terry again to call Jess Stearn because I really wanted to talk to him about possibly doing a screenplay for me. A Hollywood- type friend of Terry's drove me to meet Jess about the screenplay. Since they had both been recently divorced, all those two men could talk about was their former wives, instead of the screenplay. Oh well (win a few, lose a few, play every day to paraphrase a few buddies)!

I eventually found someone by the name of John Parisi to help me with this project which blossomed into two TV documentaries. There was also a very personal spiritual experience beyond my success in having the story of Guadalupe brought to the attention of the public, with the help of that first and so efficient assistant, John. There was another earlier John, my first assistant.

At the time when the first John was about to leave—in fact on the last day of his employment—we decided we should go and see a Mrs. Murphy, a mystic, in Norwich, CT who had a statue of St. Theresa of Lisieux which bled and sometimes, I believe, there was a message for the visitors in the blood. We finally got there and I noted with some amusement that the local garage was called, Huxley Garage. That day the statue bled seven drops; I knew that six is the number of man and seven, the number of God. That day it seemed that my spiritual path had begun in earnest.

It was the same assistant, John, who accompanied me on my first trip to the renowned mystic who had the so-called hidden stigmata, Sister Louis Bertrand, and it was a privilege for me to see her. Since she belonged to a cloistered Dominican order, it was an experience similar to that visit my grandmother and I paid to the Ursuline nun, who taught at the convent where my grandmother was sent to recuperate from malaria and also to be educated. That nun, like Sister Louis Bertrand, lived separately from the outside world, and we could only speak to her through an iron grille.

My visit to Sister Louis Bertrand on this occasion was very special. I had visited her a few times before but this time, on my fifth visit, she said, "When you embark upon your spiritual path everything and everyone on your path that you perceive to be good, God gives to you for your journey. If that person or entity is not good or you perceive it not to be good, then it should not concern you because it is between that person and God."

In other words, it seems that we should not judge others. From that fateful day, the day of my fifth visit, those words opened so many doors for me. Sister Louis must have known that we would not see each other again. After all, she was a mystic. She said those things to me when I was about to leave so I asked her, "How would I know whether these things that I am experiencing are from God? Where will I find someone like you, beloved Sister?" and she said, "Don't worry. It will be all right from now on. It will be between you and God." Through the years I have looked for another spiritual adviser which I couldn't find, except for a certain retired Archbishop in Providence, Rhode Island, whom I am still hoping to see some day. Nevertheless, I did have the privilege of meeting a Father Post, an elderly retired Jesuit priest, previously Master of vocations for the Jesuit seminarians at Fairfield University and very well revered. It was a great privilege for my husband and me to have seen him for just two years before he died.

PART III

CHAPTER THIRTY-FOUR

THE BATTLE OF
THE WOUNDED HEART

WOUNDED KNEE

There was no hope on earth, and God seemed to have forgotten us. Some said they saw the Son of God; others did not see Him. If He had come He would have done some great things as He had done before. We doubted it, because we had neither seen Him nor His works.

    The people did not know; they did not care. They snatched at the hope. They screamed like crazy men to Him for mercy. They caught at the promise they heard He had made.

-Red Cloud

I shall not be there. I shall rise and pass.
Bury my heart at Wounded Knee.

-Stephen Vincent Benét

"(Yea, a sword shall pierce through thy own soul also), that the thoughts of many hearts may be revealed" (Luke 2: 35).

This was the prophecy of Simeon concerning Mary, when it revealed to him by the Holy Ghost that the infant Jesus whom Mary and Joseph had brought into the temple according to Judaic law, was indeed the Christ. This is the meditation of the third Joyful Mystery of the Holy Rosary.

(My heart was pierced when they wrapped Patricia in
wet sheets and administered shock treatments.)

The Holy Rosary is really a series of prayers, repeated like a mantram. It was given to Saint Dominic during the 13th century, by the Blessed Mother herself. It consists of fifteen meditations on the life of Christ, seen through the eyes of His Mother: the Joyful, Sorrowful and the Glorious mysteries, which are comprised of the *Our Father*, given by Jesus to His disciples and the Hail Mary, the salutation to Mary by the angel, Gabriel when he informed her that she was going to be the mother of the Son of God.

The first series of mysteries are known as the Joyful mysteries, the fourth of which is the Presentation of the child at the altar, according to Jewish custom. Of the baby Jesus Simeon also prophesized, "Behold, this child is set for the fall and rising again of many in Israel; . . . . There was also Anna, a prophetess, "And she coming in that instant gave thanks likewise unto the Lord, and spake of him to all them that looked for redemption in Jerusalem."

On the night of January 24-25, 1938, almost one third of the world seemed to be on fire. Fire engines streamed out of cities all over Europe to combat flames which were not there. From the Arctic in the north deep into Africa, from Bermuda in the west to the Ural Mountains in distant eastern parts of Russia, millions thought it was the end of the world. (It coincided with the outbreak of World War II which ended in the use of atomic weapons.) Scientists unable to explain it, described it as some form of Aurora Borealis. But the visionary of Fatima said: "I believe if scientists investigate they will find that it could not be an aurora. It is the great sign."

Patricia, our first born, came into the world on January 25, 1952. Her birth was normal except for slight jaundice. She was a rather restless baby, a light sleeper, did not nurse too well, but was cheerful, full of spunk, and weaned at three months. Patricia lost her maternal grandmother when she was four, a great loss for us all, but particularly for Patricia since she was tremendously close to her. This loss may have affected her health more deeply than we realized initially.

Always thinking about the Joyful mystery, and the Biblical citation, "and a sword shall pierce thine own soul," my first major wound occurred with the death of my mother. But devastating though that was, the real test came with my daughter's illness, first with cancer which resulted in the amputation of her leg, and then with schizophrenia. According to Carl Simonton, the presence and development of cancer seems to appear about 17 months after a major loss. The kind of despair that followed the death of my mother promoted the cancer process physiologically almost 17 months to the day when one of our many temporary nannies told me, after bathing Patricia, during one of my periods of ill health, "Madam, I believe your daughter has a lump on her leg." Since I was very nervous anyway, I became quite alarmed. Lumps are not usually very good news, so I rushed her to the pediatrician and sneaked a peek at his report which said the lump was possibly a malignancy on her lower right femur.

What a frightening time! Panic set in. The effect of the report of a malignancy was almost as serious as the one which I experienced on my mother's death! I experienced sheer terror. That evening I prayed, "Dear God, if you can spare my daughter from cancer, I shall become a member of the Third Order of St. Francis." I had been thinking about doing this for some time, but membership presented some logistical difficulties, since the meetings were held in downtown Los Angeles and at that time I didn't have my own car.

I telephoned my best friend Laurey's mother, a very kind and caring Episcopalian lady, and asked her to pray for us. She agreed to do so and said that she would call her prayer circle together at All Saints' Episcopal Church in Beverly Hills, where my husband sang in the choir, and have them all pray for our sweet daughter, Patricia, right away. She put my daughter's name on their prayer list and those good ladies took turns in praying for her. I promised God that I would join the Third Order of St. Francis if He saved my daughter's life.

We ended up taking Patricia to the Los Angeles Orthopaedic Hospital, whose president and founder, Dr. Charles LeRoy Lowman, was a good friend of my first step-father, my good step-father, Hal Rosson, who had himself been helped by Dr. Lowman many years previously, following a bout with polio. Dr. Lowman was a kindly man and received a Medal of Freedom from President Eisenhower years later. He operated on our daughter but didn't remove the growth plate because had he done so, the leg wouldn't have grown back at all. Dr. Lowman didn't believe the tumor to be malignant, therefore he only scraped it out and her leg was put in a splint for three months. Patricia was five-and-a-half: it was June 1957.

The tumor grew back in a year's time. This time it was the opinion of Dr. Vernon Luck, then the president of the American Academy of Orthopaedic Surgeons, also connected with the Los Angeles Orthopaedic Hospital, and a tumor specialist, that the tumor was indeed malignant.

In January 1960, Dr. Luck, assisted by Dr. Lowman and two other doctors, instead of amputating, performed a radical resection on her right femur. They removed part of the femur (all of the tumor), put it into an autoclave and put it back along with bone from the bone bank, as well as bone they removed from Patricia's pelvis. She was put in a full body cast for approximately a year-and-a-half.

With the help of the devoted Anglo-Irish nanny and mother's help, Maureen Clegg, the redoubtable Mrs. Luella Simpson, the kindergarten home teacher and a full length wheelchair, we all remained in pretty good shape and Patricia's spirits appeared to be holding up in the face of this difficult situation. Mrs. Luella Simpson, who lives in Santa Monica, was a kindly but firm Kindergarten teacher. I always said to myself, if only everybody could be like Kindergarten teachers, there might be more people with sterling characters and hearts of gold!

By the summer of 1964, Patricia's right leg was still the length of a seven year old's since it did not grow as the growth center was destroyed in her first operation. It was becoming grotesque and Patricia had inadequate mobility due to cumbersome braces and a built up shoe. Dr. Frank Stinchfield of Columbia-Presbyterian performed another bone graft and also inserted a metal rod to try to promote growth. Also, while Patricia was in the hospital a birthmark was removed since it could have been irritated dangerously by use of crutches.

Patricia's spirits gradually worsened after the move East with the disastrous departure of our long-time live-in nanny, Maureen Clegg, back to California, and the onset of puberty. All signs of puberty were present at an early age except menstruation.

In May, 1965, because the right leg was about 5/8 the length of the left leg, I asked Dr. Stinchfield what could be done. After consulting with the head of the Orthopaedic department in both of the top New York University Medical Centers, it was decided to fit Patricia with a hollow prosthetic since she was fearful of an amputation. (This involved the dropping of the right foot.) The day after the first fitting for the hollow prosthetic, Patricia began to show the first evidence of psychosis by becoming extremely withdrawn, depressed and anorexic. With the help of a family pediatrician, a warm and understanding man, her spirits were raised to a minimum level of functioning, while I was desperately trying to get help. Since this was the family's first experience with mental illness it was doubly difficult, and since it was summer, all the child psychiatrists had left on vacation. In August, a very severe catatonia and anorexia forced us to put Patricia into a local custodial psychiatric hospital while looking for a better institution. After great difficulty, we found the Yale-New Haven Medical Center's in-patient psychiatric unit where she was admitted in October, 1965. She showed very little progress except from the encouragement given her by a black male nurse named Harold, who though not college educated, spoke seven languages.

However, because she was in a hospital setting, for long-term cosmetic considerations, all thought it best to amputate her withered right leg. The amputation was performed in March 1966 by the distinguished and revered orthopaedic surgeon from Yale, Dr. Wayne Southwick, colleague and protégé of Dr. Frank Stinchfield. Dr. Southwick gave one year of pro bono time to the Good Ship, Hope, and didn't charge us a cent, whereas the psychiatrists bled us dry. Incidentally, many years later when my husband was having eye surgery at Yale, New Haven, whose picture was seen hanging in the lobby? It was Dr. Southwick's, of course.

The psychotherapeutic treatment at the hospital was Freudian centered, psychoanalytic and included group therapy. Patricia was discharged conditionally in September, 1966 and sent to a boarding school not too far from home which took problem children. She regressed very much there to a very low point. Conditions were very poor: there was overcrowding; she suffered lack of sleep, etc. and so I brought her home. Patricia remained on a homebound study program with some wonderful teachers and improved gradually. After a trip to one teacher's farm and a visit with my wonderful sister-in-law Lili in California, Patricia became well enough to resume school. For her sophomore year, the teachers were very lenient and Patricia did manage to get through school, although concentration was at times difficult.

After a good summer where Patricia became a proficient swimmer, her father and I took an urgent business trip to Europe, not realizing the chronic nature of her illness. The day after we returned, after an especially hectic day involving five younger siblings, Patricia once again became mute and immobile. We were desperately trying to keep her out of the hospital because of the terrible ordeal it created for her and for the rest of the family. After two sessions of what appeared to be a standard Freudian approach, Patricia became worse. She made a slight attempt to slash her wrists and pleaded to be hospitalized. Because of a long association with the American Schizophrenia Foundation and my commitment to the new psycho-chemical approach to schizophrenia, instead of just psychoanalysis, she was sent to the first available hospital that used mega-vitamins. Almost immediately, Patricia became extremely well and lucid on a very high dosage of vitamins. But her doctor was careless and because of inadequate hospital policy and medical care, the hospital diet was poor so she didn't eat much, and not having enough calories she became nauseated from the high doses of vitamins and, after an intravenous injection of Compazine, went into a coma.

Because the doctor refused to give us any explanation about this dangerous event, Patricia was immediately transferred to a rural hospital in New York State. The nursing services there were good, but there were no young people and the doctor was not very well acquainted with the full procedure necessary in mega-vitamin treatment. After three months there and no significant improvement, we finally decided to take the risk of sending Patricia to what turned out to be a terrible hospital, but one where her doctor was the chief practitioner of mega-vitamins. She did not stay there long. She was so anxious to get out that her doctor thought she ought to go home.

Patricia improved gradually and only became worse after discontinuing vitamins and after an overly stressful Easter weekend which involved skiing. One thing we were not aware of at the time is that excess physical stress can produce regression as well as mental stress.

Because of some internal pressures at home, the result of my fatigue and problems with siblings, Patricia became violent and had to be hospitalized yet again. The hospital was a good one and close to home and, although they had no vitamins and no active program, Patricia maintained her spirits well enough that with a great deal of encouragement, she was able to persuade herself that she could go to France. Patricia had an O.K. summer in France, though she experienced cyclical regressions in a French boarding school requiring eventual hospitalization for two weeks in the South of France and then two months in Fuller Memorial with Dr. Philpott. Patricia was discharged in January, 1971.

God had answered my prayers; my daughter's life was spared from cancer but her life would be that of a suffering soul. It would be no understatement to say that what happened to Patricia has affected the course of our family's life as no other series of events could possibly have done. Much of my work during and subsequent to the events of her ordeal has been concerned with dealing with issues involving suffering, healing, redemption, rescue and survival. I had no idea that I was to be involved with such concerns, that the synchronicities in my life would invariably be tied up with the sufferings of our daughter.

On a visit to Manchester, Vermont for a conference on Holistic Health, held at the lovely Equinox Hotel, I met for the first time, the renowned researcher and clinician, Dr. Ernest T. Krebs, who developed the use of laetrile for the treatment of cancer—a great panacea for pain—but it was pooh-poohed by the FDA, representing as they did, Cancer, Inc. What else is new? Anything to preserve the mega giant profit-driven industry whose clinical application is sometimes referred to as "cut, slash and burn." Dr. Krebs had no definite answer to my queries but he encouraged me to hang on.

As I describe some of the events from the time of my mother's death onward, it should always be borne in mind that behind it all, Patricia was and still is going through her ordeal, although much, much reduced, and that her course of life has not yet been resolved. Nevertheless, we have had some answers, though many remain outstanding to our many "whys."

Some years later on a trip to Paris, my husband took me and our daughter, Suzy, to Maxim's, the fabled restaurant of 19th century lore, where I was inspired to write this French poem, ever mindful of our suffering Patricia whom we left at home.

Speech of April 10, 1985
Written during dinner at Maxim's in Paris

LES QUATRE NIVEAUX

Oh, welcome, to ye, beloved members of the fourth level, be of good cheer, members of the greatest level of God's bounty.

Les quatre niveaux:

Le premier: Ceux qui ne savent rien et qui ne saurent rien. Ce sont "les perdus."

Le second: Ceux qui aperçoivent ceux qui s'occupent du quatrième niveau et s'imaginent qu'un jour ils s'en occuperont ou partagreont au troisième niveau. Ils pensent qu'ils toujours un choix avant de devenir parmi "les perdus."

Le troisième: Face à face au quatrième niveau, ils n'ont aucun choix d'agir encore à ce niveau d'une facon ou d'une autre. Ils tâchent autant qu'ils peuvent de s'y joindre. Mais ils n'ont pas été choisis pour cela et ils le savent. Ils n'ont ni les dispositions ni le choix. Ils s'occupent aussi entièrement que possible du quatrième niveau.

Le quatrième: C'est le message principal de Jésus, le Christ. Bienaimés du quatrième niveau, D'où venez-vous? C'est la question du Sphinx! De la Passion de l'Univers; Vous êtes le col de l'Univers,

Pourquoi?

THE FOUR LEVELS

Translation of the speech in French of April 10, 1985.

The first one: Those who know nothing and will know nothing. They are the "lost ones".

The second one: Those who perceive the fourth level ones and believe that one day they will take part or will share at the third level. They think they will always have a choice before becoming "lost ones".

The third one: Facing the fourth level they have no choice yet to act on this level in any way. They try as much as they can to join it. But they have not been chosen for this purpose and they know it. They have neither the dispositions nor the choice. They dedicate themselves as thoroughly as possible to the fourth level.

The fourth one: It is the main message of Jesus, the Christ. Beloved of the fourth level. Where do you come from? It is the question posed by the Sphinx! by the Passion, by the Universe; You are the way of the Universe.

Why?

CHAPTER THIRTY-FIVE

A NEW JOURNEY BEGINS

I had been inspired to attend the conference of the Holy Spirit in New Orleans with my sister-in-law Lili in the Fall of 1987. It was a mind-blowing experience for religious people. There were 50,000 in attendance in the super-dome there. Approximately 52% were Roman Catholics and the rest included Protestants, Evangelicals and two Messianic Jewish groups. There were also a couple of groups who were specifically ministering to homosexuals who were trying to achieve celibacy. At this point I should share one of my major locutions (word of knowledge, as the Protestants call it) that I received many years ago.

At that time, I was heavily involved in attending conferences on brain functions—mostly on the West Coast—in an attempt to gain further knowledge that could lead to my daughter's recovery. The main message was the existence of a continuum of disabilities that are related since they all originate from a primitive part of the brain, the brain stem, and its neighbor, the hypothalmus. The diseases on this continuum in a roughly escalating scale of disability, are the chronic obesity syndrome, alcoholism, schizophrenia and homosexuality.

I was born with the chronic obesity syndrome. Both my father and maternal grandmother were fat. I was that cuddly, but unfortunate, fat baby. Dr. A.T.W. Simeon, a British physiologist, and colleague of the great Haldane, did much research in the biological science in the study of obesity, known as bariatric medicine. Shortly after the First World War, Dr. Simeon, a civil servant, was sent to India to treat the largely obese sons of the Maharaji. Most of them were pear-shaped and had a condition known as Orchidism (undescended testicles). Dr. Simeon was one of the foremost physiologists of his time and went on to write, what I believe to be (an opinion shared by my former beloved physician, Dr. David Sheinkin) one of the great books of the 20th century, a book entitled, *Man's Presumptious Brain*. Dr. Simeon used the classical treatment for Orchidism—injections of human chorionic gonadotrophin (HCG), in India and observed that this not only corrected the Orchidism but also the pear-shaped look was lost. The doctor wondered whether he could put these young men on a diet as well to see what would happen. He very carefully devised a diet of exactly 500 calories per day with similar proportions of carbohydrates and protein, but no fat at all; his patients were not even allowed to use cold cream on their skin. They all lost 1 lb. per day, during which time they did not feel hungry at all. They continued to lose weight until they reached their individual ideal weight. Only then did they become hungry.

In the 1930's, Dr. Simeon moved to Rome, and after World War II he became affiliated with the Hospital of Santo Spiritu where he continued his practice. Patients came from all over the world. Models from New York City, who wanted to be rid of extra inches on their hips, and couldn't do it any other way, would seek him out. I read about this in a *Town & Country* magazine in the 1950's while I was living in California, and I told myself that whenever I returned to New York, I would go on that diet, since I had a difficult time keeping my weight down, having to resort to nerve wracking amphetamines and the like, from time to time, out of desperation.

In New York City, *Harper's Bazaar* featured a female opthalmologist, probably looking to increase her income, who also practiced bariatric medicine by successfully using this HCG treatment as it was called. So when I moved back East and my husband had to go abroad for five weeks on business, I commuted into the city six days per week for five weeks and lost 22 lbs. It was like a miracle, so I continued using this method of preventing obesity until my health deteriorated after several crucial and tragic events in my life, culminating in a hysterectomy. After that, the treatment no longer worked. However, I did manage to keep my weight down through frequent visits to health spas. Chronic obesity syndrome is found where there is a lack of an appropriate fat metabolism in persons who are genetically programmed. The hypothalmus does not do its work because of that same old goblin, stress. Events in one's life that produce negative responses cause stress.

Stress may be either positive—eustress, or negative—distress. Enough distress will make a person with chronic obesity syndrome put on more weight without any changes in diet. This has been proven in many studies.

When my brother died, quite suddenly, the fact that I had hardly seen him throughout the years made it much worse, of course. I felt the tremendous sense of loss of someone whom I loved but had hardly known. It was as if all the grief of my poor brother's life could not have been redressed.

I do not know what it was, but shortly thereafter I was unable to get out of bed for almost a week. Whether this was the same malaise that afflicted Elizabeth Barrett and caused her to be bedridden before she met Robert Browning, that other great poet who took her off to the wilder shores of Italy, or whether it was the beginning of chronic fatigue syndrome, I do not know. What I do know is that during that week that I was unable to get out of bed, by some extraordinary coincidence, there was a TV presentation by two famous vitaminologists and health food buffs, Durk Pearson and Sandy Shaw, who were carrying on a flourishing business in Santa Barbara. I am sure you must have seen them. They all looked like hippies (although we were then in the '80's) with long stringy grey hair, beads, some kind of turban around their head and wearing zany smiles.

What they said made so much sense to me: "When you have

five events happen in a short period of time—A followed by B followed by C followed by D etc., you connect the dots and you sometimes get the Aha, an insight." So sure enough, when they said, "If you have these symptoms ending with not being able to get out of bed for a whole week, then maybe you are dying," it got to me. I did not say, "Aha." I said, "Uh! Oh! Maybe I am dying." That was when I knew that if I did not to do something about my health then I'd end up like my brother who was diagnosed as suffering from cancer, and three weeks later he died.

Subsequently, my husband had to make a business trip to Switzerland and I decided to tag along so that I could go to the grandfather of all health clinics, the Bircher Benner Clinic in Zurich. Dr. Bircher started this clinic around 1900, I believe, and was one of the great pioneers of what is now known as the health food movement. After all of four days there, I had this feeling that I was going to survive. The regime there included a great deal of hydro-therapeutics as well as the Bircher muesli—a wonderful creamy oat cereal made with oats soaked in pear juice the night before—with nuts and dried fruits. I then realized that I would have to continue going to these health resorts to restore my health and especially to keep my weight down.

I found such a place at the Rancha La Puerta health resort, and its younger, more lavish sister resort, the Golden Door, a spin-off of the Bircher Benner clinic, which was started in 1940 by a young woman, Deborah, then only 17 years of age. She was the daughter of health devotees who were influenced by Dr. Bircher. Deborah ran her resort with the help of her Romanian husband—a much older person—Edmond de Szekely Bordeaux, a scholar, philosopher and writer.

Because he was from a noble family, I believe de Szekely Bordeaux was able to gain access to the Vatican archives in the 1930's where he discovered a great deal about the Essenes, a religious sect which lived in the wilderness of Judaea. The Essenes purportedly trained John the Baptist to lead his ascetic life—eating locusts and wild honey (Matt.3:4)—in preparation for his ministry.

The second disease on this continuum of diseases, originating in the brain stem is, alcoholism. When I got this message I thought this was pretty interesting stuff. As Jesus said to Peter when he responded to his question, "Whom say ye that I am?" and Simon Peter answered and said, "Thou art the Christ, the Son of the living God." And Jesus answered and said unto him, "Blessed art thou, Simon Bar-jona: for flesh and blood hath not revealed it to thee, but my Father which is in heaven" (Matt. 16: 16-17). Likewise, only the "higher power" as God is called in Alcoholics Anonymous could have revealed this information to me.

Slowly, over the years, these facts have been disclosed on the front pages of the *New York Times*, of course. Where else? There are several types of alcoholism and the most prevalent, and hard to get rid of type, is found where the brain produces something called THIQ. The patient in an acute stage simply cannot stop drinking until he has had too much, and it soon becomes chronic. The result is that it wrecks that person's health and personality, as well as producing a negative impact on that of his family, to put it mildly.

It was God who told Bill W to start AA because, in the final analysis, only God could help an alcoholic to improve.

> To William G. Wilson [Bill W. Of AA]
> [original in english]
> 30 january 1961
>
> Dear Mr. Wilson,
>
> Your letter was very welcome indeed. I had no news from Roland B. anymore and often wondered what has been his fate. Our conversation, which he has adequately reported to you had an aspect of which he did not know. The reason was that I could not tell him everything was that in those days I had to be exceedingly careful of what I said. I had found out that I was misunderstood in every possible way. Thus I was very careful

when I talked to Roland B. But what I really thought about was the result of many experiences with men of his kind.

His craving for alcohol was the equivalent on a low level of the spiritual thirst of our being for wholeness.

How could one formulate such an insight in a language that is not misunderstood in our days?

The only right and legitimate way to such an experience is that it happens to you in reality, and it can only happen to you when you walk on a path, which leads you to higher understanding. You might be led to that goal by an act of grace or through a personal and honest contact with friends or through a high education of the mind beyond the confines of mere rationalism. I see from your letter that Roland H. has chosen the second way, which was, under the circumstances, obviously the best one.

I am strongly convinced that the evil principle prevailing in this world leads the unrecognized spiritual need into perdition, if it is not counteracted either by a real religious insight or by the protective wall of human community. An ordinary man, not protected by an action from above and isolated in society, cannot resist the power of evil, which is called very aptly the devil. But the use of such words arouses so many mistakes that one can only keep aloof from them as much as possible.

These are the reasons why I could not give a full and sufficient explanation to Roland B. But I am risking it with you because I conclude from your very decent and honest letter that you have acquired a point of view about the misleading platitudes one usually hears about alcoholism.

You see, alcohol in Latin is *spiritus*, and you use the same word for the highest religious experience as well as for the most depraving poison. The help therefore is: *spiritus contra spiritum.*

Thanking you again for your kind letter, I remain,

Yours sincerely,

C. G. Jung

* "as the hart panteth after the water brooks, so panteth my soul after thee, O God" (Psalm 42:1)

The third condition on this upward trajectory of the continuum is schizophrenia. In families where one of the parents or both are either over-weight or alcoholic, because of an impairment of the brain stem, there is a possibility that schizophrenia may occur.

Schizophrenia is such a complicated disease because it involves a great many other diseases and syndromes. In fact, there are few schizophrenics who are alike, as characterized by early orthomolecular researcher and clinical pioneer, New York based Dr. Alan Cott, in his book, *The Schizophrenias, Yours and Mine.* But there are certainly outstanding symptoms in the acute phase (such as hearing helicopters, for instance) as described by Dr. Carol North in her book, *Welcome Silence. I Never Promised You A Rose Garden.* It tells the story of a schizophrenic, Joanne Goldberg, in pre-tranquilizer days, goes into harrowing and horrific detail about the monsters present in her acute florid psychosis, treated successfully through the brilliant insightful talk therapy management of Dr. Frieda Fromm Reichmann. Joanne recovered and became a teacher of the deaf.

After attending a conference in London entitled, "The Biological Basis of Schizophrenia," (which was subsequently published as a book) I developed a hypothesis on schizophrenia. It seems that the genesis of this disease can be traced to certain bacteria from the gut that have escaped into and through a weakened blood brain barrier and lodge in the corpus collosum, which is the cavity separating the left and right hemispheres of the brain. This was also, no doubt, the "progenitor cryptocides," the mysterious bacterium alluded to earlier in this book in the Huxley lecture by Dr. Eleanor Alexander Jackson, concerning the discovery by her father, the brilliant researcher and neuro anatomist at the University of Buffalo, of this unknown virus. This central lesion is characterized by Dr. Lewis Thomas in his book, *Lives of a Cell*, in which he hypothesized right in the middle chapter of his book that he had a hunch that there was a central lesion involved with most disease states.

In the case of schizophrenia, the lodged bacteria can and often do manifest themselves in what I can only describe as "stuck right-brain behavior." I shared this with one of my mentors who was a pioneer in orthomolecular medicine, and a protégé of Aldous Huxley. He said it was an interesting hypothesis but I needed to prove it. (Next incarnation!—That's my usual joke. Only kidding, again.) Maybe next book.

The last on the ever ascending scale of disturbances of the central nervous system is homosexuality. I really did not understand it until two years ago when there was an article again on the front page of the *New York Times* which stated that studies showed that some homosexuals had problems with their, you guessed it, hypothalmus. Of all the people in these disease states, homosexuals suffer the most in their trip to recovery. I have a tremendous compassion for homosexuals and believe that some day they can be helped to have a better life, which will not include this terrible disability which is described as an abomination in the Bible.

CHAPTER THIRTY-SIX

SERVICE TO THE WOUNDED IN THE PUBLIC SECTOR

In the 1980's, since my husband and I had once more become involved in politics, we were called upon to give fundraisers for Republican candidates in our spacious home. One of those candidates was Prescott Bush, Junior., older brother of George W. Bush, and the elder son of the well-known Senator, Prescott Bush, Senior.

There was a fundraiser for Jim Buckley, brother of Bill Buckley, the brilliant author whom I first met at Yale and whom we saw from time to time at various functions. Not only did Bill come but also the then Vice President, George Bush. That was definitely an occasion not to forget.

We met with George Bush in Washington a few times after that. In fact, I remember that at the first Reagan/Bush inaugural, which we attended at the Hay Adams Hotel in Washington, DC, there were 202 Bushes from all over the East. I think my husband and I were the only non-members of the Bush family. George and Barbara are a gracious couple, if ever there is one.

PCMR (The President's Committee on Mental Retardation)

While campaigning for the Presidential nominee, Ronald Reagan, I was encouraged to seek appointed office in the public sector. In fact, it was the affliction of a good friend of mine—homosexuality—the very last affliction on the continuum, that prompted him to encourage me to seek office in the public health sector. His own disability made him so sensitive to the welfare of others, that he suggested that since I had acquired so much experience in the private sector in the use of alternative medicine in the care of my daughter, that I should try to work in the public sector in the area of health care for the mentally challenged or mentally ill.

It was he who encouraged me to pull out all the stops to get a public sector post, and with the help of many dear friends who wrote letters and recommendations, I was able to get a job, the closest thing I could get to taking care of the mentally ill.

My son, John was on hand to hold the Bible
for me for the swearing in

After a suspenseful waiting period, I was appointed to the President's Committee on Mental Retardation (PCMR). Since this was my very first appointment in the public sector, I was rather scared because, as you must know by now, my right brain does not inform my left brain what to do next, much of the time. Nevertheless, it was very sweet and touching to have my daughters Yvonne and Suzanne fly down to Washington DC for the swearing in ceremony. Moreover, on my reappointment, my son John was on hand to hold the Bible for me for the swearing in. I think my children thought, and rightly so, that I was doing everything I could to solve the riddle of their older sibling's affliction. On looking back, I could say that all that effort was not in vain.

Some memories of this period include some of the distinguished presenters in the field of orthomolecular medicine. During the early part of the '80's when I was at PCMR, I remember mainly that I made some very good friends. Our meetings, on the whole, were quite jovial, very much like President Reagan was himself, he who appointed us all. You could say, when we were not getting down to the business of serving the retarded community, we enjoyed each other's company very much.

I know that on the first day I was totally shocked that the computer record on me revealed that I was trying to make a movie on Our Lady of Guadalupe, with more emphasis on that instead of the Huxley Institute. That was very pleasing to me, and I guess not too surprising since the Reaganites of those years tended to be conservative Catholics and conservative Protestant Christians.

I remember Ginny Thornburgh, wife of Dick Thornburgh, Reagan's Attorney General, expressed interest in the efficacy of vitamins in the treatment of the retarded, since they had a retarded son, but I was never able to get hold of the main man in that field to lecture to us, Dr. Henry Turkel. He was the physician who devised a cocktail of vitamins to be administered in the treatment of Down's Syndrome patients under the age of 10. His remarkable treatment was totally banned by the FDA, despite evidence of its success.

Of all the members of that Committee, as many as 25% of us were interested in vitamins, and that group were mainly Californians like myself. The major accomplishment was getting Dr. Jeff Bland, Dr. Pauling's protégé, to write that famous paper on complementary medicine (a term at that time used only in British medical journals), which Dr. Bland brought to the U.S.

During my tenure on the National Council on Disability—a later appointment under George Bush—I was able to present a paper on the subject, thereby making my contribution in bringing the term Complementary Medicine to the knowledge of the general public.

CHAPTER THIRTY-SEVEN

COMPLEMENTARY MEDICINE

(A paper presented to the National Council on Disability)

I reiterate that it was my daughter's suffering that catapulted me into a search for healing and consequently into the field of health care. I became affiliated with the Huxley Institute for Bio-social Research and founded the first Chapter in Fairfield County, Connecticut. Later, finding that there was a bulwark against complementary medicine, i.e. the use of vitamins and enzymes in healing, I saw the need to start my own foundation, to address the needs of the sick and disabled planet!

A little history is in order here to understand what complementary medicine means and its relationship to disorders of the central nervous system.

The Second World War brought profound changes in the world, including the world of medicine. Prior to the Second World War, foods could not be preserved except by salting and curing. In other words, foods had to be fresh so as not to become spoiled.

Infectious diseases and sepsis of the infections from wounds had killed so many men in the First World War that much interest centered on finding new methods for, not only the preservation of foods, but the development of drugs to combat and prevent these disabling and fatal conditions in the future.

It became imperative that American industry and global industry, for that matter, find solutions to these problems so that imperishable foodstuffs could be sent to the men on the front lines and drugs could be discovered to combat infectious diseases, which invariably spread if not checked.

Sir Alexander Fleming discovered penicillin during those war years and it only became available to civilians, under extraordinary circumstances, right after the war. Because my mother's godfather, Dr. Patrick (Dinty) O'Brien, was head of research at the Rockefeller Institute, as it was then called, he was able to get some precious penicillin which saved my grandmother's life. She was then dying of blood poisoning in Paris in 1947, when I was a teenager. The experience was as scary as it was miraculous.

PIONEERS OF COMPLEMENTARY MEDICINE

Linus Pauling   Aldous Huxley

Humphrey Osmond   Abram Hoffer

The evolution of these two major discoveries, (the preservation of foods and development of new drugs) which actually helped guarantee in its way the Allied victory, paved the way for what many consider, and what the demographics and statistics indicate, the often sorry state of medicine and American health today. Americans have latched on to "Alternative" medicine, paying for it mainly out of their own pockets.

To begin at the beginning, let's consider what happens to the food that we take into our bodies. The development of new chemicals made it possible to develop a very large agricultural production—agribusiness—which over the decades culminated in depleting our soils of the vital minerals necessary for the maintenance of human health.

Furthermore, the ever growing chemical industry, which during the war had been corralled into the development of explosives and other weapons, also expanded into other fields. Profits from the weapons industry were so enormous that the chemical industry was more than happy to use its newly-developed technology in as many arenas of American consumption as possible. What to do with waste products, while of course making a profit from their disposal, became a reasonable business objective. For example, ice cream contains some of the same chemicals used to make Kleenex. If people only knew what they were eating, from most American dispensers of food, the supermarkets, fast food outlets and vending machines, they would probably gag or vomit, the latter being preferable since they would at least get these nasty chemicals out of their systems. What has the American diet become? Chemicals, chemicals, and more chemicals!

The American cigarette industry has come under a lot of attack for promoting the use of its dangerous and addictive products. Nevertheless, the assault may be more hypocritical than necessary as there are many other factors in the production of consumer food, cosmetics and other products that are equally dangerous. Smoking may not be as popular or socially acceptable as it once was, but some smarter smokers (if that isn't an oxymoron) whom I know, roll their own, including a former head of the Department of Psychiatry at a prestigious, leading hospital in New York City. It is the chemicals used in American cigarettes (as well as others made elsewhere using similar methods) which actually pose a greater threat to one developing lung cancer, emphysema and a host of other hideous diseases, than the nicotine—the amine produces the excessive endorphins which cause the addiction to the pleasurable sensation produced by an over abundance of endorphins.

But World War II brought other changes in medicine as well, most notably in the field of psychiatry. Hitler's anschluss drove a large number of psychiatrists from Germany and Austria to our shores, many of whom had been trained in the Psychoanalytic School of Sigmund Freud.

To this day, many psychiatrists in this country are still under that influence, which is now deemed irrelevant, if not baleful, in many quarters of the psychiatric establishment, as well as from complementary physicians, for the treatment of the seriously mentally ill. Freud, himself, in the last decade of his life, revealed that he thought the problems of those with serious mental illness, such as schizophrenia and manic depression, were undoubtedly biochemical in nature and would be treated as such in the later decades of the century, and he was right.

For instance, among hundreds of instances now, the researchers Ròhan and Ganguli at the University of Pittsburg found that some schizophrenias were essentially an immune disorder. This amazing discovery made its way to the front page of *USA Today* 10 years ago.

Right after the war, Swiss researchers serendipitously found the new chemicals known as phenothiazines, which had been developed for the treatment of another disease, but had a remarkable effect in that population who were also mentally ill. In other words, they got better.

At about the same time in Saskatchewan, Canada, two distinguished researchers, both M.D/Ph.D's—Abram Hoffer, who directed the Department of Psychiatry at Saskatchewan Hospital, and his colleague, Humphrey Osmond, who was a disciple of and also Aldous Huxley's personal physician in the last years of his life—, were grappling with the problem of the seriously mentally ill. They decided to look at the history of it in the literature since one of Dr. Osmond's specialties was the history of mental illness, gained from years of experience at the Maudsley Hospital in London.

They did the research and discovered that many of the psychoses in the literature were produced by people suffering from pellagra, a deficiency of vitamin B3, nicotinic acid, in the diet. Thereupon, Drs. Hoffer and Osmond made medical history, only for the cognoscenti, alas! when they administered mega-doses of vitamin B3 to acutely (or recently) ill male schizophrenics in a hospital population where they conducted a controlled study. As a matter of fact, it was the first double-blind study in the history of psychiatry as we know it today and virtually all of the male schizophrenics became well, since chronicity had not set in.

So how come this amazing medical discovery was not immediately accepted by the American psychiatric establishment? I suppose it is for the same reasons that American smokers don't roll their own cigarettes in larger numbers; ignorance, apathy and the brainwashing of doctors and patients by the greed driven drug and chemical industry.

Incidentally, this is the reason I and one-third of the American population spend upwards of $23 billion, according to 1999 estimates, on alternative or complementary medicine—an amount still largely out of our own pockets and not covered by most health insurance providers—because it works and it's cheap.

A case in point is our own, eldest daughter, Patricia, who suffers from chronic schizophrenia and has also lost a leg and uterus to cancer, but nevertheless is working slowly towards a master's degree in helping other disabled people in a holistic nutrition program. In her case, the pioneer M.D/ Ph.D, whose treatment our daughter has barely swerved from for fifteen years, is that of the late Dr. Carl Pfeiffer. He established the Brain-Biocenter in Princeton, New Jersey, after having been one of the heads of the Department of Pharmacology for the U.S. Navy during World War II.

Dr. Pfeiffer's work was heavily influenced by the pioneer researcher, Dr. Henry Schroeder, whose laboratory was located in Brattleboro, Vermont, where the air, being almost 100% pure, contributed to the conduct of experiments with greater accuracy. Dr. Schroeder had found that mineral levels affect human behavior.

Again, from the laboratory to the clinic, it is more than reasonable to lay the blame in large part, on the then woefully ignorant agribusiness, which has so successfully demineralized the soil on which the production of foodstuffs depends. Foods which would supply the minerals in normal healthy amounts to the American population do not, thereby contributing to a deleterious effect on the central nervous systems of millions of people.

The evolution of Dr. Pfeiffer's treatment is best seen at the only half-way house of its kind in the U.S. called Earth House, where so many last resort patients have come away with extraordinary results. I credit our daughter's stay at Earth House for her eventual significant amelioration of schizophrenia.

The last great pioneering scientist, who must be mentioned in discussing the holistic recovery of the mentally ill by complementary medicine in the U.S. was my friend, the late Dr. Linus Pauling, who did much to popularize the beneficial effects of Vitamin C. But Dr. Pauling's work on Vitamin C was not entirely his own original research but was largely attributed to the work of Dr. Irving Stone, who was the chief presenter at the first major conference (in 1971) of the Huxley Institute, formerly the American Schizophrenia Association, in New York City.

Dr. Stone spoke on his early research which found that humans are no longer able to synthesize their own Vitamin C but must obtain it through external means (largely supplements). Dr. Stone also found that it was crucial that enough vitamin C was present in the diet not only to combat scurvy but, moreover, because there definitely existed in the human race endemic ascorbemia, or Vitamin C avitaminosis (deficiency). This last factor accounts increasingly so for the prevalence of the common cold, allergies, many cases of cancer, which has a viral component, and, most of all, viral infections, in which schizophrenia is implicated.

The work of the late Dr. Richard Klenner, of North Carolina, at Rockefeller University in the 1930's demonstrated unequivocally in laboratory animals that a lack of vitamin C results in pronounced anomalies in health and behavior that is related to similar deleterious effects in humans.

All the preceding research results were pooh-poohed by the American medical establishment for the usual deplorable reasons, i.e., ignorance, apathy, and the lack of desire in American doctors to return to medical school for, and, inevitably, the heinous effects of the drug conglomerates on the medical school curricula. Additionally, the enormous profits drug companies were making and were willing to share, were factors.

Consequently, American physicians are still turning their backs on vitamins to the point of being silly about it sometimes, but this trend is finally changing.

Dr. Roger J. Williams, another pioneer who synthesized pantothenic acid in the forties and was a researcher at the University of Texas, Austin, wrote a book entitled *Biochemical Individuality*, as well as a paper called, "Why the Climate in Medical Education Must Change." These seminal works are more true now than ever.

We now have complementary medicine on the map in the United States, thanks in part to Dr. Jeff Bland who, when he was an intern in Dr. Pauling's laboratory, wrote the first major paper on complementary medicine called *Complementary Medicine* (appropriately enough). He wrote this paper at my behest to present while I was serving on President Reagan's President's Committee on Mental Retardation.

Subsequently, Dr. Dean Ornish funding his own research, finally produced definitive research results showing that heart disease can be reversed by diet, exercise, and supplementary vitamins and minerals in his book, *Reversing Heart Disease,* and subsequent books.

Even the *New York Times*, in June and August of 1997, published the news of the studies which demonstrated that vitamin E, folic acid, and B6 are also antidotes against heart disease. Finally, I would like to conclude with the story that people like me, a presenter, pro tempore, and former member of the National Council on Disability, like to tell about the medical philosophy of the ancient Mandarins in China. The ancient Mandarins were probably the only people of early times who were able to implement the lifestyles that are now available to the middle- and upper-classes of industrialized nations today.

The ancient Mandarins said that it is preferable to live in a fashion in which one does not become ill in the first place. In other words, I might say, "Good luck."

Secondly, if one was not able to attain this felicitous state, then one would have to consider intervention. As was the case with the ancient Chinese, intervention would be the administration of herbs following a scientific knowledge of this subject.

If one found oneself in the sorry state of not being able to escape ill health or disease by the administration of herbs, then one would have to resort to the "barbaric" measure of acupuncture. Very broadly speaking, this was the credo of the ancient Mandarins for human health.

(It was in the Huxley years that I befriended the son of the editor of the *Journal of Chinese American Medicine*, Dr. John Kao, and developed an interest in Oriental medicine. We had a party in our "historic pool house" of *Swimmer* fame, with Norman Cousins as guest of honor, as well as Dr. Kao. Chinese medicine was here to stay.)

How do we compare the modern medicine and psychiatry of America today? With the exception of accidents and acute bacterial infections and disabilities, should the case of barbaric intervention, i.e., surgery and its prohibitive costs, be replaced by a holistic approach? By a lifestyle oriented towards the primary prevention and secondary prevention (addressing the prevention of worsening of symptoms and amelioration of the disease process, especially for the mentally ill) of disease? The answer is, of course, increasingly "Yes."

We need to consider these facts in the pursuit of the truth, the truth which has the power to set us free.

CHAPTER THIRTY-EIGHT

FURTHER APPOINTMENTS
IN THE PUBLIC SECTOR

During my five-year stint on PCMR the only place I could get alternative medicine, demonstrated as being effective, was in a chapter of a book entitled, *Curative Aspects of Mental Retardation*, by Dr. Jack Stark (whose own son was retarded) and Frank Menoloscino, M.D., Head of the Department of Psychiatry at the University of Nebraska, a member of our Committee. Dr. Menoloscino, a completely charming man of Italian descent, was full of passion in the good sense of the word. He also had a passion for antique cars (as I do) and he even asked me to find some for him in Greenwich, Connecticut, at Malcolm Pray's place. Pray was a fellow Republican Eagle. Unfortunately, I wasn't able to deliver before dear Dr. Menoloscino died.

That part of the book where the doctor suggests a curative aspect of mental retardation, such as the treatment of Down's Syndrome through alternative medicine, was completely ignored by the FDA. Dr. Menoloscino restated the findings of Dr. Donald Davis, an advocate of Dr. Turkel's intravenous vitamin treatment for Down's Syndrome children under the age of ten, which from the slides of these subjects, showed promise. Under this treatment, as I have previously mentioned, the functions of Down's

Syndrome children were found to improve by upwards of 30 per cent if given an intravenous cocktail of enzymes, at the earliest possible age. Dr. Davis recommended that this "cocktail" should be administered in accordance with the guidelines of the eminent Henry Turkel, M.D., who had offices in Detroit, Michigan, and Bern, Switzerland. Dr. Turkel showed us his tapes to prove this theory. Imagine what could have been achieved if all of us in the alternative medicine movement had been able to fight the AMA, FDA, APA, and especially the drug companies. The lives of untold thousands of Down's Syndrome children and their families might have been dramatically improved. Hopefully we can achieve something in the thousand years of peace that are fast approaching—if indeed the New Jerusalem is about to appear.

Greeting Nancy Reagan

One of my presenters besought by me, at one of our meetings, was also the very brilliant Dr. Richard Kunin of San Francisco, who spoke of the importance of the use of folic acid in the prevention of many diseases, but especially for prevention of Spina Bifida. Only one or two people were interested in this since

297

Dr. Kunin's brilliance went over most everybody's head. A few years later this important piece of information was taken up when I was on the National Council on Disability (NCD) and then it took off, thank God.

I did not complete my second term on PCMR, since I felt I had done all I could do with secondary prevention of various conditions which cause mental retardation.

HUD—Committee on Housing For Handicapped Families

In 1989 in the interim period, much to my surprise I was appointed to the Committee on Housing for handicapped Families under HUD Secretary (Housing & Urban Development), Jack Kemp. Well, I thought, this is really going to be a case of thinking on one's feet (the whole point of the curriculum at the Center for Creative Leadership, in Greensboro, North Carolina) because I don't know too much about housing. Newly sworn members did the dutiful bureaucratic thing by going to the White House to meet Secretary Kemp, as well as Nancy Reagan who definitely disapproved of the way I looked. My clothes were not fresh from the cleaners and my hair was not well groomed (and I did not have any face lifts like hers).

To put it mildly, life was very difficult for me in the 80's— what with troubles with the Shroud investigation, Patricia being very sick, and the first signs of my employer's illness, I had no time for a wardrobe concièrge or a hairdresser—a symbol of status for females in the public eye.

This was an appointment for one year only, which meant that there were going to be just two meetings, the second of which coincided with an opportunity for me to meet Pope John Paul II in November 1989, so I only attended the one meeting in March.

The first committee meeting I thought was an interesting challenge. We were given an assignment, which was to describe the ideal housing for the handicapped, the answer to which had to be supplied from the top of one's head, so to speak. All of the male committee members were in one way or another connected to the building trade, and they were all in wheelchairs, so they were experienced as well as highly motivated. Since I had a handicapped daughter and I was given the opportunity to work during the Reagan administration, I was able to prove that I had a reasonable amount of creative ideas and therefore could possibly come up with some creative and productive answers as well.

I remember that in my answer to our assignment, I proposed that housing for the handicapped should be provided in buildings with appropriate multiple accommodations in a geographical area where the size of the population was large enough to justify this kind of housing. I asserted that ultimately such an arrangement would be more cost effective, but looking back on this, maybe it was not a good idea psychologically.

It was like being back in academia, providing an answer on the kind of exam which the French still dearly love. The object was to save as much as possible since in the 80's there were budgetary constraints in providing housing suitable for the handicapped, e.g. buildings with ramps and large bathrooms in a pleasant environment. If I had my way, housing for the mentally handicapped would be on farms, since they do so well in that environment.

I had to miss our second meeting in November 1989, in order to accompany my husband on a business trip to Rome. This would be an opportunity for me to meet with Pope John Paul II. So, after some deliberations as to how I could accomplish this, I decided to call his assistant, then Monsigñor Stanislaus Dziwicz, now Bishop, John Paul II's devoted right-hand man into whose arms he fell after the assassination attempt. I decided just to simply keep calling him up, speaking in French, because the Poles speak better French than English. I asked whether I could see the Pope on Wednesday morning. My husband did not think I would get in to see the Pope and neither did I, so he left on Monday to continue his business trip. It was seemingly rather hopeless, but after that phone call it occurred to me that such a miracle could only be achieved by—you guessed it—prayer.

So, in my sunny room in the Hotel Atlante (with its wonderful rooftop restaurant), I said the fifteen decades of the rosary with the special intention of seeing the Pope in his chapel, but especially directing my prayer to Polish Blessed Faustina Kowalska, of the Divine Mercy Devotions. Sure enough, with the help of my dear Bishop, on Tuesday afternoon, a very muffled voice informed me over the phone that I should be at the gate at 5.30 a.m. to wait in line for admission to the private chapel of the Holy Father for the early morning Mass that he said daily. Just as was the case with seeing Padre Pio, and now lately reading my E-mail in the early hours, getting up before dawn now has a special meaning for me.

Greeting the Holy Father

On that glorious morning of Wednesday, November 16th, when I arrived I was told to go the far right end of St. Peter's Square and stand in line before those large brass doors. We filed up the stairs leading to the hall facing the chapel where the Pope said Mass each morning at 6.30 o'clock.

Just being in the private chapel of the Holy Father was great enough, but this time the Mass was said in French and what's more there was a group of French-speaking nuns from all parts of the world, singing the most exquisite songs in French. It was like being in the presence of a choir of angels. Their singing was simply heavenly. The Pope was visibly moved and so were we all, the French speaking audience that we were. I would say that two thirds of the congregation were religious or clergy.

After Mass, those of us in the congregation, maybe 70 or 80, came to the great hall outside of his chapel to line up for the photo-op and a few words. When it was my turn, with a bit of chutzpah, I asked the Holy Father to bless my initiative concerning the Shroud of Turin. Of course, I also mentioned that I was trying to make a film about Our Lady Of Guadalupe for whom the Holy Father had great affection.

John Paul II made the first papal visit to the Tilma (the rough cactus cloth on which Mary's image is still preserved after 500 years!) in Mexico and he has been there twice since. On his coat of arms are the words "Totus tuus" [All yours (Mary).]

Some years ago the Holy Spirit inspired me to paint an icon of Our Lady of Guadalupe. It was a careful rendering of the original sacred image, since I have an almost photo retentive memory of what I see when painting or drawing. It seems that the Tilma had at least 217 colors!

After my meeting with the Holy Father, I decided to send that painting to him and got back a very nice (and brief) thank-you note from who else but Monsignor Dziwicz. His note included a brief statement from the Holy Father that making a motion picture about Our Lady of Guadalupe would be very helpful to the *cultus Marialis.*

I am still trying. I tried to get Franco Zeffirelli interested but he turned me down twice. Oh, well. Never give up. I like Monsignor Dziwicz more than I can say. Wherever the Holy Father is, he is never far away, hovering in the background. Bishop Dziwicz seemed very worried on TV recently because the Holy

Father looked particularly worn and sick during his recent visit to St. Louis, Missouri, and Mexico. I always privately celebrate St. Stanislaus' Day which is November 13th, a saint held in deep esteem by many Poles.

NCD—National Council on Disability

When George Bush was selected as Presidential nominee, the Republican National Committee (RNC) asked if we would do a fundraising for him and our celebrity draw for the event was to be Dr. Jeane Kirkpatrick. They gave me exactly 11 days to organize this fundraising event—a challenge if ever there was one! So doing what we had to do—on a dime—I think we raised a great deal of money under the circumstances, since we had had much practice in this area—giving parties! Our mailing list was still very fresh from our Reagan efforts, plus the fact that I had a lot of help from the RNC and the local people.

This event, plus the fact that I had served with President Reagan for five years and also under HUD Seretary, Jack Kemp, as well as all of my other activities. I was nominated for that very coveted position on the NCD, the top committee in the health sector. It was quite a rigamarole since this post required senate confirmation—(just like Clarence Thomas!) I had to send in forms and was subjected to FBI clearance. I believe they called 42 of my closest friends! That was a challenge—some of whom were laughing at being called by the FBI about poor old Annie and could have made up some funny things, as they told me later they were tempted to do, but fortunately refrained from doing so. Many thanks to you all.

For that fortuitous honor I was prompted to do what I always do when something of that nature comes along—give a party. My dear son, John, was able to find a nice hall at the Army & Navy Club so I gave a party for all of my Washington friends. They practically all came. Bless them. Even Jim Buckley, the dear and distinguished judge came—taking time out of his busy schedule.

They came to see me off to my first quarterly meeting which was to be held the next morning, in Las Vegas, Nevada, of all places. There is something positively surrealistic about leaving all those loyal and kindred spirits in this lovely cadre, taking a night flight to Las Vegas, going through the surreal underground of a Las Vegas night club passing, along gambling tables and slot machines—one arm bandits—on the way to my hotel room. I said to myself, "Is this what this is going to be like?" The other trips were more refreshing and edifying than this one, thank God.

The thing I loved most about this job was working on the sub-committee briefly with that wonderful ex-football player, Texan, Kent Waldrup. He became a paraplegic after an accident, as a result of which he started a foundation for paraplegics. Both he and his wife, it seemed, are from well-to-do Texas families, and Kent had a deep commitment for service. It was always a pleasure working with him. We co-chaired the committee on prevention—mainly secondary prevention, which means preventing the disability from getting worse or ameliorating it. We worked in liaison with the Centers for Disease Control and Prevention (CDC) in Atlanta and traveled there quite frequently to work with our opposite numbers in that organization. It was in that milieu, that I was able to make my best contribution. Having conferred with CDC and *Prevention Magazine* on our earlier work in the use of folic acid for the secondary prevention of disabilities, believe I influnced them enough to post bulletins at their various prevention centers, being set up that year throughout the USA, to alert pregnant young women to take folic acid.

Two years later, I noticed that that information had spread to health food magazines in this country and to British medical journals. All I can say is, "Thank God."

I did not make as many close friends as I had on the PCMR. Maybe the Reaganites were more overjoyed at being elected since it was the first time a Republican had been in power for a long while. Nevertheless, it was quite an extraordinary experience! Since the job was more powerful it was also more political and some members, not unexpectedly, resisted the idea of alternative medicine.

My job became fruitful after the election of the current President in 1992, strangely enough, when a new Director, Marca Bristo, was appointed. Marca Bristo was a nurse midwife who became wheelchair-bound after an accident. I suppose this experience also brought on some emotional problems because when I brought my handicapped daughter to meet her, something special occurred in my heart, if in no one else's. I believe Marca was moved by that meeting, and so when my time ran out in 1995, she nevertheless appointed me to be the presenter of a paper at a Summit Conference entitled, "The Future of the Disability Movement," in Texas in 1996.

The second conference on alternative medicine was held in 1997 in San Diego. At the request of my successor, Rae Unziker, who represented the mental health movement, I presented a paper which did generate the interest of quite a few people. After all, the American people are now—budgets permitting—beginning to call the shots about the manner of their health care.

CHAPTER THIRTY-NINE

THE TILMA OF GUADALUPE AND THE SHROUD OF TURIN

The image from the Shroud of Turin
and the Tilma of Guadalupe

These entities not only brought an opportunity to alleviate suffering as a response to our daughter's travails, but seemed to go hand-in-hand with an increase in my spiritual activity.

It was the year 1977 that Henry King gave me the job of finding the money to make the film *Our Lady of Guadalupe*. That same year that the Holy Spirit inspired me to launch the Fourth

World Foundation. These mysterious but awesome events, which are continually unfolding, began around the same time.

Our Lady of Guadalupe, according to Henry King's script, is basically the saga of what happened in Mexico at the time the Virgin of Guadalupe appeared to the Indian, Juan Diego, or Singing Eagle in Aztec, and the story of that apparition. The convergence of that miracle, which happened 450 years ago, and the events of today will follow. The first of my many peregrinations in finding the $1.5 million required for the production of the movie of *Our Lady of Guadalupe* was a trip to a Brother Leo.

Brother Leo was a monk who, monk or no monk, became the manager of the famous King Ranch in Texas, in those days of the 70's. Presumably he had access to all the millions of dollars flowing from this enterprise. Brother Leo was quite like the elusive Pimpernel—very hard to find—since many people were after him for the possibility of acquiring some of the money he controlled. When I managed to get hold of him in a motel in Sturbridge, Connecticut, of all places, (but that's another story) and told him of my plan, he wished me well but said that his major enterprise was to become involved with the street children of Chile. With whatever money he was able to keep, he intended to use it to rescue the children from the streets of Santiago and other large cities, who were being sold into prostitution, and care for them in a home, something like the wonderful Covenant House in New York City. I knew Our Lady of Guadalupe would say okay to that and give her blessing to Brother Leo.

Since there were only a few wealthy Catholics—in those days that was something of an oxymoron—I decided to go and see Harry John, head of the De Rance Foundation, which had the largest proportion of giving per foundation when compared with other Catholic and maybe all foundations worldwide.

I visited Mr. John at Blue Mound Road in Milwaukee, Wisconsin, and had lunch with him and his entourage, including his manservant, a poor beleaguered monk (whom Mr. John treated rather badly, I thought). He had an in-house chapel and displayed a few characteristics of the few very wealthy Catholics that I had met.

On that occasion, I also made a trip to Necedah, two and a half hours from Milwaukee, Wisconsin, where there is a shrine to Our Lady in which I was very interested. It was the abode of the late visionary, Mary Ann Van Hoof, a housewife with a large family, who had visions of the Blessed Virgin Mary, starting in 1950. Her visions were never approved by the local Bishop who had something in common with Harry John; he was a man with fixed views and opinions. In my opinion, the apparitions as seen by Mary Ann Van Hoof bore the hallmarks of authenticity, as per postcards which were painted according to her descriptions:-

One postcard depicts Alexander I of Russia slaying the dragon. Gadzooks! Is this a synchronicity or what?

Another shows Mary and Joseph and the baby Jesus on a donkey with the great pyramid of Giza in the background. This corroborates the apparition of Our Lady in Zeitoun (Heliopolis), close to where Mary and Joseph took refuge from Herod's slaughter of the innocents.

Our Lady of Zeitoun, Egypt

As far as I was concerned, these apparitions had personal meaning to me. Their newsletters are perhaps the most interesting of all apparition newsletters, since they have received knowledge of the most esoteric aspects of mysticism, as well as very down to earth advice, initially from the Blessed Virgin Mary such as: don't drive over 55 mph or consume white flour and white sugar! Thanks, Mom.

When I visited Necedah, there were plans to start a home for unwed mothers and another for homeless men. I don't know if any of these came to fruition.

Mr. John, of the De Rance Foundation, who had previously financed Roberto Rossellini's last film on Jesus, said that he might be able to finance Mr. King's movie if I could sell the Rossellini film to a distributor for $1.5 million, the money he put into it.

I decided to meet with Isabella Rossellini, while she was still married to Martin Scorsese, to try to get her permission to release her father's last masterpiece. However, when I saw the film it was much too long and needed a better soundtrack (musical background). All I could get for it was about $500,000 from an art movie distributor in the New York area.

I awaited further direction concerning that assignment which seemed to me too valuable to relinquish, as it seemed to have been given to me by God, Himself.

Meanwhile, Mr. King, who was in his 80's, had just come back to Los Angeles from a film festival at the Museum of Modern Art, in New York, in his honor. Unfortunately, on returning, he had a freak accident and destabilized very rapidly shortly thereafter and died. He had been "living on the edge," flying his own plane and going to Rumania every year to get youth shots from Ana Aslan, the fabled youth guru. Each year while he and his wife, Ida, were en route to Rumania I would meet him in the lounge of the Howard Johnson Hotel near Kennedy Airport, the best hotel at the airport at that time, to give him my fundraising progress reports—that was weirdly typical.

When I read of Henry King's death in the newspaper, I said, "Now what do I do?" I was not able to get the money from the De

Rance Foundation. As a consequence, I realized that I needed help and put an ad in the paper for a media assistant. As is usually the case, I was inundated with responses and also as usual, there seemed to be one that stood out from all the others, as reflected in "the loneliness of the long-distance runner."

This time, one J. Parisi sent his resume in with the most spectacular reference I had ever read in my life, from Robin McNeil and Jim Lehrer, who were just launching their news hour program and for which they would need a research assistant. This reference described this John Parisi as having been nearly the best intern McNeil-Lehrer had ever had. I knew this person had been sent to me by God.

During that memorable visit with Isabella in the apartment she shared with her then husband, Martin Scorsese, she showed me the pictures of Jesus and Mary above their bed. As I wandered to their large picture window in the rear of their lovely apartment, I was joined by Mr. Scorsese, and all of a sudden there was a bolt of lightning out of a clear blue sky, to which he responded almost cavalierly, "Don't worry. That happens to me."

As I was leaving, Isabella handed me a piece of paper and said, almost in an off-hand manner, "Here, this might be of some interest to you." I could not imagine what a great help that would be to me in time. It was a letter from a Will Brownell, who, at that time was civil defense editor of *Survive* magazine. He was soliciting support for his civil defense efforts. I wondered whether I should be involved in building shelters or whether I should be giving advice instead because of the Holy Spirit in my life. I was immediately inspired to write back to Will Brownell myself. To put it mildly, he was one of the most mysterious people I have ever met. It took me six months to catch up with him. We collaborated in producing a theme for this book entitled, "The Handwriting on the Wall." Then he disappeared from view for many years.

Will Brownell started a chapter in my life which was to parallel the entire enterprise of my promulgating Our Lady of Guadalupe and thereafter the Shroud of Turin. This parallel track turned out to be the world of international geopolitics and particularly the area of civil defense. At the time that Isabella Rossellini handed me that fateful letter by Will Brownell, it occurred to me that if humanity did not go down the track leading to God, i.e. the track of the Shroud and the Tilma, then surely the only other inevitable antithetical track would have to be that of civil defense and nuclear war.

The Guadalupe Research Foundation was then established after Mr. King died, with many professionals of note, such as Dr. Phil Callahan, entomologist, all-round scientist and author of many books on a bewildering array of subjects from religion to entomology. He was maybe the most brilliant man I had ever met. His credentials were impressive. He spent his leisure time trekking in the Sierra Nevada with his granddaughter.

Another member was Professor Jody Brant Smith, a Methodist minister who was obviously chosen by God to promote His Virgin Mother. These were joined by Vern Miller, the official photographer of the entire Shroud of Turin research expedition of 1978, who was also a professor at the Brooks Institute of Photography in Santa Barbara, and his colleague, Don Lynn, of the Jet Propulsion Lab in Pasadena.

While on the West Coast, I met a female lawyer by the name of Elizabeth McAdam, who was a friend of Vern and interested in all the Marian apparitions, especially the one in Zeitoun, Egypt. Elizabeth was also interested in the Shroud research project; in fact she was interested in both the religious and other facets of the supernatural. She was a very interesting and remarkable lady. She once had an amazing psychic at her home in Los Angeles, Alex Tanous, whose life story is one of the greatest psychic adventures you could ever imagine. All of this, of course, was as a precursor to the Marian apparitions of the 80's and 90's—to say nothing of the resurgence of Our Lady of Fatima. This prompted her to ask me to present a paper on the apparitions of Mary at the Los Angeles Society for Psychical Research for their meeting in January 1980. At that time, they seemed to be the only group interested in Marian apparitions. Since this was before the Medgugorje apparitions in 1981, which, if I may put it this way, put Mary back on the map of human consciousness, having been eradicated by Vatican II "Aggorniomento" which once again seems to have thrown Mother out with the bath water.

In order to get the paper written, I knew I had to "get out of the house." It just so happened that our former student barter employee, Mark Mascarenhas, a brilliant young man who had recently graduated from Fairfield University with a major in Communications, was getting married in New York City.

Mark was from a very distinguished South Indian family from Bangalore. They were all Roman Catholics and doctors and lawyers. Mark, himself, was very motivated; in fact, in terms of material success, he has come an enormously long way. He now owns all the rights to all the cricket programs on sports television for the U.K. Cricket is very popular in Britain and the British Commonwealth. I suppose that it is so because it is so enormously "elegant" in some ways, while encouraging team spirit in the players.

He was marrying a beautiful Italian girl, so people there were Indian and Italian, very merry, to say the least. I was due to fly to St. Martin that very day because that is where I proposed writing my paper on Marian apparitions. For some reason, the PanAm flight was leaving in the late afternoon and very conveniently right after the wedding.

Now, I had to get to the airport and it was snowing outside, so I wondered if I went down to the curb, whether I would be able to hail some vehicle. No sooner had I come down the steps than in pulls a large, white stretch limo. The driver rolled down his window and asked "Madam, may I take you some place?" I told him, yes, and asked him if he took me to Kennedy Airport how much that would be? The driver said "You are such a beautiful lady, it will only be $15.00." 1 said, "wow" to myself, but to him I said, "Thank you very much, sir. I appreciate it."

Now, I was a little late for my PanAm flight, it is true, and for some reason they had completely overbooked the first flight, but the people behind the counter said, "Don't worry, we're getting a second airplane." I said, "What?" And they said that yes, they were getting another 747. I was not about to ask why or any more questions, but just to accept this fact, as amazing as it was. (My husband said that maybe this was one of the reasons PanAm subsequently went out of business!) But I was very grateful and boarded the plane with one other person. I sat down in the front, since there was no one else on the plane except the crew and the other person who had boarded with me, and who sat in the rear and began to read a book.

So I sat there waiting for something to happen, such as more people and things like that. Then I asked the stewardess, "Do you think I could have some champagne?" And she said, "I don't see why not, since you are the only passenger." I and that other lady were the only passengers on that flight. I have a picture of me and the crew holding the champagne.

Frankly, I never got over that flight, but I realized it was because the Lord wanted to show me His appreciation for writing a speech about His Mother, no doubt, because I really didn't like flying at all, and this was obviously the only way to go—in your own 747!

My own private 747

The Summit Hotel where we stayed (my husband had joined me later) while on that trip was perfect. They hadn't started playing this horrible combination of music, like rock'n roll and other schlocky stuff, that lower priced hotels play at pools, such as an execrable record by Englebert Humperdink. (And I don't mean the Belgian opera, *Hansel & Gretel*.)

I went down by the pool and sometimes sitting up and sometimes lying on my stomach, during the next two days—three hours one day and four hours the next—I completed my speech on Marian apparitions (no notes or books). Had I been Shirley MacLaine, people would have called it channeling.

That paper, which was actually published by the Connecticut chapter of the *Journal of Religion and Parapsychology*, took on the famous comment from the remarkable Trevor Ravenscroft, "The woman is very powerful." In fact, that was the title of my paper.

Meanwhile, my Guadalupe project was still not off the ground. So armed with a letterhead and a few credentials, the prodigious John Parisi was able to talk NBC into financing a documentary on Guadalupe entitled, *The Guadalupe Miracle* as part of the *David Brinkley Magazine* program. The narrator was Bill Perkins and he is still going strong, I am glad to report. I see him introducing movies from time to time.

Since this documentary was to be filmed in Mexico, it was necessary for us to obtain permission from the Cardinal of Mexico and the Guardian of the Tilma, for filming and inspection of their national treasure at midnight when no one would be there.

John also prevailed upon the BBC *Everyman* series, whose principal director was Bill Nicholson, (of later *Shadowlands* fame) who made documentaries on the apparitions of the Virgin Mary, among other things, to send their crew to join NBC for the shoot in Mexico City. According to John, none of this could have happened without the efforts of a very talented producer named Angela, who was the head of the BBC production team.

This production almost didn't go through because they encountered the usual difficulties in the investigation of a sacred relic. The Tilma, like the Shroud of Turin, obviously is not an icon, but something real, a relic. It is an original, not just a reproduction. John Paul II declared the Shroud a relic. He also made the first public visit to view the Tilma of Guadalupe.

The American documentary was released on April 12, 1981. Astoundingly, on exactly the same day, the Shroud of Turin exhibit opened in Santa Barbara, California, at the Brooks Institute of Photography, where Vern Miller was a professor. This was beyond coincidence. THE ERA OF THE TWO HEARTS HAD BEGUN.

It was in the 80's that our daughter came home to live with us since she and her companions had both experienced burn out. It was that same year that we became directly involved in the Shroud of Turin. Our daughter's suffering was somehow inexorably linked with the Passion of Jesus.

On October 7, 1981, my husband and I went to the presentation of the findings to the world press by the American team; STURP (The Shroud of Turin Research Project), who had investigated the Shroud in 1978, when it was taken out of its casket and shown to the public by permission of the Holy Father.

By some amazing coincidence, that weekend of October 7, 1978, we received news in the local paper that the Californian scientist, Roger Sperry, had just won the Nobel Prize for his research in the hemispheres of the brain, and since this Associated Press release did not appear in the *New York Times* but in our local paper, I wondered how my spouse would have received it. You see the report mentioned that Sperry observed that women were much better attuned to receiving right-brain information, photographed, as he was, in his canoe during a vacation in Baja California. I held the article right up before my husband's nose as I beamed broadly; he gave me a Lucy smile.

Assuming that the Shroud studies were over and that the scientists would be interested in turning their attention to the Tilma of Guadalupe, I sought the permission of jet propulsion scientist from Granada Hills, California, Don Lynn, to make an announcement, the evening before the report of the Shroud investigation of 1978, to the world's press. I made a short speech asking if there were any Shroud scientists, now that they had finished publishing their studies (for the time being), who would be interested in investigating the Tilma of Guadalupe in the same way.

There was no substantial response forthcoming because, as usual, at that time, metaphorically and otherwise, Mary was still at the back of the bus. That was to change slowly over the years.

Finding that I was not able to raise money for research on the Tilma, I went to a fundraising professional, Mike Thompson, in Washington, DC through the recommendation of a conservative direct-mail expert. Thompson said, "Annie, you won't be able to raise any money for the Tilma, so why don't you try the Shroud?" I looked at my staff person, the prodigious Denny Brown, who was disappointed since Mary was a woman and Denny, of course, was a serious feminist. However, I got rather enthusiastic support from my husband, Harry, because, let's face it, the Shroud is about a Man!

And so, we embarked on the formation of a committee called The Shroud of Turin Exhibition Committee, which was to act as the liaison to artistic studies (my specialty, or so I thought) on the Shroud of Turin. Father Val McInnes, of Tulane University, became a member of the Exhibition Committee, through some remarkable coincidences. He was responsible for the exhibition of Vatican treasures in the United States in collaboration with Stuart Silver, the extraordinary museum director who had just finished the exhibit of King Tut at the Metropolitan Museum of Art in New York City, as well as that of the Vatican treasures. Fr. McInnes persuaded Stuart Silver to join the Board, thereby giving it extra weight and credibility. In other words, there was obviously only one act that could possibly follow King Tut and that was the Shroud of Turin.

Of course, we didn't have the enthusiastic response and support for a Shroud exhibit from the secular museum directors. We were all crazy about the Shroud. However, they were not. What else is new in a secular world (heading to perdition perhaps)?

Late in 1986, as we were proceeding on this uphill challenge, I remember the important call that Stuart made, displaying his brilliant good judgement and wisdom, which I had obviously not yet acquired. He said, "Annie, did it ever occur to you to call STURP (The Shroud of Turin Research Project) and see what they are up to before you go any further?" I replied, "Oh Gosh, no, but I will, right now."

We called and found out they needed funds to make a return visit. My husband, Harry, and I then tried to raise the funds to match my husband's generous gift so that we could send STURP back to Turin, Italy, where they could finish their investigation. This included the Carbon 14 dating, the preservation of the Shroud and, if possible, to make some observations that might suggest how the Resurrection occurred. Now, these were all tall orders, to put it mildly.

After an enormous amount of effort, and money expended, I must add, we were able to persuade Bill Buckley to lend his prestigious name to the fundraising given at the Union League Club, which was a consciousness- raising success in some ways, but not a financial success. America had already started its moral decline and museum shows about Jesus simply did not have the same appeal as King Tut, which Stuart produced as well as his subsequent exhibition entitled "Hollywood," also a fascinating and well wrought exhibit.

We had another large fundraiser at the 'F' Street Club, in Washington, DC, thanks to dear Bill Fitzgerald who, along with the President of Sacred Heart University, Thomas Melady, headed an organization called, "The First Friday Club," where Roman Catholics from Washington, DC and elsewhere would meet on the first Friday of each month at the International Club.

At this Washington fundraiser in May, 1977, it was a real challenge as to who would say grace since we had such a dazzling array of distinguished clerics. The honor went to our dear friend, Dr. Ernest Gordon, the aforementioned Presbyterian and former Dean of the Chapel at Princeton for 35 years, sender of

Bibles behind the Iron Curtain, and many other wonderful things. A strong electrical current crops up amongst clerics from time to time. We also had some Roman Catholic priests with us, too. Dr. Gordon said his grace in Latin, displaying God's great sense of humor.

This reminds me of when my husband was in Scotland on a business trip when the Maître D, at the golf club at St. Andrews, hit the gong, like at the beginning of J. Arthur Rank movies, and said, in his finest Scottish burr, "Please to say grace." On that occasion the honor went to my husband and the only grace he could think of, amongst all those Presbyterians, was a Roman Catholic grace! I smile when I think about all these things.

In any event, as we made our attempts to raise money to send the American team back to Turin to further their investigations, this time into the Carbon 14 testing of the Shroud, and also to look into the resurrection process, even with the enthusiastic support of the Papal nuncio at the time, Archbishop Pier Longhi, we were halted in our tracks by those mysterious anti-Christ forces, which in their Byzantine manner wend their way through Vatican politics.

Only shortly afterwards, however, were we told to cease and desist from all activities concerning the Shroud without any explanation whatsoever. It later turned out that there were nefarious elements within the Vatican who were anti-Christ forces and would therefore be against the Shroud project. No doubt these people were involved in the spurious 1988 Carbon 14 dating of the Shroud, which the world's secular press was only too glad to publicize to the world. The report stated that the Shroud was Medieval, not 2,000 years old, implying perhaps metaphorically that God is dead, or that the proof of His Passion and Resurrection does not exist.

Personally, I was convinced of its authenticity because of the measured scientific discoveries made in the investigation by STURP (The Shroud of Turin Research Project) in which there was irrefutable proof that on this cloth was the image of a man—

a tall bearded Semite who had been cruelly scourged, Roman style, with thongs attached to the end of a whip. He was wearing a sharp crown of thorns on his head from which blood trickled down on his face, which was corroborated in the original investigation, and was carrying a heavy object on his shoulder. There was evidence of a body wound. Finally he was crucified—death occurring by way of asphyxiation.

While the general skepticism regarding the authenticity of the Shroud has diminished somewhat, the spiritual battle against the principalities and spirits, as described by St. Paul, has increased exponentially since that time. The battle of the Wounded Heart continues.

Harry and I view the Shroud image

CHAPTER FORTY

THE WOUNDED HEART
AND THE TWO HEARTS

The confirmation of the reality of the Two Hearts came to me as I was sitting in my chair, the same chair in which I was sitting when I received news about the earthquake in Swabia, Germany. It was this brief message which came through my brain but I knew that it came from outside of me. It simply said, "My mother's and My heart are One." That same year I received confirmation of this reality of the Two Hearts in Ochre Court, Newport, Rhode Island, where I was attending Mass.

This beautiful gilded room in Ochre Court, the magnificent Administration edifice of Salve Regina University, might have been a music room in former times. Occasionally it serves as a concert auditorium but it is also used as a chapel for daily Mass. It was in this most beautiful setting that I received Holy Communion and experienced at the same time, that very overpowering scent of the presence of the Blessed Virgin—the unmistakable scent of roses and sandalwood. I am certain it was the Blessed Virgin. I have had many such experiences on previous occasions, which concur with the experiences of others who were also made aware of Her presence.

At first I did not know what to make of it, but it soon came to me that I had indeed received the Sacred Hearts in Holy Communion. It was truly the body and blood of Jesus Christ which includes that of His Mother, as stated in the apparition in Akita, Japan. "My Son is truly present in the Eucharist." Since Jesus, the Son of man was present, so was His Mother, who is part of His flesh and blood.

PART IV

CHAPTER FORTY-ONE

THE HEART OF MARY

Mary first shared her compassionate heart with me on the sorrowful night of the death of my mother; she revealed herself in her true life portrait that she left for mankind on a rough cactus cloak in Mexico City, on November 12, 1531, that of Our Lady of Guadalupe. It was this compassionate Mother, the Mother of mankind who, in her immediacy, replaced my earthly mother, and brought me through the previously described synchronicities. Through my sister-in-law's own inspiration I became involved in the project to make a movie on Our Lady of Guadalupe, which has turned out to be my life's work.

This life's work led to the formation of the foundation described in the previous chapter and to an intense involvement with many appearances of Mary on this planet. The same honored with a church in Moscow, Iberian Virgin, appeared as Guadalupe in Mexico; Fatima, Portugal, and finally in Garabandal, Spain. Other apparitions were in Medjugorje, Yugoslavia: Walsingham, England; Zeitoun, Egypt; and San Damiano, Italy. There have been manu others throughout the world.

Since the salutations of the Angel Gabriel to Mary who announced to her that she would be the mother of the Savior, and that of Elizabeth to Mary (Luke 1: 42. "Blessed are thou amongst women, and blessed is the fruit of thy womb"), it is plain that

Mary was blest among women. Since those biblical times, she has made many appearances on earth in her glorified body, which was assumed into heaven to join her spirit, like her son, Jesus.

Martin Luther wrote a beautiful paper on the "Magnificat," while he was detained in Wurtzberg Castle. The problem is that his successors threw the Mother out with the bath water of Roman Catholic and Papal excesses. This needs to be addressed as soon as possible, especially since the Father has chosen His Daughter as the Commander in Chief of the Forces of Good to combat the forces of evil in these latter days. (See John Bosco.)

> "Who is she that cometh forth as the morning rising, fair
> as the moon, bright as the sun, terrible as an army set in
> battle array?"

That England was Mary's dowry is no better illustrated than in the story of Our Lady of Walsingham:

In the reign of Edward the Confessor, in 1061 A.D., Lady Richeldis, widow of the Lord of the Manor of Walsingham, Parva, England, had a vision in which the Blessed Virgin Mary appeared to her three times and showed her a site similar to the one where the Angel Gabriel had appeared to her in Nazareth at the Annunciation. She was told to take the measurements of the Holy House and to build a reproduction of it in Walsingham. Carpenters were engaged and the question arose as to where it should be built. During the night, there was a heavy dew but in a certain meadow, two spaces of equal size ground, the exact dimensions of Holy House, remained dry. One spot was chosen on which to build a chapel. But, to the dismay of the carpenters, nothing went right in the construction. The next morning, after Lady Richeldis had spent a night in prayer, a miracle occurred—the chapel appeared completed and standing on the other dry site. It was concluded that Our Lady, with the assistance of the holy angels, had removed the House to the spot she herself had chosen.

Today, Walsingham, England, remains as a place of pilgrimage for miraculous cures and answers to prayers. It is truly an ecumenical pilgrimage site since all three Catholic religions are represented: Roman, Anglican and Orthodox.

A researcher of the events of this millennium, which began in the year 1001, concluded that nothing cosmically extraordinary seemed to have happened in the first century except the Norman conquest of England. Clearly, he was mistaken in terms of spiritual history since in that period the first apparition of Mary occurred. Revelation (or scripture)which was being written at this time, now included The Woman.

It seems as if The Woman wanted to make sure mankind got the message of the first revelation or scripture given to us by her Son and His disciples, and to make sure that the people continue to be exhorted to live the Gospel. That is why she asked for a replica of the house of the Holy Family to be built at Walsingham similar to the much later Holy House in Loreto, Italy.

Although the original basilica was destroyed by Oliver Cromwell during the post Reformation period, two columns still remain, standing as evidence of the grandeur and glory of architecture that existed before the Reformation. Oliver Cromwell destroyed many churches and chapels including the Basilica at Walsingham. England, considered Mary's dowry until those troubled Cromwellian days. In early Medieval days, Walsingham was a major Christian shrine. Now, a thousand years later, both Roman and Anglican Catholics alike, are beginning to make frequent pilgrimages to the Walsingham Center.

Some years ago the rector of the Shrine of Our Lady of Walsingham in England, Fr. Colven, visited America. I was able to meet him through his countryman, Fr. Timothy Campbell Smith, the rector of St. Paul's Episcopalian Church in Norwalk, Connecticut, where my very good friend Laurey Scott was a member. Laurey lost her daughter, Tatiana, to muscular dystrophy. She, herself, was such a great help to our children, a second mother to them and particularly to our daughter, Patricia, over the years.

She lives in Norwalk, Connecticut in the parish of the beautiful 18th century Episcopalian church, St. Paul's, with graveyard to match! Rev. Timothy Campbell Smith was close to my friend Laurey and therefore to me, too. He was a lovely person and devoted to Tatiana, who had designed the kneelers for the Mary Chapel, which is to the right of the apse, in his church, St. Paul's. I even had a ramp built for Tatiana but she was only able to use it a few times before her illness overcame her.

Fr. Timothy Campbell Smith asked me if I could give a party for some visiting Anglicans, one of whom was Fr. Colven. I invited many Episcopalian priests and other interested people to raise money for a hospice for pilgrims to Walsingham. Years later, on a trip to England, I was able to visit the church at Walsingham and although Fr. Colven was no longer the rector there, I was nevertheless very well received and was invited to return at any time.

Father Smith's parish population went downhill in terms of income, because the neighborhood had changed and so they developed fiscal problems. At about the same time in 1987, we were raising money in New York City for the investigation of the Shroud of Turin, and with Bishop Alexander Stewart so enthusiastically behind our efforts, he was able to corral rectors of many of the leading Episcopalian and Anglican churches in New York, I think maybe 10 or 12 in all. That was quite a coup. As I was heading for lunch at the Union Club with Bishop Stewart and the Episcopal priests to educate them of the tremendous significance for Christians and the whole world, about the Shroud of Turin, I asked myself, "What is a Roman Catholic housewife like myself doing among all these Anglican and Episcopalian ministers?" Well, I did my best, which was not good enough for a certain Father John Andrew, rector of the beautiful church of St. Thomas on 5th Avenue in New York, where a sign going back at least 40 years says enticingly, "Enter, rest, pray." How can anyone resist that? Well, during that luncheon at the Union Club, Father John Andrew left in something like a huff, before it was over, because I was talking about Mary.

However, when I wrote a letter to Father Andrew asking them to consider supporting Father Timothy Smith because their parish was wealthy, he did, *mirabile dictu*!! God bless him. He had remembered that very coincidentally we were dinner partners in the grand ballroom of the Waldorf Astoria, where I was inducted as a Dame of Malta and he was the head of all the Anglican Knights of Malta. Furthermore, and this was the most extraordinary part, almost two years to the day after that luncheon at the Union Club, I received in the mail an invitation to the unveiling of a statue entitled Our Lady of Fifth Avenue!!. Guess where? Nowhere else but at St. Thomas' Church on 5th Avenue, Father John Andrew's church. So there she is, a statue to Mary, the Mother of God—Our Lady of Walsingham—in the rear left of that church.

Of course I could not miss the opportunity to attend the unveiling ceremony, and took along with me, Father Timothy Smith. Cardinal O'Connor was there officiating as well, since his church, St. Patrick's, is just down the street and Fr. John Andrew beat him to the wire with a statue to Our Lady of Fifth Avenue!

When The Lady decides to go to work, she decides where she's going to go, who's going with her and she doesn't waste any time!

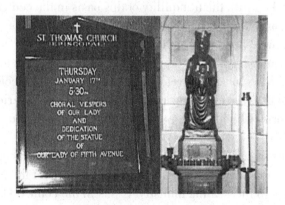

Dedicatory plaque and statue of Our Lady of 5th Ave.
in St. Thomas Church, Episcopal, New York City

CHAPTER FORTY-TWO

MEDJUGORJE
& THE QUEEN OF PEACE

F r. Michael Koonsman, rector of St. Mary's in the Bowery, was a good friend of Fr. Timothy Campbell Smith. He came to our house regularly for healing sessions conducted for the benefit of our family. He had been to Medjugorje, the site of many apparitions of the Blessed Mother, beginning June 24/25, 1981, the birthdays of our children, John and Marianne. Fr. Koonsman was so taken with the tranquility of this oasis in the center of war torn Yugoslavia, that he started a group called, Friends of Mary, in the Lower East side of New York. He was a major force for good in our lives, but his work on this plain was much too brief. He died too soon a few years later following a car accident in Yugoslavia. The following is an account of his experience in Medjugorje, which I have permission to share with you:

"I first heard of Medjugorje and Our Lady's appearances there in October of 1984. An *Anglican* priest, I had spent the previous five years in the healing ministry. It was in the context of a healing trio of Burrswood, an Anglican healing center in Britain founded by the stigmatic Dorothy Kerin, that I was first given material about Medjugorje. The way seemed immediately wonderful to me. Here was a great and prophetic teaching which already was bringing thousands of people closer to the Heavenly Throne and to one another. Here were people living out a teaching for peace in a profoundly spiritual way.

As a pastor, I began to keep the Medjugorje practices myself and then to share them with those who came to me for healing and spiritual direction. In various ways we began the three cycles of prayers, the seven cycles of prayers, the spontaneous recitation of the Creed, fasting, fuller participation in community and religious life, personal and community reconciliation, and the prayerful study of scripture and our Lady's messages. The effect was extraordinary: not only did people who had prayed all their lives find that their prayer deepened, but people who had never prayed before now could. Mary's promise that the hearts of those who followed this teaching would be changed was indeed true. None of these prayers were new, but in the context of Medjugorje they seem to carry a special spiritual grace.

Accordingly, in early March of 1985, I traveled to Medjugorje as part of my Lenten discipline for that year. While in Medjugorje I was able to be with the visionaries during the apparition and to present my concerns and petitions to Our Lady. Since that day, my life has continued to change, as have the lives of those whom I love and serve. Since the evening of my first petition in the apparition room, I have been wonderfully lifted; I am more conscious and open to the guidance of the Holy Spirit in my life than in my previous 15 years in the Priesthood.

The way of life in the village of Medjugorje also impressed me in a lasting way. Several things stand out: the compassion and strength of the Fansciscan clergy; the spiritual power of the liturgy in the parish church and the open-heartedness of the families who extended themselves so fully to myself and to other pilgrims. In summary, I was impressed by the breadth of the catholic spirit which these people embody so beautifully. It is a spirit to be cherished that is too easily overlooked in times such as these.

Returning last spring to the U.S. meant bringing home with

329

me the practices of fasting twice a week, saying the Rosary daily, and I believe, a touch of the love and simplicity and faith of Medjugorje. We now have several parishes, religious orders, individuals and families who are linking up informally with this teaching. Some are Catholic, some Orthodox or Anglican, and some Methodist, Buddhist or Presbyterian. Outwardly, we do start from different places, Yet we all share a sense that Our Lady's call to prayer and peace is an essential and central part of our lives. We call ourselves Friends of Mary—Marijini Prijatelji.

The following remarks speak of the immediacy and depth of response to this teaching from the Queen of Peace:

- " I was so glad to hear that God has a Mother. I am so happy now. It has been a wonderful surprise."
- " As soon as we started to the rosary, Mary was with me."
- " I've never prayed the rosary before. It is really changing my sense of time and eternity."
- " In fasting I am now closer to the heart of the whole world."
- " My entire prayer life is changed. I am closer now to all those for whom I pray."
- "I have waited all my life for this." (from a monk)

At this writing, I am again in Medjugorje in July of 1985. The past four months have continued to bring changes for me. I have been a secular priest for 15 full and wonderful years. I find that with this teaching from Medjugorje my spirit is moving more beyond desire, fear, materialism and selfishness in a new and powerful way. Something within me has deepened and allowed me to let go of myself. While my ministry continues in this openness I feel increasingly called to community life and to prayer and fasting with the people of Medjugorje.

The details remain to be worked out, but it is clear that these visions are central to a deepening of my own vocation. It continues to be my joy to see these practices blossom beautifully in the lives of others as well."

God rest your sweet soul, dear Anglican Father Michael Koonsman.

DIARY OF A TRIP TO MEDJUGORJE ON THE OCCASION OF THE TENTH ANNIVERSARY, JUNE 24-25, 1991

In 1991, I made a trip to Medjugorje on the tenth anniversary of the Marian apparitions there and made a diary of my experiences.

JUNE 23

The eve of first day of apparition of Medjugorje. It was a difficult start in a room next to the kitchen with no privacy. I hardly had any sleep, having to get up at 3.30 a.m. to walk up Mt. Krisevac. I was unable to go very far from lack of strength. But later in the morning I went to a beautiful healing service. Five people got out of their wheelchairs and started pushing them! It was very, very, dramatic.

I was "slain in the spirit," with a restoration of some energy, since I thought I was getting a relapse of the Chronic Fatigue Syndrome again.

The healer was an amazing priest from Chicago, Father Peter Mary Rookey (in black robes and a great mane of grey/white hair.) He said, "Sickness is due to unforgiveness or hate, our own or ancestral." He also alluded to some children in wheelchairs as "victim souls." I know what that's about. The families of victim souls need extra help and healing (like ours). There were many valuable insights about healing which will be necessary for the disabled of all kinds.

Flashback to June 17th. I had a prophetic dream (in anticipation of Knights of Malta meeting and of my upcoming trip to Medjugorje?) which was analyzed by me right afterwards, (as per the dream workshop given by Montague Ullman, the Dean of Dream Analysts at Maimonides Dream Laboratory, Albert Einstein University). The details of the dream I now largely forget, but the gist is that Harry is at the outset of a great, arduous journey that is all right for me to take near some mountains or hills. It turns out to be much tougher than anticipated (now turning out to be prophetic about arduousness of Medjugorje pilgrimage).

Anyway, towards the end, since it is a lucid dream in which I, the dreamer, can control it to an extent (the first "lucid" dream I can remember having) I asked the dreamer-me- what the dream was all about?

"Why," replied the dreamer, "this is your version of 'Indiana Jones.'"

"Indiana Jones?" What were they seeking in that amazing, dangerous adventure film that was just like my dream! So unlike my life since I am a real cream puff, very physically cowardly and phobic, probably in part since I didn't have a dad to teach me courage.

"Well, you know what they were looking for even before you had this dream. They were looking for the Ark of the Covenant."

That explains all. The litany of Mary has as one of her descriptions the Arc of the Covenant, she who brings the Christ.

That is how I must bring her forward, to those at the Knights of Malta meeting, to Ralph Martin.

On June 17th, at the reception for the Knights of Malta, I met Ralph Martin, maybe the foremost charismatic Roman Catholic evangelist, and I told him about my dream. Afterwards I wrote to him, asking him to bring Mary forward to the Protestant evangelicals, whose colleague he is, as the Arc of the Covenant. She is the Arc of the Covenant since she, the most perfect human being, brings us, the human race, to the Christ; she takes us from the darkness of sin and suffering to the light of Her Son, the Christ.

The advent of the apparition at Medjugorje has been characterized by Fr. Svetozar Kraljevic as the most important spiritual event since the days that Christ walked the earth. So on this important day, June 24th, the first of the two day celebration of the anniversary, the message of Medjugorje is that peace in the world starts with your own peace, then peace in your family, and then to the world. Since illness comes from hate, one's own or familial, healing comes from forgiveness.

This message was surely the impetus that enabled the five yesterday who left their wheelchairs. These were genuine healings, which included an Irishman whose pallor bespoke his illness and whose wasted arms shouldn't have been pushing his wheelchair.

I did not come for lagniappe (a Cajun term for that little extra) nor for signs or wonders, although tonight seeing all the doves and birds flying in joyful frenzy at the time of the apparition was wondrous enough.

No, already I have accomplished what I came for, and that is healing, in body, mind, and spirit. I have already received two slayings in the spirit, a great healing gift from the Holy Spirit which came none too soon, since the arduousness of this trip was on the verge of making me ill again.

I am hoping for distant healing, too.

The rest of the week is ahead!

JUNE 24, 1991

After badly flunking going up Mt. Krisevac, I thought I should at least try Pdrbo Hill- the Hill of the Apparition but I knew I couldn't do it unaided—too many disabilities. So to make a long story short, with a few extra dollars the wildest cab driver east of the Adriatic was persuaded to accompany me up the hill as far as I would go in the dark.

Coming back sooner than later I then decided to have a Yugoslavian moon bath. It was wonderful.

The next time we come, I believe the Seggerman family would probably want to stay only two or three days in the very nice hotel here.

The Adriatic coast is overwhelmingly beautiful, hundreds of miles of gorgeous coastline, no pollution, and hundreds of lovely little fishing villages tucked into the rocks and some beaches.

JUNE 25

Actually tonight feels a little like Encounters of the Third Kind.

My fellow housemates came in from the mountain top. No miracles except for flashing lights (as usual) at the Cross. I saw flashing lights outside the apparition room of the second story of the left tower at St. James Church which takes place everyday at 6.40 p.m. Was it flashbulbs or "lights?"

The greater miracle to me however, was reading about the Community of Jesus by Fr. Svetozar Kraljevic, in which he devotes a chapter to this community. This is an answer to my prayers on the Community of the New Jerusalem, whether or not this would be a viable endeavor here in the greater New York area. Reading this unexpectedly at this time is the answer to prayer.

JUNE 26
"TESTING MY LIMITS"

After getting up at the crack of dawn again and walking to Vicka then to Marija then through the fields to Mass in the hot sun, I didn't think I would make it through lunch.

The essential themes of today are the central messages of Medjugorje from the two seers Vicka and Marija: prayer, penance fasting, mass, confession.

I had been wondering why there had been no mention of good works and sure enough Marija mentioned good works for the first time. She said first you go to Mass, having confessed your sins and say the Rosary. It will be during your prayers and after receiving the Holy Eucharist the Holy Spirit will inform you of what good works you are to do. That answers one of my basic questions of how to corral all the energy, these millions of pilgrims to change the world in action as well as in prayer. I was thinking there should be more emphasis on action. First things first! Prayer first, action second.

JUNE 27

Up at 5.00 a.m. What else? To go to Fr. Jozo—five hours of prayer in an extremely hot church, a real penance for everybody in it. After a message that I should present Mary, at long last, to Billy Graham, whom I hoped to meet in December, I offered up this morning's penance for that cause. Each year in the first week of December I went down to St. Martin to try to see Billy Graham. After our first meeting, I would send him flowers and even sent him some books. In 1990 I sent him a copy of an article about the Fourth World Foundation wanting to have a devotion and/or a statue to St. Martin de Porres, the first black saint in the western hemisphere, to bring a consciousness to the tourists about the poor in the Caribbean. I got a nice thank-you letter from Ruth Graham. What better way to present Mary to the Protestants than through Billy Graham. Do any of them know that Martin Luther never lost his devotion to Mary?

So when the priest came up to me for the "slaying of the spirit" healing, and asked if I had any intentions, I told him that I wanted to bring Mary to the Evangelicals, especially "my friend", Billy Graham.

To a further answer to prayer about what to do about the future, in a very synchronous manner, I sat next to Martha who had the "messages" of June 24, and 25, and the Blessed Mother said that we pilgrims could now understand what we should do, following the Medjugorje messages of preparation. I guess I am slightly ahead of the game since I put the cart before the horse, or you might say, "Ready, fire, aim!"

No question at all in my mind that everything being equal, one is truly guided here and blessed—in Medjugorje!

On this special day, the Blessed Mother extends to all here and their loved ones a day of Peace, Joy, and Holiness.

This photograph was taken in Medjugorje, in the former Yugoslavia, where Our Lady has been appearing to six visionaries since 1981. The picture was taken on Apparition Hill on June 25, 1995—the 14th Anniversary of the Apparitions. The word "CHRIST" could not be seen in the sky when the photo was taken. It appeared on the negative when the photo was developed.

CHAPTER FORTY-THREE

THE APPARITIONS OF MARY

In regard to the Eastern religions, here's an insight about the universal origins of the personage we know as Mary, in corroboration with what St. Augustine said regarding her continued presence throughout time on this earth. The occasion of this insight occurred during a visit to my health clinic, "The Oaks", in Ojai, California, where at the same time, by sheer coincidence(?), the great mythologist and philosopher, Joseph Campbell, author of *The Hero With a Thousand Faces*, was giving a workshop. I had not known that he was going to be there, but naturally raced to get a seat as soon as I could for a Monday afternoon lecture.

Dr. Campbell's work, *The Hero With a Thousand Faces*, was incorporated in a presentation of a speech I made at the American Society for Psychical Research in Los Angeles, which was called, "The Eternal Female Consciousness." At the time, he was a professor at Sarah Lawrence, the all-female college (which our third daughter, Yvonne, who was a dancer, subsequently attended because of their good dance department). Dr. Campbell is a latter day mythologist, often emphasizing the female aspects of humanity and deities.

The afternoon workshop was devoted to Dr. Campbell's slides of his trips to Sri Lanka, then called Ceylon. He had slides of the famous Ajanti Cave #2 to show to those who were interested in these things. Ajanti Cave, Slide #2 showed a drawing on the wall dating 2,000 BC which I could hardly see from the back row, the only seat I could get at this workshop. But even from that distance, I was completely overwhelmed by what seemed a remarkable resemblance to a Lady I had come to know very well: Our Lady of Guadalupe. So I sent away to Dr. Campbell's office at Sarah Lawrence for a copy of that slide. All of six months later, the slide arrived and I literally fell off my seat with shock, socks flying off with dispatch. Sure enough, the Bodhisattva, Goddess of Compassion, of the Ajanti slide #2, from an Indian culture of 5,000 years ago is an uncanny dead ringer for Our Lady of Guadalupe.

Bodisattva of Compassion and Guadalupe

Now the question is, "Who is Mary anyway?" St. Augustine said, "Mary and Jesus have been around for a long time." They revealed themselves as to who they really were 2,000 years ago.

But was the woman of Revelation really revealed to us in all her power and splendor (arrayed as an army dressed for battle)?

Now, in the last ten years, there has been a new title given to the Theotokos (Mother of God) who is now referred to as Coredemptrix, Mediatrix and Advocate. She has been given the power to repel Satan in his final days on Planet Earth until he is finished for a thousand years. Who is this Woman of the Revelation, who once was Mary?

There are ongoing apparitions and messages, written and on tape, from a great many people all over the world.

One of them said we should disregard the dissension between the promulgators of some of these apparitions—professional rivalry you might say. They are not all to be denied the possibility of authenticity since they may be useful in their own way. It seems that the few inauthentic ones have already fallen by the wayside.

Those who see apparitions are often called seers. There are two seers near New Orleans, Louisiana, whom I visited. From the standpoint of a reasonably educated observer, they seemed quite prodigious in "fruits"—activities, good works and beneficial influence. As a matter of fact, as I was leaving the humble home of one of the seers, Genevieve Comeaux, I was completely overpowered by an indescribably beautiful odor of flowers. Since there were absolutely no flowers around, I had to go back and ask her about it. She replied, "Don't worry. That is a frequent occurrence. It is a sign of the presence of the Virgin and her blessings on you."

These two seers in Louisiana seem to be part of a growing network of seers and increasingly are forming newsletter networks in which the messages are very similar. One of these seers is as far away as Woolagong, Australia.

The message is the same: UNLESS WE RETURN TO GOD WITH PRAYER AND PENANCE, WE SHALL HAVE A NUCLEAR WAR at the least, and/or the unleashing of severe planetary disruptions.

The frightful description of a global nuclear war by one of

the seers is distressingly similar to many apparitions, some approved by the Church.

The important apparitions for now are behind the Iron Curtain countries of Yugoslavia and Nicaragua. The Nicaraguan apparition does not have much of a following yet in this country, but deserves much more, since it has become a source of great consolation to the suffering Nicaraguan people. A lovely lady, a pious Episcopalian, who lives in Nicaragua, brought this to me through contacts with two women in New York. This lady's sister-in-law is a nun who took down the messages from the seer, a humble Nicaraguan peasant, now a priest.

The apparition at Medjugorje, Yugoslavia is undoubtedly the most famous one at present, although it is still controversial. Nevertheless, books in many languages have been written about it, which is all the more remarkable because the apparitions are so recent, having been delivered to six young people who have seen them. Even Protestant fundamentalists have been impressed. Is it a sign that Mary has returned to stay to establish the New Age or the Age of her Immaculate Heart in which her Son will reign? In any event, she announced this would be her last apparition on earth. Many cried when they heard this. It's like losing your best friend. This must mean that the time is short and we'll be on our own. ARE WE READY?

In another apparition, which occurred in San Damiano, a small Piedmontese village, of St. Francis of Assissi fame, the Virgin appeared to a humble peasant woman, Rosa Quattrini—this is the story.

Each week, at San Damiano, the Blessed Virgin came, spoke and bestowed abundant graces, showing herself more than ever the 'MOTHER OF ALL.'

On October 16, 1964, Rosa Quattrini, 60 years old, a humble and uneducated peasant, but an honorable, pious and courageous mother, who had previously been favored with supernatural graces and miraculously cured after returning from the hospital and dying, saw publicly for the first time the blessed Virgin above a little pear tree in her garden.

Our Lady said: "MY LITTLE DAUGHTER, I COME
FROM VERY FAR. TELL THE WORLD THAT ALL
PEOPLE MUST PRAY, BECAUSE (sic) SALVATION OF
ALL MEN, GOOD AND BAD. I AM THE MOTHER OF
LOVE, THE MOTHER OF ALL, YOU ARE ALL MY
CHILDREN. THEREFORE, I WISH EVERYONE TO
BE SAVED. THIS IS WHY I CAME TO LEAD THE
WORLD TO PRAYER, BECAUSE A CHASTISEMENT
IS AT HAND. I SHALL RETURN EVERY FRIDAY, AND
GIVE YOU MESSAGES AND YOU MUST ANNOUNCE
THEM TO THE WORLD."

Since then, every Friday and on Her feast-day, our 'HEAV-
ENLY MOTHER' keeps her rendezvous with the world. She calls
all her children—good or bad, rich or poor, learned or uneducated, saved or lost, old, adult or young—at this particular site
which she calls her little Garden of Paradise. There, Heaven and
earth meet, not through a vision but through faith, prayer, sacrifice and an abundance of spiritual graces. Pilgrims come at the
feet of someone they do not see but know her presence by the
word of this humble woman everyone can approach and address,
for she spends her days helping them and her nights praying
and suffering for souls.

Here, as with all religious/psychic experiences, we must
examine for ourselves the authenticity of these apparitions, since
most of them are seen by one or only a few persons. There are a
few experts in this field so we have to judge for ourselves for
the time being, since this is process theology. And even Roman
Catholics, for whatever it is worth, have permission to believe
in these apparitions, if it does not harm in faith or morals. In
this regard, I quote from the frontispiece of the book, *Voices
From Heaven.*

Regarding apparitions that have not been approved by the
Church, Pope Urban VII, who reigned upon the Throne of Peter
from 1623 until 1644, once had this to say:

"IN CASES LIKE THIS (apparitions), IT IS BETTER TO BELIEVE THAN NOT TO BELIEVE, FOR, IF YOU BE-LIEVE AND IT IS PROVEN TRUE, YOU WILL BE HAPPY THAT YOU HAVE BELIEVED, BECAUSE OUR HOLY MOTHER ASKED IT. IF YOU BELIEVE AND IT SHOULD BE PROVEN FALSE, YOU WILL RECEIVE ALL BLESSINGS AS IF IT HAD BEEN TRUE, BE-CAUSE YOU BELIEVED IT TO BE TRUE."

We must judge them (apparitions) according to the fruit they bear. One of the greatest mystical authorities of them all, St. Ignatius Loyola, in his book, *The Spiritual Exercise of St. Ignatius Loyola,* in a lengthy discourse paraphrased the words of Jesus, from Matthew 7:16, "YE SHALL KNOW THEM BY THEIR FRUITS."

What are the fruits of these apparitions? At the apparition site of Necedah, Wisconsin, as a result of their inspiration there were plans to build a home for unwed mothers and a clinic for the aged and homeless. I do not know if these objectives have been accomplished. Nevertheless, thousands who pray there find hope, determination and faith, and receive good advice.

The messages themselves are controversial. There have been probably dozens or even hundreds of reported miracles: base metal rosaries turning to gold, very miraculous or inexplicable photographs and many healings and conversions.

Once again, in spite of conflicting or negative reports, one must look to the fruits of the apparitions. At the apparition sites, such as Bayside, New York, thousands, probably hundreds of thousands, have been praying the rosary since thousands cel-ebrate the vigil of each of the 34 annual Marian feasts.

It must be mentioned the Mother of Christ is inextricably linked to the prayer known as the rosary. This is the prayer she gave to St. Dominic in the 13th Century. It is a series of repeated prayers, or mantra, as they are known in the Indian religious traditions, a meditation of a series of mysteries of the life of her son, Jesus and also on her own life. A Methodist minister, J. Neville Ward, wrote a very fine book, on the rosary, *Five For Sorrow, Ten For Joy*, that he recommends especially to his fellow Protestants.

CHAPTER FORTY-FOUR

THE WOMAN IS VERY POWERFUL

I refer you to a comment made to me by one of my dearest and most advanced mystical friends, the late Trevor Ravenscroft of Great Britain. At my first meeting with Trevor, I was so impressed that he appeared as a great magical Orson Wellian Mr. Rochester to my timorous, trembling Jane Eyre. I told him I was "supposed" to make a film on one of the appearances of Mary, Our Lady of Guadalupe. The last remark Trevor made to me at the end of that meeting was, "THE WOMAN IS VERY POWER-FUL." That phrase succinctly identifies my message to you and was the title of my presentation at the Los Angeles Society for Psychical Research.

Certain followers of Martin Luther completely ignored his beautiful treatise on the Virgin entitled, "The Magnificat," and in their strict desire to reform, threw out Mother with the bath water. Therefore, in deference to those of us who do not have a full cosmic exposure to Mary, The Woman, by way of introduction I would like to speak first about our beloved Master, her son, Jesus.

Much has been written about Jesus and much has been written about what Jesus said. As a matter of fact, most of the sacred writings of our Christian civilization came from Jesus and his disciples.

There has always been lively speculation about what Jesus was really like as a person. My own opinion is that the best description of who Jesus really was and what He did, is offered by parapsychologist, Frank Tribbe, in his book, *Portrait of Jesus— The Illustrated story of the Shroud of Turin.* Dr. Tribbe once gave a lecture at the New York Society for Psychical Research on his fascinating book about the Shroud, the purported burial cloth of Christ. This important relic has been extensively examined by a team of world-class scientists using the latest technologies and their findings have been reported to the world press. Many of these scientists were agnostic, Jewish, or had no specific convictions regarding Jesus. Most of them became profoundly Christian after the investigation. One only, whom I have decided must be the required resident "Doubting Thomas," Walter McCrone, of Chicago, has remained a vociferous skeptic.

From the best of the 19th Century scientific methodology and the best of 20th Century technology, the evidence is conclusive that the man on the Shroud was a tall, handsome, bearded Semite who lived approximately 2,000 years ago in Palestine, who was scourged in the horrible Roman style, crowned with thorns, pierced with a lance, carried a cross, was finally crucified, and lastly, and inexplicably, left his likeness to be discovered and authenticated only in our time.

If this man was Jesus and his image was left on this cloth in a miraculous or inexplicable fashion, and the scientific analysis and implication is the authentication of the entire mystery of the Passion and Resurrection, then our attention must immediately turn to another miraculous image—to that of the amazing and beautiful image on the Tilma (cloak) of a Mexican peasant, Juan Diego. The cloth with the likeness of Mary hangs in the Basilica of Mexico City, and is known as the Tilma of Guadalupe.

This phenomena of the impressed images on the Shroud and Tilma are so interrelated that I was invited to lecture on the Tilma image of Mary to that team of investigating scientists of the Shroud in New London, Connecticut, before the release of their findings to the world press on October 11, 1981. The result is that a few of those scientists became interested in the investigation of the miraculous image of Our Lady on the Tilma of Guadalupe, which has been hanging in the cathedral in Mexico City for 450 years.

That fact alone defies science. This fiber's average lifespan, once woven, is 25-40 years in Mexico's normal hot and humid climate. The image and the story about it are well known to most Mexicans and Mexican-Americans. For those of you who do not share that heritage, I will relay the amazing true story of Our Lady of Guadalupe.

In December of the year 1531, the Blessed Virgin Mary appeared and proclaimed her identity four times to a 57-year-old man whose name was Juan Diego. She directed him to go to the bishop of the area with the message that she wanted a church built there in her honor. The bishop told Juan Diego to ask for a sign. In response, Our Lady told Juan Diego to go to Tepeyac Hill. There, unheard of in winter, were beautiful roses which Juan Diego gathered in his cloak and brought to the bishop. When Juan Diego opened the cloak before the bishop there appeared on it an image of Our Blessed Lady. The church was built and the image remains today at Tepeyac at the shrine known as Our Lady of Guadalupe, a shrine which continues today as the second most visited shrine in Christendom after St. Peter's. At Tepeyac, Our Lady described herself as the merciful mother of all who dwell in this land, who desire to hear and who seek her help.

The Codex, the contemporaneous copies made of Aztec pictographs of this story, can be seen in the Museum of the American Indian in New York City.

The Shroud and Tilma are the cornerstone of the apparitions of Mary and Jesus on our planet. Why? Because they provide the physical evidence to overcome skepticism to help make the necessary leap of faith.

A few in this field, myself included, might speculate that at the moment of His resurrection Jesus joined His "light body" and that it was recorded on the Shroud. The Shroud is physical evidence of that which was promised—the resurrection of Christ. The Nicene Creed pledges belief in that promise, "I believe in the resurrection of the body . . . "

> "Jesus said unto (Martha), I am the resurrection, and the
> life: he that believeth on me, though he were dead, yet
> shall he live:" (John 11:25).

The light body is capable of appearing on earth, hence the possibility of Jesus and Mary appearing to us visibly from that other dimension.

There are currently some 200-plus apparitions of Mary, many authenticated by the Roman Catholic Church. However, I shall focus on the more interesting ones from the point of view of both parapsychology and the millennium fever surrounding the year 2000.

I now present a hypothesis, a hunch, a bicameral insight, that, as yet, has not been confirmed by anything that I have read. But here it is: the onset of the Eschaton or Latter Days began in earnest in the mid-19th Century. Why? Because most of the major Marian apparitions, mainly in France, Belgium, and Ireland, started in the 19th Century: Banneux, Beauraing, Lourdes, Pontmain, La Salette, the Miraculous Medal, Our Lady of Knock, etc.

Paralleling these apparitions, Joseph Smith, founder of the Mormon religion, had his vision from the angel Moroni, the guardian angel of America, in mid 19th Century. Although many facets of the Latter Day Saints of Jesus Christ, the religion that he started, had gone awry, such as the practice of polygamy, no doubt because the Indians might have polished off too many men, much of what they do makes a lot of sense—to survive and add strength and hope to our country in these dangerous times.

Also during the 19th Century, the baleful adversary, Satan, the ol' boy, began his work in earnest through the twin-headed monster that the great philosopher Rudolf Steiner characterized as Lucifer and Ahriman. These are described in Steiner's prophetic literature as the Red Dragon and the Black Panther, or the evils brought on by the excesses of the Industrial Revolution or the materialism of the West and the dialectical materialism, otherwise known as the Evil Empire of the East, which is Fascism/Communism: Red inside/Brown outside (Nazism), Brown inside/Red outside (Stalinism). These twin evils are to be fought by the "children of light."

The Woman who made all these appearances in the 19th Century called herself, ultimately, the Woman of Revelation. She identified herself in this way to the Italian, Bruno Carraclaolia, in 1922, after he had converted from persecuting Christians, much like Saul of Tarsus, who became St. Paul.

John Haffert, in *The Woman of the Apocalypse*, quotes The Bible and has this to say:

A great portent appears in the heavens:

"A WOMAN WEARING THE SUN FOR A MANTLE,
WITH THE MOON UNDER HER FEET, AND WEAR-
ING A CROWN OF TWELVE STARS." (Apoc. 12:1)

The Church applies this passage of the book of the Apocalypse (now generally known as the book of Revelation) to the Mother of Jesus.

What title should we give to her as she appears clothed as it were in atomic power, crowned with stars and about to give birth to the reign of her Divine Son?

The battle is squaring up between this Woman, whose dominion is the kingdom of her father, God; spouse, Holy Spirit; and son, Jesus, versus the same twin-headed monster, this time in the nature of Communism/Facism and materialism in the kingdom of man.

The late Malcolm Muggeridge, in a television program, made a point that was particularly interesting: "Christians do not have to fear a nuclear war!" Well, it helps if you're 80 years old and living in Sussex, England. It helps even more if when people say "the end of the world is at hand" (the old world which Satan unquestionably has been ruling in one way or another), they add that "the Kingdom of God is also at hand."

Many, not all, facets of the so-called New Age address much of the radical shift of consciousness, a shift to compassion, that must take place if we are to survive as a viable species in the future. Our loving consciousness must overcome the soulless technocracy which produced "the Bomb," germ warfare and genocide.

And that is indeed the message of the greatest of miracles of the end times and series of apparitions that occurred at Fatima, Portugal from May to October, 1917: We must develop a loving consciousness and return to God with prayer and penance.

This Fatima apparition is known to Roman Catholics of a certain age, shall we say over 39, but has been for the last 30 years largely ignored by the secular press and secularized Roman Catholic clergy. Shortly after the Fatima apparition were the events, which led to the Communist Revolution.

Bishop Fulton Sheen, the greatest moral genius and orator of our times, concerning Marian apparitions, from his book, *Life is Worth Living* had this to say in the chapter entitled Fatima a paraphrase of which is as follows:

> Our modern world with its great crises began on October 13, 1917. Three cities will quickly be visited to see what happened on that day: Moscow, Rome, and a little village in Portugal called Fatima.
>
> October 13, 1917—*Moscow*: Maria Alexandrovich, a young Russian noblewoman, was teaching religion to a class of two hundred children in the *Church Of The Iberian Virgin*. Suddenly there was a disturbance; horsemen entered the front door, rode madly down the middle aisle, vaulted the communion rail, destroyed the icons, the statuary, and the altar, then turned on the children, killing many of them.

Maria Alexandrovich ran out of the church scream-ing. Knowing there was an imminent revolution and sus-pecting the leader of them all, she went to him, saying, "A most terrible thing has happened. I was teaching cat-echism to my children when horsemen came in, charged them, and killed some of them. I, The revolutionist leader, said, "I know it. I sent them." Such was one of the events that heralded the beginning of the terrible Communist Revolution that has since harassed the world.

October 13, 1917—*Rome*—the same hour of mid-day: Church bells are ringing throughout the city, her-alding a joyful event: the consecration of a bishop. His name—Eugenio Pacelli—a man who then was not very well known, but who one day would become the greatest spiritual force in the world against the revolutionary tyranny of Communism.

October 13, 1917—*Fatima:* Near the little village of Fatima three little children, Lucy, Jacinta, and Francis, were gathered, expecting a revelation. They had said that Mary, the Mother of God, had appeared to them. It would not be surprising if she had, not only because the Lord come through her, not only because through her He worked His first miracle, and not only because from the Cross He commended us to her with His kind words, "BEHOLD THY MOTHER," but above all, because be-ing the Mother of mankind she should have a motherly interest in our troubles during the twentieth century.

The children said the Lady had appeared to them before, on April 13, May 13, June 13, July 13, August 19 and September 13. In the course of these earlier revela-tions, something very interesting was said which goes to show that our world conditions are determined by the way we live, rather than by politics.

The Lady said that the present World War, which was World War I, would end in a little over another year.

The United States went to war on Good Friday of that year, 1917. Actually, the war did end in a little over another year, on November 11, 1918.

The Lady told the children that there would come an era of peace to the world: If the world would only return to God; Russia in that case would be converted. But she added, "IF PEOPLE DO NOT STOP OFFENDING GOD, ANOTHER AND WORSE WORLD WAR WILL HAVE ITS REMOTE BEGINNING DURING THE REIGN OF THE NEXT PONTIFF." This, it was disclosed, was the Civil War in Spain. World War could have been prevented by penance and prayer and return again to God. For the failure of the world to return to God, the Virgin foretold another World War: "RUSSIA WILL SPREAD HER ERRORS THROUGHOUT THE WORLD, PROMOTING WARS AND PERSECUTIONS. THE GOOD WILL BE MARTYRED, THE HOLY FATHER WILL HAVE TO SUFFER MUCH, AND VARIOUS NATIONS WILL BE ANNIHILATED."

The Blessed Virgin promised the children that on October 13, 1917, she would give a sign that her revelation was true. Seventy thousand people gathered at Fatima on that rainy day with the children, awaiting a sign. Most of them were unbelievers. Portugal in those days was an anarchistic, Communistic, anticlerical, and atheistic nation. Most of the people come out of curiosity, not out of faith. They doubted that anything would happen, but the children assured them that the Heavenly Lady would show a great sign as a proof that she had actually appeared. The proof was what has since been called the "MIRACLE OF THE SUN." The testimony of these 70,000 people, as well as the records of the atheistic and anarchistic newspapers of the time which I have read, attested the fact of what happened.

The Blessed Mother first appeared to the children and then

pointed to the sun as a rift in the clouds made it visible. The sun seemed almost to detach itself from the heavens, becoming like a great silver ball; shooting sparks in all directions, it seemed to descend to the earth as if about to precipitate itself upon the people. Immediately they all cried out to God in prayer and supplication, in sorrow and in contrition. Three times the sun became a whirling mass of flashing silver and, spinning on its axis, cast off beams of multicolored light, as it plunged and zigzagged its way to the earth. The crowd shrank in fear and clamored for mercy as the molten mass seemed about to destroy them. And though it rained all day, after the miracle of the sun had taken place three times, everyone discovered that their clothes were dry.

From that time on, Fatima became a kind of gathering place of all the people of the world who believed that peace is made somewhere else than at the tables of the politicians.

At this point, one might pause and wonder at the enormity of the implications. First of all, when a person who has reached the age of reason with sufficiently unimpaired thinking ability can sit back and reflect on this set of events (very much as one would reflect on the state of the weather or the stock market report or the world political situation, in other words thinking in one's left brain), the implications are staggering. Persons from another dimension altogether have come to speak to humanity, very much as the Greeks believed in pre-Revelation times, like the gods from Mt. Olympus. This person, in this case the Woman of Fatima, caused the sun to dance at Fatima, a miracle which was seen by multitudes, photographed and recorded in the world press. She gave a specific message—that the Soviet Union would be the cause of great danger to mankind because of the sins of the world—a message given even before the Bolshevik revolution in 1917.

Should we not pay heed?

*   *   *

What about the other apparitions? What were the messages there and why were they given?

Briefly, here are some other major apparitions which occurred from the time of those at Fatima in 1917 and the more interesting or even spectacular aspects of each. The Woman is not only powerful, she is exceedingly mysterious. To prove my point, I shall proceed directly to the mysterious and awesome apparition of Zeitoun, Egypt, which began during the month of April, 1968.

Some workmen, who were Moslems, were making repairs on a garage across from a church of the Egyptian Coptic Rite, in the town of Zeitoun, formerly known as Heliopolis, the spot through which the infant Jesus, Mary, and Joseph passed to escape the slaughter of the innocents, King Herod's attempt to kill the newborn King of the Jews.

One of these workmen saw a very bright light above the ramparts of this church, then it seemed this light appeared as the form of a woman—a woman transfigured, so to speak, into a light body.

Many mysteries are attached to this apparition, photographs of which were in all the Egyptian newspapers.

The first mystery is that the apparition preceded the historical Camp David Accords. I had several amazing synchronocities that pointed to the fact that this Lady wished to be known not only as the Lady of Peace, but also as the Lady of Silence, since she said nothing. It could be that her presence alone in this once holy spot was the message to the Moslems and Coptic Christians who were her main audience.

Indeed, one of the great synchronicities is that Mary chose to appear at Fatima, Portugal, since Fatima was the name of Mohammed's oldest daughter, who started the branch of Islam known as the Fatimids, which formed the nurturing environment for the flowering of the great intellectual, and artistic Moslem culture of the 13th Century. The mystical tradition of the Moslem culture is now carried into Sufism.

The apparition at Zeitoun, however, presents the greatest mystery of cosmic proportions when considering these facts: Zeitoun or Heliopolis is very near the immeasurably immense mystery which is the Great Pyramid at Giza. The apparitions and subsequent miraculous picture of the Lady of Guadalupe also took place in a location outside of Mexico City and very close to the great Aztec pyramids of the sun and moon, formerly at the heart of Mexico City.

Mexico City is at the exact geographical center of the Western hemisphere, including North and South America, and the great pyramid at Giza is speculated to have been at the exact geographical center of all land masses known as the Eastern hemisphere prior to the great flood. Some Egyptologists of several countries concur that the Great Pyramid could only have been built using technologies and energies our civilization no longer possesses and that knowledge of these energies was lost with the destruction of the great, but increasingly decadent civilizations of Atlantis and Lemuria, not to mention the poor sinners who surrounded Noah and his ark.

> "But as the days of Noah were, so shall also the coming
> of the Son of man be. For as in the days that were before
> the flood they were eating and drinking, marrying and
> giving in marriage, until the day that Noah entered into
> the ark . . . " (Matthew 24:37-38).

Similarly, the Aztec pyramids and technology are a marvel to researchers now, but the Aztec route to superior knowledge was lost as that culture became decadent, which included unspeakable human sacrifices. It was as much Hernan Cortez's devotion to God and his resolution to stop these atrocities as it was with his greed for gold, which brought about the destruction of the Aztecs, as their own prophets had foretold.

We can guess why the mysterious and powerful Woman chose to appear at these crucial and parallel sites. I quote from a letter from a Guadalupan colleague, Ed Schaffer of Silver Spring, Maryland:

I have received slides from Mexico prepared by an accredited astronomer which show the stars on Our Lady's mantle match the configuration of the stars in the heavens as of 10:40 a.m., December 12, 1531. The Northern Constellations are on her right side; the Southern Constellations on her left side. What is surprising is that they match the star 'map' as seen from above; from another galaxy rather than from the Earth looking up. If you orient the Lady's Image to the East (as were the Aztecs; to the rising Sun), and superimpose that Image on a topographical map of Mexico, several Aztec symbols for 'hill' or "mountain" which appear on her rose-colored gown, fall EXACTLY over the locations of obvious volcanic areas. Further, the 'hill' symbol occurs on either side of her white cuffs; indicating to the Aztec, 'white mountain.' They fall directly over the two sacred (to the Aztec) snow-capped mountains, Popocatepetl and Ixtacciuatl. The white at her throat is also shown in conjunction with a "hill" and falls over La Malinche.

The Aztec sign for movement, the "nahul-ollin," falls directly over Tepeyac. And it is the only nahui-ollin on the robe. Also, the constellation Virgo falls over her hands and the constellation Leo, recognized almost exactly as the Greeks saw it, is the Aztecs' celestial nahui-ollin and ALSO falls over Tepeyac. The angles of the sash, extended out to the East, are the angles of the Winter Solstice and the Vernal Equinox!!

The three stars in a vertical line at the bottom left of her mantle, in conjunction with two or three other Aztec pictographic symbols, 'spell out' the Aztec date—113 coyote—interpolated into our Gregorian calendar, that is 1531! She dated her Image!

The most remarkable and prodigious apparitions all deal with the possibility of the coming Apocalypse and what to do about it, including the third of the trio of Iberian apparitions, since it was the Church of the Iberian Virgin that the Bolsheviks attacked in their first public act of terror. The only difference between this, the third Iberian Marian apparition at Garabandal, Spain, and the other two, Fatima, and Guadalupe, is that it has not been officially sanctioned by the Roman Catholic Church. This is probably for no other reason than that they are all very recent, in fact some are taking place right now, such as Medjugorje, Yugoslavia. It generally takes the Church decades to do what is necessary to validate an apparition, which is understandable.

Despite the reluctance of the Church to readily validate these apparations, the leader of the Roman Catholic Church, Pope John Paul II, who made his first trip and first public homage as Pope to the Shrine of Guadalupe, is truly a child of Mary. He pulls no punches concerning changes which must be made amongst the wealthy, uncharitable capitalists of North America and especially of South America. Nor does he pull punches with what is appropriate to God's holy priesthood. This man is living the Gospel, and he is such a threat to both the twin Satans of Materialism and Communism that it almost cost him his life, when in St. Peter's Square he was almost fatally shot by a Bulgarian terrorist in the pay of the Communist rulers in Moscow at that time. May we pray the powerful Blessed Mother will protect him once again as she did twice on May 13th, the day of the first apparition of Fatima (which happens to be my birthday!).

The third Iberian apparition took place in Garabandal, Spain, a small mountainous village in the northeastern province of the Estremadura. Here, as is almost always the case, the apparition of Mary was preceded by the appearance of an angel.

The apparition in Garabandal, Spain, in the sixties, to four girls, (I have met one of them and discussed it with her) is more specific about the nature of the unfolding of the Apocalypse. The main message is that Jesus, who revealed himself as the King of Mercy to Sister Faustian in 1931, would give us some time for repentance and some signs to convince even the hard hearted. The first of these signs would be a warning—the famous warning of Garabandal. This warning will take place before the great miracle which will be seen at all the Marian shrines of the world.

The Great Miracle will probably be a sign in the sky and many conversions and cures will take place. The warning which precedes this will be a brief period of time in which every human being will, like a dying man, see his whole life before him, all the evil he has done, all the good he did not do, and it will come as a great psychosomatic shock.

* * *

So now it is time to consider the Great Warning of the Garabandal prophecy:

A passage in the book on Fatima, *Life is Worth Living* had turned my attention to Garabandal. Well, Fatima and Guadalupe have certainly become intrinsic parts of my life, so the third part has to be Garabandal: the third part of the triumvirate of Iberian apparitions of the Blessed Virgin. I hadn't thought about Garabandal for some time and for some reason I felt an urge to contemplate it—about its significance. That very night on the satellite TV (which I seldom watch but just happened to be turned on) by another "coincidence," was the Life of Oscar Wilde. I said, "Of course, I have it!" The warning of Garabandal will be very much like, *The Picture of Dorian Gray*.

If anyone wants to know (but in a very reduced degree) what it's like to look upon your sins, just take a look at *The Picture of Dorian Gray*, (first version) when Hurd Hatfield looks at the state of his soul and actually dies from the shock of seeing the state of his soul as reflected on the unspeakably hideous "picture" of himself, after confessing his sins, of course.

The great warning of Garabandal, "and so somewhere along the line the entire human race will have this mini judgment." Many of us who have not been going to church regularly, and are not being good, not staying out of trouble, and breaking any of the Ten Commandments are going to contend with the fact that

357

seeing our souls the way God sees them may kill us from fright. So, I admonish the readers to clean up their spiritual act as quickly as possible if they have the will to survive.

CHAPTER FORTY-FIVE

THE MAYPOLE

At the moment of our creation, in the ineffable moment of creation, God who knows us as only the Creator can, gave us His Spirit in which we are created in His image and likeness. The variables in our development are due to the genetic and environmental nature of our free wills and the wills of our ancestors, who preceded us and gave us our traits and characteristics, the worst of which we can choose to ameliorate or overcome.

The thread connecting that ineffable moment with the events of one's life is like a maypole in the dance of life. The persons holding those threads weave in and out until finally there is, hopefully, the triumphant multicolor braid. The streamers are attached to the pole but how are they to be braided? I have been given in the last year a blueprint for the maypole that comprises this part of the book. This blueprint is the one given to us by Our Eternal Father to all of us. It is to live in the divine Will.

The Kingdom of the Divine Will was the name and subject of messages given to the mystic who, bedridden for 64 years, was given what I consider to be the ultimate message from the eternal Father to human kind. She, Luisa Picaretta, was instructed by the Father to take down the message of His Divine Will, in the Kingdom of the Divine Will. This message, written in 36 books, was given to her in dictation by God, and was descriptive of the purpose of our human drama which fell away from the divine world, alas, with Adam's fall.

God in his act of consummate love of creation declared that act as a first of three fiats given to us in our human/divine history. After the first fiat of creation, God gave His love freely, and in turn, this was meant to be expressed freely in what we humans have as free will. Love freely given must be returned freely. In the case of Adam, love for love was not returned. Adam fell and as they say, the rest is the history of the human race.

God found in the maelstrom of the poor choices of the free will, one just man, Noah, and his family (Gen. 7:1).

The prophetic communication from God to his people, replete in the continuing maelstrom, will once again be heard when God declares his love for mankind. But for this to happen, He, himself, would have to come down to His people as one of them and take on their iniquities so they could return to their Creator.

In the second person of the Trinity, God or Abba becomes Jesus. So the second fiat is the incarnation of Abba, with the humble acceptance of She who once was Mary and is now the Queen of Heaven. After two millennia we are on the eve of Love's third great fiat, the coming of the Kingdom.

Because of my blueprint in the act of my creation, I always knew that some day I would be a herald, one of many, of that fiat pointing to the New Jerusalem where Love's will shall be done on earth as it is in heaven.

At Hawthorne in Beverly Hills, California, where I was a student from the fourth to the eighth grade, I remember maypoles only too well since I could never figure them out and I always ended up going in the wrong direction, or messing up the braid. My blueprint was not an earthly maypole dance. It was to the tune of the music of the spheres, an experience I later had in a workshop under the tutelage of Paul Solomon, the "successor to Edgar Cayce."

As a young child, I had an imaginary friend who was an angel, and who later appeared to me as St. Michael the Archangel in the toll booth leaving NYC in 1978. This also explains the synchronicities of my life, the rainbows, the earthquake, the prophetic dreams, even the project, unheard of for an ordinary housewife, and when that blueprint said once and for all "The New Jerusalem" (Rev. 22).

It is said in the story of the divine will as given to Luisa Picaretta that there is a very broad consensus among latter day prophets and visionaries that a large part of the human race might be destroyed, to achieve this third fiat. How can we get these wayward humans to understand that God's will must be done on earth as it is in heaven, which means the complete absence of sin as in heaven?

Right now that seems to be too tall an order. John Paul II has declared this year, the *Year of the Father*, in response to his own mystical guidelines.

In His instructions, which the mystic also beautifully took down, God the Father wants His creation to venerate Him in a manner that His creation never has done before. It is specifically to celebrate His feast on the first Sunday in August.

Above all things, with the message of Fatima second only to this, this fiat will give human kind a chance to mitigate the chastisement which must come before the new heaven and new earth can be realized.

CHAPTER FORTY-SIX

THE MARIAN MOVEMENT
OF PRIESTS

I shall conclude by recounting the story of this particular Marian devotion. Father Stefano Gobbi of Milan started this movement led by the Holy Spirit to counteract the evil of our times (as manifested in the sex education curriculum in the public schools, which caused me to start this devotion here in 1989).

On the 8th of May in 1972, Father Gobbi was commissioned by the Blessed Mother to gather her priests for her in the Latter Days in what is known as the Marian Movement of Priests. The story is as follows:

At Fatima, in the little Chapel of the Apparitions, Don Stefano Gobbi was praying for some priests who, besides having personally given up their own vocations, were attempting to form themselves into associates in rebellion against the Church's authority.

An interior force urged him to have confidence in the Immaculate Heart of Mary: Our Lady, making use of him as a humble instrument, would gather about the Pope those Priests who would accept her invitation. Thus, a powerful cohort would be formed, with a strength that springs from silence, from prayer and from constant fidelity to one's duties.

Father Don Stefano asked Our Lady for a little sign. A month later, she gave it to him punctually, at the Shrine of the Annunciation in Nazareth.

Concretely, what was he to do? In October of the same year, a timid attempt was made, by way of gathering of three Priests for prayer and fraternal sharing, in the Parish of Gera Lorio (Como, Italy); a notice of the Movement was given in some papers and Catholic reviews.

By March, 1973, the number of Priests inscribed was about forty. That same month, the undersigned came to know about the Movement and also asked to join, with no inkling of the responsibility that Providence had reserved for him.

In September, 1973, at San Vittorino, near Rome, the first national gathering took place, with about twenty-five Priests taking part, out of the eighty who had been inscribed by that time.

By 1985, the Marian Movement of Priests had grown to 24,000 members.

After our failed attempt to raise money to send the Shroud scientists back to Turin (having been stopped in our tracks by the antichrists in the Vatican, "the Black Panther,") and because I was well known to the local media, due to the star quality of my Huxley Institute board which included Paul Newman and Joanne Woodward (et al), when they heard about the Shroud they were very intrigued and sent a photographer. They were always looking for interesting stories about the locals, and that was me all right—a local with interesting stories. There was a beautiful picture of Harry and me holding that Holy face of Jesus.

Like my Huxley connection, that picture generated a response from a group of parents whose children were being educated in the Westport Public Schools System. They asked me if I could help them in some way to rid the Westport public school system of the lurid and frightful sex education that was being taught there. I suppose that they thought that anyone who had the privilege of holding a picture of the Shroud of Turin could be of some service.

Incredible as it might seem, this was how my association with the Marian Movement of Priests later developed.

So we began holding regular meetings, including parents who had children attending schools in various Fairfield County towns. I called our group, Christians Anonymous.

After having a few meetings in our home in our attempt to address this sex education problem, not only in our town, but also in other towns in Connecticut. and New York, I met a great number of people who were involved in this issue. The most important to me was Edward Eichel, a sexologist of repute and also a believing Jew. Mr. Eichel had been sent, with others in his profession, to a meeting in Amsterdam to discuss the sex education curriculum which was developed by a group that would send recommendations to SEICUS (Sexuality Information and Education Council of the United States), and was to be introduced into the U.S. public school system under the auspices of New York University, the headquarters for SEICUS. One of the alarming things was his discovery that the Amsterdam group was allegedly run by a large percentage of people who were pederasts. I immediately thought that the International Left might have something to do with that. I have never researched this thoroughly but there are certainly clues to that effect, since this would be very helpful in destroying the American family, a view held by W. Cleon Skousen in his book, *The Naked Communist*.

It is a known fact that what is known as the homosexual agenda, is indeed a leftist strategy to bring down the American family. Naturally, the curriculum did reflect a homosexual viewpoint. Hence, unspeakable things were taught to our children—that it was okay to do some unspeakable things, not only homosexual acts, but every other kind of sexual perversion. All I can say is that if your hair were straight, then those revelations would make it turn curly and vice versa. I attended many conferences at which Edward Eichel was the speaker. So I created a file, entitled, "Sex Education," and along with another which I call "My Satanist File," I put it in an obscure cubby hole, since I never had any staff with guts enough to help me follow up this research, except for one feisty grandmother, Alice Benson, my favorite volunteer.

Nevertheless, Goliath won this particular battle with David.

Unfortunately, after many meetings and conferences with professionals, parents and students, we could not budge this monster. I knew in my heart of hearts that the only way was prayer, and that the answer could come only from the spiritual realm which was in accordance with the tenets of the Fourth World Foundation.

During my involvement with the sex education problem, I also met a woman who had started to counteract the liberal and feminist tendencies that were pervading Catholic women to the detriment of the solidarity of the Catholic family through a religious group, the Marian League of Catholic Women. I told her that the only way we could do something effective was by starting a spiritual movement, (we concurred) and with her help and that of two other faithful stalwart and intelligent women, we made some headway. Through the Holy Spirit, it was gradually revealed to me that the organization I would have to create would be a Cenacle of the international movement just described, "The Marian Movement of Priests." I started such a Cenacle on my birthday, May 13, 1989, when we had our first meeting. That was the beginning of seven wonderful years of spiritual activity.

CHAPTER FORTY-SEVEN

MOTHER TERESA

Her influence on my life really began when I read, *Something Beautiful for God*, by Malcolm Muggeridge and published by Lady Collins whom I met in London in 1977. This was at the time of the formation of the Fourth World Foundation and the recruiting of board members. Since the creation of the foundation was really a right-brain event—and the right brain doesn't tell the left brain what it is doing until the time is right, I really didn't know what this was all about. But I was told that Mother Teresa's definition of the fourth world was, "the poorest of the poor and the most disenfranchised of the disenfranchised (including the mentally ill)." Of all the definitions of which I was aware, hers was the closest to my heart.

Mother Teresa's influence was broad and penetrating into all areas of my life, it seems. In the late summer of 1992, I was once again moved by forces outside of myself to be moved to alarm concerning the candidacy of the current President as the Democratic candidate. The week after the Democratic convention (at which they decided the presidential nominees) I called my friend, Maureen Flynn, who publishes the most comprehensive Catholic End Times newsletter in the U.S. (and therefore the whole world!), I voiced my alarm at the situation of the current President. She knew that I was semi-mystical, not like the visionaries whose whole lives have been taken over by signs and wonders, but one foot in mysticism and the other on terra firma, in an oft times negative environment. So I told her that we should do something fast because time was short and she agreed.

We mounted an ad hoc organization entitled, "Save the Children" because we knew that the current President was a pro-abortion candidate which would bode poorly for the country in "tribulation" terms, were he to become president. I managed to scrounge some finances from my various sources of income to help Maureen send out a newsletter to all priests, Bishops and Cardinals, asking them to urge their congregations to pray for a pro-life leader. This was tricky because it could be said that church and state should be separate, but it was the Founding Fathers who said, "In God we trust." Alexis de Tocqueville in his book, *Democracy in America* said, "America will remain great if she will remain good." We thought that America's greatness could be compromised by someone like the current President with his spurious track record, if he became our leader.

Mother Teresa of Calcutta

Because it was a life and death issue for the unborn, we decided that we needed the approbation of the greatest pro-lifer in the world, namely, Mother Teresa. So, after a furious scramble in October 1992, which lasted about three days (during which time I doubt whether Maureen and I got much sleep, if any), we were finally able to fax a letter to Mother Teresa via the concierge of the Oberoi Hotel, in Calcutta, India. It was just across the street from Mother Teresa's Headquarters, and was the only place with a fax machine in that town. We prevailed on the concierge to take the letter, in the middle of the night—Calcutta time—across the square to wake Mother Teresa to get her to sign a letter for us and fax it back to us, since it was our daytime. Her response was immediate and beautiful and it brought joy to our hearts.

Though our efforts were in vain, I sincerely thank my friend Maureen Flynn for her dogged determination in helping me to get Catholics aware of our nation's predicament.

For many years, Maureen Flynn has been the editor and publisher of the *Signs of the Times*, a Catholic newsletter on the end times. Within the last year she has started another publication, "Catholic Prophecy Update." Maureen is probably more in tune to the path the Lord has chosen for me than anyone else I know. She is truly a kindred spirit. Maureen did not turn her back on anything of a "right brain" nature and therefore on that fateful day of October 16, 1992, when we received the letter from Mother Teresa, we became friends and semi partners for life.

Maureen's husband, Ted, went into producing TV documentaries on the latter days, Catholic style. On the cover of one of their newsletters, similar to the vision I received years ago, is a white cross in the sky. Somewhere in these latter days we will be seeing the white cross in the sky; whether it will be part of the great miracle of Garabandal I don't know, but surely based on a broad consensus of visionaries we will experience this extraordinary phenomenon.

Maureen and Ted came to one of our Cenacles to explain their work and were very well received by the audience.

CHAPTER FORTY-EIGHT

CENACLES

Our meetings under the auspices of the Marian Movement of Priests were called Cenacles, named for the upper chamber where the Holy Spirit descended on Mary and the disciples on the day which is known as Pentecost, the birthday of the Christian Church. They were glorious affairs and we had something like eight the first year. Our remarkable Bishop Egan, the local Bishop from the Bridgeport, Connecticut Diocese, presided over one wonderful Cenacle concelebrating with other priests on May 13, 1990. We also had many well-known mystics from around the world. Inspired by the picture of Jesus and Mary always at my side, I was able to have regular meetings of the Marian Movement of Priests in our backyard on the feast days of the Virgin Mary. Sometimes our meetings were held during the warm months, as well as the rest of the year, depending on the weather and circumstances, when we had as few as 40 and as many as 800 attendees.

Many remarkable incidents occurred during these Cenacles but one of the most memorable is that during one of the early ones, my friend, Michael H. Brown, author of *The Final Hour*, *Prayer of the Warrior*, *After Life* and other books, went public with me when he acknowledged that we both had seen or felt the presence of St. Michael, the Archangel.

It was obvious during the years 1989-1997 that the messages

from various visionaries, who came into our midst, indicated in ever clearer terms what the human race could expect from the hand of the Father which could no longer be held back in the name of justice. Nevertheless, it was during those precious years in spiritual development that I learned of the Divine Mercy.

The Divine Mercy as revealed to a nun, Sister Faustina, is a sign of God's forgiving love. When Jesus revealed Himself to her in 1931, He made some requests which, if obeyed, would constitute the devotion to the Divine Mercy which would earn mankind some measure of protection from the just wrath of God.

First, He requested her to paint His image as she saw it with the inscription: "Jesus, I trust in You." Then as a further sign of His forgiving love Jesus requested that His image be blessed on the first Sunday after Easter and that day should be designated the Feast of Mercy. Thirdly, He asked that this Feast of Divine Mercy be preceded by a Novena to the Divine Mercy which would begin on Good Friday, and finally in 1933, God gave Sister Faustina a striking vision of His Mercy, as a result of which she understood that God blessed the earth for the sake of Jesus. She found herself saying a special prayer in an attempt to prevent the Angel of God's wrath from striking the earth. This prayer, known as the Chaplet, is promised to grant the penitent great Mercy at the hour of death.

He said, "I want the whole world to know My infinite Mercy. I want to give unimaginable grace to those who trust in My Mercy." Therefore, there is hope for those of us who heed His wishes.

We had one Cenacle the second year. I remember this because there was a priest who was in the hospital the same year as my employer and, sure enough, we agreed that it was in 1990 that my employer became very ill for the first time. He was placed in intensive care and everybody rushed from every part of the country to his bedside. The rehabilitation process took a long time.

Thereafter, my employer found himself in various precarious health situations. I now know that the Blessed Virgin smiled on us all these years and preserved us in spite of this. A famous holistic doctor whom we visited a few years ago said, when he saw my employer, "What! You are still alive?" This explains why I have a memory block about

1990. Not only did I also have to contend with the rehabilitation of our daughter from her long-standing schizophrenia, but in addition, I also had to deal with a recurrent bout of her cancer which resulted in the loss of her uterus. It was like in the Old Testament times or like being married to an actor. Some years were good and some were lean. The frequency or lack of those Cenacles seemed to reflect what was going on in the background, of our private lives.

The Cenacles remind me of my first meeting with Buckminster Fuller, among whose many books is one called, *I Tend To Be A Verb*. I have always asked God to accept my work as prayer. I dislike pilgrimages almost as much as I dislike graveyards. There are simply too many people, too much stuff going on. The closet is a much better place for prayer and contemplation. Maybe this has something to do with my Chronic Fatigue Syndrome which plagues me off and on.

One of our best Cenacles was in 1995. What I specifically remember about that occasion was that it was the first time that the remarkable Ukrainian dissident from the atheistic Soviet rule, Josyp Terelya, said that he could make it also. By some Providential happenstance, my nephew had been married by Fr. John Houle, S.J.(Fr. Houle's miraculous recovery from cancer, attributed to Claude de la Columbière, led to the beatification of Blessed Claude. The ceremony took place only last year in Rome). Fr. Houle was incarcerated in a Japanese concentration camp, along with Ignatius Cardinal Kung, the official Roman Catholic Cardinal of China under the aegis of the Holy Father, and not the Patriotic Catholic Church sponsored by the Communist Government and the People's Liberation Army.

By some amazing happenstance, my nephew called me just a few days before the Cenacle. So I asked him if he thought Father Houle could persuade Cardinal Kung, who lived in retirement in Stamford, Connecticut, to join with Josyp Terelya, the Ukrainian, who himself had been incarcerated by the Russian Communists for 20 years, at our Cenacle. Josyp was a leading Ukrainian dissident whose life had been spared on a couple of occasions through the intervention of the Blessed Virgin. On one famous occasion, as described in his seminal book, *Witness*, she prevented him from freezing to death in his very cold jail cell. This is how the Communists decided to kill him since they could not succeed in any other way without actually shooting him, which they could not do because, even at that time, he was very famous, and they didn't want to run the risk of being accused of murdering him.

So on May 15, 1995, on our podium which was built by an eccentric Moslem Hungarian carpenter, Tony Szabo, stood those two men who had been incarcerated for a total of 50 years by the Communists. Fr. Bill McCarthy, our very dear friend and renowned charismatic priest and founder of the retreat center, "My Father's House," and Cardinal Kung officiated at the Mass. To say that this was a very enthralling experience would be an understatement, despite the fact that the weather was quite cool. As usual, yours truly did not even have the time to take a bath or even change her clothes or wear stockings, or make-up for that matter. Nobody noticed, of course.

A Cenacle! The extraordinary Mass concelebrated by
the late Ignatius Cardinal Kung, Roman Catholic
Primate of China, Fr. Bill McCarthy, of My Father's
House, joined by the Ukranian patriot and mystic,
Josyp Terelya. The Cardinal and Josyp between them
had spent 50 years in Communist prisons!

One memorable Cenacle was the one where we had the (controversial?) mystic, Vassula Ryden. That was in 1996. I received a telephone call from my friend, Tom Carroll, who had been coming to our Cenacles over the years. He said that he was Vassula's representative and that she was supposed to be speaking at a church in Waterbury, Connecticut, but at the last minute that church could not accommodate her. Vassula's background is quite remarkable. She is Greek born, Orthodox, and a very good tennis player. In fact, she was seeded #2 among the diplomatic community while she lived in Bangladesh. She also speaks something like seven languages. I actually went to visit her at her apartment in Lausanne where there was a group of holy people. It was very thrilling. The famous Belgian priest, Father Spies was there. He was the spiritual adviser not only to Vassula but also to Julia Kim of Naju, Korea. Julia Kim not only has the stigmata but also feels the pain of those mothers going through abortions and also the pain of the aborted foetuses. Her suffering is indescribable. Fr. Spies just said to me, "Annie," which he followed with a look as if to say I had quite a lot of work to do on myself, and that was true. I was not the type to get the stigmata or to do any of those things. On the other hand, I had tried to do my bit.

The woman who called me about Vassula was a very nice Episcopalian lady (who was thinking about becoming a Roman Catholic). She asked me to help find a place for Vassula to speak. I said no, initially, to my friend Tom as well as to this woman about letting Vassula use our backyard for her conference since the time was too short. The Waterbury church had turned down Vassula because they said she was Orthodox and not Roman Catholic, that she had been married twice, plus all the bureaucratic excuses one could think of to keep her out. This was four days before Vassula's scheduled appointment.

The Episcopalian woman then went on to say that she had been driving West along the Merritt Parkway when she had to pull over because of a flat tire. A man stopped to see what he could do. That man was none other than Tom, Vassula's representative. He told her his story and he said that he was trying to find a forum for Vassula. There was a church in Southport which could not accommodate them because they were having an AA meeting that night. After this remarkable "coincidental" meeting they both came to me and told me what had happened and of their disappointment in not finding a church where Vassula could speak. Then they looked at each other and then at me. I said, "Uh, oh," and then, of course, had to say, "Yes." In four days busloads of people from Long Island, where Vassula has quite a following and from other places, arrived en masse. About 600 people turned up in our backyard. However, I don't think this was very pleasing to our neighbors. They objected to the buses coming through our streets and also to the signs that we had placed along the route to our home. Nevertheless, the event was a very extraordinary one. One Presbyterian lady said that she saw the Blessed Virgin. Many others said that they saw Jesus. These visions allegedly occur when Vassula is around. I believe it. After all, she was chosen by God because she is Orthodox, because she is beautiful, very fit—she has to be because she has to take dictation of all her messages from Jesus on her knees—and because she can speak all those languages and because she can speak to the Protestants as an Orthodox. Her messages from Jesus are very beautiful, almost too strong for the secular-minded, to be sure.

Another memorable Cenacle was that of June 2, 1997 when Josyp Terelya returned, along with Maureen Sweeney (now Kyle) of the Apostolate of Holy Love. The Blessed Virgin gave a message. Right after that Josyp Terelya healed a woman of liver cancer. So many prodigious things happened but since I was running the show I was not privy to most of them, but I had done my job.

I am thinking of some of the mystics who came to speak in our home: Debra of Australia, whose authenticity, as far as I was concerned, was only briefly clouded by the fact that initially the people around her in Australia exhibited an aggressiveness that seemed to display a distinct lack of holiness and Christian charity. She, herself, was beautiful, cheerful, kind and loving, though her life was quite filled with intense suffering through her family. At that time she was living only on the host, except on Marian feast days.

Debra came through an ice storm to speak at our home where we had expected 400 but instead only about 40 of these braved the weather, but they were the remnant anyway, they reminded me. Debra told me just out of the blue sky, "We have to fight the Black Panther these days." I said, "What, how did you get that name?" She replied, "That is the name of human secularism." I said, "I know, because that is the same name Rudolf Steiner (and I) used for it!"

Debra knew I was writing this book. And she said, "I want you to tell me all you know about herbs." Coming from Australia she knew she would be in a position to survive all the destruction in the Northern hemisphere, especially since she was commissioned by God to build the first Basilica to the Blessed Mother by her title, Co-Redemptrix, Mediatrix, and Advocate, in her part of Australia.

Later on she said, "Forget about the herbs for now. Your job is to fight the Black Panther." That now is coming to pass.

The youngest group that comes to mind, of all the remarkable Cenacles that we had, are the two Patricks from Ireland. Being in their presence is almost like being visited by Jesus, Himself. Their humility, piety, simplicity, and, of course, care for the poor everywhere is truly like the compassion of Jesus. I don't even feel worthy to have them back because I have not yet made a good enough headway with my anti-poverty programs.

Our Cenacles as we knew them were soon to be halted. The Marian Movement of Priests leadership in Maine had become rather bureaucratic, maybe because the movement is so large. Quite suddenly in 1997 we received a letter from the Headquarters of the Marian Movement of Priests in St. Francis, Maine, stating that the Cenacles should be limited to the Consecration, prayer, the Rosary and Mass. There were to be no outside speakers.

My role was like that of a religious Sol Hurok, if possible, a well-known impresario on Broadway years ago, someone I was exposed to while growing up. Well, I shared that message from Headquarters with the faithful in Fairfield County. Of course I could not attract people to our Cenacles if I followed this directive. In fact, Father Gobbi himself also had his last visitation from the Virgin Mary at Christmas 1997. In view of these two obstacles to the way in which we conducted our Cenacles, I began ruminating, or rather I prayed to God to direct me how to bring the many aspects of the Gospel to Southern New England. That door closed and a two year tenure as president of the local Division of the Blue Army of Fatima opened.

Long before the Cenacles had ceased however, it had been in my heart to bring in a leading Episcopalian charismatic evangelist, of whom I had heard. He was Fr. Everett Fullam, a notable leader in the national Episcopalian charismatic movement. I eventually brought him into our midst through a particular venue that my foundation would be able to organize.

Josyp Terelya and Harry standing
behind the late Cardinal Kung

CHAPTER FORTY-NINE

FOSTERING ECUMENISM

Many years ago my brother-in-law, Fred Seggerman, came to live with us as he was having some problems in his life. Fred is somebody of whom I am extremely fond. He has a very kind and giving soul. I remember that he was just thirteen when his brother and I were married and even at that young age, he was as beautiful inside as he was outside. Indeed, all the Seggerman brothers were handsome but Fred, by far, was the most handsome of them all. I also remember at that time, that he liked Gilbert and Sullivan, as I did at his age, so I gave him a special book on Gilbert and Sullivan that my grandmother had given me many years before.

When Fred came to live with us, we had a friend called Helena whom we met through her volunteer work for the Huxley Institute in the 70's. Helena had a daughter with the same problem as ours and demonstrated such efficiency at the Institute that I hired her as a secretary, and over the years she did some terrific work for me until she became too sick to work any longer.

However, her great forte was that she was a Christian in deed as well as in thought and word. So she took Fred under her wing and sooner or later he followed the call which really came so naturally to him, maybe unlike the rest of his family, and he became a Christian.

Helena also asked me if I could arrange to attend various healing ceremonies with her, which at that time was something new within the burgeoning Evangelical movement. The first one I attended was in the mid 80's in Stamford, Connecticut, at a time when I was first experiencing the throes of Chronic Fatigue Syndrome, which people who have it, can confirm how very debilitating it can be at times. I remember clearly two things about these healing meetings: The first was that a group of very fine and tall men surrounded me and laid their hands on me. They were praying in tongues, asking Jesus for a healing. Whether a healing occurred or whether it was just a placebo effect, who knows? For sure something happened because I felt better for the next few weeks. I was definitely free of all symptoms, which was a blessing.

The second thing that comes to mind is the problem of evil. It is a phenomenon I have encountered in many healing ceremonies, be it Evangelical or Catholic. Invariably there appears to be someone present who is possessed by demons and starts screaming or, as it happened in Medjugorje, speaking in a foreign tongue in fearsome staccato—like phrases in contrast to the soft murmur of the Holy Spirit. Since I have the gift of discernment of the presence of demons during such ceremonies, I was inspired, during their first healing meeting, to lead a fledgling ecumenical prayer group, part of the local Episcopalian church, away from the so-called Toronto Blessing, into a grace-filled organization which subsequently became known as "Healing of the Shepherds." This is before the organization of the present group that meets from time to time in the Oratory, an Anglican and Episcopalian Prayer Center in northern Conncticut.

The second healing meeting that I remember attending with Heléna and others was in Long Island at a service held by a group, The Vineyard, started by the well-known Evangelist from Anaheim, California, John Wimber. This was truly a grace-filled Evangelical group if ever there was one that did everything, as far as I know, even without the benefit of the sacraments. John

Wimber himself was not only a great speaker but also a great man. The extraordinary event during that weekend in Long Island was the presence of the so-called Kansas City prophets with the particularly charismatic speaker, Paul Cain.

Paul, like Terry Fullam, was a genuine mystic with all the hallmarks of that calling. His grandmother predicted that he would be a great and holy man some day and his mother was visited by angels before his birth. Paul's life has been marked by suffering, not unlike all great mystics born with grace, but he also has an enormous amount of humor which makes him a very charismatic speaker.

Last year when it was announced that Paul would be coming back, after a hiatus of 15 years, as part of the Conference to be conducted by Evangelical entrepreneurs from Texas, I was thrilled. That conference produced the greatest outpouring of the Holy Spirit that I have ever experienced in my life. We were singing, and clapping, and praying and dancing. Quite frankly, I thought we would all fly through the roof. We were on a high that no hallucinogen could ever produce. It was terrific. Paul said something which seemed quite strange—that he experienced revival in two places, Norway and Connecticut! Well, maybe we all have been doing something right after all.

The prayerfulness, kindness and enthusiasm of Evangelicals as well as their *outreach*, especially during the National Day of Prayer of which I was very blessed to be the leader in 1998, caused me to wonder whether, as in early Christian times, we Catholics are like the Jews. We seem to care about too many laurels and not enough about the admonitions as stated in the book of James, "Pure religion and undefiled before God and the Father is this, To visit the fatherless and the widows in their affliction, and to keep himself unspotted from the world" (James 1:27), and " . . . .faith, if it hath not works, is dead, being alone (Ibid 2: 17)." Maybe it is because I have had so much experience with the Protestants, as well as with the Catholics that I have such an open mind. In the words of that driver on the Los

Angeles freeway who was beaten up by the Police, "Why can't we all get along?"

In 1987, always under the guidance of the Holy Spirit, since I did not have any other reason for doing this at the time, I was inspired to attend a meeting in New Orleans entitled, The Conference of the Holy Spirit, 1987. I had never attended any charismatic conferences before but there was something about this one that really attracted me, even to the extent of dropping everything and going down to New Orleans and asking my sister-in-law in California to join me there. She and I were buddies since we had earlier teamed up to work on a project to make a film about Our Lady of Guadalupe. After all, it was her father who knew Henry King. This is how that started a decade earlier.

With the exception of the very first charismatic conference held at Purdue University, this one has certainly turned out to be the grand-daddy of all charismatic conferences. It was held in the superbowl stadium where approximately 55,000 people were in attendance. About 55% were Roman Catholics, I was told; the other 45% comprised mainly Evangelicals and other mainline Protestant groups, two Messianic Jewish groups and a couple of tables representing homosexuals, who were turning to Jesus instead of to other agencies which most serious Christians consider supportive of homosexuality. The only representatives of Mary amidst this whole group of religious people were the Evangelical Sisters of Mary, a wonderful group of Lutheran nuns, headed by the remarkable German nun, Sister Basilea Schlenk, who started her order in a place called, Canaan, in the Arizona desert.

If you ever saw the film, *Lilies of the Field*, which I strongly recommend that you do, then you would see that Sister Basilea is a softer version of the nun portrayed in that movie. I hope that like the nun in that movie, she is fortunate enough to have had somebody as marvelous as Homer, (played by Sidney Poitier) who did most of the building.

For me, the most memorable event was the segment of the conference which was presided over by Rev. Everett Fullam who, with his congregation, was speaking in tongues. There is no way to describe the atmosphere when there is a congregation genuinely speaking in tongues. It is definitely a very worthy experience, and equally so, when they are singing in the spirit, which I happen to prefer—as I had once experienced in an evangelical service in Cathedral City, CA (near Palm Springs).

There is a book, *Miracle in Darien*, which tells how Rev. Fullam was called by God to start a charismatic movement in the Episcopalian congregation of St. Paul's Church in Darien. The congregation, while under his leadership, grew many times over, who knows, maybe one hundred fold? and the enthusiasm, beauty and joy manifested during his services were unmatched anywhere. His sermons were also the best I have ever heard. Indeed, if St. Paul were to return, in our midst, I imagine he would sound something like Terry (his nickname).

In 1997 we were fortunate enough to be able to put on a revival under a huge tent on the campus of Sacred Heart University in Fairfield, Connecticut. Approximately 1,400 people signed up, but a somewhat smaller amount actually came because in the typical fashion of spiritual warfare, there were the evil forces in the form of horrible winds accompanying Hurricane Bertha. This, on July 13, was very early for the hurricane season but the winds did not blow down that large tent.

Our speakers included Rev. Fullam, Dee Jepsen, wife of former Senator from Iowa, Roger Jepsen, a Lutheran and President of her own foundation, "Enough is Enough," which was set up to address pornography in order to prevent children, women and even families from becoming victims of sexual violence. But above all, for us Roman Catholics, she is known as the author of the book, *Jesus Called Her Mother*. The third speaker was our very own, Fr. Bill McCarthy, director of "My Father's House," the center in Moodus, CT., which is mainly, but not exclusively for Roman Catholics. Moodus is a town which before the war, had been the predecessor of the Catskills as a mainly Jewish retreat headquarters, since it is hilly and close to the Connecticut River, and also because of its somewhat proximity to a large urban Jewish population.

Our conference was remarkable in a number of ways. To begin with, it was the first ecumenical conference of this kind that I had ever heard about, in New England, and furthermore, because of the winds and rain accompanying Hurricane Bertha, there was up to one foot of water in some parts under the tent where there were live wires, but miraculously nobody was electrocuted. As soon as this was discovered, the sound man got to work and effected the necessary repairs. We should never forget that in spiritual warfare God wins.

The following year, in 1998, we wanted to repeat our success but did not achieve our goal. Our very outstanding speaker, Rev. Fullam suffered a very serious stroke and was unable to attend. We had some remarkable speakers nonetheless such as: Professor Courtney Bartholomew, Professor of Medicine at the University of Trinidad, who has written two books. His first, *The Ark of the Covenant*, has photographs of the same Shekinah glory as described in the Old Testament, which is the sheaf of a cloud, the manifestation of the presence of God, the Holy Spirit. I have received messages from visionaries also experiencing the vision of a long shaft of light, signifying the presence of God.

Another outstanding speaker was my friend, Margaret Heckler, who may be in some ways the woman in the U.S. with the most remarkable track record. She unseated Joe Martin (Democrat), former U.S. Senator from Massachusetts for 16 years!! Later, she was unseated by Barney Frank!! She became the Secretary of Health and Human Services and tried to warn the nation about the encroaching problem of AIDS long before anybody else was doing so. Finally, she was appointed Ambassador to the Republic of Ireland, a post for which she was truly qualified since, among many other great gifts for the post, her maiden name was O'Shaugnessey. Experiencing the miracle of her rosary turning to gold sparked her conversion process and made her a woman of even greater faith. She was inspired to spread the Gospel, this inspiration having been confirmed by the many visionaries whom she sometimes welcomes to her apartment in Virginia.

Her speech was also one of the most extraordinary ones I have ever heard, was later confirmed in an article in the *New York Times* which stated that our best knowledge is received, not through our heads, but in our hearts.

One of our original researchers of the Guadalupe Research Committee, who was involved with the NBC version of the 1981 documentary, was Professor Jody Brant Smith, Professor at Florida State University. Although he was a Methodist, he eventually became one of our enthusiastic supporters of Our Lady. I have always admired Methodists, including Elsie Kelsel, the judge from Ohio, who sat with me on the President's Committee on Mental Retardation (PCMR). She was one of my best buddies while serving on that Committee under President Reagan.

My husband's step-mother's sister was married to John Foster Dulles, an elder in the Presbyterian church. It was his son, Avery, who became a Roman Catholic priest and wrote an absolutely lovely short book about his conversion, *A Testament to Grace*.

In late May 1999, I went to a seminar during my husband's 50th reunion at Princeton, entitled, "Taking God to the Princeton Campus." The first speaker was an Indian oceanographer, a creative student whose parents had taken in Ghandi once and they told him that as a young lawyer in South Africa, he fought for citizens' rights and was beaten up. The people who cared for him after this attack were Catholic missionaries. After that, Ghandi always had a picture of Jesus on his wall. The young Indian remembered what his parents had told him and became an Evangelical at Princeton. He is one of the very few who are spearheading what you might call the return of God to the Princeton campus. This is based on a similar movement at Harvard University, entitled, "Veritas."

So the conundrum remains. Is the church the one which was founded by Jesus, and given to St. Peter to head in Rome, whose bones have actually been found in excavations far below the main cupola in St. Peter's Cathedral? Is this the religion of which Jesus said, "The gates of Hell shall not prevail against it?" What are they about and whom are they for? In the words of Mother Angelica, as she describes one of her programs, "Questions not promises."

CHAPTER FIFTY

THE JEWISH CONNECTION

Our Jewish driver was bringing us back from a trip to our monthly meeting with a New York State psychiatrist for Kim, a very sweet young man who lives on the property and who is a friend to our daughter. I thought to myself, "So where are we? Are we anywhere near Mamaroneck?" I must have spoken this aloud without realizing it because the young man said, "Yes. It is north of here." North was on the way home, so I said, "Good." Mamaroneck is the home of the best, and as a matter of fact, the only fresh caviar you can buy outside New York City, that I know of. Now that was one of my jobs which I never got around to doing. It was to buy caviar for our tax accountant (and myself) which I usually do every year, since he, like myself, has Russian and Jewish blood and likes caviar. It is a very special, almost genetic taste, you might say.

So we went to this place to get some. The new owner was a large bear of a man whose name was Fortier. I thought he was French Canadian, but when he saw my cross he said out loud, "Son of David, Have mercy upon us." It was my Edith Stein cross which caught his eye. David Rothbard, former whiz kid attending Jesuit Fairfield University while working for me, actually left the university before graduating to start his own think tank. Later he returned and obtained his diploma. David acquired my Edith Stein cross for me fifteen years ago when I sent him, in my stead, to a meeting of the Edith Stein Guild. Edith Stein was a German Jewish philosopher who had studied some Catholic Philosophers, and over the years became intrigued with Catholic philosophy. Eventually she became a Roman Catholic. This was during the 1930's while Adolf Hitler was gaining power in Germany. Being a Roman Catholic lay person was not enough for someone like Edith Stein with her personal and intense religious feelings. So finally, she joined the Order of Carmel and became a Carmelite nun.

When Hitler over-ran all of Europe she knew in her heart that she had to return to the scene of his crimes, to be a witness for God at the crimes of the Holocaust. She was imprisoned by the Nazis and was soon sent to her death at Auschwitz. She was recently beatified by Pope John Paul II amid some controversy.

I don't remember how I became a member of the Edith Stein Guild. It was inevitable under the circumstances, but David Rothbard brought back this cross to me and I have worn it ever since. The only person to notice it besides Mr. Fortier was Clare Booth Luce, in a church in Washington, DC., for some ceremony I no longer recall. As I was leaving she came up to me and said, "This is a very unusual cross. Please tell me about it," and I did.

I did not tell this to Mr. Fortier but I thought that my Jewish driver would be impressed that I was wearing such a cross. I believe that his wife thinks that I have the gift of prophecy, like the Old Testament prophet. Maybe that is what Elisha had inherited from his predecessor, Elijah. Maybe that was part of the double portion, which the spiritual healer John Gargiullo apparently discerned about me during a healing session at our home.

John Gargiullo conducts or conducted a healing service every Tuesday night at St. Maurice in Stamford, Connecticut, which I attended once. His style of being slain in the spirit leaves me in amazement at his "passion." One shouldn't forget, though, that he is Italian! Gargiullo is part of Helena Willett's network of Christian activists. Helena is a born-again Christian, who has offered her enormous sufferings over the last few years to Jesus Christ as an atonement for the sins of the world, just as Roman Catholics are adjoined to do.

My husband had been ill off-and-on for the last few years and one of the healers who prayed for him was John Gargiullo. I remember one occasion very well when he came into our library, which is my own family's healing space. It has two stained glass windows, one with an image of Jesus and another with an image of Mary. (By the way, these images stirred up much antagonism in my atheist neighbor who could see them over a high brick wall as he rode by on his horse.) Gargiullo laid his hand on my husband and started speaking in the spirit. Lo and Behold! I recognized that he was speaking in old French. Afterwards, I asked him whether he was aware of this. He said no, but he also said that I must have the Charism of the Holy Spirit, the gift of interpretation of tongues. Some day I shall comprehend the full import of this. We are obviously on some spiritual wavelength which is still being played out. John Gargiullo also told me that he perceived that I had the double "portion" that Elijah gave to Elisha, his successor. Since I am not a Bible scholar I had to research this story. I still did not know what that meant in my life but it is becoming clearer now. All of these incidents took place in 1994.

Back to my trip home from Mamaroneck: my Jewish driver drove me home with the caviar and as I ruminated on the events at the grocery store I knew, inevitably, that there was a connection with the Jews in my life, which is part of the tapestry that is being woven.

It was sometime in 1991, that I once again heard that mysterious voice telling me, just before waking up, "You should call John Jackson." That is all the voice said. I knew I had to acknowledge this familiar prophetic voice, so I called John Jackson, the principal investigator and instigator of the Shroud Team in 1978, and told him the truth. I told him I had just had a dream in which I was instructed to call him. John Jackson has a great sense of humor and said that only to somebody like him could I call with such a message.

At that time I was in the process of forming the CCJU (Center for Christian Jewish Understanding) at Sacred Heart University, in Fairfield, Connecticut. In 1980 I tried to launch the Center for Marian Studies at Sacred Heart University but it had not taken off at all, since people in those days were not very interested in Mary. Things changed only after the full significance of Mary's apparition in Medjugorje, in June 1981 was revealed. So in 1991. I said to myself, "Maybe I can start a Center for Christian Jewish Understanding, since Mary is the Jewish Mother of mankind, Miriam of Carmel."

Father Val McInnes was a member of the Shroud of Turin Exhibition Committee, also Head of the Tulane Center for Judeo-Christian Studies and a good family friend. He gave me the model and so much help by coming up from New Orleans to attend the early formative meetings held in our home. I also met with Rabbi Wallin, a faculty member at Sacred Heart University (SHU). At that time, Rabbi Wallin was the rabbinical advisor, just before the departure of the soon to be ex-President of SHU, Dr. Thomas Melady, who had been appointed by his friend, George Bush, as Ambassador to the Vatican. I happened to sit next to the distinguished Stamford, Connecticut Rabbi, Joseph Ehrenkranz at a going-away luncheon party in Stamford, in honor of Ambassador designate Melady.

When I told Rabbi Ehrenkranz of my inspired desire to launch a Center for Judeo-Christian Understanding, just like the one my friend, Fr. Val McInnes, started at Tulane University, he was very interested. He also informed me that he was about to lead a tour group of Catholics and Jews to Rome and Israel, and inquired whether I would like to join them. I said I would like to go but could only spare a week, which happened to be the week they were to spend in Rome.

As Rabbi Ehrenkrantz became more involved with the formation of the CCJU, he retired from his post as Rabbi to the congregation in Stamford, Connecticut. The distinguished and well-known Rabbi

Edward Bemporad (who looked very much like my half-brother, whose name was also Edward), worked alongside with Rabbi Ehrenkrantz and they became a team to direct the formation of the CCJU. There were a series of meetings in which major participants in the Jewish and Catholic communities attended. Eventually we were able to give a very successful fundraising dinner, at which many illustrious persons spoke. Even those among the Cardinals of the Catholic Church got involved. There is a picture with the original Rabbis and the Holy Father himself. For yours truly, adhering to the principle of remaining in the closet to do the good works, this was no exception, since I was excluded from all the photo ops.

I believe this very successful CCJU became a model for the formation of the Mark Tanenbaum Foundation (The late Rabbi Tanenbaum was a leading person on the board of my foundation as well as in the Catholic Jewish rapprochement), which also became an outstanding success. It is more secular, you might say, than the CCJU, but the goals are similar, establishing a rapprochment between Christians and Jews. Only recently was I able to contribute a gift which ended up by being matched by Steven Spielberg himself, probably through his Righteous Persons Foundation.

It was, as I said in 1991, at the time of the formation of the CCJU that I got that mysterious message in my dream to call John Jackson. I told John that I would soon be going on a trip to Rome, but could not stay for the whole tour which would last two weeks. John said that he really needed to go to Rome with his new assistant, Rebecca Hadassani, a Jewish convert, because they wanted to find out if they could get permission to have a meeting in Rome about the Shroud. I said, "Oh well, maybe that is why I am supposed to call you. Maybe you and Rebecca would like to come along," and come along they did. I believe the high point of the trip for both John Jackson and Rebecca Hadassani was their private meeting with Cardinal Angelini, who was wearing a ring with the face of the Shroud on it. That was sufficient to let us know where his sentiments lay.

John and Rebecca, now his wife, subsequently attended a

meeting with the Cardinal, who in turn invited them to a symposium on the Shroud which he organized. This was in 1998.

The response to the replica of the Shroud in Moscow, where they have set up a center, of which I am very much in favor for very obvious genetic (and political) reasons, is good. Such positive support is still lacking in non-Catholic countries which are still influenced by the spurious 1988 Carbon 14 dating (might I suggest as possibly an allegedly rigged investigation conducted under the auspices of certain persons at an English university).

On our way to Rome, for no obvious reason, I said that one could expect a high while we were in flight because of the altitude. I then blurted out a question to John and Rebecca. I asked, "Have you ever heard of Lilith?" (I had no idea where that came from). Rebecca said that she was some ancient goddess figure in the Cabalistic Hebraic writings and that was all.

A few months later, I requested an internet search on this character since I thought there might be some connection between this ancient goddess and the increasing number of women who were murdering their unborn babies—Medea style. It was only recently during a deliverance ceremony did this name come up again, and as they say in the movies, I thought I was on to something. It is Lilith, a female demon, who is behind all these abortions. I will discuss this in greater depth towards the end of the book, or maybe in a subsequent book. I will talk about the problem of evil since I always seem to be on the front lines, fighting it wherever I go.

> "Be not overcome of evil, but overcome evil with good"
> (Rom. 12:21).

A year after our trip to Rome, the Jacksons were married. I was invited to be the best lady but I could not fulfill this role since I was then visiting the Island of St. Martin, and it would have been too long a trip back to the U.S.

In 1992 there was a Shroud symposium in Rome which the

Jacksons attended, along with many others including the Russian Baptist physicist, Dimitri Kousnetsov. I was able to finance one year's investigative work at the Moscow laboratory run by Dimitri, and working jointly with John, they were on the cusp of making a joint discovery, which would refute the 1988 Carbon 14 tests. Just at that time, I ran out of money and the program could not go forward. However, political events soon caught up with us and are now converging with the spiritual ones.

CHAPTER FIFTY-ONE

THE THREE GRIDS

The first grid describes geopolitical realities, a dangerous triad; the rearming of Russia?, the arming of China, worldwide, and the Islamic terrorist surrogates, and concomitantly, the decline of morals, the increase in decadence, particularly in the United States at this time.

The second grid is made up of prophecies of destruction and chastisements upon this planet particularly predicting weather changes, violent storms, and even comets and boloids smashing into the earth, mitigated or delayed by prayer, as retold by visionaries, the re-emergence of signs leading to the End Times such as American Indian prophecies, the return of the lost tribes of Israel, and prophecies from the Bible both Old and New Testaments, as well as prophecies from Nostadamus, et. al.

The third grid, the antidote to the evils of the other grids is, as the Blessed Mother would say, "pray, pray, pray." This also redresses the balance between the "haves" and "have nots", from the micro to the macro, from the First to the Fourth Worlds, as well as a return to God, to *Godliness*, to living the Gospel worldwide.

By means of these three grids I would like to demonstrate that the third grid or the spiritual grid is of a positive nature, and includes good things we can do as God has directed through His various visionaries and through the Holy Scriptures. This grid has a direct effect on the activities of first grid—of the activities on planet earth—and will have an impact on wars and rumors of wars and the sins and suffering of mankind.

To clarify the situation I would like to cite three examples showing how that grid seems to have worked in the past. Because of the enormous impact of the apparitions of the Mother of God in Fatima, Portugal in 1917 on the visionary environment, if you could call it that (read *The Fatima Prophecy* by Tom Petrisko) I shall start there.

In the aforementioned book you will see that two monasteries at ground zero in Hiroshima were left standing amidst absolute devastation within a five mile radius. The only reason given for this is that the monks in those monasteries, founded by St. Maximillian Kolbe, said the rosary non-stop for two years (See Rosary of Hiroshima).

On a scientific level, the famous Canadian healer, Ambrose Worrall, conducted a study to determine the effect of his thoughts on the progress of cancer cells, the best study of its kind at that time. He demonstrated that his positive thoughts or prayer for the healing of the cancer cells actually produced the desired result. The positive effect of prayer and its corollary, good works, has a direct impact on grid #1 which I have mapped out with the words—volcanoes, earthquakes, insurrections. The meaning of natural disasters cannot always be explained in terms of cause and effect. Maybe a majority are amazingly cause and effect, but not all.

For the first time in the late 20th century in recorded seismological history some new faults are becoming active in the Los Angeles basin. These were not known faults, yet existed for many years. Suddenly they became active, specifically on January 17, 1994, resulting in an earthquake, which caused great devastation. Its epicenter was in Northridge, California which at that time was the center for pornography on this planet. Whether the people who were in charge put two and two together, I don't know. It seems to me that unless the movie/TV industry cleans up itself, chances are that "the big one" may arrive sooner rather than later.

Two monasteries at ground zero in Hiroshima were
left standing amidst absolute devastation within
a five mile radius

A very esteemed deliverance minister who, with his wife, has
written many books, speaks of the spirits not only of people and
places but also of cities and countries as if to say these ego-
entities need to be delivered of the presence of evil. This is
something you can only believe if you believe in the presence of

evil or in the presence of the Prince of Darkness, Satan, the Father of Lies.

This now brings us to the current phenomenon of leadership in the US the "right wing conspiracy" alleging its involvement in, at last count, at least 102 deaths (not including, possibly, the Oklahoma bombing and related disasters and as yet unconfirmed connections). From the last two pieces of information of the supernatural or preternatural as Maureen Dowd of the *New York Times* prefers to call it—(last year she made a "preternatural" 180 degree turn about, interestingly enough, in this regard)—two very incomprehensible factoids have emerged. One is the very uncanny resemblance between the current President and the Roman Emperor, Nero, whose behavior matched that of our President as demonstrated in the *Apocalypse* segment of the TV documentary series, *Mysteries of the Bible*. The second is that a Messianic Jewish internet group has made it known that in the Greek and Hebrew systems of numerology, our President's name adds up to 666. You figure.

PART V

PART 4

CHAPTER FIFTY-TWO

THE DAWN OF POLITICS

It was in the early days of our marriage. I was pregnant with our first child, Patricia, while we were living in New York City in this wonderful apartment two flights up at 8 East 92nd St. I was taking a bus downtown to St. Patrick's Cathedral for first Saturday devotions, which the Blessed Mother asked of us in her apparition at Fatima, Portugal, in reparation for the sins of mankind. She said in effect that if her requests were heeded, and if mankind turns back to God, then there will be peace. If not, "Russia will spread her errors throughout the world and several nations will be annihilated. But eventually my Immaculate Heart will triumph." Somehow or other, I got hold of the Fatima message, maybe through Bishop Sheen, or from a speaker somewhere. Whatever my source, I was determined to answer Our Lady's call so that at the very least, several nations would not be annihilated by the enemy, Communism, which Our Lady identified to three little children, on that fateful day in Fatima, Portugal in 1917, even before the Bolshevik revolution.

So I got on a bus going down Fifth Avenue, but had to hold on to the rail because all the seats were taken. I believe I was five months pregnant, maybe more. It was during fall and my pregnancy showed. This kindly looking black woman was sitting down and looked up at me and said, "Oh please take my seat". We struck up a conversation. I accepted gladly and I told her where I was going and why, and she said, "Oh, I am too." I always remembered that. It was part of the weaving in and out of my life of the black presence and the black consciousness.

These were the early days of our marriage. Along with the Fatima devotions, part and parcel of which were the dire political implications, we also made regular treks to presentations given by famous Communist dissidents and drop-outs from the Communist Party USA such as Elizabeth Bentley, Bella Dodd, and Sydney Hook. The latter was the primary inspiration of the Jewish anti-Communist and largely Democratic neo-conservatives including Midge Decter and husband Norman Podhoretz, Irving Kristol, Ben Wattenberg et al, who were anti-Communists with whom we worked so harmoniously 30 years later during the Reagan administration. We also heard some other speakers—champions such as: Rep Walter Judd of Minnesota, Congressman Tom Dodd, Senator Chris Dodd's father (would you believe this?) and the redoubtable physician, Dr. C. Fred Schwarz, whom we were to meet a few years later in Los Angeles where he spoke regularly. Schwarz was a very perspicacious Australian physician who realized the dangers of Communism, and came to warn the West, which in this case was East (and North) of his homeland. He was my first early mentor on the nature of Communism. His famous phrase and title of his book was, *You Can Trust A Communist to be a Communist.* That's still true now and helps me deal with the dilemma presented by much of the leadership of the Western world at the present moment, which is becoming mostly socialistic.

It was also at this time during my pregnancy that I remember walking up stairs in the west side of New York City, unlikely neighborhoods, promoting the presidential candidacy of General Eisenhower, of whom my husband and I were great admirers and supporters.

We shall fast forward to the political realm to the 1970's because the intervening years were taken up with having children and addressing the tremendous situation concerning our eldest child. I didn't realize at the time that she was implicated so intimately in the apparition of Fatima, or for that matter that my birthday, May 13th ,was involved. I didn't know at that time that Patricia would be the Great Sign for our family. It was in fact when it dawned on me sometime in the late 70's, I wrote The Grand Design, which appears later in this book, describing the situation.

Beginning with the arrival on our front door one Spring day in 1979 of a stalwart and bon vivant sailor, Eben Graves, who came from a fine old Southport, Connecticut family and had lived close to Senator Prescott Bush Sr., father of George Sr., and Prescott Jr. As he stormed through our front door, Eben, in his typical right-brained fashion, declared that we would have to give a party for John Connally's presidential campaign. I had not done anything politically at all since the early 50's, except for a brief foray as precinct captain while we were in Los Angeles, and later, a very strong preference for fellow Californian, Richard Nixon, over the Easterner, Nelson Rockefeller.

It was in those early days in Los Angeles, when I was a precinct captain for the Republican party, I used to do my doorbell ringing in fancy Holmby Hills, home to assorted "fat cats," if I may say so. (I much preferred walking up the stairs of the houses in the west side of New York) One of the people who was "under" me was the mother of a school chum of mine, Jane Browne, now a successful book editor in Chicago. Jane went to the same eastern school, Ethel Walker's, and was in attendance at our 50th reunion last year. She and I were both chosen to tell our stories to the class since we'd both had interesting lives. The most interesting thing about her story that I remember was that one of her clients was the one and only Mickey Cohen, the famous West Coast gangster, no doubt a colleague of our former acquaintance, Bugsy Siegel. He'd offer her anything to get his book published, but I think she turned him down even as she hilariously put it, that she'd been offered "a free hit."

Her mom, a very interesting lady as well, lived in West Los Angeles, and had regular meetings of Catholic intellectuals, which

Harry and I attended with great pleasure since our intellectual life was woefully wanting in those early years when we were living in Beverly Hills.

Another early political memory of that era was being in the Nixon-Lodge motorcade for those of us who spoke Spanish including Ginger Rogers, stalwart conservative that she always was. We saw her in Washington at fundraisers working for Reagan many years later. So here we were in an open convertible throwing flowers to the (few!) people who would line the streets to see us in the semi barrio of East Los Angeles and shouting "Viva Nixon", Ginger Rogers and I and eight other people. Was that funny or what?

Back to Eben Graves. Dealing with him was always a big laugh, I assure you. Through some extraordinary peregrinations and backing and filling, we finally got John Connolly to show up for this fundraiser, an unlikely event, but in order to make it a success we had to have a "heavy hitter." Eben, Harry and I huddled almost football team style and came up with the only person we thought could be the heavy hitter we needed—Henry Kissinger.

In order to ensure that John Connally would show up, we had to actually get him out of the shower, and come to the phone from his home in Texas. I remember that very well. Only someone like Eben Graves could pull this off.

Getting Kissinger was somewhat harder, somewhat easier. Easier, I suppose, because I had met Kissinger at a Jewish committee function at which Abba Eban, formerly an Israeli foreign minister, was a keynote speaker. I think Kissinger remembered seeing me at a Republican Eagles convention in Beverly Hills. The Eagles are large contributors to the Republican party. After then I saw Mr. Kissinger who seemed to have connected me with Jewish causes.

In any event, he did show up with his lovely wife, Nancy, their car, flanked by a pair of motorcycle outriders carrying little flags on their motorcycles. Would you believe it? Poor Nancy had a very bad cold. However, the evening was a great success. We had all the local politicians and about 600 people and the TV networks. It was quite an event. The high point of the evening was Kissinger's introduction of John Connolly. When a reporter asked Kissinger why he was supporting Connolly, he replied, "ve people vit accents must stick togezzer" in his deep German drawl. It was memorable and one of my husband's favorite jokes. Eventually, this kind of political activity contributed to my being appointed to serve in health care in the public sector a few years later.

After that famous fundraiser we had for John Connally in 1979, Ronald Reagan got the nomination. So we worked for him since he was a better candidate anyhow, and thus we began our latest political careers. After we joined the Eagles, we went to all kinds of parties all over the place. I remember one in particular at the Rancho Mirage where Jonas Savimbi, the freedom fighter from Angola, who regretfully later lost to the Communists, was the speaker. On another occasion, Ian Smith, the then Prime Minister of Rhodesia (now called Zimbabwe) was the speaker when we went to the Biltmore for yet another fundraiser with Robin Moore, who authored *The Green Berets* and the *French Connection*. Robin blurted out a strange thing. He first introduced me extemporaneously to the hundreds who were present in the Biltmore dining room, then went on to say that I was Rhodesia's best friend in the U.S. Did he know something that I didn't know? (This could partially explain why Rhodesia was lost to the Communists?!)

Robin and Mary Olga Moore

In those glorious early Reagan years, we had the time of our lives. Our daughter, Patricia, was in the care of a couple with whom she lived in Thomaston, Connecticut. She was doing well, going to colleges and even studying to be a nurse, which alas proved too physically challenging for her. She also drove about two to three hundred miles a week from Thomaston to Waterbury or Hartford, depending on which college she was attending, and then back down to Fairfield to spend the weekends with us. She was really prodigious, driving through ice storms, everything.

We were determined to have as much fun as possible since, frankly, we hadn't had very much fun over the years. We became friends with John Lodge, former ambassador, governor, congressman, and his delightful wife Francesca, who eventually joined the board of the Fourth World Foundation. One of the Lodges' closest friends was Robin Moore and his lovely new wife, Mary Olga, who was of some Russian heritage. We became very friendly with the Moores. Robin and I hit it off for some reason, maybe both of us were right-brained. I really appreciated him and was really in awe of our little charmed circle—the Lodges, Moores and us—because we all wanted to have a good time, among other things.

We became friends with John Lodge,
and his delightful wife Francesca

John Lodge had been an actor in his earlier years—he was actually a good actor, added to that he was extremely good looking, and personable too. He was in a film called *The Scarlet Empress* with Marlene Dietrich, which was about my ancestor, Catherine the Great, and how she took Orlov as her lover since Romanoff couldn't have children or something like that. In any event, this film was shown at an event I had originally wanted to do, Walter Mitty-style, called the John Lodge Film Festival, which was actually finally organized by Robin in his home.

Robin and Mary Olga bought their house from the well-known local Hungarian artist, Steve Dohanos, one of the founding members of the Famous Artists' School, a designer of many of the American postage stamps and a very fine painter in the order of Norman Rockwell. His wife, Margie, had been on the board of the Huxley Institute since they had a schizophrenic son. We were friends until Margie died. Steve was a very lovely man too and was much missed by us when he, too, passed on. I've always enjoyed Hungarians, you know.

Later, after John Lodge died, there was a ceremony dedicating a portion of the Connecticut Turnpike to him. You can see the sign if you look carefully. But since he was a conservative, the sign was probably smaller than it had to be. Nevertheless, John Lodge was a Renaissance man if ever there was one. I have to confess that once on a train on the way down to Washington, he asked if I would go with him and Francesca to Marbella where they had a summer home, and where he wanted me to take down his memoirs. But as my husband says, I wasn't cut out to be an amanuensis. Still, what an honor to be considered for the part of a Boswell to John Lodge's Dr. Johnson.

Robin joined us at the reception after the dedication ceremony at the Longshore Country Club, Westport's official country club. This is where our friend, Nancy Pettee, (from Albertus) took us many years before and successfully talked us into moving to Connecticut from New York in 1960. It's a lovely place but frankly, compared to say the Pierre, or the roof of the St. Regis, rather plebeian. After a lot of speeches, Robin was getting bored and so was I, so we went up to the mezzanine overlooking the assembly and consoled ourselves with a few dry martinis. I wondered if this famous man had something up his sleeves. Of course, he did. He was simply a better "spy" than me. He successfully talked me into throwing the only really large party I ever hosted, not for a charitable or political cause. Of course I'd thrown parties for the Huxley Institute and later for the activities on behalf of the Blessed Mother. What Robin wanted me to do was to throw a party for the Greek part of the island of Cyprus, and, of course, after those martinis, I had to say, yes.

That party was almost indescribable. We had the Cypriots dancing with glasses on top of their heads and the woman who managed it was our household manager at the time, Francesca Fiore, a remarkable woman who showed enormous compassion to our daughter, Patricia. She had been a caterer and had manufactured her own pepper jelly. It was hot! She successfully masterminded getting 160 people seated with gold chairs, candlelight, etc. It was amazing. But frankly I didn't have too much fun because there were too many people.

Eventually the government of Cyprus, after much pressure, decided to reward us. So accompanying my husband on his way to the Mideast on business, we stopped off at Cyprus and had someone official take us around to see all the sites. The most memorable site for me was seeing the rock from which Aphrodite purportedly emerged, memorialized by Botticelli as a giant shell in a famous painting hanging in the Museo Uffizzi in Florence. That picture engendered an interest in me that never bore fruit, namely to start a single's club called Club Aphrodite on St. Martin. The locals on St. Martin actually approached me on this idea. I hadn't approached them. They either spoke French or English but not both, so I had to translate. But that idea didn't come about, I suppose, because of too many hurricanes. The place we wanted had a rock like the one in Cyprus with a restaurant called The Waves on it. But this place had too many waves. (Next, you know what—I'm only kidding.)

CHAPTER FIFTY-THREE

FATIMA'S WRITING ON THE WALL

Here is Will Brownell's take on Fatima. Brownell, coincidentally, was Robin Moore's ex-nephew-in-law; his first wife was Robin's niece.

Daniel 5: 1-6

Belshazzar the king made a great feast to a thousand of his lords, and drank wine before the thousand.

Belshazzar, whiles he tasted the wine, commanded to bring the golden and silver vessels which his father Nebuchadnezzar had taken out of the temple which was in Jerusalem; that the king and his princes, his wives, and his concubines, might drink therein.

Then they brought the golden vessels that were taken out of the temple of the house of God which was at Jerusalem; and the king, and his princes, his wives, and his concubines, drank in them.

They drank wine, and praised the gods of gold, and of silver, of brass, of iron, of wood, and of stone.

In the same hour came forth fingers of a man's hand, and wrote over against the candlestick upon the plaster of the wall of the king's palace; and the king saw the part of the hand that wrote.

Then the king's countenance changed, and his thoughts troubled him, so that the joints of his loins were loosed, and his knees smote one against the other.

IBID: 13-14

Then was Daniel brought in before the king. And the king spake and said unto Daniel, Art thou that Daniel, which art of the children of the captivity of Judah, whom the king my father brought out of Jewry?

I have even heard of thee, that the spirit of the gods is in thee, and that light and understanding and excellent wisdom is found in thee.

IBID: 16-17

And I have heard if thee, that thou canst make interpretations, and dissolve doubts; now if thou canst read the writing, and make known to me the interpretation thereof, thou shalt be clothed with scarlet, and have a chain of gold about thy neck, and shalt be the third ruler of the kingdom.

Then Daniel answered and said before the king, Let thy gifts be to thyself, and give thy rewards to another; yet I will read the writing unto the king, and make known to him the interpretation.

IBID: 23-28

But hast lifted up thyself against the Lord of heaven; and they have brought the vessels of his house before thee, and thou, and thy lords, thy wives, and thy concubines, have drunk wine in them; and thou hast praised the gods of silver, and gold, and brass, iron, wood and

stone, which see not, nor hear, nor know; and the God in
whose hand thy breath is, and whose are all thy ways,
hast thou not glorified:

Then was the part of the hand sent from him; and
this writing was written.

And this is the writing that was written,
MENE, MENE, TEKEL, UPHARSIN.

This is the interpretation of the thing:

MENE; God hath numbered thy kingdom, and finished it.

TEKEL; Thou art weighed in the balances and art found
wanting.

UPHARSIN; Thy kingdom is divided, and given to the
Medes and Persians.

The beginning of the First World War was not the series of
events that took place in 1914, nor any other series of events
which are generally cited as leading to the beginning of that
conflict. Rather, the world war as we understand it, must be described as a *word* war, a war of the spirit against the machine, the
lotus against the robot and the genie of man against the devil of
the universe.

This conflict was unleashed in earnest on the 13th of October of 1917, when Lenin's thugs assaulted the Church of the
Iberian Virgin, and simultaneously as the Virgin *in* Iberia declared the devil to be coming into an ascendancy. The rest of the
century was to become essentially a duel between these two forces,
a conflict that would sweep from Siberia to Spain and would spill
over onto all other continents and regions and which would
threaten, by the latter half of the century, to engulf and destroy
the bulk of the human race itself.

Bishop Fulton J. Sheen has written concerning these events
that they seemed to usher in the modern era.

Lenin's assault on the Church of the Iberian Virgin was the opening salvo of the great conflict between the sword and the spirit, between the robot and the lotus, between pragmatic materialism and visionary Christianity. Since that opening salvo, there have been increased skirmishes, confused struggling, and the proverbial clash of armies fighting in the night. Amid it all, there is no one today who can claim to be sure of the extent of the battles before God's final triumph and, indeed, there are few today, who would even venture more than a few guesses. The doomsdayers and soothsayers on the one hand are forming a Greek chorus to say that all is doomed and all are damned, while in the meantime, the pious idealists and hemophiliac liberals chatter among themselves most amiably about how all systems may accommodate one another, and how the lambs and lions may lie down together in peace. In point of fact, however, modern history since 1917 has been one global war of the lotus against the robot; of man's strivings for his better essence, against his tendency for a far lower level of being.

The purpose of this part is to offer a history, chronicle, record, account or memoir of this struggle, with its reverses and stalemates, partial victories and defeats, and with their ramifications and implications for the present and beyond. For the events in Moscow at the Church of the Iberian Virgin on that day in 1917 were not isolated. Simultaneously, on the 13th of October, in the Iberian Peninsula itself, the Virgin Herself appeared to three prophet children with a message of things to come.

It is not our purpose here to tell the well-known story of that day. As is known, some 70,000 persons gathered to test whether these prophet children were lying. The children claimed they had seen the Virgin on previous occasions on the 13th day of each of the preceding five months: May 13, June 13, July 13, August 19, (six days later because the children were incarcerated by the authorities) and September 13. The newspapers and various groups had become involved and the issue of the apparitions had become something of a cause célèbre. Rumors abounded about what the Virgin had allegedly said to the children on the previous occasions. Garbled versions of the reports indicated that there had been some statement about another world war to follow the present conflict, and also that there had been mention of Russia itself, and the idea that at some future moment entire nations might be "annihilated." At this moment, however, almost no one had any idea of an atomic bomb. A science fiction writer, H. G. Wells, had written about it in one passing reference, and a young scientist named Albert Einstein had hypothesized a theory which would seem to indicate that such destructive devices could exist. With such weapons, whole nations could be destroyed. But all this was in 1917 and this set of concepts was imagined only in a few dozen minds on earth. To most pragmatic and practical people, the idea of whole nations being annihilated was prima facie evidence that the prediction came from a demented source. Also the idea that there might be another world war to follow this world war was considered utter nonsense. World War I was "the war to end all wars," the war to make the world safe for democratic government. It was "the Great War," and in the minds of very practical people, the story coming out of the mouths of the children was just that: children's tales.

What then transpired at Fatima in Portugal, when the Virgin appeared to the three Iberian children, was in a sense an answer to the materialistic challenge which Lenin and his cohorts had delivered to the Church of the Iberian Virgin in Moscow. As Bishop Sheen described it:

> . . . The Blessed Mother first appeared to the children
> and then pointed to the sun as a rift in the clouds made

it visible. The sun seemed almost to detach itself from the heavens, becoming like a great silver ball; shooting sparks in all directions, it seemed to descend to the earth as if about to precipitate itself upon the people. Immediately they all cried out to God in prayer and supplication, in sorrow and in contrition. Three times the sun became a whirling mass of flashing silver and, spinning on its axis, cast off beams of multicolored light, as it plunged and zigzagged its way to earth. The crowd shrank in fear and clamored for mercy as the molten mass seemed about to destroy them. And though it rained all day, after the miracle of the sun had taken place three times, everyone discovered that their clothes were dry . . . . . .

While much has been written or suggested about the Fatima apparition, one particular aspect has failed to receive due emphasis and here we refer to the secret message from the Virgin to the shepherdess Lucia dos Santos, and from her to the Portuguese bishop in Leiria, who conveyed it to the Archbishop of Coimbra, who in turn relayed the message to Rome, where it was brought before Pope Pius XII.

The Pope read the message with what was reported as "a look of dismay." He then ordered that it be sealed and put away—which of course was done. Years later there was some possibility that he would re-open the message and let it become public, but he died just a few days before this was to be done.

Pope John XXIII, who succeeded him, did not make it public and made it clear, in 1963, the reasons why. "The third message of Fatima will remain a secret of the Vatican. It cannot be made public because its contents would cause a world-wide panic."

Of course, the best source on the third message of Fatima

would be the girl Lucia Dos Santos herself, but she has been extraordinarily reticent regarding details of the secret. Shortly before the third message was given to the Pope in Rome, Lucia was questioned by a high-ranking church dignitary about what she, Lucia, felt was transpiring. Her statement merits being quoted in full:

> " . . . I tell you, Father, Satan is about to win the decisive battle. What is so troubling to the heart, in all of this, is the martyrdom of so many decent men and women. Of course you know that there are many religious people and priests who are neglectful of their calling and their work. I say we must all change our lives, for the Devil is about. He wishes to seize our souls, he attempts to undermine them in order to have them lead others to a state of total unrepentance. He is using every trick and device to get us to leave the pathway of faith and righteousness. Because of this, our inner lives are often so dry, the world is so cold, and there are so few who devote themselves totally to God.
>
> I tell you, Father, that the Mother of Jesus is suspended as if between two choices and two swords . . . . She sees the hardening and stubbornness of mankind . . . She sees how many of us remain unbelievers, so sensual and pleasure-seeking and materialistic . . . .The Mother of Jesus told me clearly that we are coming to the End of Time:
>
> We must become aware of the terrible truth of what is to come."

But Lucia is not recorded as having said any more than this since approximately 1920. Did she retire into silence in terms of her own inner path? Did she receive instructions to maintain silence, in terms of her authorities' known fear that the third message of Fatima would cause a worldwide panic? Both explanations are entirely plausible and indeed, there are those who have argued that both are simultaneously correct. In whatever event though, there have been fragments of the third message which have come to light at one moment and then at another, and like the pieces of a broken mosaic, can be reassembled into a proper whole.

The Marian Apparition on October 13, 1917 was clearly warning about the savage and unanticipated growth of communism in the 20th Century and in this context it is meet and fitting that one consider the multiple reasons. It was not just the fact that Lenin and his cohorts had launched the first symbolic (and real) attack against the churches of Russia on just that date, when they attacked the Church of the Iberian Virgin. The Virgin, in her apparition in Iberia, was clearly identifying communism as a supreme and menacing evil which threatened not just a part of the globe but, indeed, the human race itself. Reverend Richard Wurmbrand elaborates upon this concept in his 80-page essay entitled, *Was Karl Marx a Satanist?*

*   *   *

Marx wrote as a young man, "I wish to avenge myself against the One who rules above." Other references from Marx's early years include poems with such lines as:

"Wish to build for myself a throne . . . ."

And, even more revealingly, there is a five-line section of a poem by Marx, a poem titled "The Fiddler," which seems to go as far as Marx would admit it publicly:

"The hellish vapors rise and fill the brain,
Till I go mad and my heart is utterly changed.

> See this sword?
> The Prince of Darkness
> Sold it to me."

In this context, the reader must be reminded that the major initiation rites of the Satanic Mass involve an enchanted sword which guarantees the candidate's success. (In return for this guarantee, the candidate must sign a covenant in blood taken from his very wrists, a covenant that his soul will belong to Satan after he, the candidate, dies.)

When did this transformation take place in the life of Karl Marx? No one is utterly certain, but evidence would seem to indicate that before 1837, the young Marx was fairly Christian and sometimes even devout, but that after the autumn of that year, something had happened and some change had taken place. Marx wrote his father on November 10 of that year: "A curtain had fallen. My Holy of Holies was rent asunder and new gods had to be installed."

We do not find too clear an indication of how the Holy of Holies had been rent asunder. Marx's father wrote a fatherly letter earlier that year about how he hoped that Marx's heart would remain pure and that "no demon will be able to alienate your heart from better feelings . . . ." But there is considerable evidence that some demon *did* alienate his heart and, in this context, one should consider Marx's poem "The Pale Maiden," which reads:

> Thus Heaven I've forfeited,
> I know it full well.
> My soul, once true to God,
> Is Chosen for Hell.

Marx's attitude of vehement allegiance to Hell and the Devil became a tenet of Marxist/Communist dogma and, however much some communists would appear to have abandoned some aspects of Marxism, they have been steadfast and true to this one. As Reverend Wurmbrand succinctly stated the case: "When the Soviets in their early years adopted the slogan, 'Let us drive out the capitalists from earth and God from heaven,' they were merely fulfilling the legacy of Karl Marx." And some relatively orthodox Marxists seem to have at least tacitly noted the possibility of Marx's Satanism One such observer was the biographer of Marx, Franz Mehring, who was himself a Marxist and who wrote of Karl Marx's father that "Karl Marx's father . . . seems to have observed with secret apprehension the demon in his favorite son. Henry Marx did not think and could not have thought that the rich store of bourgeois culture, which he handed on to his son Karl as a valuable heritage for life would only help to deliver the demon he feared." And the demonic quality of Marxism seems not only to have been transferred throughout the movement to everything that it touched, it also was acknowledged as demonic by many of its more eminent victims. Bukharin himself, whose death served as a literary theme for Arthur Koestler's definitive condemnation of Stalinism, Darkness at Noon, said shortly before he was executed: "My life ends. I bow my head under the ax of the henchman. I feel all my lack of power before this infernal machine . . . ."

In so referring to Stalin, he may have been alluding to Stalin's actions in general, or possibly to Stalin's quality in particular. (Stalin's pseudonym at first was "Demonoshvili," or "the Demoniac." Only later was it changed to "Stalin," or "Man of Steel.") His prime henchman, Yagoda, was wont to shoot at the images of Christ and the Saints, in clear imitation of Satanist ritual. His prime predecessor, Lenin, exulted in the manner in which they were all cutting loose from the past, and in their guilt in relation to the standards of the era. "We all deserve to be hanged on a stinking rope," Lenin wrote in 1921.

It was U.S. President, Ronald Reagan, who with courage pulled the wool up long enough to let the world see world communism for what it is. Reagan called it, "The Evil Empire," a phrase that reverberated around the world and even led many average Russians to reconsider the course of their country.

CHAPTER FIFTY-FOUR

THE EVIL EMPIRE

The politics of the 1980's, which led up to the destruction of the Berlin wall and the seeming dissolution of the Soviet Empire, in retrospect, were merely a breather before the huge warfare which might soon occur on the planet. A look back at Czarist Russia will enable us to find out the origins of the Evil Empire.

Did the Evil Empire start with the early Bolshevik assassination of the first cousin of my great, great grandfather, Czar Alexander II, in that very first awful act of terror? Russian historians, including my husband's fellow Princetonian, James Billington, the author of *The Icon and the Axe*, and the current Librarian of the Library of Congress, have described in their own way the events leading up to the Bolshevik takeover in 1917. Billington, in his own inimitable style, provides an account which is as different as all the others who have written about this period. This is understandable because of the complexity of the unfolding historical events, which, from my point of view, is the ongoing struggle between the forces of good and evil of our time. When looked at in that way it does simplify the issue by seeing that the Czars, famous for their repression of the serfs, their anti-Semitism, and the cruel autocracy of the Russian Court which my cousin Alexander II attempted to reform, were nonetheless battling the forces of evil in their own country. When Alexander II liberated the serfs, those evil forces retaliated by assassinating him.

Americans who watch documentary TV programs are probably more aware of the injustices of the late Romanoff Court, but they were not made aware of Nicholas II's great desire and the initial measures he instituted to try and reunite the Eastern and Western churches of Christendom. In the battle for the good, this would indeed have been the right thing because God, the Father has made it known through His visionaries that He desires His churches to be united under the banner of His Son, aided and abetted by The Blessed Mother.

The very active forces of evil started gathering more and more fuel in their combined attempt to strike back, this time through the Anti-Christ forces now known as the New World Order. This is an outgrowth of a movement which actually started in the great temple of Jerusalem, shortly after the crucifixion and resurrection of Jesus Christ.

Providentially and synchronistically, my information concerning this far older movement came to me as a result of my first visit to the great basilica in Mexico City, which is the original housing of the Sacred Image of the Mother of God, the Tilma of Guadalupe. I was escorted to a building in an enclave next to the Basilica where an order of nuns, called the Minims of St. Francis resided. This order was founded by a nun, Mother Dorothea, who was also quite an extraordinary mystic, to take care of the poor of Mexico City. She was also led to reside next to the Basilica which houses the picture of the Patroness of the Poor, Guadalupe. Mother Dorothea had been to Rome for permission to start the Order and was granted same by Pope Paul VI, but by the time of my visit to her headquarters, she was dying of cancer.

Next to the Convent was a Friary, run by Franciscan monks, who helped the nuns with their ministry. I met the head of this group of friars who took me aside and said he had a story which needed to be told to the outside world. It was about the very origins of the New World Order, an Anti-Christ movement for the last 2,000 years.

He said that in the Great Temple of Jerusalem a meeting was held between Herod Antipas, who was part of the team that organized the crucifixion of Jesus and Ciaphas who had a grudge against Jesus since his followers did not recognize the religious establishment to which he belonged as the ruler of the Jews. Jesus was the king of the Jews, but there was no room in the hierarchy of Judah for this revolutionary interloper. If Jesus and His followers were allowed to hold sway, then that would have inevitably jeopardized the standing of those who were a part of the establishment. In short, they would have lost their jobs. Therefore, in or around 37 A.D. Herod and Ciaphas decided to start a movement of their own to weaken the growing strength of the Christians. At first there were only a few followers, yet they were behind some of the massacres of the Christians that took place in the great arenas for the entertainment of the Romans.

This new movement endured through the Dark Ages merging with occult groups and, in some desultory fashion, emerged during the Middle Ages as Stone Masons, a Guild, from which evolved a branch, or "cover," the Freemasons, their express purpose all the while, being to bring down the Christians. After the great era of cathedral building of the 13th Century in which real masons were involved, and following the aftermath of the plague of the 14th Century, and the beginnings of the Renaissance, the Free Masons dwindled to just a few members.

In 1517 their headquarters were in Holland, where in the era of the Post Protestant Reformation, they decided not to attack Christians as a whole, but just the Roman Catholic Church, weakened after the Reformation. In this atmosphere they knew they could enlist help from the non spirit-filled Protestants, who were basically more interested in political gains rather than spiritual goals. Their aim was to get rid of the church, which was founded by Peter, the first Bishop of Rome.

From those very dark beginnings they have today evolved

into what is now known as Freemasonry, the majority of whom have been shielded from this occult knowledge. I suppose that is why the 33rd Degree Masons have "secret" knowledge.

I must repeat once more the aetiology of the ever unfolding scenario. In the 19th Century the German occultist, Adam Weishaupt had been dabbling in Satanic activities and decided to commandeer that erstwhile Anti-Christian group now operating as Anti-Catholic forces into a new movement which he called the "Illuminati." At that moment, the Illuminati were really aligned to the real enemy of Christ, Satan himself, which employed them to bring about his evil intentions, all the while, operating under cover; which is the reason why this history is not known. This group subsequently evolved in this century into the New World Order. Their purpose was not only to bring down the followers of Jesus, but also the institution that was established by Jesus, who designated as his successor, Peter, the Bishop of Rome. They also aimed to acquire the power needed to forward their cause.

This New World Order, whose members as adherents of an Anti-Christ movement, managed to enlist powerful bankers (as indicated by Professor Antony Sutton, formerly of the Hoover Institution, in many books), such as the Rothschilds, the Schiffs and many of the families of great wealth, who would provide them with the resources with which they could acquire world domination. They decided to forward this goal of world domination yet again by bringing down the Czarist families. This was achieved through Karl Marx, a Satanist, who became the leader of the Communist movement, and who, through the infusion of occult powers, was enlisted by the group to do away with the czars, and foment wars. This essentially was the beginning of the new anti-God movement called dialectical Marxist Communism.

Rudolf Steiner, the great philosopher of the early 20th Century, wrote of the two heads of evil being the *Red Dragon* or dialectical anti-God communism and the *Black Panther* or secular humanism, or nowadays, the "New World Order."

In the month of April, 1999, we saw the raw face of Satan's work as exhibited by the Communists in Yugoslavia under the leadership of their Serbian President, Slobodan Milosevic, a personification of the force of Satan. Milosovic's wife, not incidentally, is the head of the Serbian Communist Party, who, with the support of other followers of the Prince of Darkness, determined to depopulate enclaves of non-Serbs and enslave the residents with tyranny.

Brigadier General Ben, the keynote speaker at a recent preparedness conference delivered a major speech on the topic that the (Communist) revolution and the New World Order are one and the same." Marxists and The Group, as it is sometimes referred to, share a common goal, in the destruction of religion in general, be it the theocratic nation of Tibet, the persecution of Christians worldwide, or doing away with Christianity in particular. The New World Order is already revealing its horrible face to us as shown in the great narrative, "Report From The Iron Mountain." One of their stated goals was a selective depopulation of the planet using such methods of wars or terrorism.

This New World Order is manifesting itself both on a material and on a spiritual level. It started with the death of Jesus and the birth of the Christian religion and is alive as an active adversary to this day.

In the Fatima (Portugal) apparition of 1917, the Mother of Jesus told the children that a new more terrible war would begin, following the great sign of January 25, 1938. That war did occur. It was instigated by Adolf Hitler (also aided by the elite of the New World Order), the leader of the spirit of Anti-Christ, responsible for millions of deaths, since one of Satan's goals is to destroy the human race. At the end of the 19th Century, Pope Leo XIII was given by God the prophetic vision in the Vatican Chapel that Satan was given 100 years to see if he could wrest the planet from God or be banished forever. There is no doubt that he is doing a very good job, but we know through Scripture that in the end Satan will lose and be thrust into the lake of fire with all the evil angels. Things are indeed heating up, both temperature wise and in the realm of spiritual warfare.

The Evil Empire is not dead, and rumors of its demise have been concocted to misinform the world. Vladimir Lenin, the great communist strategist, put out a six-point plan which is well enunciated in the books, *New Lies for Old* and *The Perestroika Deception* by Anatoliy Golitsyn.

This plan was reconfigured by the Italian, Antonio Gramsci, who defined a new style of war. It was not the Stalinist style of General Von Clausewitz which is confrontation and complete bloodbaths but the Eastern style as set out by Sun Tzu in his book, *The Art of War*: the only way to win a war over a powerful enemy such as the West, and particularly the U.S., is by deception. One should pretend to be weak, pretend to advocate peace, and that would be the only war. The communists did just that, to the extent of installing a leader in a very high place, and garnishing him with a lifestyle guaranteed to tarnish and even demoralize U.S. citizens, especially Christians.

This leader has been successful in achieving many of the group's goals, via people of great wealth and power. One of their great resources is the drug trade, which produces billions, if not, trillions of dollars for its various purveyors. Please read *Red Cocaine*. To refer to my husband's question, "But what could we do?" I have come to the conclusion that as of October 13, 1998, and indeed, more so in the present time, the anniversary of the great miracle of the sun in Fatima, Portugal, all we have left is Fatima (Mary) herself, her Son and our Father.

We have to keep in mind that the enemy of Christ in 30 AD is the same in 2000 A.D.

423

CHAPTER FIFTY-FIVE

BREAKFAST WITH A FRIEND

During my tenure with the NCD (National Council on Disability), I was having breakfast on a Tuesday in a diner across from my hotel in Arlington, Virginia with my friend, Margaret Heckler, recent U. S. Ambassador to Ireland. It was the only day I was not having a meeting and was the one morning that she could spare some time to see me. We were talking about our shared interests in religion, politics, health, and other things. We were talking about some of the things that were going on under our very noses, alas, and I said, "Oh, it must be the signs of the times." My friend Margaret gave me a real fright when she suddenly jumped up and said, "Oh Yes, you must meet my friend, Maureen Flynn, the publisher of a magazine in Herndon, Virginia, called *Signs of the Times.*" This magazine addresses all subjects concerning these times from a Catholic point of view, especially messages from various visionaries who have been having apparitions of Mary and Jesus, some approved by the Church and some not.

It was very providential that at the very last minute Maureen was able to send her very faithful Filipino driver to pick me up and drive me all the way from Arlington to Herndon and back again, so that I could spend some time with her that day before going back to my hotel in Washington where I was attending a NCD quarterly meeting. This occurred in the Spring of 1992.

Maureen and I, as I have pointed out, had a great deal in common since we are great devotees of the Virgin Mary and were trying to live the Gospel in our various ways, but especially by spreading the messages which Mary has been sending to mankind these days. It was this new relationship that got me thinking that we had to do something to try and stop the Democratic presidential nominee from being elected.

I knew that I would not have much longer with the NCD since with each change of administration there is a cyclical guillotine at work. Were it not for my affiliation with the other side, I would have gotten things done, but politics prevailed.

Mother Teresa was of the opinion that if abortions were allowed to continue we would be at risk of nuclear war. ("The fruit of abortion is nuclear war.") Keeping this in mind, I made it a point of making a public statement about abortion by picketing a couple of times in front of City Hall and in front of the abortuary in the City of Bridgeport. I remember my first demonstration. It was on Holy Saturday and there was a young man with a cross which he lugged along behind him as he walked with us from the abortuary to City Hall and back again. By the end of the day, the police had joined our side and were helping us in our endeavors. I believe that most policemen have their hearts in the right place. This year on the anniversary of Roe v. Wade I arrived late with my banners of Jesus and Mary and ran into a priest who had been at our very first Cenacle in 1989, Fr. Douglas Tufaro. Since I had been walking with him, I asked him, "What do you think of Y2K?" "Oh," he said, "It is a catalyst." That is all he said—all he needed to say because it seems that it is indeed more than a catalyst which is a wake-up call in disguise for the Remnant, as we are called, prevailing over what would be for some, cataclysmic events which might come in the future.

CHAPTER FIFTY-SIX

MESMERIZED BY EVIL

During the early morning hours, I spend time reading the latest works from the visionaries with whom I have had contact since 1989, the year I became coordinator of the Fairfield, Connecticut, Cenacle of the Marian Movement of Priests. Since 1973, Our Blessed Mother has guided her priests and laity in this movement through prayer and locutional teachings given through Fr. Stefano Gobbi, to a clear, concise understanding of the Church and of God's will for these "latter days" or "end times."

Since 1989, the spirit of "fiat," or doing God's will, a number of major prophets/seers have spoken to large audiences at Cenacle gatherings at our home: Vassula Ryden, Josyp Terelya, Debra of Australia, Maureen Sweeney, being the most well known. Their message is the same as the Holy Father's message, the same as the seers of Medjugorje—fast, pray, repent, convert, love, forgive and be at peace.

At a Marian Conference held at My Father's House Retreat Center in Moodus, Connecticut, the keynote speaker was Dr. Tom Petrisco. His book, *Call of the Ages*, I believe to be the finest commentary on Marian apparitions to date. He had just finished his latest book on the seer, Christina Gallagher. She displays signs of being a major visionary/locutionist with the stigmata of

Christ, as well as many other signs. The extraordinary sign of the stigmata is not a new occurrence for mystics all through Church history. But with the evolution of the latter days, and the intensification of evil in this century, mystics exhibiting these extraordinary phenomena have multiplied. Our Lady told the visionaries in Medjugorje that if need be, she would appear in every household to call her children back to God. Christina has given many insights about her mystical experiences of heaven, hell and purgatory, which were revealed to her by the Blessed Virgin. I think it is important for you to know what she said about a certain dark-haired man with piercing eyes. She describes him in detail, saying that she saw this man several times without knowing who he was—encounters which left her with a feeling of horror. Finally, the Blessed Virgin tells her it is the Anti-Christ himself. Christina goes on to say there will be many Anti-Christs before this scripturally foretold embodiment of Satan himself, manifests in one human being.

For me, and certainly for many others, it is extraordinary to believe that so much prophecy foretold in the Holy Scriptures is now being revealed in our time. But Scripture tells us that God gave extraordinary signs and graces for those present at the time of His first coming, for those who had faith. So in the time of His second coming, would He give signs and wonders? In the words of Scripture and in the visionaries that follow, it is very evident that God's help is for those who believe in Him, who are obedient and faithful.

Concerning the arrival of many Anti-Christs who are to precede the man who is called Anti-Christ, a series of coincidences led me to understand that as God was using His saints to connect His dots, so Satan was at work in the world using his advocates to do his work. As I have mentioned, a book was given to me titled, *Marx and Satan,* (and referred to by Will Brownell) written by Richard Wurmbrand, the Jewish-Lutheran pastor incarcerated by the Russian Communists for 17 years. This pastor, after much research on the topic, wrote that after leading a religious life for many years, Karl Marx turned to satanic worship, which in turn led him to dialectical atheism, namely Communism. I recommend this book to anyone who is interested in the dual nature of the well-named "Evil Empire." It appears that too few Americans are interested in this subject. This apathy, born of the sinful and apathetic practices of the new American death-culture, is one reason we may indeed have not only a forerunner of the Anti-Christ as a leader in our country, as well as the predicted chastisement of God on our nation as well.

In our country today, there are representatives of Anti-Christ forces in leadership positions. Who are these precursors of the Anti-Christ? St. Paul describes these times in his sixth letter to the worldly Ephesians: "For we wrestle not against flesh and blood, but against principalities, and powers, against the rulers of darkness of this world, against spiritual wickedness in high places" (Ephes. 6:12).

Who are these men and women representing evil genius as described by the Canadian visionary, Jim Singer, as the "Shining Darkness?"

Clearly, unfortunately and awfully, such persons increasingly appear to be part of the current leadership of the United States. We have only to look at its record to realize that it is indeed, a "Shining Darkness." What are the fruits of this leadership? Every evil has increased in this country since then: the proliferation of abortion; the latest outrage—the veto on the ban on partial abortion, which is infanticide; the lessening of controls of the rampant surge of homosexuality, increasing the spread of AIDS; teenage suicide and killings; murders in which our leadership may even be implicated, according to some very powerful video tapes; and last but not least, an enormous increase in the use of illegal drugs. By actions and words, our leadership has encouraged a way of life which breaks each of the ten commandments, and encourages and advocates, in the words of John Paul II, a "culture of death."

We are all sinners, and a great many of our citizens break the commandments habitually, but for persons who claim to be Christian and to love God and country, and who have taken an oath to preserve the Constitution, to be responsible for these sins and incriminated for crimes on such a scale, is to say the least, appalling. Anyone with eyes to see and ears to hear has to ask, "why are they getting away with this?"

Why do the American people appear to be mesmerized by this evil? What is it about evil power that mesmerized whole countries like Germany and Russia? Is it that we have not heeded the famous call of St. Paul to the Ephesians?

Why is it that so many young adults of this generation have lost their sense of morality and justice? Do they not realize that if we are not for God, then we are against Him? It looks like our current leadership not only disobeys God's laws but goes so far as to fling His laws arrogantly in the face of a democracy "under one God." And sadly, they are championed. Have not the American people espoused this philosophy, supporting our leaders, despite documented evidences warning us against its heinous policies? Have the American people turned a deaf ear to the prophesies of God's chastising justice against a country which espouses evil? Are the American people mesmerized by evil?

CHAPTER FIFTY-SEVEN

CIVIL DEFENSE

As I write this we are currently at war in Yugoslavia, headed up by a known Totalitarian dictator of the Communist variety, Slobodan Milosevic.

I know that this political part of the book is important because of a question put to me by my faithful and dedicated assistant in religious affairs, Madeline, whom, on this occasion, I have hired to put on a conference, an area in which she has proved her really consummate skills. So she asked me, "When are you going to put down on paper some guidelines on how to survive a nuclear war?"

My response was, that with the arrival of the consciousness of the presence of God, The Father, I have been given the wisdom and even the foolhardiness and confidence, if you will, to demonstrate it by way of a large map showing three major unfolding scenarios for the end times. The result will, of course, partly depend on when and where to deploy my intrinsic knowledge of surviving a nuclear war. To simplify matters and probably to overstate the case, I was a leader in civil defense in the 1980's when I was working for Ronald Reagan in the health sector. Other top women in this field were Nancy Greene and Dr. Jane Orient, M.D., and now the Utah based, Sharon Packer.

Nancy Greene and I met at civil defense conferences in the '80's. Nancy, now the widow of Lorne Greene (Star of Bonanza), was part of a brilliant team which included her husband and others who were what I would call, members of the neo-conservative movement. They were mainly Jewish Democrats who were able to take a good hard look at the real situation about Communism in general and the Soviet Union in particular. Nancy once told me that she and Lorne were inspired to commission scripts for a TV program depicting scenes after a nuclear war on American soil. There were two versions(!!), one *with* civil defense and one *without*. Only one was shown by the leftist producers and that one showed what America would look like after a nuclear war without civil defense. Nancy is an expert in civil defense, and her version of the *Day After*, which was the name of her TV documentary, had a script about America after a nuclear war without civil defense. The difference between the two scripts was like night and day. Anyone who saw the *Day After* might have known about the famous, but incredible story by Neville Schutte of the doomsday scenario for planet earth, portrayed in the movie, *On the Beach*, there was a scene where the survivors were gathered together on a beach in Australia as if to say they were the only ones to survive on the planet, and even they didn't make it.

I remember later, a particular meeting in a hotel room in Washington, D.C. with my assistant, David Rothbard, the brilliant Orthodox Jewish student who was attending the Jesuit-run Fairfield University. He subsequently set up Bridgeport Urban Gardens (a project to help the inner city) for my Foundation and did some other praiseworthy work. He then went on to set up his own think tank which is still going strong. The next day, following our meeting there was an important civil defense conference for which I made a big sacrifice in order to be present. That event was also heralded by my being awakened at 5.00 a.m. by "Sleepers Awake." What a synchronicity!

The day of the civil defense meeting coincided with the anniversary of my grandmother's birthday. It was November 19,

1985 and my Aunt Suzanne honored the occasion with a big gathering for family and friends in Paris. Aunt Suzanne doted on her mother. I gave up this very important trip to Paris in order to attend this civil defense meeting in Washington, D.C. I sent my daughter Suzy instead. In an emotional sense, it was my loss but Suzy's gain. This is how it should be, because looking back on it emotionally speaking, my work has to be more important than my psychological state at any time. Suzy's gain was that by being there she was able to establish a warm and loving relationship with our French family.

While in that hotel room in Washington, D.C. with my assistant, David, I remember Nancy saying to him, "What are we doing with this Mushinegga blond?" Neither they, nor I for that matter, knew at the time that my father was a Belgian Jewish doctor. Maybe somebody could have guessed. I think I asked David to come and meet Nancy since they were both very conservative Jews and I knew they would get along. This occurred on the eve of that very important civil defense conference.

Let me go back to the early years of our marriage when we were living in Beverly Hills in my mother's house on Chevy Chase Drive. I had become the driver for French speaking visitors (mainly African) for the first International Music Festival in Los Angeles held at the University of California at Los Angeles (UCLA) and also I was the official driver for the Los Angeles World Affairs Council, always driving my beat-up old Dodge. Since we lived so close to UCLA I used to go there and do things. I was very involved with their activities. I remember that there was a Picasso 60th birthday (how young that seems now!) exhibition and I loaned them my Picasso which they accepted as genuine. I subsequently sold it for a song to a Frenchman in San Francisco to help out a family member in financial straits. As a result of that sale I lost, possibly, a few million dollars. Oh, well! Putting that aside, much more to the point, was the fact that UCLA in the 50's held conferences given by famous people. One I particularly remember was given by my mentor on civil defense, Herman

Kahn, author of *Thinking the Unthinkable: On Thermonuclear War*, who at that time was working at the Santa Monica based Rand Corporation. There was also, thank God, Edward Teller, that great Hungarian physicist and expert in civil defense who was a part of the Manhattan Project and helped develop the Atom Bomb. In fact, he called himself the father of the Hydrogen Bomb. What a family to be the father of!! This time in UCLA he decided to give a series of lectures on the relativity theories of Albert Einstein. If you think I could have resisted that, think again. Things being what they were in my house, I only managed to make it to the first one, "The Special Theory of Relativity."

In the words of this brilliant pedagogue with his almost incomprehensible Hungarian accent, to explain the theory of relativity we will use the example of a man going into space. What else? The man is going to the Andromeda galaxy, where else? He goes to Andromeda and comes back in earth's time which is 200 years. But when he comes back, he is not 200 years older but only five years older, whereas everybody on earth has been gone for several generations since he left. Now how is that possible? This is where the special theory of relativity comes in. How do you explain the fact that this man is only five years older? This is actual science. The first thing to understand is that what we think about time and space is not necessarily the reality of time and space that we are "accustomed to." In this case, time depends on space. So you ask yourself, what is time and what is space? Time is the passing of events and is the measurement of events; the measurement changes when the speed at which you are traveling changes. Professor Teller put it this way: This man's body was being propelled to Andromeda at the speed of light. His body was passing through space much faster than earth's passage of events. In space everything was speeded up. The trick in understanding this is to see how much time your body lingers in any particular space. If it lingers for less than earth's time, your time changes so when you return to earth everybody is 200 years older but you are only five years older. That made a lot of sense to me then as it does now. Unfortunately, I missed the lecture on the general theory and would give anything to get a copy of that lecture which was delivered again, no doubt in Professor Teller's delightful Hungarian accent. However, when it comes to civil defense, there is no greater pedagogue than Professor Teller, with the exception perhaps, of Herman Kahn. Everything I learned about civil defense is purported to be fundamentally unchanged, except for the new addition of defense against chemical and biological warfare and is available in the bibliography of those books, some of which are still in print. What has definitely changed is the terminology; ultimate war is now referred to as CBN (Chemical Biological Nuclear Warfare Syndrome). This is quite recent, having been coined with the development of suitcase bombs, Islamic terrorism, and the escalating development of Bio-Preparat.

Let's start with nuclear war. You want to be able to gauge when, where and why nuclear war will be conducted. Also, that will determine the length of time to expect a major disruption of society. It was pretty cut and dried in the late 70's when the Hoover Institution on War, Revolution and Peace hired Joseph D. Douglass, Jr. and his colleague, Amoretta Hoeber, who was then employed at the Department of Defense, to write their seminal book, *Soviet Strategy for Nuclear War*. The important point made in the book, as far as I was concerned, was something called the correlation of forces which analyzes when the enemy will decide the optimum time for the first strike, and when they will be ready to wage a protracted war, a war to the end they can win. At the time Dr. Douglass wrote his book, there was a rather well-defined scenario in which the Soviets would gather and then deploy their tanks across the North German Fulda plain and then over-run Europe. (Not a hard thing to do when you consider the lifestyle of the French, or the Parisians anyway.) This tactical war would gradually escalate to a nuclear war. That was the plausible scenario for a third world war in the early 50's. Dr. Douglass also wrote the books, *Red Cocaine* and *America the Vulnerable*. Must reading!

What is the new correlation of forces? First of all chemical and/or biological warfare is so much cheaper than conventional warfare. Therefore, due to the fact that the Soviets are so broke (all their money has gone into their war machine), they might want to conduct a third world war to win their ultimate goal of world domination, using chemical agents in order to survive, rather than to pursue their present conventional course. The latter would be a continuation of their revolution which in fact never really ended. Are they going to organize and deploy some surrogate Islamic terrorism with biological warfare or is it their intention to conduct nuclear war?

Now for the first time, let's take a look at this map, I mentioned earlier, the idea of which I received by way of inspiration. It is the map of a developing scenario for end times. On the left you will have the current geo-political situation, in the middle you will have the doom and gloom prophecies of proliferating visionaries of the planet, as well as Biblical prophecy, and on the right side, thank God, is hopefully the news currently given to us by the visionaries which is in line, as is always the case, with devotions to God the Father in our lives. John Paul II, who is our greatest mystic, of course, took it upon himself through his mystical inspiration to inaugurate the years leading to the great jubilee of the millennium of 2000, as special periods of prayer and worship. He started with 1997, which he dedicated in honor of the second Person of the Holy Trinity, Jesus Christ. We did not get involved at the time since this had not yet received much publicity. But by the time 1998 rolled around, it was the year of the Holy Spirit. I did not know this when I gave this conference which I named the Conference of the Holy Spirit. This was the second of two, but as I say those of us in this field seem to get the same messages at the same time.

The year 1999, is the year of God the Father and this is the first time, with maybe a few exceptions not well publicized, that visionaries are being given messages from God about the meaning of His presence in our lives as Father. There are a few visionaries who have been blest with the presence of God the Father in their lives in a mystical way (See *Conversations With Heaven* by Eileen George).

Therefore, where do we stand when it comes to nuclear war? You will make three impressions on Map # 3. You will record political events and trends. In spite of events, which show that the Adversary is doing so much damage, the Eternal Father is still in charge. How will these events be changed by the spiritual initiatives of Map #3? In other words, where will this present war lead? Will it become nuclear? When will the terrorists strike?

CHAPTER FIFTY-EIGHT

SOME ANTI-CHRIST ACTIVITIES

The frequency of Apocalyptic events is increasing exponentially. Is this the time to convince the uninformed and the ignorant? Is this the time to transform the apathetic and to lead the remnant to safety? Maybe it is time to do some triage, which is a term used in war for medical purposes to determine which of the wounded should be saved. First you attend to those who can easily be saved; then you turn to those who might be saved; finally if there are any resources left, you consider those who are helpless or dying. Normally in the battlefield, in those circumstances, you let them go. Is that the case here?

My natural inclination is to serve the underdog, those least likely to succeed, the disenfranchised and the most desperate of sinners since the battle of the principalities and the spirits is being manifested more and more to the material senses. Maybe this is no longer possible and I simply have to lead the remnant or the elect to safety through this book—physical safety, that is—since presumably God has chosen the elect for this generation. It is God's choice, and ultimately, their choice, whoever they are. Maybe they are the only ones I can help now.

When Ronald Reagan became President, it seemed as if the cold war was over. I was not totally at ease in believing this to be wholly true. Knowing what I knew about Communism, and also because of the increasing prophetic messages to visionaries world-wide about the approaching end times, I could not be at ease.

It was only when I started connecting the dots about our leadership that I realized that something was afoot. It was like reading *The Perestroika Deception*, a sequel to a book entitled, *New Lies for Old*, written in the 1960's by the important Russian defector, Anatoly Golitsyn. In that book he states that all that is going on in the so-called former Soviet Union has been a deception to fool the West. In Lenin's words, "Give them enough rope and they will hang themselves." That is exactly what we have done. We have done it especially because of the events in the administration over the last six years.

I was inspired to hold a meeting in a motel room in Virginia with some strategic analysts including Joe Douglass, the author of *Red Cocaine*, recommended by Will Brownell, who stated that the book was totally ignored by the West at its own peril. That book shows how the Communists used drugs to bring down the West just as the Chinese did in Korea.

After that meeting, I had some hunches and followed them up by doing some research which led me to the ineluctable conclusion that members of our leadership were acting like Communists.

At this point, I return once again to the dictum of C.J. Jung that when you produce a series of facts, as often as not, you will obtain an insight called, an "Aha!" One of the persons who also was connecting the dots in this record was Emmett Tyrell, editor of *American Spectator*.

After many internet searches and conversations with Dr. Paul of Missouri, a leading amateur Kremlinologist in our country, it seemed that our leadership was connected with a famous family, which is connected in many ways to the history of what is known as the New World Order. This famous family are all, by and large, Masons and are related to this leader who is also known to be a member of the de Molay, originally a French Masonic organization.

According to some sources, Georgetown University is implicated in the education of this leader who went on to become a leader of the Communist front group in Britain during his student days.

We also know that this person studied with the leaders of the Czechoslovak Communist Party many years ago and that allegedly there are tapes where he professes his allegiance to communism.

It is an established fact that a close member of his family is a convicted drug dealer and seems to have been involved in drug running in the south central US.

There is another book out with circumstantial evidence that this person is not a sociopath but a psychopath, since he fits the description stated in a book by a behavioral psychologist who specializes in psychopathic behavior in criminals behind bars and elsewhere.

In the course of this new collaboration, I learned that members of the American Communist Party spoke of a plan to foist a stealth Communist as a leader in the USA. This is what Jeff Nyquist found out while he was a student in California in the 1980s because he was able to join Communist cells at that time.

Therefore, I am still wondering whether it makes any difference at all that as the simple messenger I am, whether I knew these plans or whether it has any relation to current events. This has also been made very clear through visionary experiences and writings of others that as many people as possible should be saved. This is clear—triage or no triage—we have to save as many people as possible, body and soul.

CHAPTER FIFTY-NINE

THE HEAT IS ON

As the battle between the Principalities and the spirits (spiritual warfare) warms up exponentially, you might say that the heat is on—not only in the spiritual world but also in the physical world.

Global warming is no longer a figment of the imagination of radical environmentalists. It exists. It is here now and unless I am very much mistaken, it is increasing exponentially. This means that the excessive heat experienced in some parts of the U.S. in the Summer of 1998 will be something akin to living in a frying pan in 1999 (Texas)! It was!

Global warming syndrome is a metaphor for the material level on which great changes are taking place on planet earth—on a material level but with a spiritual cause. I am convinced, there being enough proof to declare with certainty, that the sinfulness of mankind as defined by events in the U.S.—once the hope of the world—is leading to God's punishments. These are seen through natural phenomena: global warming, terrible weather conditions, such as floods, earthquakes, tornadoes, increased activities of El Niño etc. Other punishments are war, as once stated in the great apparition in Fatima, Portugal, in 1917, "Wars are punishments for man's sins," and "God is using that poor country (Russia) as a punishment for the sins of mankind." So we will also have wars as well as rumors of wars, be they the conventional kind, such as those that are taking place right now in the Eastern Hemisphere, or the new kind of war with new weaponry with biological and chemical components. This brings us to the subject of bacterial warfare for which the Russians are still preparing, as discussed in the PBS TV documentary, *Plague Wars*, featured by "Frontline" on October 13, 1998. Almost like the typical average American (which he is not), my husband asks, "Well, what can we do?"

How do you escape bacterial warfare? Those persons who have the means, (or those whom the government deem worthy of being saved) through some very stringent triage, should acquire body suits complete with gas masks and a supply of oxygen. In addition, they should also have an underground refuge—sealed chambers with an independent oxygen supply and sufficient sustenance for the inhabitants for the period of time required for the termination of any threat from airborne bacteria.

The most desperate move I have made to date is the acquisition of nine fallout suits in preparation for possible biological, chemical or nuclear warfare. Thank God they exist! They must be Israeli. If the Israelis can live with this possibility, why can't the Americans do so in fortress America? We need to toughen up as our ancestors did in the 18th and 19th Centuries. They fought disease, famine and unfriendly forces.

In the case of regular nuclear war fighting, the means of survival are the same as they were 20 years ago. The demands on one's resources will be much the same due to radio-active fallout. The expected period of time in total underground conditions should not exceed two weeks. After that period, forays to the outside should be carefully conducted so as to avoid the contamination of the shelters on re-entry. For more information on this important lengthy topic please consult the bibliography.

The major factor, never implemented, as far as I know, is the need for education in the area of long-term agriculture. But the threats from bacterial warfare are much greater than those from natural warfare, since the devastation wreaked is considered greater and cheaper to deliver.

How are we doing? I shall answer, "Not so well," but help is on the way.

CHAPTER SIXTY

FORTRESS AMERICA

Pray God that a President, whom we so desperately tried to prevent from ascending to this post, will not be succeeded by more of the same.

In this last year, I have received many newsletters that are quite apocalyptic in nature. They seem to agree that there is a possibility of a worldwide final depression, and, of course, the specter of biological, chemical or nuclear warfare from a whole possible panoply of delivery systems.

In one of the newsletters, "Chaostan," which is produced by a Richard Maybury, there is a map of the world showing those countries where there is either chaos or war. Most of the Eastern hemisphere is drawn black, and therefore is in Chaostan, while the area covering the Western hemisphere is clear, so far. Immediately, I thought of what Pope Pius XII, the Pope of my youth, said in 1950. He said that as long as Guadalupe is venerated as Queen of the Americas we will remain unharmed. The Iberian Virgin is once again our best defense against the terrors that possibly await us in the future.

CHAPTER SIXTY-ONE

THE PROBLEM OF EVIL AND THE FRONT LINES

Certainly there seems to be much evidence that mysterious and still unfathomed factors exist in the esoteric sciences, some of which are psychotronic warfare, particle beam energy deployed for evil purposes, and mind control. Such phenomena demonstrate how our so-called advanced technologies could possibly contribute to the downfall of our present civilization.

In the case of the particle beam energy, the Philadelphia Experiment demonstrated that there are various sources of energy that can be deployed by anyone for good or evil purposes (such as dematerialization). The use of particle beam energy for evil purposes has resulted (based on some educated hypotheses) in some child killings that are now taking place in the US.

On the tape entitled, "The Montauk Project," there is mention that a vast concentration of this energy was deployed in the Denver area, which is near the scene of the Colombine High School massacre.

Remember I said that one would have to "get out of one's regular mind," and into another state of consciousness, in order to understand Einstein's special and general theories of relativity? In other words, it's just not a case of getting out of your left brain and into your right brain, you have to get into what some characterize as a cosmic mind in order to understand what is going on. We have not been talking about this cosmic mind, but I did have a revelation through the intervention of Sister Barbara Igo, the well-known Catholic metaphysician and charismatic healer. I wanted to find out who my real father was and she told me to go to my "level" (one's altered state of consciousness). Having gone through a course of Silva Mind Control, I knew what she was talking about. Immediately, I knew that Dr. Boullay was my father and not Curtis Crellin. This was the working of the cosmic mind.

The cosmic mind is also the super conscious mind that Jung describes as the source of prophetic dreams. The Ashakic records are accessed by the cosmic mind. These are words we used in our workshops with Paul Solomon, successor to Edgar Cayce. This does not in any way contradict Christianity. It only completes it. Perhaps you could call it esoteric Christianity which will be revealed to us in the New Age of the New Jerusalem, the age of the Immaculate Heart when the full gifts of the charisms of the Holy Spirit will be revealed to us and rained upon all. At that time, the mystery of iniquity will also be revealed to us by the Blessed Mother, according to many visionaries of today.

The problem of evil is something to which I was exposed from my very early days. It began with the fact my real father was not known to me and furthermore my "foster" father, my mother's unfortunate first husband, had so many problems that he was asked to leave the U.S. Added to that were the problems of my step-fathers who had to deal with either addiction or evil in their lives. But beyond that, we inherit the sins of our fathers. I suppose I can start in my own family tree with Catherine the Great of Russia, whose lifestyle left something to be desired, to put it mildly, according to historical sources.

Growing up, I was exposed to the cruelty of my own family, as well as that of our so-called babysitters, who visited their special evils on my poor brother but which I managed to escape through my own constant renewal of a prayer life. Maybe this was why I had the compunction to say 12 Our Fathers and 12 Hail Marys as I walked everyday the seven blocks on Rexford

445

Drive to and from Hawthorne School, in Beverly Hills in the 1940's. That was my primary means of survival.

Our daughter's afflictions also visited enormous physical and moral evils on us. Her afflictions were in themselves tremendous, especially the cruelty, insensitivity and greed of some of her psychiatrists.

Rudolf Steiner, in addition to being a philosopher, was one of the great 20th Century proponents of the cosmic mind. It was characteristic of him, as recounted by the mystic, Trevor Ravenscroft, to be Hitler's No. 1 enemy because of his visionary experiences of the dangers of the 3rd Reich.

Steiner understood the very nature of evil in our time because of his shamanistic training and because he had received the gifts of the Holy Spirit—wisdom, counsel, and metaphysical energy attending all these gifts.

I visited the Steiner headquarters in Darmach, Switzerland on the border of Austria, Germany and Switzerland where it had stood for almost 50 years until a fire brought it down. Fortunately, it was rebuilt according to Steiner's model. Its architecture was distinctively unique. In some ways it was similar to Gaudi's cathedral, La Familla Sagrada in Barcelona, which is also quite unique. Steiner's building, called the Goetheanum, has statues of the Black Panther and the Red Dragon. I would like to add that some features of the architecture of Frank Lloyd Wright seem to be present in the Steiner headquarters. Frank Lloyd Wright adopted some of this fusion architecture into his own work, in which the forms of the building are part of the natural environment so that lines are not squared off. It is very much like a garden where the gardener creates and molds and brings his own personal energy into his creation, which is really God's creation.

God is reflected in nature. Man makes, builds and collaborates with God to truly form the garden. When there was no evil, there was a Garden of Eden, and after evil is destroyed in the New Jerusalem, this will once more be a garden.

CHAPTER SIXTY-TWO

A QUESTION OF MYSTERIES

With the advent of the preparedness shows, people who have been accepting of mysterious agenda are beginning to come out of the woodwork. One such person is the author of a tape called, "The Montauk Project." This is some of the most important stuff that has come across my desk and when you consider the contents of books such as, *Angels Don't Play This Haarp*, about psychotronic warfare which I have previously mentioned, one simply has to believe it.

There are advanced technologies on this planet that are kept hidden from most of us. This kind of knowledge sometimes smacks of the supernatural and while mankind is generally not privy to it , yet it may be useful to us now.

We don't know where Jesus went between the ages of 12 and 30. There is no mention of this in the Gospels. The Mormons think that he went to the Northern Hemisphere and across the Americas, teaching many of the Native American tribes. The East Indians think that he visited them, too, and they called him Issa.

Do you remember my account of how I visited Terry Moore when she was in bed with a cold and I made her chicken soup? Well, on my next visit, I was with my husband. Being a very handsome man, I guess made her more inclined to spend some time with us. So she took us to her Mormon Temple and showed us pictures of Jesus in North America. Jesus said, "He that believeth on me, the works that I do shall he do also; and greater works than these shall he do; because I go unto my Father" (John 14:12). Furthermore, John stated in his Gospel, "There are also many other things which Jesus did, the which, if they should be written every one, I suppose that even the world itself could not contain the books that should be written" (John 21:25).

We are beginning to get an inkling of these mysteries, in the words of the scientists and philosophers and especially the philosopher-scientist Teilhard de Chardin, "We are indeed on an upward evolution scale." That may be true, everything being equal, but let's face it, everything is not equal and humankind is still as ever in need of redemption? Can the answer be found in a grand design given to us by Our Creator, in alignment of our will to His?

PART VI

PART VI

CHAPTER SIXTY-THREE

THE GRAND DESIGN

All the children love our home in St. Martin, battened down as it has been by hurricanes Luis and Lenny. Hurricane Lenny was a strange November storm coming up out of the West, maybe like the storm in the book, *A Perfect Storm*, by Sebastian Junger, also an atypical November storm out of the West.

It was on the Island of St. Martin that I wrote a paper titled, "The Grand Design," which deals with my perception of the spiritual design for our family:

Matthew Arnold, the English poet, wrote in the poem, "Dover Beach" . . . ."We are here as on a darkling plane, where ignorant armies clash by night . . . " St. Paul wrote in his letter to the Corinthians (13:11-12), "When I was a child, I spake as a child, I understood as a child, I thought as a child; but when I became a man, I put away childish things. For now we see through a glass, darkly; but then face to face; now I know in part; but then shall I know even as also I am known."

Until the morning of October 30th, the month of the Rosary of Our Lady, in the Year of Our Lord 1984, the overwhelming vision was of armies clashing through the dark glass. At long last, much like the flash which overwhelmed St. Paul, came the vision of the "Grand Design."

When did I even get the notion that there could be such a thing as a Grand Design for a person's life. Well, when I was a little girl, people used to say, "What do you want to be when you grow up?" or, in other words, what is your philosophy of life? To me it was always very simple—then as now, it is the second question in the Baltimore catechism, the question being, "Why are you here?" and the answer to that question is, "To love and serve God so as to be happy with Him in this life and forever in the next." To a child's mind that seemed like a very worthy and probably, a reasonably simple goal.

The worthiness of this goal has never been in question. The simplicity of it is called the cross, which has been outlined in other papers, books, chapters, insurance, hospital records, etc.

Emerging like the chrysalis from its cocoon, the furious armies of anguish and despair, injustice, cruelty, illness, and unkindness seem to be playing out the conflict against a backdrop. The armies cast their shadows on this backdrop into which gradually emerges a light which shines brighter over the years.

Essentially the grand design is the backdrop and is the light that St. Paul describes in speaking to the Corinthians; it is the Word of God, which in visual terms is the pure light of God's Love. The armies are still there, and like soldiers in a conventional army who fight wars with the aid of an operational plan (O.P.) as set out in their military manuals, I have an O.P. which is the Grand Design for my life.

It is very hard to explain to people who have not experienced the fullness of God's Love (in their right brain and in their hearts) which, from time-to-time, manifests itself in signs, miracles, and "synchronicities." Most people use their left brain in their average waking state, crossing the street without getting hit by a bus (I have trouble with this sometimes!), non-abstract math, rational thought, linear, mechanistic thinking. The synchronicities serve very well to illustrate there is something beyond that which most people see most of their waking hours. Through synchronicities, the invisible world becomes visible. The left brain skeptics, agnostics (not atheists—they're taking a position), the couldn't-care-less type of people would balk at these synchronicities.

For instance, starting at home:
1) I was born on May 13th, the day of the great miracle of Fatima.
2) My husband was born on August 15th, the feast of the Assumption of Mary.
3) Our daughter, Patricia, whose illnesses started us on this path, was born on the day of the great sign of Fatima, January 25th. (Also the feast of the conversion of St. Paul.)
4) Suzanne was born on August 13th, the fourth scheduled apparition day of the apparitions in Fatima, Portugal. (The Blessed Mother did not appear on that day because the policemen took the three children away. But She did return on August 19 when they were released.) August 13 is also the feast of the Mystical Rose.
5) Marianne and John were born on the feast days of St. John the Baptist and of the great latter day apparition in Yugoslavia at Medjugorje, June 24 and 25.
6) Yvonne was married on the official birthday of the Virgin Mary, September 8 (not the actual day of August 6 as recently revealed at Medjugorje).
7) Henry was born on March 18th, which was also the day on which the Blessed Mother appeared to the major seer at Medjugorje. It has been stated in a newsletter, *Caritas*, the unofficial Medjugorje journal published in Alabama, USA, that March 18 would be a crucial day in the unfolding of events predicted at Medjugorje, events for the latter days.

Almost to make sure that I wouldn't forget about all these amazing events, God saw to it that I had mystical experiences connected with my children.

The week of May 15, 1978 was the most amazing week of my life. I was scheduled to meet my older son, Henry, to view an independent film in the basement of the Hilton Hotel on 7th Avenue in New York. This was the year that I purchased my favorite convertible, which subsequently became our "trashmobile," as Henry called it. By the time that car got into Henry's hands, one door did not close and the other did not open. I took it to a body shop in Stamford, Connecticut. Stamford was quite different in those days. There were no high-rises. On Canal Street there were several car repair shops. When I took it to the repair shop they told me to give them two hours to check it out. Since I lived quite a distance, I decided to walk around the area. When I returned the door of the shop was closed but I could hear laughter from within. When they opened the garage door there was rope tied around the car (to prevent the door from opening). They charged me $10 for that rope and sent me on my way. We needed to sell it, and wording the advertisement was quite a challenge. Henry rose to the occasion and we sold the car for $50.

Anyway, I had an interesting experience that day that I was going to the Hilton to meet Henry in that car before it became "trashed". There was a violent cloudburst which slowed me down quite a bit. I was already running late and worried because I had been attempting to placate Henry, who had been having fights with his father because of the Ho Chi Minh beard he was wearing that year. The year before he wore an Alexander Solzhenitsyn beard—which was better, at least politically. According to my watch, I was more than an hour late, but I decided to push on anyway. When I finally arrived I glanced at the clock at the Hilton basement lobby. I was on time. What happened to the "lost" hour? This was a bit of a surprise but I had been reading about these experiences which were described as a "time warp." It is something that occurs when one is in synch with another dimension. It is an example of dominion over time and space through the higher consciousness of the exaltation of prayer. These miraculous experiences have occurred in connection with my other children as well.

Another similar unexplained experience occurred with my younger son, John, when I was driving him to his school in Watertown, Connecticut, about 80-100 miles away from our home. It was also raining that day and on my return through back roads I noticed that the gas gauge had not moved since the beginning of the trip! This phenomenon has also occurred to my staffer, Madeline, a prayerful Roman Catholic.

My most meaningful experience connected with our children involved our youngest daughter, Suzy. I was returning home to Fairfield after visiting her at school in Pomfret, also in Connecticut. I was in a most relaxed state because it was usually a very happy experience for me to visit my children when they were away at school. On this occasion, I had the most extraordinary experience. All of a sudden, as I was approaching Glastonbury, Connecticut, just West of Hartford, I felt a presence, like a vibration, but much stronger. It was like a lightning bolt coming out of the sky. I knew that that was God, the Father, and that the palpable but unusual vibration I was sensing was the intensity of His love for us. That is the only time that I have ever had that kind of experience. However, I am reminded of it as we celebrate this year ordained by John Paul II as the *Year of God, the Father*, as part of the Jubilee of the year 2000.

With our daughter, Patricia, from time-to-time there have been many mystical experiences, the most pronounced of which is "the odor of roses". In the words of "the little flower," St. Theresa of Lisieux, holiness is not prayer and good works; holiness is suffering.

In the world of mysticism and psychic phenomena there is usually a follow-up occurrence as a confirmation of a mystical experience. One year later, I accompanied my husband on a business trip to the Middle East, a trip that included Morocco and Turkey. We stayed at the Istanbul Hilton in Turkey. I did not like Istanbul because it was full of smog and, furthermore, I did not like the Tokapi Palace since that Moslem palace itself revealed the low status of women, amongst other things. We also visited Santa Sophia Cathedral which had been turned into a mosque. In the nave were some mosaics purportedly of two saints, St. Sophia and St. Michael. In order to see these windows, one had to climb up a staircase of some well-worn cobbled stones which had deteriorated—worn by centuries of pilgrims' boots. I wanted to see what St. Michael looked like through the eyes of an 11th Century artist. When I got to the spot, I looked up and saw exactly that same being that appeared to me in that toll booth in New York City—same clothes, same curly hair and the same blue eyes!

In the ensuing years I have had dreams, which C. J. Jung referred to as break-through dreams and which Christians call prophetic dreams. Since I suffer from a lack of Vitamin B6, I do not have much dream recall (according to Dr. Carl Pfeiffer), except for these break-through dreams. One night I heard a disembodied voice giving me a long lecture ending with the words, "And thou shalt be didactic." I replied, "Who are you anyway?" The reply was, "I am St. John, the Evangelist," and I saw him. He appeared as a young man wearing bangs. He had blondish hair and was wearing a long white robe. I sat up in my bed and awakened my husband to find out what "didactic" meant. He told me that it means to teach.

A year after this dream, we went to Ireland, my husband, oldest daughter, younger son and I. One night we went to a wedding and it was such a good experience because the people were so warm. On the last day of our trip, my husband, playing the role of part-time businessman and part-time father touring with the kids, and I, set out for a resort on the West Coast; on the way there was a sign saying, "This way to Knock—100 Km", which caught my eye. I knew that The Blessed Virgin had appeared in Knock. Mirabile dictu! I managed to persuade everybody to take this long detour and see this beautiful apparition site. The story goes that it was during the potato famine when some children saw three personages at Knock, St. Joseph, St. John the Evangelist and Our Lady. There was a beautiful re-creation of the scene in a glass house whose transparency gave a realistic effect of how these personages appeared to the children. This visit confirmed my dream/vision of St. John. He appeared just as I saw him in my dream, with bangs and a long white robe.

CHAPTER SIXTY-FOUR

CONCERNING OUR CHILDREN

How can I demonstrate to the reader that like everything else in my life, my children are not the children of a "business as usual" kind of family? Maybe there is no such family. Maybe there isn't the little white house with the picket fence and the dog wagging its tail at the gate, where the mother gets breakfast for her children and her husband then sees the children off to school and the husband to his work. If that exists somewhere, that is wonderful, it is surely rare. It has never existed for me.

Instead, I ponder the famous observation of Leo Tolstoy that all happy families are alike and that unhappy families are all different. Then I think about the very Catholic point of view about the value of suffering and the salvation of souls. This stance is diametrically opposed to the modern philosophy of "Jesus Prosperity", and good times with Jesus. Where does the truth lie in all of this? I have to come to the conclusion that our lives must be premised on the life of Jesus, His Passion and Resurrection. The times in which we are living are not only the times of the Revelation of St. John, which I will skip over because of controversial interpretations, but more directly, the times described in Chapter 24 of the Gospel of St. Matthew (the end times).

Thinking about all these things, I always wonder about our family's connection, in one way or another, with Marian feast days, on which they were born, or in one instance, married, as illustrated in "The Grand Design."

About five years ago, a woman by the name of Tamara, who lives in the St. Juan Islands, off the coast of Washington State, called me. She said she needed to meet me because of my involvement with Guadalupe. She had been in touch with a priest in Mexico who received a message that if a sonogram were used on the Tilma of Guadalupe, it would manifest a living presence. He commissioned her to enlist support for this investigation. May I say that this is really "far out", something similar to the Mexican Bishops' request that NASA test the Tilma with their ultra modern equipment. They finally got their wish and it is alleged that the image manifested immanent life (presumably because, the image on the Tilma which appeared 13 days before Christmas, historically deemed to be the birthday of Christ—depicted Mary as a pregnant woman.

The great American scientist, John Jackson, who was part of the STURP team (Shroud of Turin Research Project) of 1978 disparaged the idea of a sonogram test because of the possibility of a sonogram injuring the Tilma. Tamara eventually visited our home and we spent a couple of days together. Before leaving she gave me the name of a person of a mystical bent, connected with this enterprise. His name was Fred Tumminia. After she left I did nothing for a while, but afterwards I contacted this gentleman because he seemed to be a rather *rara avis*. American mystics are usually women. Most male mystics tend to be non-American such as the Canadian, Jim Singer, the Ukranian, Josyp Terelya and the German, Franz Kieler. It is only recently that male American mystics are coming to the fore, there being two in the State of Connecticut and one that I know of, in New Jersey.

I called Fred and asked him if he could account for the fact that each member of my family was either born on or in some other way connected with Marian events, especially Fatima. He said that it was because we will need special angels to protect and guide us through our lives since Mary is the Queen of Angels. That figures, since I am from the place called Nuestra Signora de Los Angeles, or L.A. There you have our connection. I hope our special angels are gathering together to bring us out of all the dark situations that have afflicted us as a family, into the place of Light. Through the guidance of God, and our friendship with Jesus, we will be protected under the blue mantle of our Mother Mary and enlightened by the Holy Spirit. That is her space, the place where I have always envisioned family life. Since I never had a real family, the Holy Family was the only one I ever knew. When I was a child, I asked them to adopt me, and they did. However else can I account for all those experiences of a religious nature that I have had over the years?

I used to have trouble telling my children about these things. They always fobbed me off as a religious fanatic. But things are changing now since humankind is being painted into a corner by virtue of the events occurring on our planet, which are so clearly described in Matthew 24.

The year 1999 was the year of God the Father. I was not given any inspiration as to what part I should play in this magnificent and glorious year as designated by our Leader, John Paul II, whose call has already been taken up by so many of us in the Catholic remnant. I have made references elsewhere in this book to God, the Father as being felt as a great light. That is true. In my mind I see our environment more and more permeated with this great light. I believe that the time of the Immaculate Heart has already arrived. Incrementally, little pieces of light are being wedged into the dark desert—the dark places of sin and suffering.

All of this enlightenment came as a concern for all our children, the children afflicted with the dangerous sex education curriculum and our pervasive violent culture of death.

Our children, in order of their ages, from oldest to youngest, from back left to right, Patricia, Henry and Marianne. In front from right to left Yvonne, Suzanne and John.

Harry and John   Patricia and Suzie

461

CHAPTER SIXTY-FIVE

THE MUSIC OF THE SPHERES

The music of the spheres actually exists—a heavenly phenomenon—which can be heard by us mortals in this physical
realm. The first time I had the opportunity of encountering this
reality was in a workshop conducted by Paul Solomon, the
Lutheran minister turned psychic, and self-proclaimed successor to Edgar Cayce, the sleeping prophet.

I haven't dwelt much on Cayce except for meeting the author
of the biography of Cayce, Jeff Stearn, whom I visited in Malibu
Beach while in search of a scriptwriter for my proposed movie
about Our Lady of Guadalupe.

Cayce was an entrepreneur who taught Sunday School. He'd
been a poor student, but then after an illness he found that just
by sleeping with a book under his pillow, he knew the contents
the next morning. That prodigy expanded when he went into
self-induced trances and did "readings" on his patients' state of
health with unexplainable physiological accuracy. Then Cayce
went on to make predictions about earth changes that would occur in the U.S. Some of them have partially come to pass such as
the flooding of the Mississippi basin. But the inundation of the
West Coast hasn't occurred yet. Perhaps if people pray enough
(my remedy) then it won't happen.

Paul Solomon started off as a Lutheran minister and then led a wayward life. After a serious reversal, he had a Saul of Tarsus experience which made him realize that he was to become a messenger of God, by utilizing gifts similar to those demonstrated by Edgar Cayce.

I first met Paul on a TV show that we shared, amazingly enough. I touted vitamins and he talked about earth changes just like Cayce. Also, like Cayce, he received messages in a trance state, and then went on to give workshops in what I suppose you would call spiritual development. One of these workshops was conducted in an out-building of the medical offices of my dearly beloved Dr. David Sheinken and some other holistic physicians and their patients and/or friends.

We were all told to lie on the floor. This was in the 70's when many of us, myself included, had a lot of training in deep meditation work, a kind of self-hypnosis in which you reach an altered state of consciousness.

This is an experience akin to being "slain in the spirit", except that when you are slain in the spirit, you are in an intense spiritual condition, often experienced by Evangelical Christians and Charismatic Roman Catholics. Roman Catholic saints sometimes refer to it as the third stage of meditation.

There we were on the floor in a deep meditative state, and Paul said in his inimitable hypnotizing fashion, "and you will begin to hear the music of the spheres." It's hard to describe but you really can hear music in your mind, even the notes and especially the instruments. Whenever I hear the music of the spheres, I hear the brass section. Don't ask me why. It is the resonance—bold and brassy. I was so bold to say this exists on the physical realm. Let me explain.

We know that there is energy out there which the Chinese call Chi, the Japanese call Ki, and Hindus call Prana, and what Nicola Tesla, the great Yugoslav physicist probably had in mind when he described the results of his great experiment "free energy". We know that through studies, all matter/energy has a vibration. This vibration becomes music. You can hear it if you're highly tuned, if you are a "sensitive", which many of us were in the 70's. As I get older and my physical system (I hate to admit it) is beginning to shut down slowly, my experiences of hearing the music of the spheres are diminishing. But it is as Greta Woodrew said, you "hear the colors and see the music".

Keeping this in mind, follow me as I recount the beginning of this musical journey of mine from the age of six when I started playing the piano. How ridiculous since I was so nearsighted that I could hardly see the music, if at all, and so short, I couldn't reach the pedals until I was twelve! But Miss Peery, the wonderful Indian princess, my first piano teacher of note, changed all that. She said, "you can achieve the impossible if you think you can, just do it, especially in music." So I became a semi-accomplished musician in some respects, and was certainly highly appreciative of music, even to the extent of dragging my grandmother and godfather to whatever concert happened to be in Los Angeles during the war years. There was one concert where Arturo Tuscanini conducted excerpts from *Tristan und Isolde*, which I swooned over as only a nine-year-old can.

Later, the thrill and excitement of taking those two subways to the master classes in Paris right after the war with the great Bach interpreter, Albert Lévèque, was second to none.

I suppose this was the beginning of the manifestation of the physics of resonance in my life. Somewhere in my body there were cells that resonated with the music of J. S. Bach. First, his music was truly spiritual, ahead of its time, sophisticated, syncopated and unexpected. It was because of Bach and his music that I met my husband on the occasion of a Bach concert (who might have been truly spiritual, ahead of his time, sophisticated, syncopated and unexpected!).We continued going to Bach concerts for the rest of our lives, occasionally including Alexander Brailovsky playing Chopin for good measure one summer in France, also Harry hearing Pablo Casals, my seeking out all the best that came to Los Angeles during the years we lived there, including the first U.S. recital by the great Russian pianist, Sviatoslav Richter.

I have since discovered that Bach was also dear to a British osteopath of the old school and also a healer, Dr. Viola Frymann, whose practice included a large population of the mentally retarded, especially Down's Syndrome children who showed a significant rate of improvement due to her technique of cranial manipulation (which, twenty years later, is only now becoming popular) together with her own healing powers, no doubt. What is also memorable about this woman was that in a small spare room with its door closed, she had a pianist playing classical music—especially by Johann Sebastian Bach—all day long. Many of us are aware of the healing qualities of Bach's music.

This harkens to the famous laboratory experiments conducted by the University of Colorado 35 years ago, and described in the outstanding book, *The Secret Life of Plants*. These were controlled experiments to determine the effect of various forms of music on plant growth. Identical plants were exposed to three types of music viz. Indian Raga music, Rock-n-Roll, Johann Sebastian Bach, and no music at all. Would anyone like to guess the result? Well, the plants did the best under Raga music, which doesn't surprise me at all. Second were those under the influence of Bach and Rock-n-Roll came in last, at the bottom of the heap, of course. I clearly remember my experience with Raga music on one occasion when I went to pick up my husband's new Mustang from the dealer in Greenwich. I was playing some newly purchased Raga tapes—don't forget these were the Huxley days when I was investigating New Age and Eastern philosophies—which was an almost dangerous thing to do since they could produce in a keen listener, a state of consciousness not always conducive to safe driving on I-95.

Since I had an ear for music from a very early age, I had a love for classical dance but this was an art form I could never master since my body was not built for it. However, I did occasionally indulge in what my husband referred to as "snoopy dancing" to disco music like Saturday Night Fever, to Salsa and such.

465

It was such a great joy and pleasure when our third daughter, Yvonne, became a ballet dancer and then a choreographer. She was truly an amazing five footer: she became the head of the student dance department at Sarah Lawrence College, specializing in leaps, especially leaping off the top of a human pyramid which made me gasp in fright and awe. She went on to perform off-Broadway, and also in the (slightly) absurd theater. In one such performance she played Mary Jo Kopechne in a play about Howard Hughes called "Exhausting the Possibilities!!" This was definitely off off Broadway, but very hilarious.

She met a stage fight dancer; they danced a so-called Apache dance in Tribeca. Not long after that they got married, had three beautiful children, and ran an outdoor performing arts company. The future will have much in store for that sweet family.

Yvonne was born in Los Angeles during our seven-and-a-half year sojourn in my mother's house. During this time we would go to the Ojai Music Festival in Ojai, California—a festival known for its innovative qualities. There we heard the latest music of Igor Stravinsky, some conducted by Stravinsky himself and later by his protégé, Robert Kraft. After we returned East I went back to Ojai, and on one occasion heard an unforgettable concert aptly entitled, "East meets East" which included the most famous Koto player from Japan, as well as the well-known Indian musician, Ravi Shankar, playing Raga music on his sitar. It was extraordinary!

The year after that concert, Lukas Foss came to play the Bach Brandenberg Concerto #5 in which the crescendo of the cadenza in the 2nd movement reminded me of the climax of the one act play *Don Juan in Hell* by George Bernard Shaw, in which an interplay of words and ideas comes to a crescendo as the characters played by Charles Boyer, Sir Cedric Hardwicke, Tyrone Power and Agnes Moorhead, joust with each other using Shaw's best words to a dazzling climax. Never have I witnessed such a theatrical performance before or since. The sparks were flying. This same kind of dazzling crescendo was displayed by Lukas Foss in the 5th Brandenberg, during the cadenza in the second movement.

During the intermission of that Bach concert I remember espying dear Lukas Foss behind the amphitheater, resting on a bed of old rubber tires. It looked rather natural and rather comfortable besides. It was in those California days of the 50's while Foss was playing in the International Music Festival for which I was the driver, using our beat up old car. That was a lot of fun. One of my passengers was Tikhon Krennikov, a Soviet composer still known to Russians. Only recently I met a Russian TV producer in the lobby of the Westside Holiday Inn, in New York City, of all places, on his way back from the Turin Shroud Center of Colorado in Colorado Springs; he was interested in the Shroud of Turin, and had not only heard of Krennikov, but liked him. That is well enough, of course, if you happen to like Soviet music. Another passenger was the wonderful Carlos Puig who wrote some memorable classic music. Perhaps he was related to the Puig family my grandmother befriended.

There is a connection, strangely enough, between Lukas Foss and the great pyramid of Giza. It was during one of three trips to Egypt when my husband was developing a potential pool of investors in the Middle East to the mutual fund operated by a large company of which he was the director of international funds.

Developing these contacts was a slow process since it was an awesome challenge to get countries like Abu Dhabi and some other Trucial states to invest in an American-run mutual fund. Somehow or other, we made the acquaintance of an Egyptian living in Brooklyn with his American wife who happened to tell us of a soiree being given in the home of a friend in honor of Lukas Foss, who was the Director of Music at the Brooklyn Academy of Music. Mr. Foss was presenting an interesting program which included, "The Four Seasons," by Paul Hindemith (one of my favorites). I knew in my heart that sooner or later Lukas Foss was destined to become a board member of my foundation. I thought that that was probably the night that destiny had arranged for me to meet Mr. Foss and ask him to join the board of the Fourth World Foundation.

So when the opportunity for me to actually meet him arose I knew that I had to ask him to join my board. I did get to meet him at the party and afterwards managed to hitch a ride home to my hotel in Manhattan with him and his lovely wife. Before alighting the car, I said, "Oh, Mr. Foss, would you grant me the great honor of joining the music committee of my foundation?" I thought that was harmless, seeing that his wife was present. He looked at me and said, "You are a singer, aren't you?" I said, "Yes." In fact I had studied music at the Opera Comique in Paris. He said, "Since you are a musician, then I would be happy to do so." This was both good news and bad news. The bad news was that singers are more often than not overweight, so he might have been assuming my profession merely from my appearance; the good news is that he joined my board.

Some years later I read that he had composed a moving musical tribute to the victims of the holocaust. He was a good Jew whom I always considered a junior Leonard Bernstein, of whom he was a good friend. I found this out later when our daughter, Suzy, became a friend of the Bernstein family.

While here in Connecticut, we've been going to ballet and Bach concerts. The last ten years or so we've brought down the New England Bach Festival to Fairfield University, the B minor Mass and St. Matthew Passion, two years running. We had quite a good attendance for these events. If nobody was going to perform those beautiful works down here in Fairfield County, then by golly we would make it happen ourselves! The redoubtable Blanche Honegger Moyse presided; she was a great violinist who married Marcel Moyse, one of the founders of the Marlboro Music Festival along with Adolf Busch and Rudolf Serkin and is now the director of the New England Bach Festival. This was great music with great musicians and anything remotely attached to these wonderful events was exciting and wonderful.

Listen now to strains of "Night on Bald Mountain" by Modeste Mussorgsky—you know, the one used on Walt Disney's classic movie, *Fantasia*, where everything is spooky and somber and ends up being heavenly with celestial music. Pray God that the denouement of our lives and our children's lives will be to that tune.

CHAPTER SIXTY-SIX

SHRINES

La Capilla de Todos Los Santos,
Sangre de Cristo Mountains

As part of an ongoing effort to promote a heavenly harmonic convergence on earth! I have become involved with the developments of various shrines in whose path the Almighty Father has put me, accompanied by synchronistic and mystical experiences. It was on one of my many trips between East and West, going West to California, to my warm health spa, that I was called to remember the words of a disembodied voice that I have heard both in waking and sleeping dreams. This voice had said to me, one morning in Connecticut thirty years ago, "You must go to the Sangre de Christo mountains." This was the same voice that told me to call John Jackson. This voice came from the same place, of a waking dream in which I, the party giver, (similar to the juggler of Notre Dame, the character in the story by Guy de Maupassant) offered to the Blessed Mother what I had—the know-how to organize parties—and that She came down from her pedestal and offered me a golden apple. I was trying to conjure up all sorts of explanations for the meaning of it; I thought of Eve, Snow White and the Seven Dwarfs, and Midas. I even went to a restaurant known as the Golden Apple on the Island of St. Martin and wondered if the place would give up some of its secrets to me. No luck. Eventually, I came across the book, *Apples of Gold*, that I acquired in the gift shop of the hospital where my daughter Patricia was hospitalized. Finally the mystery of the golden apple was solved; it had to do with the cross of my daughter's life with which all of us in my family have been afflicted, which has taken to book form. "A word fitly spoken is like apples of gold in pictures of silver" (Prov.25:11). This, hopefully, is also "didactic," similar to the exhortation in a prophetic dream from St. John the Evangelist, "Be thou didactic," which I mentioned earlier.

I kept this message about the Sangre de Christo mountains for many years knowing that eventually there would be some sort of confirmation.

That confirmation came on a wintry day about twenty-five years ago, when the pilot of our westbound plane said (and I have never heard this before or since), "we are now flying over the Sangre de Christo mountains." And I said to myself, "Oh, thank you God, the Sangre de Christo mountains exist after all and are there somewhere in Colorado." You see, I had no idea that these mountains ever existed.

We'll now fast forward to my early encounter with John and Rebecca Jackson, after our famous trip to Rome together, when our relationship was cemented and I visited them at their home in Colorado Springs for the first time. On their coffee table in their modest living room was a flyer, a modest black and white flyer which said, "Come visit our shrine in the San Luis valley in the heart of the Sangre de Christo mountains in Colorado." I was shocked. "Where did you get this?" I asked Rebecca. She said, "Oh, a friend gave it to me and I want to go down there since I have a hunch that some of the inhabitants are descendants of one of the lost tribes of Israel." Now Rebecca Hadassani Jackson is nothing, if not very Jewish, having a very strong consciousness of her heritage, which is why God put her and

John, a Catholic, together. One of her best lectures ever was "The Jewishness of the Shroud."

And so the Jacksons and I embarked on our first of three trips we took to the San Luis Valley in Colorado, two-and-a-half hours south of Colorado Springs. Pueblo is about halfway there, as I recall. With baited breath I soon expected, after so many years, to finally enter the domain of the Sangre de Christo mountains. Magical it was. The panoply of those snow-covered peaks in the distance, so near and yet so far, was simply breathtaking, unlike any mountains I'd seen before because of their seeming quality of going back into infinity with a certain ineffable quality they possessed of always receding in the distance and yet always strangely accessible.

The priest in charge of the shrine, actually the priest who founded it, was one of the most extraordinary priests I have met over the years. Father Pat Valdez, a Mexican–American, is a member of the Theatine order which was founded by St. Cajetan, and the Western head of the order. On my first visit, the shrine consisted of a hill with the stations of the cross positioned along the path to the top. The stations consisted of the most extraordinary bronze statues that may have ever been cast East of the Appalachias or the Tiber, for that matter. Certainly the most extraordinary bronze statues I have ever seen, perhaps anywhere on the planet. Of course, the stations of the cross, which denote the Passion of Jesus Christ, have a great affinity with the Shroud on which is etched the face of the Passion. There was an immediate kinship between Fr. Valdez and the Jacksons lasting to this day.

As for my message about the Sangre de Christo mountains, two other women who came to some of our Cenacles had the same messages!! One couple, after they retired, actually moved to San Luis, and they were also named Jackson. They were a very loving couple who have endured the hardships of loneliness, cold winters and other rather primitive conditions, on a barren mesa 8,000 feet up, known as the "solar capital of the world" because of the large amount of annual sunlight. Fr. Valdez laid out his plans for us. He wanted to increase the visitors to the shrine. He already had a shrine garden to the Virgin of Guadalupe, but he wanted to build a visitor's center and eventually a chapel at the top of the hill.

When Pope John Paul II visited Denver for his Youth Conference, wearing gold sneakers! on his mini-treks in the backyard of the Rockies, we all thought it would be grand if he'd come visit San Luis. So I immediately dispatched a letter to Cardinal Keeler of Baltimore who was in charge of the Holy Father's visit. Would he please visit what would one day be the greatest shrine in the United States? (And maybe a very large refuge for the Remnant) Cardinal Keeler was very gracious in his reply, turning us down, of course. Meanwhile, on subsequent trips to Colorado Springs, we continued to visit Fr. Valdez.

The last time I visited San Luis was on the occasion of the dedication of Fr. Valdez' beautiful chapel called, Capilla de Todos Los Santos which is perched right on top of the hill, with the backdrop of the magnificent Sangres.

The Jacksons and I, amongst others, were honored guests which, for me, was to be expected since I had made a contribution, to what I thought was important, which was the affixation of a bronze plaque with the appropriate prayer for each station of the Cross.

Remember the architecture of the Goetheanum of Rudolf Steiner that I talked about, which is similar to the Capella la Familia Sagrada in Barcelona, a combination of free form with maybe a touch of the Eastern Byzantine? Well this chapel had this mix and is perhaps one of the most beautiful chapels I have seen in my life. Every artist in the San Luis Valley seems to be inspired by God's special inspirational force.

Because I fancied myself something of a community builder, as well as a benefactor of the shrine, I was interested in purchasing some property immediately beyond the shrine on the same hill. I was, and am keen to build a hospice for priests and or pilgrims. However, that is not yet to be. I thought possibly that San Luis would be the center of one of the largest of the Remnant communities, especially if a chastisement would take place according to the prophecies of Edgar Cayce, Paul Solomon and now Gordon Michael Scallion. All of them have prophesized the eventual inundation of the whole Southwest, pretty much right into central Colorado. We'll see.

Apparently, Fr. Valdez is something of a mystic too, for on the date of the dedication of the chapel, the plaque displaying the names of all the donors included none other than the Fifth World Foundation! This Indian priest knew full well that the fifth world of the Hopi Indians is coming soon, will be the New Jerusalem and that San Luis will no doubt be one of its headquarters.

Shrine to St. Martin de Porres, St. Maarten, Dutch Antilles

St. Martin de Porres

Coming down out of those mountains and off that great high mesa in Southern Colorado, we fast forward a bit to the island of St. Martin, which is very mountainous. The highest peak, Pic Paradis, looks volcanic, since it is an almost perfect cone. I knew that eventually I'd have to build a shrine to St. Martin de Porres.

The genesis for the development of a Shrine to St. Martin de Porres came about because the Fourth World Foundation was launched initially for the express purpose of addressing poverty and its endemic problems of malnutrition, and starvation in developing and underdeveloped countries which make up the third and fourth world nations. We have been given the opportunity, as well as the divine encouragement, to erect a Shrine to St. Martin de Porres on the island of St. Maarten in the Windward Islands specifically to highlight and address the problems of the poor in the Caribbean.

After receiving the support of leading journalists on the French side of the island, we had hoped to find a site there for the erection and building of a large statue on top of a hill, but when I tried to actually acquire a hilltop, after much backing and filling, I was met with total resistance. We were turned down by landowners in French St. Martin. But The French and Creoles are a pretty secular bunch: I'll leave it at that. However, there was one very bright spot in the person of the one and only priest on the French side, Fr. Cornelius Charles.

It is by a strange providence, a well-disguised blessing, that my employer who was down in St. Martin at the time, became ill, and while he was in the hospital on the Dutch side, I was chauffeured to visit him, by a very gregarious and compassionate taxi driver who knew everybody in town. While he drove me to and from the hospital, I shared with him my desire to build a shrine and he said that given enough time, he could introduce me to the people who could make it happen.

Now this was a time of travail, so to cheer myself up, I took a delightful room in the Bel Air Beach Hotel (almost within walking distance of the hospital) where they had an Australian tour desk, of all things. They were very friendly and helpful when I told them of my plight. I told them, "You know, I need to get on a boat and go around the island and see if I can find any mountain tops that would be suitable for a shrine and a statue." Being Australian, always gung ho for anything and everything, even with eccentric middle-aged housewives, they said, "Why not?" They had a boat and so I hired it. And there I was, in this boat with a bunch of Australians who were sailing it and that was fine and there did seem to be two or three mountainous candidates for shrinehood, viewed from afar on that boat.

Now, as it happened, the cab driver who ended up taking me everywhere, especially to the hospital and back, was a very friendly chap. O'Neal was his first name. He seemed to know everybody and before you knew it he was my official appointed agent to find a mountain top for the shrine, one that could be seen by all the cruise ships in the principal harbor of Philipsburg, the capital of the Dutch side of the island. We did find one good Catholic named John, who said his family owned a mountaintop, and he said he'd lease it to me reasonably and said further that the shrine would be good for everyone, tourism, and that was a blessing for his family as well.

Over a period of about four years, through amazing coincidences and divine interventions, the Shrine may now become a reality since the Dutch Government of St. Maarten has OK'd the allocation of the necessary funds for the road which they owned. I have done all of the spade work—with a great deal of help from the pious people who live on that part of the island—in finding a very suitable location on the top of a mountain where there is an existing road (of sorts). The top seen from the harbor where cruise ships dock, and from the sky, by airplanes. The local parish priest, who was very much in favor of the project, made a formal request to the government, which was granted.

We even found a Bulgarian sculptor who could make the statue; he had a lot of experience with statues, putting them up on hills in his own country during the Soviet period. He'd had to put up statues of the Soviet oppressors, of course, but he'd actually been an Orthodox Christian, but that's how he made his living. We even got local government permission to help pave the roadway linking the existing road to the top of the hill and then, whammo! Hurricane Lenny. This is what might be called unfinished business, including a couple of other shrines which I hope to talk about some time in the future, maybe even during the era of peace. Once again, we'll see.

Lyford Cay, Bahamas

Since our home in St. Martin is rented most of the year, we needed a second choice to satisfy our need to go south. Occasionally we would come to New Providence Island, and eventually it occurred to me that if a shrine could be built in St. Martin, then why not have one in such a felicitous location as New Providence Island? As expounded in the enclosures, the purpose of the shrine is to recognize the fact that St. Martin is the first Black saint to be canonized, which was done by Pope John Paul II in 1993. Furthermore, he is considered the foremost of all the patron saints of the poor. While other saints are often called on to help us through prayer for their intercession, St. Martin is one of the most powerful saints in Heaven whose intercession in our lives can be very powerful, to which I can attest from personal experience.

It was on May 12, 1993, as a matter of fact, that I wrote a letter to the Superior of the Augustinian monastery in Nassau, asking him if he would be interested in our project. God must have favored this request since, on that very day, we had a rainbow around the sun which made the headlines of the two local newspapers.

Unfortunately, Brother Elias, a monk who took a real interest in this, died a couple of years ago. However, Monsignor McManus of St. Paul's Church for the Catholics in and around Lyford Cay, said that he would accept a statue in the esplanade behind the church where there is an entrance. Monsignor McManus has had great success in building a hall and field for the young people of Lyford Cay.

A statue would be very lovely for the Catholic residents of Lyford Cay. Obviously there will be many people—like those in French St. Martin—who, initially, will not be enthusiastic, but it is only the people as a whole who can bring this idea to pass so that American and European tourists, who are so inclined, may visit the shrine, leaving a donation to the appropriate development and relief agencies, which could help bridge the gap between the haves and have nots. It is this very gap that is helping to exacerbate tensions between East and West.

CHAPTER SIXTY-SEVEN

ONCE IN A BLUE MOON

The year 1999 was a very unusual one in that only once or twice this century have there ever been two blue moons. A blue moon occurs where there are two full moons in the same month. In 1999 we had two such occurrences in January and March.

This month has been very unusual for me in other ways. I believe it has something to do with the presence of the Father's arrival, finally, in our lives in a formal way. I can't remember experiencing a better day in my whole life than this first day of Spring. This came about while I was still basking in the glory and sheer pleasure and joy of a beautiful experience on the Island of St. Martin.

Father Cornelius Charles, a brilliant and erudite pastor from the French side of St. Martin (originally from St. Lucia), delayed the opening of his new church in the town of Grand Case for six months when fortunately, I could make it. I can't really remember everything that led to that little ceremony. It was as if I were in a trance or in some altered state of consciousness.

Well it all started with Hurricane Luis in 1996. You might say that that hurricane did a number in the consciousness of all the Christians living on that island. They knew that it was a sign from God, as described in Matthew 24. Fr. Charles' church in Grand Case was blown down. In fact, he took a direct body blow in everything. Many of his parishioners were made homeless; his radio antenna was destroyed. It was the worst hurricane this island had ever experienced since they started recording them, and one of the strongest ever felt in the Caribbean with winds of up to 220 mph. The devastation was severe. One of the videotapes made clearly indicated this. Fr. Charles understood very well what the hurricane meant; so, as soon as he could, he commissioned all the painters he could find on the island, including the Haitians who are very good artists, to paint the fourteen stations of the cross for his main church in Marigot, the capital of French St. Martin. Remembering that I had some absolutely beautiful photographs of those magnificent bronze sculptures of the Fourteen Stations at the shrine in St. Luis, CO, I thought that if Fr. Charles wished to decorate his other church, maybe I could have those photos blown up and framed. That is exactly what happened. I got them blown up and then took them to St. Martin where, with the help of Kendall, my local caretaker par excellence, I got them framed (6 feet by 4 feet) and deposited rather unceremoniously in Fr. Charles' living room.

When I went back some months later, Father Charles said he was waiting for me. I made several trips after that, each time spending only a couple of days. Fr. Charles waited six months for me. This is pretty much the first time that anything of this nature has happened. According to the Scriptures, we should quietly go about our work. I remember the work I put in to bring the CCJU into being. Those concerned subsequently went off to see the Pope without me. They seemed reluctant to publicly acknowledge my involvement with the CCJU and I never said anything (not until my Bishop acknowledged me in public). But that is how it should be. In fact, virtually everything of this nature that I have done has usually been kept in the closet. My experience with Fr. Charles is the first of its kind. Maybe I ought to thank St. Martin de Porres since he seems to be in charge of everything I do on the island.

The congregation applauded me and then I gave a little speech in French and then in English.

On my return home to Connecticut the week before the week of the blue moon, the church down the street from our home, St. Timothy's, notified me that they were having a ceremony on March 21, the first day of Spring, for the installation of their new organ. Of course I had to go since I encouraged them to do this some years ago, and they finally did it. They are such a nice group of people down there! Sure enough, the last piece of music that the organist played was the Toccata from Charles-Marie Widor's Symphony No. 5. Perhaps this is the most magnificent piece of music written for the organ. What an experience for me!

The many Biblical references to God and His angels in terms of light, have led me to believe that any expression of God must be manifested in light. On this premise, gratitude must be an attribute of God because of the effect on me of those acts of gratitude by Father Charles and the members of St. Timothy's. It was like a beam of light shining into my being overshadowing the darkness of the many challenges which daily confront me.

ENDGAME

And so I am gazing at my authentic Portuguese statue of Our Lady of Fatima, sculpted from the description given by Sister Lucia (the last surviving visionary) of what Mary looks like. (She looks like Our Lady of Guadalupe, of course, same Lady.)

And then it dawns on me that what makes this likeness different is her crown! Other likenesses have rosaries, white and blue gown, bare feet etc. and crowns. But this crown is different. How is it different?

Her crown is the onion dome of the EAST. Is Fatima the most important of all apparitions (except for Guadalupe) not only for the conversion of the Red Dragon (Communism) and its corollary the Black Panther (the secular humanistic New World Order), but also for the conversion of the third part of the triad of danger to the planet—Islamic fundamentalists? Is that why She is Fatima, named after the well-beloved daughter and successor to the great prophet himself, Mohammed? Is our Mother—East meets West? Her love encircles the globe as she appears in various countries from West to East bearing messages for the welfare of all mankind.

As I gaze at Her image I think of that *New York Daily News* journalist's caption, under that picture of me and my husband descending the stairs of St. Vincent Ferrer's Church on our wedding day: "East mates West". Under Her guidance, this union has led to my involvement in global activities. She, who stood at the foot of the cross and watched the intense suffering of her first born, has supported me in the suffering of my first born as only a mother can. Her Love for me and my family, that same Love that encircles the globe, points to supernatural events, which will someday be the natural order of the New Jerusalem, when mankind lives in total accord with the Divine Will. I am getting ready.

The pilgrim statue of Our Lady of Fatima which
wept real tears while on tour in New Orleans

BIBLIOGRAPHY

This bibliography is intended for supplementary reading and research. Not all of the titles presented are referenced in this book.

Ackroyd, Peter. *Blake*. New York : Knopf : Distributed by Random House, 1996

Alighieri, Dante. *The Divine Comedy*. New York : Alfred A. Knopf, 1995.

Andersen, Christopher P. *The New Book of People* : photographs, capsule biographies, and vital statistics of over 500 celebrities. New York, N.Y. : Putnam, c1986.

Beckley, John L. *Working With People*. Fairfield, N.J.: Economics Press, c1985.

Bedford, Sybille. *Aldous Huxley*: a biography. 1st American ed. New York : Knopf : distributed by Random House, 1974.

Beecher, Charles Rev. *Patmos; or, The Unveiling*. Boston, Lee and Shepard, 1896.

Begg, Ean. *The Cult of the Black Virgin*. Rev. and expanded ed. London; New York: Arkana, 1996.

Bennett, William J. *The De-valuing of America*: the fight for our culture and our children. New York : Summit Books, c1992.

Bennett, William J. [ed] *The Book of Virtues*: a treasury of great moral stories. New York: Simon & Schuster, c1993. 831 p.: ill.; 24 cm.

Benson, Herbert. *The Relaxation Response*, with Miriam Z. Klipper. New York: Wings Books, c1992.

Blakeslee, Thomas R. *The Right Brain*: a new understanding of the unconscious mind and its creative powers. 1st ed. Garden City, N.Y. : Anchor Press / Doubleday, 1980.

Blofeld, John. *Bodhisattva of Compassion*: the mystical tradition of Kuan Yin. Boston : Shambhala ; [New York] : Distributed in the U.S. by Random House, 1988, c1977.

Bordeaux, Edmond S. *The Soul of Ancient Mexico*, Edmond S. Bordeaux. [San Diego, Calif., Academy Books, c1968]

Bromfield, Louis. *Pleasant Valley*; with an introduction by Gene Logsdon, and drawings by Kate Lord. Wooster, Ohio : Wooster Book Co., 1997.

Broun, Janice. *Conscience and Captivity*: religion in eastern Europe, Grazyna Sikorska. Washington, D.C.: Ethics and Public Policy Center ; Lanham, Md. : Distributed by arrangement with University Press of America, c1988.

Brown, Dee. *Bury My Heart At Wounded Knee*: an Indian history of the American West. 1st Owl book ed. New York: H. Holt, 1991

Brown, Raymond [ed]. *Mary in the New Testament*: a collaborative assessment by Protestant and Roman Catholic scholars; from discussions by Paul J. Achtemeier . . . [et al.] ; sponsored by the United States Lutheran-Roman Catholic Dialogue. Philadelphia: Fortress Press, 1978.

Browning, Robert. *Selected Poetry*; edited, with an introd., by Kenneth L. Knickerbocker. New York, Modern Library [1954, c1951]

Bucchner, Frederick. *Open Heart*: a novel. 1st Harper & Row pbk. Ed. San Francisco: Harper & Row, 1984, c1979.

Buckley, William F. Jr. *God and Man at Yale*: the superstitions of "academic freedom"; introd. by John Chamberlain, with a new introd. by the author. South Bend, Ind. : Gateway Editions, [1977?] c1951

Buckley, William F. Jr. *Gratitude*: reflections on what we owe to our country, 1st ed. New York: Random House, c1990.

Buzan, Tony. *Speed Reading*. 1st ed. New York : E.P. Dutton, c1984.

Campbell, Joseph. *The Hero with a Thousand Faces* (Mythos: Princeton / Bollingen Series in World Mythology, Vol. 17), Princeton Univ. 1990.

Cayce, Edgar. *Earth Changes*: past, present, future. [Virginia Beach, Association for Research and Enlightenment Press, 1963]

Cayce, Edgar. *Home Medicine Guide*, [Virginia Beach, Association for Research and Enlightenment Press, 1983]

Chambers, Whittaker. *Witness*; preface by Robert Novak; foreword by Milton Hindus. Washington, DC : Regnery Pub., 1997.

Charell, Ralph. *How to Make Things Go Your Way*. New York : Cornerstone Library, 1981, c1979.

Chinmoy, Sri. *Arise! Awake!* Thoughts of a Yogi. New York, F. Fell [1972]

Chinmoy, Sri. *The Garland of Nation-souls* : complete talks at the United Nations / Sri Chinmoy. Deerfield Beach, Fla. : Health Communications, c1995.

Chinmoy, Sri. *The Silent Teaching* : a selection of the writings; with an introduction by Alan Spence. Edinburgh: Published by the Sri Chinmoy Centre in conjunction with Aum Publications, Jamaica, N.Y., 1982

Clark, Linda A. *The Ancient Art of Color Therapy*: updated, including gem therapy, auras, and amulets. Greenwich, Conn.: Devin-Adair Co., 1992, c1975.

Connelly, Marc. *The Green Pastures*, a fable suggested by Roark Bradford's southern sketches, "Ol' man Adam an his chillun,", with illustrations by Robert Edmond Jones. New York, Farrar & Rinehart, incorporated, 1930.

Council For Defense and Freedom. *A World Without Communism*

Das, Pankaj K. & De Cusatis, Casirner M. *Acousto-Optic Signal Processing*: fundamentals & applications; with contributions by Sergey V. Kulakov. Boston : Artech House, c1991.

Dass, Ram & Gorman, Paul. *How Can I Help?* : stories and reflections on service. New York : Knopf, 1985.

Dass, Ram a.k.a. Alpert, Richard. *Be Here Now, Remember*. San Cristobal, N.M. : Lama Foundation ; New York : distributed by Crown Pub., c1971, 1974 printing.

DeCharms, George. *John in the Isle of Patmos*; stories of Revelation. [2d ed.] Bryn Athyn, Pa., Academy of the New Church Book Room, 1955.

Dehan, Emmanuel. *Megiddo Armageddon*. POB 3238, Tel Aviv, Israel

Denton, Jeremiah A. Jr. *When Hell Was in Session*, with Ed. Brandt. Washington, D.C. : Morley Books, 1997.

Douglass, Joseph D. Jr. *Red Cocaine* : the drugging of America ; introduction by Ray S. Cline. 1st ed. Atlanta, Ga.: Clarion House, c1990.

Douglass, Joseph D. Jr. and Livingstone, Neil C. *America the Vulnerable* : the threat of chemical and biological warfare. Lexington, Mass. : Lexington Books, c1987.

Douglass, Joseph D. Jr. and Amoretta M. Hoeber. *Conventional War & Escalation*: the Soviet view, New York: Crane, Russak, c1981.

Douglass, Joseph D. Jr. Amoretta M. Hoeber *Soviet Strategy for Nuclear War*; foreword by Eugene V. Rostow. Stanford, Calif.: Hoover Institution Press, c1979.

Drosnin, Michael. *The Bible Code*, Simon & Schuster, 1998.

Ebben, Mary. *The Urantia Book Basics*. Lafayette, Colo.: M. Ebben, c1994.

Epstein, Edward Jay. *Deception* : the invisible war between the KGB and the CIA. New York : Simon and Schuster, c1989.

Feldenkrais, Moshe. *Awareness Through Movement*; health exercises for personal growth. [1st ed.] New York, Harper & Row [1972]

Ferguson, Marilyn. *The Aquarian Conspiracy*: personal and social transformation in the 1980s ; foreword by Max Lerner. 1st ed. Los Angeles : J. P. Tarcher ; New York : distributed by St. Martin's Press, c1980.

Finder, Joseph. *Red Carpet*. 1st ed. New York: Holt, Rinehart, and Winston, c1983.

Firmin-Didot. et cie *Poètes Contemporains*; anthologie. [Paris] Firmin-Didot et cie [1938]

Foster, William Z. *Toward Soviet America*. New York, Coward-McCann, Inc. [c1932]

Foundation for Inner Peace. *A Course in Miracles*. Mill Valley, CA: Foundation for Inner Peace, 1999.

Foundation for Inner Peace. *Supplements to A Course in Miracles*. New York, N.Y., U.S.A. : Viking : Foundation for Inner Peace, 1996.

Fowler, Gene. *Good Night, Sweet Prince*, the life and times of John Barrymore. New York, The Viking press, 1944.

Frankl, Viktor E. *Man's Search for Meaning*; an introduction to logotherapy. A newly rev. and enl., ed. of From death-camp to existentalism. Translated by Ilse Lasch. Pref. by Gordon W. Allport. Boston, Beacon Press [1963, c1962]

Fuchs, Victor R. *Who Shall Live?*: health, economics, and social choice. Expanded ed. Singapore; River Edge, NJ : World Scientific, c1998.

Fynn. *Mister God, this is Anna*; illustrated by Papas. Thorndike, Me.: Thorndike Press, 1991, c1974.

Gallwey, W. Timothy. *The Inner Game of Tennis,* [1st ed.] New York, Random House [1974]

Garrett, George. *The Liar's Craft*, assistant editor, Stephen Kendrick. 1st ed. Garden City, N.Y. : Anchor Press, 1977.

Georg Holzherr. *Einsiedeln*: Kloster und Kirche Unserer Lieben Frau: von der Karolingerzeit bis zur Gegewart. 1. Aufl. München : Schnell & Steiner, 1987.

Gifford, Barry & Lee, Lawrence. *Jack's Book* : an oral biography of Jack Kerouac. New York : St. Martin's Press, c1994.

GOD. *The Holy Bible*. New American Catholic ed. [English. 1961. Confraternity version.] With the pronouncements of Pope Leo XIII and Pope Pius XII on the study of Scriptures, historical and chronological index, a table of references, and maps. New York, Benziger Bros. [1961]

Golitsyn, Anatoly. *New Lies For Old*: the Communist strategy of deception and disinformation. 2nd ed. Atlanta, Ga.: Clarion House, c1990.

Golitsyn, Anatoly. *The Perestroika Deception*: memoranda to the Central Intelligence Agency. London; New York: Edward Harle, 1995.

Goodman, Jeffrey. *We Are the Earthquake Generation*: where and when the catastrophes will strike. 1st ed. New York: Seaview Books : trade distribution by Simon and Schuster, c1978.

Gordon, Ernest. *Miracle on the River Kwai*, London, Collins, 1973.

Grenet, Rev. Paul. *Teilhard de Chardin*. Choix de textes, bibliographie, portraits, fac-similés. [Paris] Éditions Seghers [1961]

Gribbin, John & Rees, Martin. *Cosmic Coincidences*: dark matter, mankind and anthropic cosmology. London: Black Swan, 1991 (1992 printing)

Hammarskjold, Dag. *Markings*; translated by Leif Sjöberg & W.H. Auden; with a foreword by W.H. Auden. London: Faber and Faber, 1966.

Hassrick, Royal. *The Sioux*; life and customs of a warrior society. In collaboration with Dorothy Maxwell and Cile M. Bach. [1st ed.] Norman, University of Oklahoma Press [1964]

Heller, Milchail. *Cogs in the Wheel*: the formation of Soviet man; translated by David Floyd. 1st American ed. New York: Knopf, 1988.

Hoffer, A, Osmond, H. *Megavitamin Therapy* : in reply to the American Psychiatric Association Task Force report on megavitamins and ortho-molecular psychiatry / A. Hoffer, H. Osmond. Regina, Sask. CANADA: Canadian Schizophrenia Foundation, [1976]

Hutchinson, Gloria. *A Retreat with Gerard Manley Hopkins and Hildegard of Bingen*: turning pain into power. Cincinnati, Ohio : St. Anthony Messenger Press, c1995.

Huxley, Aldous. *Letters of Aldous Huxley*. Edited by Grover Smith. [1st U.S. ed.] New York, Harper & Row [1970, c1969]

Huxley, Aldous. *Island*. Point Roberts, WA : Hartley & Marks, 1999.

Huxley, Laura. Archera *This Timeless Moment*: a personal view of Aldous Huxley. Millbrae, Calif. : Celestial Arts, 1975, c1968.

Isaac, Rael Jean & Armat, Virginia C. *Madness In The Streets*: how psychia-try and the law abandoned the mentally ill, New York: Free Press; Toronto: Collier Macmillan Canada; New York: Maxwell Macmillan International, c1990.

Isherwood, Christopher. *Vedanta for the Western World*; edited, and with an introd., by Christopher Isherwood. Hollywood [Calif.] Marcel Rodd Co., 1945.

Jaynes, Julian. *The Origin of Consciousness in the Breakdown of the Bicam-eral Mind*, Boston : Houghton Mifflin, c1990.

John Paul II. *Crossing The Threshold Of Hope*, New York: Random House Large Print in association with A.A. Knopf, 1994.

Johnson, Paul. *Modern Times*: the world from the twenties to the nineties. Rev. ed., 1st Harper Perennial ed. New York, N.Y. : Harper Perennial, 1992.

Johnston, Francis. *The Wonder of Guadalupe*: the origin and cult of the miraculous image of the Blessed Virgin in Mexico. Chulmleigh, De-von, UK: Augustine Pub. Co., 1981.

Jung, C. G. *Memories, Dreams, Reflections*, Vintage Books, 1965

Jung, C. G. *Synchronicity—An Actual Connecting Principle*, Translated by R. F. C. Hull. [1st Princeton/Bollingen paperback ed. Princeton, N.J.] Princeton University Press [1973]

Kahn, Herman. *The Coming Boom*: economic, political, and social. New York: Simon and Schuster, c1982.

Kahn, Herman. *Thinking About the Unthinkable in the 1980s*. New York: Simon and Schuster, c1984.

Kahn, Herman. *On Thermonuclear War*. Westport, Conn.: Greenwood Press, 1978, c1969.

Kahn, Herman. *Herman Kahnsciousness*; the megaton ideas of the one-man think tank. Produced by Jerome Agel. New York, New American Library, 1973.

Kahn, Herman, Brown, William, and Martel, Leon *The Next 200 Years* : a scenario for America and the world, with the assistance of the staff of the Hudson Institute. New York: Morrow, 1976.

King, Francis X. *Rudolf Steiner and Holistic Medicine*. York Beach, Me.: Nicolas-Hays : Distributed by S. Weiser, Inc., 1987, c1986.

King, Nicholas. *George Bush*, a biography. New York : Dodd, Mead, c1980.

Koestler, Arthur. *The Roots of Coincidence*; with a postscript by Renée Haynes. New York, Vintage Books [1973, c1972]

Kunz-Bircher, Ruth. *Eating Your Way to Health*, Baltimore, Md., Penguin Books [1972]

Lafaye, Jacques. *Quetzalcóatl and Guadalupe*: the formation of Mexican national consciousness, 1531-1813 ; with a foreword by Octavio Paz ; translated by Benjamin Keen. Chicago : University of Chicago Press, 1976.

Laing, R. D. *Self and Others*. 2nd ed. [reprinted] Harmondsworth, Penguin, 1971.

Laing, R. D. *The Politics of Experience*. New York, Pantheon Books [1967]

Leon-Portilla, Miguel. *Aztec Thought and Culture*; a study of the ancient Nahuatl mind. Translated from the Spanish by Jack Emory Davis. [1st ed.] Norman, University of Oklahoma Press [1963]

Lesser, Michael, M.D. *Nutrition and Vitamin Therapy*, 1st Evergreen ed. New York: Grove Press: distributed by Random House, 1980.

Lewis, C. S. *Out of the Silent Planet*: a novel [Space Trilogy Part I]. New York: Scribner Classics, 1996.

Lewis, C. S. *Perelandra*: a novel [Space Trilogy Part II]. New York: Scribner Paperback Fiction, 1996.

Lewis, C. S. *The Pilgrim's Regress*; an allegorical apology for Christianity, reason, and romanticism. Grand Rapids, Eerdmans [1959? c1943]

Lewis, C. S. *The Problem of Pain*. Macmillan Paperbacks ed. New York: Macmillan, 1962.

Lewis, C. S. *That Hideous Strength*: a modern fairy-tale for grown-ups. [Space Trilogy Part III] 1st Scribner Classics ed. New York, NY : Scribner Classics, 1996.

Lewis, C. S. *Miracles*: a preliminary study. New York: Macmillan, 1978, c1947.

Lewis, C. S. *The Great Divorce*. 1st Touchstone ed. New York: Simon & Schuster, 1996.

Lorenzo. *The Relaxation Sensation*: the no. 1 success factor in life; photos by Joan Riggi.New York: Prema Books, c1981

Lowen, Alexander *The Betrayal Of The Body*, New York, Macmillan [c1967]

Luther, Martin. *The Magnificat*, trans. A.T.W. Steinhaeser, Minneapolis, Augsburg Pub. House [1967]

MacGreggor, Geddes. *Reincarnation in Christianity*: a new vision of the role of rebirth in Christian thought. Wheaton, Ill.: Theosophical Pub. House, c1978.

Manteau-Bonamy, Fr. H. M. *The Immaculate Conception and The Holy Spirit*: the Marian teachings of Father Kolbe; pref. of G. Domanski; introd. by J. F. Villepelée; translated from the French by Richard Arnandez. 1st American ed. Kenosha, WI: Prow Books, 1977.

Markovna, Nina. *Nina's Journey* : a memoir of Stalin's Russia and the Second World War. Washington, D.C.: Regnery Gateway; Lanham, MD: Distributed to the book trade by National Book Network, c1989.

Martin, Malachi. *The Final Conclave*. New York: Stein and Day, 1978.

Martin, Malachi. *The Decline and Fall of the Roman Church*. New York: Putnam, c1981.

Martin, Malachi. *The Jesuits*: the Society of Jesus and the betrayal of the Roman Catholic Church. New York: Linden Press, Simon & Schuster, 1987.

Martin, Malachi. *The Keys of This Blood*: the struggle for world dominion between Pope John Paul II, Mikhail Gorbachev, and the capitalist West. New York: Simon and Schuster, c1990.

Martin, Malachi. *Windswept House*: a Vatican novel. 1st ed. New York: Doubleday, c1996.

Martini, Teri. *Treasure of the Mohawks*; the story of the Indian maiden Kateri Tekakwitha. Paterson, N.J., St. Anthony Guild Press, 1956.

Marx, Karl and Engels, Frederick. *The Communist Manifesto*. Authorized English translation, edited and annotated by Frederick Engels. New York, New York Labor News Co., 1939.

May, Rollo. *Love and Will*. [1st ed.] New York, Norton [1969]

McFadden, Charles J. *The Philosophy of Communism*, preface by Fulton J. Sheen New York, Boston [etc.] Benziger Bros., 1939.

McGuire. *The New Baltimore Catechism & Mass*, A catechism in Christian doctrine, New York, Cincinnati, Benziger brothers, 1933]

Medved, Michael. *Hollywood vs. America*: popular culture and the war on traditional values. 1st ed. New York, NY: HarperCollins; [Grand Rapids, Mich.]: Zondervan, c1992.

Menolascino, Neman & Stark. *Curative Aspects of Mental Retardation*: biomedical and behavioral advances, Baltimore: P.H. Brookes, c1983.

Merton, Thomas. *Seeds Of Contemplation*, New York: New Directions Pub. Corp., [1986], c1949.

Merton, Thomas. *The Asian Journal of Thomas Merton*, Edited from his original notebooks by Naomi Burton, Patrick Hart & James Laughlin. Consulting editor: Amiya Chakravarty. [New York, New Directions Pub. Corp., 1973]

Mesarovic, Mihajlo & Prestel, Eduard. *Mankind At The Turning Point*: (2nd Report of the Club of Rome), 1st ed. New York : Dutton, 1974.

Moore, Robin. *The French Connection*; the world's most crucial narcotics investigation. [1st ed.] Boston, Little, Brown [1969]

Moss, Robert and de Borchgrave, Arnaud. *Monimbó*: a novel. New York : Simon and Schuster, c1983.

Muggeridge, Malcolm. *Something Beautiful For God*: Mother Teresa of Calcutta. London, Collins, 1971.

Neihardt, John. *Black Elk Speaks*, 1997-1998, University of Nebraska Press.

Newton, Isaac. *Isaac Newton's Observations on the Prophecies of Daniel and the Apocalypse of St. John*: a critical edition / edited by S.J. Barnett ; with preface and biblical studies notes by Mary E. Mills. Lewiston: E. Mellen Press, c1999.

Nouwen, Henry J. M. *The Wounded Healer*; ministry in contemporary society. Illus. by Roel de Jong. [1st ed.] Garden City, N.Y., Doubleday, 1972.

Novak, Michael. *The American Vision*: an essay on the future of democratic capitalism. Washington: American Enterprise Institute for Public Policy Research, c1978.

Packard, Vance. *The Ultra Rich*: how much is too much? 1st ed. Boston: Little, Brown, c1989.

Pauling, Linus. *Vitamin C, The Common Cold & The Flu*,. San Francisco: W. H. Freeman, c1976.

Pearlsman, Ida. *The Messages of Lady Of All Nations*, Queenship Pub Co, 1996.

Penfield, Wilder. *The Mystery of the Mind*: a critical study of consciousness and the human brain, with discussions by William Feindel, Charles Hendel, and Charles Symonds. Princeton, N.J. : Princeton University Press, [1975]

Penkovskiy, Oleg. *The Penkovskiy Papers*. Introd. and commentary by Frank Gibney. Foreword by Edward Crankshaw. Translated by Peter Deriabin. [1st ed.] Garden City, N.Y., Doubleday, 1965.

Piccarreta, Luisa. *The Gift of the Divine Will*: The Luisa Piccarreta Center for the Divine Will, Jacksonville, FL 32210

Podhoretz, Norman. *The Present Danger*: "Do we have the will to reverse the decline of American power?". New York: Simon and Schuster, c1980.

Powell, S. Steven. *Covert Cadre*: inside the Institute for Policy Studies; introduction by David Horowitz. Ottawa, Ill. : Green Hill Publishers; New York: Distributed by Kampmann, c1987.

Pytches, David. *Some Said It Thundered*: A Personal Encounter With The Kansas City Prophets, Oliver-Nelson Press, Nashville, TN, 1991.

Raphell, Katrina. *Crystal Enlightenment*: the transforming properties of crystals and healing stones. New York, N.Y. : Aurora Press, 1985.

Ravenscroft, Trevor. *The Spear of Destiny*; the occult power behind the spear which pierced the side of Christ. [1st American ed.] New York, Putnam [1973]

Ravenscroft, Trevor. *The Cup of Destiny*: the quest for the Grail. 1st American ed. York Beach, ME.: S. Weiser, 1982.

Ravenscroft, Trevor, Wallace-Murphy, Tim. *The Mark of the Beast* : the continuing story of the Spear of Destiny. York Beach, ME.: S. Weiser, 1997.

Reisner, Bob and Kapplow, Hal. *Captions Courageous*: or, comments from the gallery, London ; New York : Abelard-Schuman, c1958.

Sakharov, Andrei D. *My Country and the World*; translated by Guy V. Daniels. 1st ed. New York: Knopf: distributed by Random House, 1975.

Salinger, J. D. *Nine Stories*. 1st Modern library ed. New York, Modern Library [1959]

Salinger, J. D. *Franny and Zooey*. London: Heinemann, 1962, c1961.

Sandoz, Mari *Crazy Horse*. New York : MJF Books, 1997.

Schwarz, Fred. *Communism, the Deceitful Tyranny* : (you can trust the communists—to be communists). Long Beach, Calif.: Chantico Pub. Co., c1966.

Satinover, Jeffrey. *Cracking the Bible Code*, Wm. Morrow, 1998,

Scott, Cyril. *Bone Of Contention*: life story and confessions, London, Aquarian P., 1969.

Scott, Cyril. *Music, Its Secret Influence Throughout The Ages*, [New and extended ed.] London, Rider [1958]

Scott, Cyril. *Cancer Prevention*: fallacies and some reassuring facts. London, Athene Publishing, 1968.

Scott, Cyril. *Cider Vinegar*: nature's great health-promoter and safest treatment of obesity. 6th ed., entirely revised, enlarged and reset. London, Athene Publishing, 1968.

Scott, Cyril. *Crude Black Molasses*: a natural 'wonder food'. Completely revised, enlarged & reset. London, Athene Publishing, 1968.

Scott, Cyril. *Doctors, Disease, and Health*; a critical survey of therapeutics, modern and ancient. London, Methuen & Co., ltd. [1938]

Shainherg, Maurice. *Breaking from the KGB*: Warsaw ghetto fighter, intelligence officer, defector to the West. 1st ed. New York, NY: Shapolsky Pub. of North America, 1986.

Sheen, Fulton J. *Life Is Worth Living*: first and second series; illustrations by Dik Browne. San Francisco: Ignatius Press, 1999.

Shevchenko, Arkady N. *Breaking with Moscow*. 1st ed. New York: Knopf, 1985.

Shultz, Richard H., Godson, Roy. *Dezinformatsia*: active measures in Soviet strategy. Washington : Pergamon-Brassey's, c1984.

Simonton, O. Carl, M.D., Matthews-Simonton, S., and Creighton, James. *Getting Well Again*: a step-by-step, self-help guide to overcoming cancer for patients and their families, Los Angeles: J. P. Tarcher; New York: distributed by St. Martin's Press, c1978.

Sirneons, A.T.W., M.D. *Man's Presumptuous Brain*; an evolutionary interpretation of psychosomatic disease. [London] Longmans [1960]

Skousen, W. Cleon (Willard Cleon). *The Naked Communist*. Salt Lake City, Ensign Pub. Co. [1958]

Skousen. Mark. *Economics on Trial*: lies, myths, and realities. Homewood, Ill.: Business One Irwin, c1991.

Sladek, Marti. *Two Weeks With The Psychic Surgeons*, Chicago: Doma Press, c1976.

Stein, Jean. *Edie*: American girl; edited with George Plimpton. 1st pbk. ed. New York, NY: Grove Press, 1994.

Steiner, Rudolf. *World Economy*, the formation of a science of world-economics. [London] Steiner Pub. Co.; New York, Anthroposophic Press [193-?]

Stuart, Gene S. *The Mighty Aztecs*; photographs by Mark Godfrey ; paintings by Louis S. Glanzman; prepared by the Special Publications Division, National Geographic Society, Washington, D.C. Washington, D.C.: National Geographic Society, c1981.

Terelya, Josyp. *Josyp Terelya, Witness to Apparitions and Persecution in the USSR* : an autobiography.; with Michael H. Brown. Milford, Ohio: Faith Pub. Co., 1991.

Tinbergcn. Jan. *Reshaping the International Order*: a report to the Club of Rome; Anthony J. Dolman, editor: Jan van Ettinger, director. London : Hutchinson, 1977.

Tolkien, J. R. R. *The Two Towers*: being the second part of The Lord of the Rings. 2nd ed. Boston : Houghton Mifflin Co., [1986], c1965.

Tolkien, J. R. R. *The Annotated Hobbit*: The hobbit, or, There and back again; illustrated by the author; introduction and notes by Douglas A. Anderson. Boston: Houghton Mifflin Co., 1988.

Tolkien, J. R. R. *The Fellowship of the Ring*: being the first part of The Lord of the Rings. 2nd ed. Boston: Houghton Mifflin Co., [1986], c1965.

Tolkien, J. R. R. *The Return of the King*: being the third part of The Lord of the Rings. 2nd ed. Boston: Houghton Mifflin Co., [1986?], c1965.

Turner, James S. *The Chemical Feast*: The Ralph Nader Study Group Report on Food Protection and the Food and Drug Administration, 1976, Penguin

Urantia Foundation. *The Urantia Book*. Chicago, Urantia Foundation, 1955.

Valladares. Armando *Against All Hope*: the prison memoirs of Armando Valladares / translated by Andrew Hurley. 1st ed. New York: Knopf; Distributed by Random House, 1986.

Van Buren, Elizabeth. *Rainbow Round the Sun*. London; New York: Regency Press, c1979.

Vine, Phyllis. *Families in Pain*: children, siblings, spouses, and parents of the mentally ill speak out / Phyllis Vine; foreword by C. Christian Beels. 1st ed. New York : Pantheon Books, c1982.

Vonnegut. Mark *The Eden Express*. New York: Praeger, 1975.

Ward, J. Neville. *Five For Sorrow, Ten For Joy*: a consideration of the Rosary. Rev. ed. / with a new introduction by the author. Cambridge, MA : Cowley, c1985.

Washburn, Del. *The Original Code in the Bible*, Madison Bks., 1998

Werfel, Franz *The Song of Bernadette*; translated by Ludwig Lewisohn. New York: St. Martin's Press, [1989], c1942.

Wilde, Oscar. *The Picture of Dorian Gray*. 1st Modern Library ed. New York: Modern Library, c1985.

Winston, Stephanie. *Getting Organized*: the easy way to put your life in order. Updated and rev., Rev. ed. prepared with the assistance of Marnie Winston-Macauley. New York, NY: Warner Books, c1991.

Woodrew, Greta. *On a Slide of Light*. New York : Macmillan, c1981.

Woodrew, Greta. *Memories of Tomorrow*. 1st ed. New York: Doubleday, 1988.

Wouk, Herman. *Don't Stop the Carnival*. Back Bay pbk. ed., with new introduction. Boston: Little, Brown and Co., 1999.

EGG

Wurmbrand, Richard. *Marx & Satan*. Bartlesville, OK: Living Sacrifice Book Co., c1986 (1990 printing)

Zeffirelli, Franco. *Zeffirelli*: the autobiography of Franco Zeffirelli. 1st American ed. New York: Weidenfeld & Nicolson, 1986.

Zukav, Gary. *The Dancing Wu Li Masters* : an overview of the new physics. 1st ed. New York: Morrow, 1979.

ENDNOTES

NOTES: PART I

1   Luther Burbank, 1849-1926, **self**-taught horticulturalist and naturalist, credited with the development of many improved varieties of fruits and vegetables.

2   See Bibliography.

3   Ellsworth, William L., "Earthquake History, 1769-1989" in USGS Professional Paper 1515, Robert E. Wallace, ed., 1990 and USGS earthquake catalogs list three earthquakes over 6 point magnitude on the Richter scale in southern California during 1940, the greatest reaching a 7.1 magnitude was the Great Imperial Valley quake which struck the area at 4:36 am.

4   Julian Jaynes, see Bibliography, from which derive the idea of right and left brained consciousness of a bicameral mind and other influential ideas.

5   by St. Thomas Aquinas, a pivotal work in Catholic Christian theology.

6   See David Pytches, see Bibliography. According to the Apologetics Index of Christian Associates International, the Kansas City Prophets were a controversial group of prophets, including Bob Jones, Paul Cain and John Paul Jackson who, in the mid 1980's, were associated with the Kansas City Fellowship. Their teachings and practices have strong ties

to the Latter Rain movement of the 1950's popularized by Franklin Hall, William Branham, George Warnock, John Robert Stevens and others. Elements of Latter Rain teachings are today being taught within certain renewal and revival movements. The Latter Rain or Dominion theology teaches a restoration of a purified church prepared to rule, out of which will arise a cadre of leaders who will possess the "Spirit without *measure*" and whom will purge the earth of all wickedness and rebellion.

7   Related to a genetic theory of Dr. Ernst Krebs Jr. concerning the uncontrolled growth of cancer and the growth in the placenta.

8   by J.R.R. Tolkien. See Bibliography.

9   by Carlos Castaneda, Simon & Schuster, 1972.

10 a symbol for world communism attributed to Rudolf Steiner

11 Armando Valladares, See Bibliography.

12 Jeremiah Denton, Ed Brandt, See Bibliography.

13 Sanscrit for psychic powers.

14 French for "a must"

15 The dating, identities of the builder(s) and even the uses of the pyramids and Sphinx of Giza are foci of controversy and speculation to this day. Some authorities have dated these monuments to more than 10,500 BC. The date given here is the most conservative and widely accepted dating for Cheops who either built or restored the great pyramid of Giza.

16 D. Scott Rogo is the author of many books on parapsychological, psychic and spiritual subjects. Many of his works are also out of print or otherwise comparatively hard to find.

17 *Fairfield Citizen's News*, July 9, 1980

18 *No Strings*. Words and music by Richard Rodgers opened prior to its run on Broadway on February 27, 1962 in the Shubert Theatre in New Haven, Connecticut. Rodgers had opened the production in Detroit, but brought it to the Shubert for a break-in engagement before presenting it in New York.

Richard Kiley and Diahann Carroll were the stars. Joe Layton
staged the production and created the dances.

19 Editor at large for *The Washington Times*.
20 Editor of the *McAlvany Intelligence Report* and the *McAlvany
Intelligence Advisor* newsletters.
21 McKeever Institute of Economic Policy Analysis
22 Comet Kohoutek (1973 E1) failed to live up to initial expec-
tations but developed into a bright naked eye comet showing
a full range of cometary activity. Only low altitude and poor
weather in the early part of 1974 spoilt a good apparition.
Some members beat the weather by taking one of two special
flights to view the comet in January

NOTES: PART II

23 Aldous' first wife Maria died in 1955. A year later he married Laura Archera. Aldous died in 1963 on the same day
President Kennedy was assassinated. Aldous' remains were
cremated and his ashes were spread over his parents' graves
in England.
24 Silva Mind Control is still an active self-help movement. Hans
DeJong is one of its current proponents. See his *Silva Mind
Control for Success and Self Confidence*, an audio book read
by the author and published by Audio Renaissance Tapes.
25 See Bibliography.
26 See Bibliography.
27 See Bibliography.
28 Founded in 1977.
29 1998, H. J. Kramer. See also Diet for a Small Planet by
Frances Moore-Lappe, 1991, Ballantine.
30 1976, St. Albans.

31 A phrase credited to Jack Kerouac but used frequently by Timothy Leary to represent the Hippie Generation.

32 Ken Keyes Jr. *The Hundredth Monkey* has been placed in the public domain on the internet and elsewhere by the author. He seems to want to let everyone know about this phenominon.

33 1971-72, Harper & Row, New York, etc.

34 Formerly Jack Rosenberg, founder of *EST*, headquartered in San Francisco. *Est* is Latin for "it is" but also stands for "Erhard Seminar Training" and from 1971 was one of the most successful enterprises in the human potential movement.

35 His full name was Richard Buckminster Fuller (1895-1983), one of the greatest inventors of the 20th century; philosopher, visionary, architect, engineer, mathematician, poet, cosmologist, and more; a futurist, author of over a score of books, was highly influential on many other people, coined words like "synergy" and made them into household words.

36 See Bibliography.

37 Ray Krok was the founder of the fast food chain, McDonald's.

38 published in the journal, *Science*, July, 1968

39 William Dufly's classic book on the highly addictive properties of common processed sugar, Warner Books, 1993.

40 part of Section 409 of the Federal Food, Drug, and Cosmetic Act of 1958. That act focused public concern on the presence of carcinogenic residues that may be found in foods and called for a "zero cancer risk" for all food. Much of the stringency of this clause and its effects on food labels was amended in a 1996 act that turned over discretionary control of the allowable percentages of alleged carcinogenic substances in food to the EPA.

41 See Bibliography.

42 AA's tradition of the anonymity of its members included that of its two founders back in 1935 in Akron, Ohio, Bill W a stockbroker and Dr. Bob S., a surgeon, both of whom were self-confessed alcoholics.

43 Op. cit. Julian Jaynes

44 Op. cit. Julian Jaynes' paradigm has been very useful to me in helping to explain much about varieties of human consciousness. I am still testing the applicability of this paradigm in practically any given situation.

45 This word, "metaphrand" appears to have originated with Julian Jaynes as a coin to describe the use of a term for one thing to describe another because of some similarity between them or between their relations to other things; the "metaphrand" describes the new thing, the "metaphier" describes the thing being referenced from familiarity. Therefore McLuhan's objection to Jaynes seems to be that there are far too many new objects (metaphrands) than can ever be reduced to familiarity by any one person's set of metaphiers. Well, one can never convince everyone.

46 For those out there who still may not know, the famous actor, Paul Newman and the famous actress, Joanne Woodward have been famously married since 1958. Joanne is Paul's second wife. Together they have three daughters and celebrated their 40th anniversary in January 1998. Paul's first wife was Jackie Witte with whom he had two daughters and a son.

47 An early 1970's best selling allegorical tale by Richard Bach about a seagull that leaves the flock of scavenger birds to see what lies beyond the horizon.

48 See Bibliography under Drosnin, Satinover, and Washburn for books on this subject.

49 this word refers to "end times" studies.

50 Dr. David Smith was founder of The Haight Ashbury Free Clinics in San Francisco out of which has developed Smith House, a social-model, early onset alcohol and drug detoxification inpatient program for women, staffed exclusively by women in recovery.

51 See Bibliography for a few of T. Ravenscroft's works.

52 Richard Wurmbrand, Marx and Satan presents some compelling information on the linkage between Satanism and Communism. See Bibliography.

EGG

53 San Sebastian De Garabandal is a small hamlet located in the Cantabrian Mountains of northwest Spain. It was the site of the apparitions of the Blessed Virgin Mary under the title of Our Lady of Mount Carmel, a title she first used in her appearances in Aylesford, England in 1251. The first apparition in Garabandal reportedly occurred on July 2, 1961, when Our Lady showed herself to four peasant children: Conchita Gonzalez (12), Jacinta Gonzalez (12), Mari Cruz Gonzalez (11) and Mari Loli Mazon (12) —while they were playing on the outskirts of their village.

54 Jose Arguelles and Brian Swimme, Bear & Co., 1997

55 See Bibliography for Neihardt.

56 The monograph <u>Ashes of the Red Heifer,</u> Stephen M. Yulish, Ph.D.: www.corp.direct.ca/trinity/ashes.html

57 Luisa Piccarreta, 1865-1947, Dominican Tertiary, bedridden for most of her life, wrote down the 36 volume <u>Book of Heaven</u> which has recently been translated into English. She has been nominated for canonization.

58 By this process, one's ancestors may be restored to a state of grace; rescued from Purgatory, etc. A similar notion is involved in the Mormon's "proxy baptism" for ancestors which is why the Mormons have such a strong interest in genealogy.

59 op. cit. José Arguelles and Brian Swimme.

60 See Bibliography.

NOTES: PART III

61 Bury My Heart At Wounded Knee, Dee Brown: p.439

62 Ibid:Preface

63 Matt. 6: 9-13 (King James Version)

64 Luke 1: 26-28 (King James Version)

65 Luke 2:34-38 (King James Version)

66 John M. Haffert, <u>Too Late</u>? Chapter 2. Not widely available except through Catholic booksellers.

67 II Maccabees 12:44-46

68 J.B.S. Haldane (1922) Sex-ratio and unisexual sterility in hybrid animals: "When in the F_1 offspring of two different animal races one sex is absent, rare, or sterile, that sex is the heterozygous [heterogametic] sex.".

NOTES: PART IV

69 See Martin Luther in Bibliography

70 Catena Legionis antiphon,

71 The Story of Walsingham Shrine, by Edward L.T. Lyon   May be out of print.

72 At the marriage in Cana, Jesus addressed his mother as, "Woman." See John 2: 4.

73 Joseph Campbell, see Bibliography.   Campbell also wrote the famous Masks of God series.

5 Ida Pearlsman, see Bibliography.

74 John Osee, <u>The Virgin Mary Present At San Damiano.</u> The Christopher Publishing House, 1977

75 Rev. A.M. Weigl. <u>Voices From Heaven</u>: Frontispiece, Pax Christi Publishing Ltd., 1983.

76 From the 450th Anniversary Commemorative Issue of Queen of the Americas Guild: Gaithersburg, MD.

77 The "light body" is used here as a metaphor for that which must be taken on faith to represent all that an individual being is beyond the merely temporal..

78 See Scripture – King James Version

79 John Haffert, <u>Who Is The Woman of the Apocalypse?</u> (AMI International Press, 1983).

80 Bishop Fulton J. Sheen. <u>Life Is Worth Living.</u> Image Books, 1954

81 "I will stop these atrocities or die in the attempt to stop them, so help me God!" Hernan Cortez. <u>The Conquest of New Spain</u> by Bernal Diaz is an eye-witness account and should be considered authoritative on the deeds, character and outcome of the conquest of Mexico by Hernan Cortez.

82 Fr. Gobbi, <u>The Marian Movement of Priests,</u> Preface, p.V., 1977.

83 Rodney King, in 1992, though not entirely innocent of the behavior which led to his beating by Los Angeles police, did manage to make these words a call for greater tolerance and understanding.

NOTES: PART V

84 Diane Books, Glendale, CA: 1977

85 See Rakovsky papers

86 Videotape - "Plague Wars": Frontline 1998. Boston Public Television

87 The US Government still denies that any of these experiments ever took place. Nevertheless anyone enlisted in the US Navy who even mentions it is subject to the most severe punishment.

88 Continuing experiments following the Philadelphia Experiment also officially denied by the US Government.

89 Nick Begich, 1997, Earthpulse Press

NOTES: PART VI

90 Synchronicities, C.J. Jung: Beyond Coincidence, Arthur
Koestler

INDEX

H

EGG

I

J

K

L

M

S